# JAVA® PROGRAMMING 24-HOUR TRAINER

*Continues*

# Java® Programming

## 24-HOUR TRAINER

# Java® Programming

## 24-HOUR TRAINER

Yakov Fain

Wiley Publishing, Inc.

Java® Programming 24-Hour Trainer

Published by
Wiley Publishing, Inc.
10475 Crosspoint Boulevard
Indianapolis, IN 46256
www.wiley.com

Copyright © 2011 by Wiley Publishing, Inc., Indianapolis, Indiana

Published simultaneously in Canada

ISBN: 978-0-470-88964-0

Manufactured in the United States of America

10 9 8 7 6 5 4 3 2 1

For general information on our other products and services please contact our Customer Care Department within the United States at (877) 762-2974, outside the United States at (317) 572-3993 or fax (317) 572-4002.

Wiley also publishes its books in a variety of electronic formats. Some content that appears in print may not be available in electronic books.

Library of Congress Control Number: 2010942181

*In memory of my friend, Felix Rubinchik.*

# ABOUT THE AUTHOR

 **YAKOV FAIN** works as a software architect for Farata Systems, a company that provides consulting services in the field of development of enterprise applications. He has authored several technical books and lots of articles on software development. Sun Microsystems has awarded Mr. Fain with the title of Java Champion, which has been given to only 150 people in the world. He leads the Princeton Java Users Group. Yakov's Twitter ID is @yfain.

# ABOUT THE TECHNICAL EDITOR

**ELLIOTTE RUSTY HAROLD** is originally from New Orleans, to which he returns periodically in search of a decent bowl of gumbo. However, he currently resides in the Prospect Heights neighborhood of Brooklyn with his wife Beth, dog Thor, and cat Marjorie. He is the author of numerous books including *Refactoring HTML*, *Java Network Programming*, *Java I/O*, and *Processing XML with Java*. His open source projects include the XOM Library for processing XML with Java and the Amateur media player.

# CREDITS

**EXECUTIVE EDITOR**
Robert Elliott

**PROJECT EDITOR**
Charlotte Kughen, The Wordsmithery LLC

**TECHNICAL EDITOR**
Elliotte Rusty Harold

**PRODUCTION EDITOR**
Kathleen Wisor

**COPY EDITOR**
Sadie Kleinman

**EDITORIAL DIRECTOR**
Robyn B. Siesky

**EDITORIAL MANAGER**
Mary Beth Wakefield

**FREELANCER EDITORIAL MANAGER**
Rosemarie Graham

**MARKETING MANAGER**
Ashley Zurcher

**PRODUCTION MANAGER**
Tim Tate

**VICE PRESIDENT AND EXECUTIVE GROUP PUBLISHER**
Richard Swadley

**VICE PRESIDENT AND EXECUTIVE PUBLISHER**
Barry Pruett

**ASSOCIATE PUBLISHER**
Jim Minatel

**PROJECT COORDINATOR, COVER**
Katie Crocker

**COMPOSITOR**
Jeff Lytle, Happenstance Type-O-Rama

**PROOFREADERS**
Nancy Carrasco
Jen Larsen, Word One New York

**INDEXER**
Robert Swanson

**COVER DESIGNER**
Michael E. Trent

**COVER IMAGE**
© FotografiaBasica / iStockPhoto.com

# ACKNOWLEDGMENTS

**FIRST OF ALL** I want to thank my family for understanding that stealing time from family to write a computer book is OK.

I'd also like to thank Elliotte Rusty Harold from Google for his valuable comments during a technical edit of this book. Elliotte himself has authored more than 20 computer books (see http://www.elharo.com) and is respected in the Java community around the world. His comments on my lessons ranged from the philosophical to a simple "I don't agree with this solution." I have addressed all of them.

Three people volunteered to help me with the book: Nick Golubyev (Singapore), Dmitry Danileyko (Russia), and Viktor Gamov (USA). They wrote several code samples for the book, which really saved me time! Thank you, guys!

Big thanks to the Wiley editors for doing a great job of editing and for not cursing me for not meeting deadlines.

# CONTENTS

# INTRODUCTION

**IT DOESN'T TAKE** a rocket scientist to notice the recent serious decline in the publishing of computer books, to say nothing of computer magazines. I enjoy reading books about software and visit the nearby Barnes and Noble at least twice a month. During the last three years the number of bookcases dedicated to computer books has shrunk substantially.

Today newly baked programmers prefer Google to books. They don't realize that Google is OK when you know what you are looking for, while books can give you a new perspective on how other people develop software.

During a recent visit to a major bookstore I noticed a series of books on digital photography. I'm one of the legions of people who are thinking of replacing a point-and-shoot camera with a digital SLR such as a Nikon D90. There were about 10 different thin books on that shelf, and I picked the one on the D90. It was about 65 pages long. I quickly skimmed the pages, learning that compared to a pocket camera one of the main advantages of D-SLR is the ability it gives you to change lenses. On top of that, these cameras use a small mirror that enables you to see exactly what you're shooting, plus you can take more shots per second. Not much information for a $25 book.

The secret was that the book came with a DVD, which contained 80 minutes of instructional videos! The printed part of the book and the DVD complemented each other. The wannabe photographers don't want to read books.

The new generation of computer programmers doesn't want to read either. They want to watch videos. They can be YouTube videos on how to do something, or screencasts. The material has to be prepared for easy consumption.

But because not everything in the world of software can be videotaped, future computer books will still include several hundred pages — some code samples and short instructions will go there.

Remember those 1,500-page Bibles on software? It seems that their days are over. These days a 500-page computer book can be considered thick. Five years from now a 200-page software book will become the standard. But books will come with DVDs on which the authors walk you through all the examples mentioned on paper.

I like this new 24-Hour Trainer series from Wiley Publishing. This is not to say that you can learn the software covered in these books within 24 hours. It's about having a trainer that's with you 24 hours a day. Each book in this series is a set of short chapters containing a minimum of theory but accompanied by an instructional DVD with screencasts recorded by the author.

## WHO THIS BOOK IS FOR

This book is for anyone who wants to learn how to program with the Java language. No previous programming experience is expected.

This tutorial can be used by Java developers looking for simple working examples that use certain features of the language.

Accomplished Java developers can also use this book as a refresher while preparing for a technical job interview.

This tutorial can be used by university students who are interested in learning from a practitioner who has spent 20-plus years developing enterprise software for a living.

College professors should appreciate the fact that each lesson ends with a "Try It" section — a prepared home assignment for each lesson.

## WHAT THIS BOOK COVERS

To be called a Java developer, a person has to know not only the core syntax of this programming language, but also the set of server-side technologies called Java EE (Enterprise Edition). This book covers both. At the time of this writing, the latest version of core Java is 6, and the latest release of Java EE is also 6.

Java is a general-purpose language — you can program applets running under control of a Web browser, stand-alone applications that run independently on the user's computer, and applications that connect to remote servers. Java is used for writing applications running in mobile devices, cars, or in household appliances.

The first 25 lessons of this book cover a program that can run on users' computers. The next 12 are about Java EE technologies used for Java programs that run on servers. The final lesson is dedicated to the process of getting prepared for Java technical job interviews.

This book doesn't cover Java programming for mobile devices.

## HOW THIS BOOK IS STRUCTURED

This book is a tutorial. Each lesson walks you through how to use certain elements and techniques of the Java language or gives an introduction to the server-side Java EE technologies. The "Try It" sections serve as continuations of materials explained in the lessons. The screencasts included on the DVD usually illustrate how the author compiles and runs code samples included in the lessons. You can choose to read the lesson and then try to run the example on your own, or you can read the lesson, watch the video, and then try to run the examples. After this part is done, start working on the assignments from the "Try It" section.

This book contains 38 lessons, which are not formally broken into sections. The first 25 lessons cover Java SE topics. Lessons 26 through 34 cover Java EE topics. Lessons 35 and 36 introduce you to popular third-party frameworks Spring and Hibernate. Lesson 37 demonstrates an application that utilizes several Java EE technologies. And, finally, Lesson 38 helps you to get prepared for the technical interview when you decide to look for a Java-related job.

The lessons are short and to the point. The goal is to explain the material quickly so you can start applying it hands-on as soon as possible. Some readers may feel that more explanation of certain subjects are required, and they are encouraged to do some extra research; there are lots and lots of online materials available on any Java-related subject. But the coverage of the material given in this book definitely helps in understanding what to focus on and what to look for.

## WHAT YOU NEED TO USE THIS BOOK

To do the examples in this book, you do not need to purchase any software—freely available software is used here. Installing Java Development Kit and Eclipse IDE is explained in the first two lessons, and this is all you need for Lessons 1 through 25. In Lesson 26, you install Java Application Server GlassFish, which is used for explanation of the materials in Lessons 26 through 34. If you decide to learn third-party frameworks Spring and Hibernate, you need to download and configure their software libraries as explained in Lessons 34 and 35. Whenever you need to download certain software, detailed instructions are given in the book and/or in the screencasts included on the DVD.

From the hardware perspective, you can use either PC running Windows or one of the Apple computers running Mac OS. Linux fans are also able to run all book samples. You should have at least 1GB of RAM on your computer to run all code examples from this book. But adding more memory can make your Java compiler and Eclipse IDE work faster.

## HOW TO READ THIS BOOK

This book is a tutorial, and I assume in each lesson that the reader is already familiar with the materials from those that came before it. If you are new to Java, I highly recommend that you read this book sequentially.

Each lesson except the last one has a corresponding video screencast on the accompanying DVD, in which I either work on the assignment from the "Try It" section of the lesson or simply install and configure some software. Ideally, you should try to do all the assignments from the "Try It" sections on your own, and use the videos only if you get stuck or don't understand the instructions. But if you prefer to learn by following the instructor, just watch the video first and then try to repeat the same actions on your own. Whatever works is fine.

Java is a multi-platform language and programs written for Microsoft Windows, say, should work the same way in Mac OS or on Linux computers. I'm using a Mac, but also have special software that enables me to run Microsoft Windows. In this book I use the open-source Eclipse Integrated Development Environment, which exists on all major platforms and looks pretty much the same on each. So regardless of your preferred operating system, you'll be able to run all the code samples from this book.

## CONVENTIONS

To help you get the most from the text and keep track of what's happening, we've used a number of conventions throughout the book.

> *Notes, tips, hints, tricks, and asides to the current discussion are offset and placed in italics like this.*

> *References like this one point you to the DVD to watch the instructional video that accompanies a given lesson.*

As for styles in the text:

➤ We *highlight* new terms and important words when we introduce them.

➤ We show file names, URLs, and code within the text like so: `persistence.properties`.

➤ We present code like the following:

```
We use a monofont type with no highlighting for most code examples.
```

## SOURCE CODE

As you work through the examples in this book, you may choose either to type in all the code manually or to use the source code files that accompany the book. All of the source code used in this book is available for download at `www.wrox.com`. You will find the code snippets from the source code are accompanied by a download icon and note indicating the name of the program, so you know it's available for download and can easily locate it in the download file. Once at the site, simply locate the book's title (either by using the Search box or by using one of the title lists) and click the Download Code link on the book's detail page to obtain all the source code for the book.

**Available for download on Wrox.com**

Listings include the filename in the title. If it is just a code snippet, you'll find the filename in a code note such as this:

*Code Filename*

> *Because many books have similar titles, you may find it easiest to search by ISBN; this book's ISBN is 978-0-470-88964-0.*

After you download the code, just decompress it with your favorite compression tool. Alternately, you can go to the main Wrox code download page at `www.wrox.com/dynamic/books/download.aspx` to see the code available for this book and all other Wrox books.

The author will also maintain up-to-date code samples in the code repository hosted by Google at the following address: `http://code.google.com/p/practicaljava/`.

This website also contains a sample online store application contributed by Nick Golubyev. Even though this application was not used in the book, it serves as a good example of an end-to-end application developed with Java EE 6 technologies. You can find the application by clicking the Source tab in the folder `java-ee`. You can find instructions on building the online store under the tab Wiki.

## ERRATA

We make every effort to ensure that there are no errors in the text or in the code. However, no one is perfect, and mistakes do occur. If you find an error in one of our books, like a spelling mistake or faulty piece of code, we would be very grateful for your feedback. By sending in errata you may save another reader hours of frustration, and at the same time you will be helping us provide even higher quality information.

To find the errata page for this book, go to `www.wrox.com` and locate the title using the Search box or one of the title lists. Then, on the book details page, click the Book Errata link. On this page you can view all errata that has been submitted for this book and posted by Wrox editors. A complete book list including links to each book's errata is also available at `wrox.com/misc-pages/booklist.shtml`.

If you don't spot "your" error on the Book Errata page, go to `wrox.com/contact/techsupport.shtml` and complete the form there to send us the error you have found. We'll check the information and, if appropriate, post a message to the book's errata page and fix the problem in subsequent editions of the book.

## P2P.WROX.COM

For author and peer discussion, join the P2P forums at `p2p.wrox.com`. The forums are a Web-based system for you to post messages relating to Wrox books and related technologies and interact with other readers and technology users. The forums offer a subscription feature to e-mail you topics of interest of your choosing when new posts are made to the forums. Wrox authors, editors, other industry experts, and your fellow readers are present on these forums.

At p2p.wrox.com you will find a number of different forums that will help you not only as you read this book, but also as you develop your own applications. To join the forums, just follow these steps:

1. Go to p2p.wrox.com and click the Register link.

2. Read the terms of use and click Agree.

3. Complete the required information to join as well as any optional information you wish to provide and click Submit.

4. You will receive an e-mail with information describing how to verify your account and complete the joining process.

> *You can read messages in the forums without joining P2P but in order to post your own messages, you must join.*

Once you join, you can post new messages and respond to messages other users post. You can read messages at any time on the Web. If you would like to have new messages from a particular forum e-mailed to you, click the Subscribe to this Forum icon by the forum name in the forum listing.

For more information about how to use the Wrox P2P, be sure to read the P2P FAQs for answers to questions about how the forum software works as well as many common questions specific to P2P and Wrox books. To read the FAQs, click the FAQ link on any P2P page.

# 1

# Introducing Java

Today Java is one of the most popular programming languages for everything from programming games to creating mission-critical applications such as those for trading on Wall Street or controlling Mars rovers. In this lesson you are introduced to some of the very basic Java terms, and you will download and install the Java Development Kit (JDK) and compile your first program.

## WHY LEARN JAVA?

The Java programming language was originally created in 1995 by James Gosling from Sun Microsystems (currently a subsidiary of Oracle Corporation). The goal was to provide a simpler and platform-independent alternative to C++. You'll see what *platform independence* means a little later, in the section "The Life Cycle of a Java Program." For now, let's look at some of the reasons why Java can be your language of choice.

Java is a general-purpose programming language that's used in all industries for almost any type of application. If you master it, your chances of getting employed as a software developer will be higher than if you specialize in some domain-specific programming languages.

There are around six million professional Java developers in the world and the majority of them are ready to share their knowledge by posting blogs and articles or simply answering technical questions online. If you get stuck solving some problem in Java, the chances are very high that you'll find the solution on the Internet.

Since the pool of Java developers is huge, project managers of large and small corporations like to use Java for the development of new projects — if you decide to leave the project for whatever reason, it's not difficult to find another Java programmer to replace you. At this point you may ask, "Does that also mean that my Java skills will be easily replaceable?" To improve your value and employability you need to *master* not only the syntax of the language, but also the right set of Java-related technologies that are in demand (you'll learn them in this book).

Not only is Java open-source, but there are millions of open-source projects being developed in Java. Joining one of these projects is the best way to get familiar with the process of project development and secure your very first job without having any prior real-world experience as a programmer.

The Java language is *object-oriented* (OO), which allows you to easily relate program constructs to objects from the real world (more on this in Lessons 3–7).

There are plenty of technical features that make Java the right choice for many projects, and you'll have a chance to see this for yourself while reading this book, watching the screencasts from the accompanying DVD, and deploying all code samples from the book on your computer.

## SETTING THE GOALS

The goal of this rather slim tutorial is to give you just enough information about most of the Java language elements, techniques, and technologies that are currently being used in the real world. The first half of the book is more about the Java language itself, while the second is about server-side Java technologies, and this is where Java shines in the enterprise world.

The brevity of some of the lessons may make you wonder if it's even possible to explain a subject in just 10 pages while there are whole books devoted for the same topic. My approach is to cover just enough for you to understand the concept, important terms, and best practices. Prerecorded screencasts on the DVD will help you to repeat the techniques explained in the lesson on your own.

There are plenty of additional materials online that will help you to study any specific topic more deeply. But you'll get a working and practical knowledge about Java just by using the materials included with this book.

The goal of this book is not just to get you familiar with the syntax of the Java language, but to give you practical Java skills that will allow you to develop business applications either on your own or by working as a team member in a larger-scale project.

## THE LIFE CYCLE OF A JAVA PROGRAM

There are different types of programming languages. In some of them you write the text of the program (aka the source code) and can execute this program right away. These are interpreted languages (e.g., JavaScript).

But Java requires the source code of your program to be compiled first. It gets converted to either machine-specific code or a bytecode that is understood by some run-time engine or a virtual machine.

Not only will the program be checked for syntax errors by a Java compiler, but some other libraries of Java code can be added (*linked*) to your program after the compilation is complete (deployment stage).

In this lesson you write a very basic Java program that will output the words "Hello World" on your computer's screen.

Technically you can write the source code of your Java program in any plain text editor that you prefer (Notepad, TextEdit, vi, etc.), but to compile your program you'll need additional tools and code libraries that are included in the Java Development Kit (JDK).

## JDK AND JRE

If you are planning to use a specific computer to develop Java programs, you'll need to download and install JDK. If you are planning to use this computer only to run Java programs that were compiled somewhere else, you just need the Java Runtime Environment (JRE).

If you have JDK installed on your machine, it includes JRE.

Java's platform independence comes from the fact that your Java program doesn't know under which operating system (OS) or on which hardware it's being executed. It operates inside the preinstalled JRE that is pretty much the same on every platform.

Since you'll be learning how to develop Java programs, download JDK from the following website: `http://www.oracle.com/technetwork/java/javase/downloads/jdk6-jsp-136632.html`.

## JAVA SE AND EE

But before rushing to the downloading process, you need to get familiar with two more terms: Java SE (Standard Edition) and Java EE (Enterprise Edition). The latter includes the server-side tools and libraries that you'll get familiar with starting in Lesson 26.

For now, just download the latest version of the JDK SE Development Kit. (The letter U followed by a number represents the update number of Java 6.)

Select the platform (Windows, Linux, Solaris) on which you are planning to develop Java programs and continue the download process.

> *JDK for Mac OS X is preinstalled on Apple's computers and no additional installing is required. The current version of JDK, which comes with computers running Snow Leopard, is JDK 6. It's located in directory /Library/Java. In this book we'll be using Java for the Windows OS, but Java is cross-platform and the book examples will work under MAC OS and Linux as well.*

## DOWNLOADING AND INSTALLING JDK IN WINDOWS

After selecting the Windows platform and clicking the Download button you'll see a Login for Download screen, which is optional: You can skip this step.

Click Save File on the pop-up screen, as shown in Figure 1-1 (the file name depends on the version of JDK).

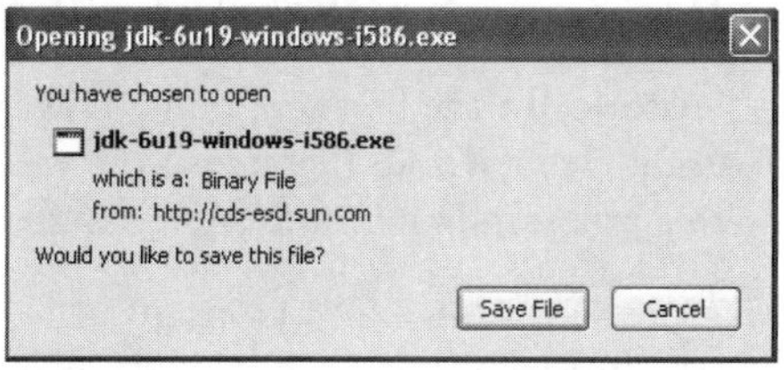

**FIGURE 1-1**

After the file is saved, start this executable and the installation wizard will lead you through the process. Read and accept the license agreement and click the button Next. Note the item at the bottom of the left box in Figure 1-2 — it is an open-source database management system (DBMS) called Java DB. You'll need JavaDB for Lesson 22.

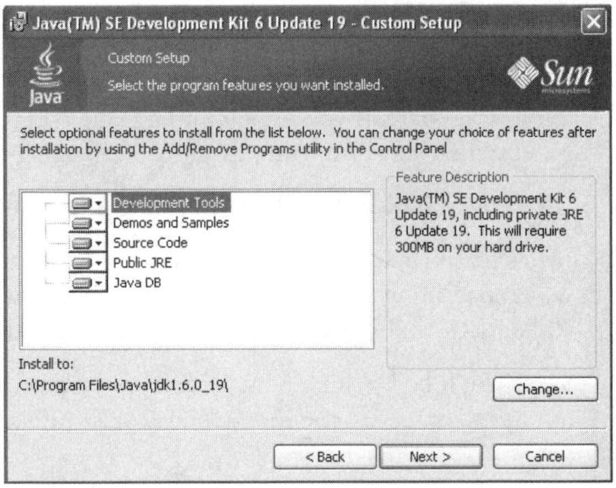

A couple of minutes into the installation process you'll see a pop-up window asking you where to install JRE. I'll assume that you've accepted the default directory (`c:\Program Files\Java\jre6`), but you can select a different one. Shortly, you should see a message telling you that installation was successful. Click Finish.

**FIGURE 1-2**

At the end of the installation process you'll see a website suggesting you register the install. This step is optional.

If you have previous versions of JDK installed on your computer, each of them will be sitting in its own directory, e.g., `c:\Program Files\Java\jdk1.6.0_019`. But for a sanity check, I always open a command line window and enter `java -version` at the command prompt. Figure 1-3 shows the confirmation that I really have JRE 1.6.0_19 (Java 6 is also referred to as Java 1.6).

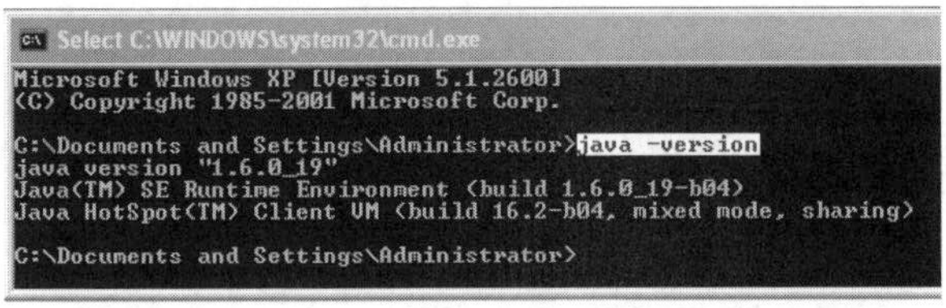

```
Microsoft Windows XP [Version 5.1.2600]
(C) Copyright 1985-2001 Microsoft Corp.

C:\Documents and Settings\Administrator>java -version
java version "1.6.0_19"
Java(TM) SE Runtime Environment (build 1.6.0_19-b04)
Java HotSpot(TM) Client VM (build 16.2-b04, mixed mode, sharing)

C:\Documents and Settings\Administrator>
```

**FIGURE 1-3**

Congratulations! Your JDK and JRE are installed.

## YOUR FIRST JAVA PROGRAM: HELLO WORLD

Historically, the first program you write while learning a new programming language is the program Hello World. If you visit the website `www.helloworldexample.net/` you'll see how to write this program in many different languages, including Java.

To start writing a Java program you could use any plain text editor — I'll use Notepad. The file that contains Java code must be saved in a file with its name ending in `.java`.

Enter the following code in the text editor.

**LISTING 1-1: HelloWorld.java**

```
public class  HelloWorld {

    public static void main(String[] args){
            System.out.println("Hello World");
    }
}
```

Create a directory, `c:\PracticalJava\Lesson1`, and save the program you just created in the file `HelloWorld.java` (if you use Notepad, select All Files in the Save as Type drop-down to avoid auto-attachment of the `.txt` suffix).

Keep in mind that Java is a case-sensitive language, which means that if you named the program HelloWorld with a capital *H* and a capital *W*, you should not try to start the program helloworld. Your first dozen syntax errors will be caused by improper capitalization.

What follows is a really short explanation of some of the terms and language elements used in the HelloWorld program. You'll get more comfortable with them after mastering the first several lessons in this book.

Our first program contains a *class*, `HelloWorld`. Give the Java class and its file the same name. (There could be exceptions to this rule, but not in this simple program.) While writing Java programs you create *classes*, which often represent objects from real life. You'll learn more about classes in Lesson 3.

The class `HelloWorld` contains a *method*, `main()`. Methods in Java classes represent functions (actions) that a class could perform. A Java class may have several methods, but if one of them is called `main()` and is declared (if it has a *method signature*), as in our class, this makes this Java class executable. If a class doesn't have a method `main()`, it can be used from other classes, but you can't run it as a program.

The method `main()` calls the method `println()` to display the text "Hello World" on the screen. Here is the method signature (similar to a title) of the method `main()`:

```
public static void main(String[] args)
```

This method signature includes the access level (`public`), instructions on usage (`static`), return value type (`void`), name of the method (`main`), and argument list (`String[] args`).

➤   The keyword `public` means that the method `main()` can be accessed by any other Java class.

➤   The keyword `static` means that you don't have to create an instance of this class to use this method.

➤   The keyword `void` means that the method `main()` doesn't return any value to the calling program.

➤   The keyword `String[] args` tells us that this method will receive an array of characters as the argument (you can pass external data to this method from a command line).

The `main()` method is the starting point of your program. You can write a program in Java SE that consists of more than one class, but at least one of them has the method `main()`, otherwise the program won't start. A Java class can have more than one method. For example, the class `Employee` can have the methods `updateAddress()`, `raiseSalary()`, `changeName()`, etc.

The *body* of the method `main()` contains the following line:

```
System.out.println("Hello World");
```

The preceding `println()` method is used to print data on the system console (command window). Java's method names are always followed by parentheses.

`System` here represents another Java class.

The dot notation `System.out` means that the variable out is defined inside the class `System`.

`out.println()` tells you that there is an object represented by a variable called `out` and it has a method called `println()`.

You will be using this dot notation to refer to class methods or variables.

## Compiling and Running Hello World

Now you need to compile this program. The `javac` compiler is a part of JDK, so open a command window on your PC, change the current directory to `c:\PracticalJava\Lesson1` and try to compile the program:

```
cd PracticalJava\Lesson1
javac HelloWorld.java
```

Oops. I got an error telling me that `javac` is not recognized as an internal or external command, operable program, or batch file. The OS doesn't know where `javac` is located. You need to add the directory in which the `javac` compiler resides to the system variable PATH. In Windows OS, go to Control Panel, click the System icon, select the tab Advanced, and click Environment Variables. Edit the system variable PATH so it starts with the following: `C:\Program Files\Java\jdk1.6.0_19\ bin;` By the time you'll be reading this book the Java version number may be different so check the name of the directory before modifying the system variable PATH.

Restart your command window and now the OS should be able to find `javac`. Get into the directory where `HelloWorld.java` is located and repeat the compilation command.

You won't see any confirmation of a successful compilation; just type `dir` to confirm that a new file named `HelloWorld.class` has been created. This proves that your program has been successfully compiled.

If the program has syntax errors, the compiler prints error messages. In this case fix the errors, and recompile the program again. You may need to do it more than once until the file `HelloWorld .class` is successfully created.

Now run the program by typing the command

```
java HelloWorld
```

Note that this time we used the term `java`, which starts the Java Virtual Machine (JVM). The words "Hello World" are displayed in the command window. In Figure 1-4 is a screenshot that shows the compilation command, the content of the folder after the compilation, and the output of the HelloWorld program.

```
C:\WINDOWS\system32\cmd.exe                                    _ □ ×

C:\PracticalJava\Lesson1>javac HelloWorld.java

C:\PracticalJava\Lesson1>dir
 Volume in drive C has no label.
 Volume Serial Number is F4DA-B746

 Directory of C:\PracticalJava\Lesson1

04/11/2010  06:39 PM    <DIR>          .
04/11/2010  06:39 PM    <DIR>          ..
04/11/2010  06:39 PM               425 HelloWorld.class
04/11/2010  06:39 PM               141 HelloWorld.java
               2 File(s)            566 bytes
               2 Dir(s)  90,760,175,616 bytes free

C:\PracticalJava\Lesson1>java HelloWorld
Hello World

C:\PracticalJava\Lesson1>
```

**FIGURE 1-4**

# TRY IT

In this lesson your goal is to write your first Java program that outputs the words "Hello World."

## Lesson Requirements

For this lesson download and install the current version of JDK from `http://java.sun.com/javase/downloads/index.jsp`. Set the value of the system `PATH` variable to include the `bin` directory, where your Java compiler (`javac`) and other executables were installed.

## Step-by-Step

1. Open a plain text editor of your choice and enter the text of the Hello World program.

2. Save the program in the file `HelloWorld.java`.

3. Compile the program in the command window using the command `javac HelloWorld.java`.

4. Run the program by using the command `java HelloWorld`.

> *Please select Lesson 1 on the DVD to view the video that accompanies this lesson.*

# 2

# Eclipse IDE

While your first Java program was written in a plain text editor and compiled from a command window, this is not a productive way of developing software. Professional programmers use one of the Integrated Development Environments (IDEs), which include an editor, a compiler, type-ahead help, a debugger, and a lot more (you'll get familiar with these features later in this lesson). There several popular Java IDEs, such as Eclipse, NetBeans, IntelliJ IDEA, and RAD. Some are free, and some are not.

Eclipse is by far the most widely used IDE, and I'll be using it for compiling and running most of the examples in this book. But switching from one IDE to another is a pretty simple process, and if you see that in some areas one IDE makes you more productive than the other, just use the best one for the job. For example, NetBeans IDE can offer great help if you'll be developing the server-side Java EE applications explained later in the book (starting in Lesson 26).

## INTRODUCING ECLIPSE IDE

Eclipse IDE is an open-source product that was originally created with a substantial code donation by IBM to the Java community, and from that moment Eclipse was a 100% community-driven product. It started as an IDE for developing Java programs, but today it's a development platform used for building thousands of tools and plug-ins. Some people are using its Rich Client Platform (RCP) API to develop user interfaces (UIs) for applications. Other Java languages are also supported by Eclipse. Visit the downloads page to see a just a portion of the Eclipse-based products available: `www.eclipse.org/downloads`.

Besides being an IDE, Eclipse supports plug-in development, and each developer can add only those plug-ins that he or she is interested in. For example, there is a plug-in to display UML diagrams, another offers a reporting system, and there are plug-ins for developing applications in C, Adobe Flex, and others.

## DOWNLOADING AND INSTALLING ECLIPSE

At work, I use Eclipse IDE for Java EE Developers. Each version of Eclipse IDE has a name. At the time of this writing, the current version is called Helios. In Windows OS, my first download window looks as shown in Figure 2-1 (note `jee` in the file name).

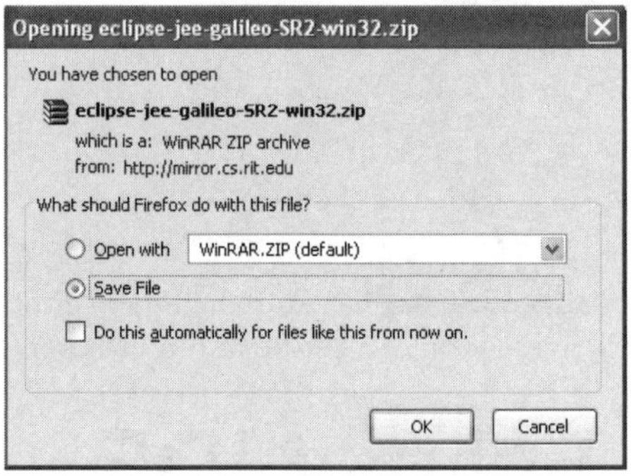

The installation of Eclipse IDE comes down to a simple unzipping of the downloaded file into a disk drive of your choice. You'll find the file `eclipse.exe` in the Eclipse folder — just run this program. You'll immediately see a pop-up window asking you to select a *workspace*, which is a directory on your hard disk where one or more of your *projects* is going to be stored.

**FIGURE 2-1**

If you want to create an application in Eclipse, you start with creating a project. In the real world, the source code of a decent-size application can consist of several Eclipse projects.

For this book I selected the following workspace directory: `c:\PracticalJava\workspace`.

Eclipse Java EE IDE starts with a Welcome panel — just close it by clicking the little x on the Welcome tab. Figure 2-2 is a snapshot of the freshly installed IDE with an empty workspace.

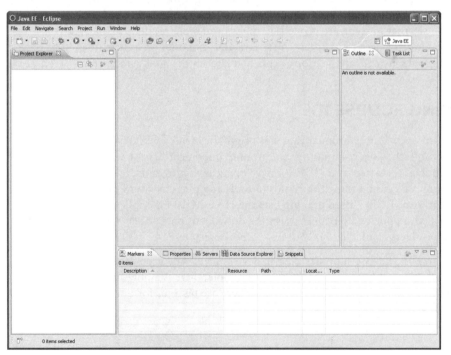

**FIGURE 2-2**

To be precise, you are looking at Java EE *perspective* (note the Java EE tab at the top), which is a collection of *views*. On the left you see a Project Explorer view. The area in the middle is reserved for the code editor view — you start using it as soon as you create your first Java class. The Outline view is on the right — you'll see the names of your classes, methods, and variables (see Lesson 3) there when they are available.

There are many other views that you can open and close by yourself by selecting Window ⇨ Show View. These include Console, Search, Servers and others.

Since you are just starting to learn the language, there is no need to work in the Java EE perspective — you can get by in the Java perspective. Click the little icon with the plus sign by the Java EE tab and select "Java perspective." You'll see a slightly different set of views with the Package Explorer and Hierarchy views on the left, Task List on the right, and Problems, Javadoc and Declaration tabs at the bottom, as shown in Figure 2-3.

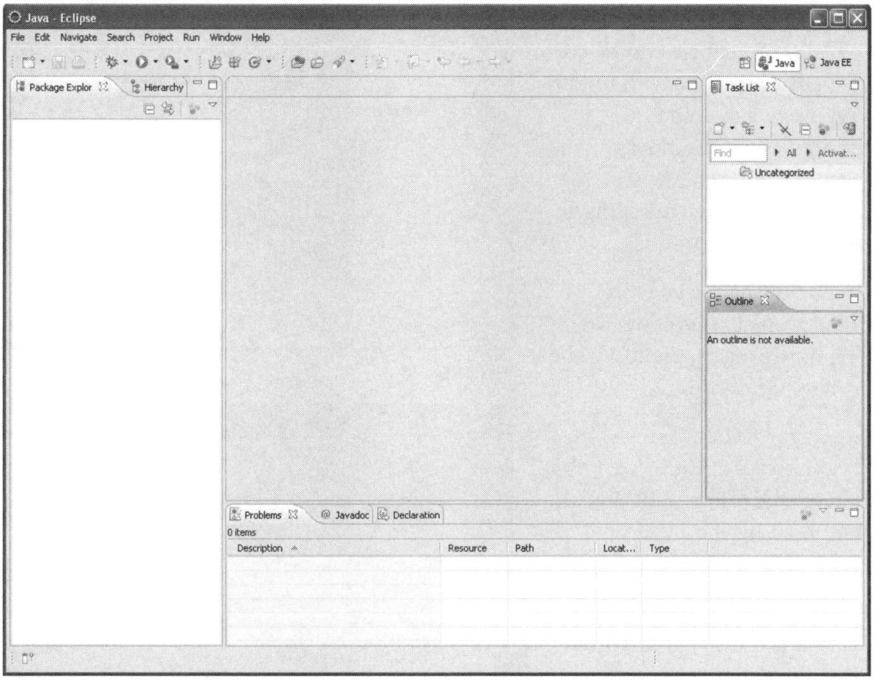

**FIGURE 2-3**

## CREATING HELLO PROJECT IN ECLIPSE

In Lesson 1 you simply created the class `HelloWorld`, but in Eclipse you have to create the project first. Select File ⇨ New ⇨ Java Project and enter `Hello` as the name of the project in the pop-up window, as shown in Figure 2-4.

You can select the version of the JRE you want to work with. In Lesson 1 I've installed the JDK and JRE of version 1.6.0_19, but you may have more than one version of JRE, and Eclipse can compile the code that will run in another version of JRE. This is a pretty nice feature of Eclipse IDE — it doesn't come with its own JRE, but it allows you to pick the version that fits your needs. In some cases you have to compile the code with older versions of JRE if you know that this program will have to run in the older JVMs.

After you click Next, the next window will ask you to specify the folder where compiled Java classes of the Hello project should be created. By default, Eclipse creates a Hello folder for this project with a `bin` sub-folder for compiled classes and an `src` sub-folder for the source code. In Lesson 1 both `HelloWorld.java` and `HelloWorld.class` were sitting in the same folder, which is a bad practice.

Don't change the name of the output directory — just click Finish on that window. In Figure 2-5 you see a new project, Hello, in the Package Explorer view of Eclipse.

This project has an empty folder, `src` — you can save the source code of `HelloWorld.java` there when ready. The JRE folder contains all required libraries supporting the JVM where HelloWorld will run.

These library files have `.jar` in their names. Java SDK comes with a jar utility that allows you to create a file archive that contains one or more compiled classes. While the JRE folder contains classes created by developers of the JRE itself, most real-world applications consist of groups of files (packages) located in one or more jars.

It doesn't make much sense to put the only `HelloWorld` class inside the jar, but as your sample applications grow, you'll see how to group and compress files in jars.

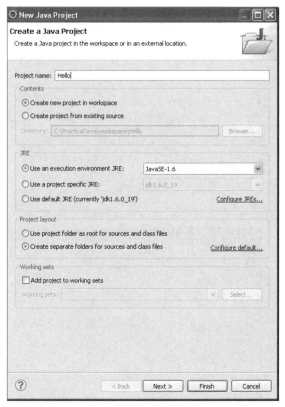

**FIGURE 2-4**

**FIGURE 2-5**

## CREATING THE HELLOWORLD CLASS IN ECLIPSE

Our Hello project will contain one Java class: `HelloWorld` from Lesson 1. Select File ⇨ New ⇨ Class and enter `HelloWorld` in the Name field in the pop-up window shown in Figure 2-6.

Then enter `com.practicaljava.lesson2` in the Package field. This is a new addition that was not present in the previous version of `HelloWorld`.

## JAVA PACKAGES

Packages in Java are used to better organize multi-file projects and for data protection. It's not unusual for a project to have several hundreds of Java classes. Keeping them all in one directory is never a good idea. Hence the files will be located in various directories and sub-directories.

What are the naming conventions for packages? Java developers use so-called *reverse-domain name* conventions. Let's say you work on a project called Sales for a company called Acme, which has an Internet site at `acme.com`. Then every package name will start with the reverse URL of the company, followed by the project name: `com.acme.sales`.

**FIGURE 2-6**

All Java classes that belong to this package would be stored in the following directory structure: `com/acme/sales`.

If some of the Java classes are specific to domestic sales, while others are used in international sales, you will create two more sub-directories: `com/acme/sales/domestic` and `com/acme/sales/international`.

While directory names are separated by a forward slash or backslash, the corresponding Java packages are separated with periods. Java has a special keyword package, and its declaration has to be the first line of the class (program comments don't count). For example:

```
package com.acme.sales.domestic;
```

Let's assume that you work for a company called Practical Java on project Lesson2; the name of the package will be `com.practicaljava.lesson2`, which is exactly what I've entered in the Package field shown in Figure 2-6.

Besides being used for better organization of Java classes, packages help in controlling data access. You learn about this feature in the section "Access Levels" in Lesson 6.

## COMPLETING CODE GENERATION

You may have noticed that I also checked off the box asking Eclipse to generate the main method for me.

Click Finish, and in a couple of seconds Eclipse will generate for you the initial code for the class `HelloWorld`, as shown in Figure 2-7.

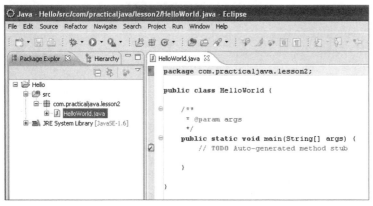

**FIGURE 2-7**

The generated code is shown in Eclipse's editor view. It starts with the `package` statement, and the class declaration with the method name goes next.

Type in the line `System.out.println("Hello World");` under the `TODO` comment (comments are explained in the next section), and save the code by pressing the little diskette image on the toolbar or using the Ctrl+S key combination.

As you type in the code, Eclipse displays context-sensitive help suggesting a selection of possible values, minimizing guesswork and typing errors. I made a snapshot, shown in Figure 2-8, right after entering `System.o`:

**FIGURE 2-8**

By default, saving the code results in an invocation of the compiler. If you didn't make any syntax errors, Eclipse will create `HelloWorld.class` in the `bin` directory of the Hello project. In case of compilation errors, Eclipse puts a little red round bullet in front of problematic lines.

Now you can run the program by pressing the round green button on the toolbar. The output of the program will be shown in the Console view panel in the lower part of Eclipse IDE, as in Figure 2-9.

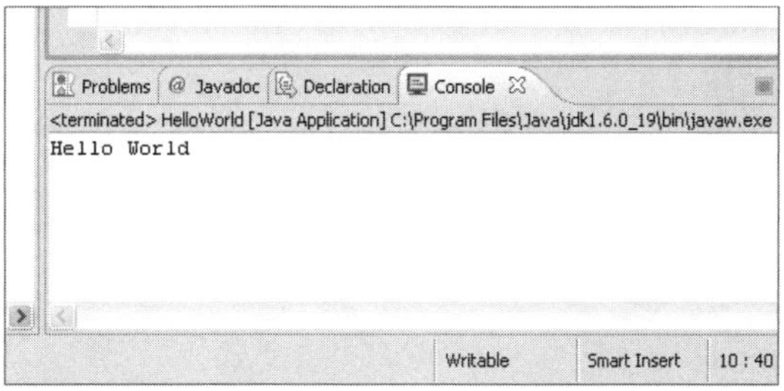

The format of this book doesn't have space for more detailed coverage of all the features of Eclipse. The good news is that there are plenty of tutorials describing every feature of Eclipse at `www.eclipse.org/documentation`.

**FIGURE 2-9**

## TRY IT

In this lesson your goal is to write, compile, and run HelloWorld in Eclipse IDE.

## Lesson Requirements

For this lesson download and install the current version of Eclipse IDE for Java EE Developers from `www.eclipse.org/downloads`.

## Step-by-Step

1. Create the Hello project in Eclipse IDE.

2. Create a new Java class, `HelloWorld`, with the method `main()`, as described earlier.

3. Compile the program by clicking Save.

4. Run the program by clicking the green button in the Eclipse toolbar.

 *Please select Lesson 2 on the DVD to view the video that accompanies this lesson.*

# 3

# Object-Oriented Programming

Starting from this lesson you'll be studying various elements of the Java language with brief descriptions to get you started programming in the shortest possible time. But you are certainly encouraged to refer to the extensive Java documentation that's available online at `http://java.sun.com/javase/6/docs/`.

## CLASSES AND OBJECTS

Java is an object-oriented language, which means that it has constructs to represent objects from the real world. Each Java program has at least one class that knows how to do certain things or how to represent some type of object. For example, the simplest class, `HelloWorld`, knows how to greet the world.

Classes in Java may have methods (aka functions) and fields (aka attributes or properties).

Let's create and discuss a class named `Car`. This class will have *methods*, describing what this type of vehicle can do, such as start the engine, shut it down, accelerate, brake, lock the doors, and so on.

This class will also have some *fields*: body color, number of doors, sticker price, and so on.

---

**Available for download on Wrox.com**

**LISTING 3-1:** Class Car

```
class Car{
    String color;
    int numberOfDoors;

    void startEngine {
        // Some code goes here
    }
    void stopEngine {
        int tempCounter=0;
```

*continues*

**LISTING 3-1** *(continued)*

```
        // Some code goes here
    }
}
```

Lines that start with double slashes are comments, which will be explained later in this lesson.

Car represents common features for many different cars: All cars have such properties as color and number of doors, and all of them perform similar actions. You can be more specific and create another Java class called Car. It's still a car, but with some properties specific to the model James Bond. You can say that the class JamesBondCar is a *subclass* of Car, or, using Java syntax, JamesBondCar extends Car.

**LISTING 3-2:** Class JamesBondCar

```
class JamesBondCar extends Car{
    int currentSubmergeDepth;
    boolean isGunOnBoard=true;
    final String MANUFACTURER;

    void submerge {
        currentSubmergeDepth = 50;
      // Some code goes here
    }
    void surface {
      // Some code goes here
    }
}
```

But even after defining all the properties and methods for the class JamesBondCar you can't drive it, even on the computer screen. A Java class is like a blueprint in construction or engineering, and until you build real objects based on this blueprint you can't use them.

Creating objects, aka *instances*, based on classes is the equivalent of building real cars based on blueprints. To create an instance of a class means to create the object in the computer's memory based on the class definition.

To instantiate a class (to put one more car on the road), you'll declare a *variable* of this class's type, and use the new operator for each new instance of the car:

```
JamesBondCar car1 = new JamesBondCar();
JamesBondCar car2 = new JamesBondCar();
```

Now the variables car1 and car2 can be used to refer to the first and second instance of the JamesBondCar respectively. To be precise, declaring the variables pointing at the instances is needed if you are planning to refer to these instances in the program. The statement new JamesBondCar() creates the instance, too. You can create many cars based on the same specification. Even though they all represent the same class, they may have different values in their properties — some of them are red, some of them have two doors while others have four, etc.

## VARIABLES, CONSTANTS, AND DATA TYPES

Some values representing an object can change over time (variables) and some remain the same (constants). This section will shed more light on the use of both types.

## Declaring Variables

Java is a statically typed language: The program *variables* must be declared (named and typed) first, and then you can assign them values either at the time of declaration or later on in one of the class methods. For example, the variable `isGunOnBoard` has been initialized during its declaration in Listing 3-2, and `currentSubmergeDepth` got its value in the method `submerge()`.

The class `Car` from Listing 3-1 defines a *variable* color of type `String`, which is used to represent text values.

## Constants

To store values that never change, you need to declare a *constant* — just add the keyword `final` to the declaration line, as in Listing 3-2:

```
final String MANUFACTURER;
```

Java developers usually render the names of constants in upper case. The value of a constant can be assigned only once, and since you are creating an instance of a specific car, its manufacturer is known and can't change during the life span of this object:

```
MANUFACTURER = "J.B. Limited";
```

Even though you don't have to initialize final variables during their declaration, it is a good practice to follow. The preceding example should be written as

```
final String MANUFACTURER="J.B. Limited";
```

## Primitive Data Types

There are eight primitive data types in Java: Four are for integer values, two are for values with a decimal point, one is for storing single characters, and one is for Boolean data that allows only either `true` or `false` as a value. Following are some examples of variable declarations and initializations:

```
int chairs = 12;
char grade = 'A';
boolean cancelJob = false;
double nationalIncome = 23863494965745.78;
float hourlyRate = 12.50f;    // add an f at the end of
                              //float literals
long totalCars  = 46372836483921;  // add an l at the end
                                   // of long literals
```

The following table summarizes some characteristics of the Java data types.

| PRIMITIVE TYPE | SIZE | MIN VALUE | MAX VALUE | WRAPPER CLASS |
|---|---|---|---|---|
| byte | 8 bits | –128 | 127 | Byte |
| short | 16 bits | –32,768 | 32,767 | Short |
| int | 32 bits | –2,147,483,648 | 2,147,483,647 | Integer |
| long | 64 bits | –9,223,372,036, 854,775,808 | 9,223,372,036, 854,775,807 | Long |
| float | 32 bits | Single precision floating point; see Java language specification at http://bit .ly/9nlwjh | Single precision floating point; see Java language specification at http://bit .ly/9nlwjh | Float |
| double | 64 bits | Double precision floating point; see Java language specification at http://bit .ly/9nlwjh | Double precision floating point; see Java language specification at http://bit .ly/9nlwjh | Double |
| char | 16 bits | Unicode 0 | Unicode 2 in a power of 16 value | Character |
| boolean | - | false (not a min) | true (not a max) | Boolean |

Have you noticed that the char data type uses two bytes of memory to store the data? This allows you to store character sets that have a lot more symbols than traditional alphabets because a single byte can only represent 256 characters, while two bytes can represent 65,536 characters.

Following are some examples of variable declarations and initializations:

```
int chairs = 12;
boolean cancelJob = false;
double nationalIncome = 23863494965745.78;
float hourlyRate = 12.50f;
long totalCars  = 4637283648392L;
```

The last two literals in the preceding list end with the letters f and L to indicate that you want to store these data as float and long data types correspondingly. But most likely, the double datatype should fit all your needs in non-integer calculations.

## VARIABLE SCOPE

If you declare a variable inside any method, the variable has a local scope (for example, adjustedTax in Listing 3-5 is local). This means that it's only visible for the code within this method (calcTax). When the method completes its execution, all local variables are automatically removed from memory by Java's *garbage collector*. Actually the scope is tighter than that.

It's accessible within the method only after the variables are declared, and only within the block in which it is declared. For instance, a variable declared inside a `for` loop will not be excessive outside the `for` loop even inside the same method.

If a variable has to be accessible from more than one class method, declare it on a class level. Listing 3-5 shows the class Tax, where grossIncome, dependents, and state are *class or member variables*. These variables are "alive" while the `Tax` object exists in memory. They can be shared and reused by all methods within the class and they can even be visible from external classes.

> *If a variable is declared with a static qualifier (see Lesson 4), it's shared by all instances of the class.*

## WRAPPERS, AUTOBOXING, AND UNBOXING

All primitive data types have corresponding *wrapper classes* that contain useful methods dealing with respective data types. The wrapper classes serve two purposes:

**1.** They contain a number of useful functions for manipulation with their primitive counterparts. For example, the class Integer offers such useful methods as conversion of a String into an int, or turning an int into a float, and more. The `Integer` class also allows you to set the minimum and maximum values for the number in question.

**2.** Some Java collections can't store primitives (such as `ArrayList`) and so primitives have to be wrapped into objects. For example,

```
ArrayList myLotteryNumbers = new ArrayList();
myLotteryNumbers.add(new Integer(6));
myLotteryNumbers.add(new Integer(15));
```

You don't need to explicitly create a new instance for every primitive as in the preceding code snippet. You can simply write `myLotteryNumbers.add(6);` and the primitive value 6 will automatically be wrapped into an instance of the `Integer` class. This feature is called *autoboxing*.

On the same note, the next line is also valid:

```
int luckyNumber= myLotteryNumber.get(23);
```

Even though `get(23)` will return the value of the 24th element (the numbering in Java collections starts with zero) as an `Integer` object, that object will automatically be converted into a primitive. This is called *unboxing*.

## PROGRAM COMMENTS

While writing code in Java, you should add comments, the text that explains what the program does. Programs are being read a lot more often than they are being written. At some point, other software developers will read and try to understand your code. Be nice and make their job easier. A typical software developer doesn't like writing comments (regardless of what programming language he or she uses).

I can suggest to you a simple technique: Write comments first and only then the code. By the time your program is written it's already commented. You can write comments pretty much everywhere — before or inside the class, or inside the methods.

In Java you can use three types of comments:

➤ Block comments that contain more than one line of text located between the symbols /* and */. For example:

```
/* This method will calculate the cost of shipping, handling,
      and all applicable taxes
*/
```

The compiler ignores the text in comments and you can write whatever you want.

➤ If you want to write a short comment that fits on a single line, just start this line with two forward slashes (//). For example:

```
// This method will calculate the cost of shipping
```

➤ Some comments start with /** and end with */. These are used by a special utility, javadoc, that can automatically extract the text from these comments and create program documentation. To get a feeling for what javadoc can generate, look at the documented API for Java itself http://java.sun.com/javase/6/docs/api/overview-summary.html.

If you'd like to learn how to use the javadoc utility, refer to its program documentation at http://java.sun.com/javase/6/docs/technotes/guides/javadoc/index.html.

# First Useful Program

It's time to write a program that does something more useful than print "Hello World." This program will emulate the calculation of state tax. The goal is to show you how Java classes communicate, how methods are called, and how variables can be used.

First you need to decide what Java class(es) you need to write for the task at hand. Then think about the properties (class variables) and methods (functions) these classes should have.

## Declaring a Tax Class with Properties

Since you are planning to calculate tax, it doesn't take a rocket scientist to figure out that you need to define a class called Tax. Start with the class name and curly braces — this is the simplest class you can create:

```
class Tax{
}
```

What data does this class need to perform tax calculations? You'll definitely need to know the gross income of a person for the tax year. This is a good candidate for a property of this class. Properties in Java are represented by *variables*. Pick one of the numeric data types. Gross income is not always an integer number, so let's use the `double` data type, as it's a number with a decimal point. You could use `float` instead, but you expect to process some very large incomes:

```
class Tax{
        double grossIncome;
}
```

You also need to know what state the person lives in — taxation rules vary by state. These are some of the abbreviations for the states in the USA: NY, NJ, CT. Use the data type String for storing text data:

```
class Tax{
        double grossIncome;
        String state;
}
```

Add one more property for dependents of the taxable person. `Integer` will work just fine here — a person can't have two and a half dependents:

```
class Tax{
        double grossIncome;
        String state;
        int  dependents;
}
```

## Adding a Method to the Tax Class

Variables store data, and methods perform actions. It's time for actions. The first method, `calcTax()`, will calculate the state tax based on the values of gross income, number of dependents, and state:

**LISTING 3-3:** Class Tax

```
class Tax{
        double grossIncome;
        String state;
        int dependents;

        public double calcTax() {

            return 234.55;
        }
}
```

The `calcTax()` method signature tells the following:

➤ Any external class can access this method (`public`).

➤ This method will return a value of type `double`.

➤ The name of the method is `calcTax`.

The empty parentheses after the method name mean that it does not have any arguments or, in other words, it does not need any values from outside `Tax` to perform calculations. As a matter of fact, this version of `calcTax()` doesn't use any data for calculation — it just returns a hard-coded tax value of $234.55.

How do you decide if a method should return a value? If your method performs some calculations and has to give a value back to a calling program, it has to return a value. If a method directly modifies the class variables or simply outputs data somewhere (monitor, disk, server) it may not need to return any values. You still need to declare a "no return" in a method signature by using a special keyword, `void`:

```
public void PrintAnnualTaxReturn() {

    //Code goes here
}
```

With the Java `return` statement a method can return data contained in a variable to a calling program, for example:

```
return calculatedTax;
```

Keep in mind that if you declare a return type in the method signature but forget to include the `return` statement in the body of the method, the Java compiler will give you an error.

## Declaring Another Class: TestTax

`Tax` will know how to calculate tax, but in a real-world application you'll have many classes that represent the various workflows of this process. For example, you may need to create a class called `Customer`. Depending on the type of employment or income, accountants use many different forms to file taxes, and each form can be represented by a separate class: `Form1040`, `Form1099`, and so on.

Each of these classes represents some entity, but none of them is an executable program — none of them will have the method `main()`. You need to create one more class to start the application and instantiate other classes as needed. I'll call this class `TestTax`. The class `TestTax` should be able to perform the following actions:

➤ Create an instance of the class `Tax`.

➤ Assign customer's data (gross income, state, dependents) to the class variables of the class `Tax`.

➤ Call the method `calcTax()`.

➤ Print the result on the screen.

The class `TestTax` will be stored in a separate file named `TestTax.java`.

**LISTING 3-4:** Class TestTax

```
class TestTax{
    public static void main(String[] args){
        Tax   t = new Tax(); // creating an instance
```

```
        t.grossIncome= 50000;  // assigning the values
        t.dependents= 2;
        t.state= "NJ";

        double yourTax = t.calcTax(); //calculating tax

        // Printing the result
        System.out.println("Your tax is " + yourTax);
    }
}
```

In the preceding code we've declared a variable, t, of type `Tax`.

The method `main()` is an entry point to the tax-calculation program. This method creates an instance of the class Tax and the variable t points to a place in your computer's memory where the `Tax` object was created. From now on, if you want to refer to this object use the variable t.

The following three lines assign values to the properties of the object `Tax`:

```
        t.grossIncome= 50000;  // assigning the values
        t.dependents= 2;
        t.state= "NJ";
```

After that you can calculate tax by calling the method `calcTax()`, and the result returned by this method will be assigned to the variable `yourTax`. The method `calcTax()` still returns the hard-coded value, but you'll fix this in the "Try It" section of this lesson. The last line just displays the result on the system console.

At this point we already have two classes communicating with each other (`TestTax` and `Tax`).

## Conditional Statement if

We make decisions all the time: "If she says this I'll answer with that, otherwise I'll do something else." Java has an `if` statement that determines whether some condition is true or false. Based on the answer to this question the execution of your program will be routed.

If the condition expression returns `true`, the code between the first curly braces will be executed; otherwise the code after the `else` statement will take place. For example:

```
if (totalOrderPrice > 100){
        System.out.println("You'll get a 20% discount");
}
else{
        System.out.println("Order books for more than a" +
                            " $100 to get a 20% discount");
}
```

Because this code sample has only one statement to execute in the `if` and `else` clauses, using curly braces is not a must, but they make the code more readable and prevent you from introducing hard-to-find bugs if, later on, you need to add more code in an `if` statement.

## switch Statement

The switch statement is an alternative to if. The case label in the switch condition (taxCode) is evaluated and the program goes to one of the following case clauses:

```
int taxCode=someObject.getTaxCode(grossIncome);
switch (taxCode){
   case 0:
     System.out.println("Tax Exempt");
     break;
   case 1:
     System.out.println("Low Tax Bracket");
     break;
   case 2:
     System.out.println("High Tax Bracket");
     break;
   default:
     System.out.println("Wrong Tax Bracket");

}
```

The preceding code will call only one println() method. Do not forget to put the break at the end of each case statement so the program will jump out of the switch statement after processing a case; otherwise the code will "fall-through" and print more than one line even though a taxCode can have only one value.

## Inheritance

In object-oriented languages the term *inheritance* means an ability to define a new class based on an existing one (not from scratch).

Imagine that the class Tax calculates tax properly in all states except New Jersey, which has introduced new educational tax deductions. If you have a kid in college, this makes you eligible for an additional $500 deduction from your taxes. In this case you have to either change the method calcTax() in the class Tax to introduce a special case for New Jersey, or create another class based on Tax and add this new functionality there.

Every person inherits some features from his or her parents. A similar mechanism exists in Java. The special keyword extends is used to indicate that one class has been inherited from another:

```
class NJTax extends Tax{
}
```

The class NJTax will have all the features the class Tax has, plus you can add new properties and methods to it. In such a setup, the class Tax is called a *superclass*, and NJTax is called a *subclass*. You can also use the terms *ancestor* and *descendent*, respectively. This new class will have access to all variables and methods of its superclass, unless those have a private or package access level, which will be discussed in Lesson 5.

Let's extend the behavior of the class `Tax` in `NJTax`. The latter will have a method called `adjustForStudents()`:

**LISTING 3-5: Class NJTax**

```
class NJTax extends Tax{

    double adjustForStudents (double stateTax){
        double adjustedTax = stateTax - 500;
        return adjustedTax;
    }
}
```

To use this new method, the `TestTax` class should instantiate `NJTax` rather than `Tax` as it did in Listing 3-4:

```
NJTax  t= new NJTax();
```

Now you can call methods defined in the class `Tax` as well as those from `NJTax` using the reference variable `t`, for example:

```
NJTax  t= new NJTax();
double yourTax = t.calcTax();
double totalTax = t. adjustForStudents (yourTax);
```

I've added a new functionality to the tax-calculation program without changing the code of the class `Tax`. The preceding code fragment also shows how you can pass a result of processing from one method to another. The value of the variable `yourTax` was calculated by `calcTax()` and is passed to the method `adjustForStudents()` as an *argument*.

# Method Overriding

Yet another important term in object-oriented programming is *method overriding*. Imagine `Tax` with 20 methods. Most of them work fine for all states, but there is one method that is not valid for New Jersey. Instead of modifying this method in the superclass, you could create another method in the subclass *with the same name and argument list*. If a subclass has that method with the same name and argument list, it will override (suppress) the corresponding method of its ancestor.

Method overriding comes in handy in the following situations:

➤   The source code of the superclass is not available, but you still need to change its functionality.

➤   The original version of the method is still valid in some cases and you want to keep it intact.

➤   You use method overriding to enable polymorphism, which will be explained in Lesson 7.

You'll have a chance to try method overriding in the "Try It" section. In Lesson 4 you learn about method overloading, which is a completely different animal.

## TRY IT

In this section you create in Eclipse the tax-calculation application described in this lesson, and then modify it to replace the hard-coded value returned by the method `calcTax()` with some calculations. After this is done, you'll subclass the class Tax and override `calcTax()`.

## Lesson Requirements

For this lesson you must have Eclipse IDE installed.

>  *You can download the code and resources for this Try It from the book's web page at www.wrox.com. You can find them in the Lesson3 folder in the download.*

## Hints

This lesson has only brief introductions to basic Java language constructs. The online Java tutorial may be handy while completing this and future assignments. It's available at `http://download .oracle.com/javase/tutorial/java/index.html`.

## Step-by-Step

1. In Eclipse, create a new project named Lesson 3.

2. Create a new `Tax` class (File ➪ New ➪ Class). Enter the code shown in Listing 3-3.

3. Create another class, `TestCalc`, and input the code from Listing 3-4.

4. Save both classes and run `TestCalc` (right-click and select Run As ➪ Java Application). The console view should display "Your tax is 234.55," as shown in Figure 3-1.

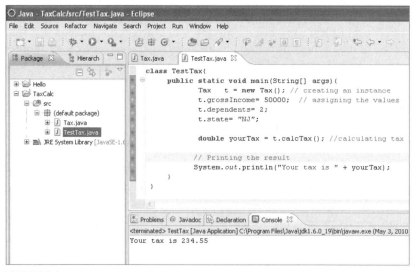

**FIGURE 3-1**

**5.** Replace the return of a hard-coded value with some tax calculations. Let's say that if the gross income was less than $30,000 you will deduct 5 percent for state tax. If it's greater than $30,000 you will deduct 6 percent. Modify the code of calcTax as follows. Run the program several times, modifying the values of the class variables of the class Tax. Make sure that the tax value on the console is properly calculated.

```
public double calcTax() {
      double  stateTax=0;
      if (grossIncome < 30000) {
        stateTax=grossIncome*0.05;
      }
      else{
        stateTax= grossIncome*0.06;
      }
        return stateTax;
  }
```

**6.** Create the NJTax class shown in Listing 3-5.

**7.** Change the functionality of calcTax() by overriding it in NJTax. The new version of calcTax() should lower the tax by $500 before returning the value.

**8.** Modify the code of the TestTax class to instantiate NJTax instead of Tax. Observe that the $500 deduction is properly calculated.

To get the sample database files you can download Lesson 3 from the book's website at www.wrox.com.

> *Please select Lesson 3 on the DVD to view the video that accompanies this lesson.*

# 4

# Class Methods

Methods contain code for actions or functions a class can perform. In this lesson you'll learn how to declare and call them.

## METHOD ARGUMENTS

Each class method performs some functionality, such as calculating tax, placing an order, or starting the car. If a method requires some external data to perform its function, such data can be provided in the form of arguments or parameters, as in the function `adjustForStudents()` shown in Listing 3-5, which has one argument: `stateTax`.

In the method signature you need to declare the data type and the name of each argument, for example:

```
int calcLoanPayment(int amount, int numberOfMonths, String state){
    // Your code goes here
}
```

When you call a function, Java run time tries to find the function that has been declared with the specified signature. For example, if you try to call the preceding function like this:

```
calcLoanPayment(20000, 60);
```

Java compiler will give you an error complaining that no `calcLoanPayment()` function has been found that expects just two arguments.

## METHOD OVERLOADING

If you want to allow the calling of a function with different numbers of arguments, you need to create multiple versions of this function. For example, you can create a function that will use the state of New York to spare developers from providing the state as an argument. If most of the loan calculation is done for New Yorkers, such a function may be a good idea.

```
int calcLoanPayment(int amount, int numberOfMonths){
    // Your code for New York loan calculation goes here
}
```

*Method overloading* means having a class with more than one method having the same name but different argument lists. A method can be overloaded not only in the same class but in a descendant too. For example, the class `LoanCalulator` can have the function `calcLoanPayment()` defined with three arguments, while its descendant `MyLoanCalculator` may have a two-argument version of `calcLoanPayment()`.

Why overload methods in your classes? To provide users of these classes with a more flexible application program interface (API). In Lesson 1 you use the JDK function `println()` declared in the class `PrintStream` (see Figure 4-1 or its JavaDoc description at `http://java.sun.com/javase/6/docs/api/java/io/PrintStream.html`). The function `println()` has been overloaded there to give Java developers the freedom to call "the same" method with different types of arguments. In reality they are calling different methods with the same name.

| | |
|---|---|
| void | **println()**<br>Terminates the current line by writing the line separator string. |
| void | **println(boolean x)**<br>Prints a boolean and then terminate the line. |
| void | **println(char x)**<br>Prints a character and then terminate the line. |
| void | **println(char[] x)**<br>Prints an array of characters and then terminate the line. |
| void | **println(double x)**<br>Prints a double and then terminate the line. |
| void | **println(float x)**<br>Prints a float and then terminate the line. |
| void | **println(int x)**<br>Prints an integer and then terminate the line. |
| void | **println(long x)**<br>Prints a long and then terminate the line. |
| void | **println(Object x)**<br>Prints an Object and then terminate the line. |
| void | **println(String x)**<br>Prints a String and then terminate the line. |

**FIGURE 4-1**

## CONSTRUCTORS

When a program creates an instance of a class, Java invokes the class's *constructor* — a special method that is called only once when the instance is being built with the operator `new`:

```
Tax t = new Tax();
```

Parentheses in the preceding code snippet mean that this code calls a no-argument constructor on the class Tax. Even if you didn't declare a constructor on a class, Java will create a no-argument constructor for you.

Constructors have the following characteristics:

➤ They are called when the class is being instantiated.

➤ They must have the same name as the class they're in.

➤ They can't return a value and you don't specify the keyword void as a return type.

Typically constructors are used to assign initial values to class variables, and in the next code snippet a three-argument constructor is defined:

**LISTING 4-1: Class Tax with constructor**

```
class Tax {
    double grossIncome; // class variables
    String state;
    int dependents;

    // Constructor
    Tax (double gi, String st, int depen){
        grossIncome = gi;  // class variable initialization
        state = st;
        dependents=depen;
    }
}
```

Creating an instance of this class can look like this:

```
Tax t = new Tax(65000,"NJ",3);
```

Note the difference in the initialization of the class variables: Here you pass the values during the class instantiation via the constructor's arguments, while in Listing 3-4 it took four lines of code to create an instance of Tax and then initialize the variables. If a constructor with arguments has been defined in a class, you can no longer use a default no-argument constructor — you have to explicitly write one if needed.

The code snippet above declares the variable t that points at an instance of the object Tax in memory. To refer to any specific field or call a method on this instance, you'll need to use so-called dot-notation — the name of the reference variable followed by a dot and the name of the field or a method. For example,

```
Public static void main(){
...
Tax t = new Tax(65000,"NJ",3);
t.dependents = 4;  // changing the number of dependents from 3 to 4
...
```

## THE KEYWORD SUPER

If a method is overridden in a subclass, there are two versions of the method with the same signature. If you just call a method by name, e.g. `calcTax()` in the class `NJTax` from Lesson 3, the JVM will call the overridden version of the method. Once in a while you may need to call the ancestor's version of a method. The keyword `super` enables you to explicitly call the method or a constructor from the ancestor's class, for example `super.calcTax()`.

If one class is inherited from another, each of them may have its own constructor explicitly defined. As with any other class method, a constructor of a subclass can override the constructor of a superclass. But sometimes you may need to add into the subclass's construction some functionality that has to be called after the ancestor's constructor code. In this case just add the explicit call to the constructor of a superclass, as shown in Listing 4-2. Invocation of the constructor of the superclass must be the first line in the constructor.

**LISTING 4-2:** Calling the constructor of the ancestor

```
class SmallerTax extends Tax{
    // Constructor
    SmallerTax (double gi, String st, int depen){
        super(gi,st,depen);
        System.out.println("Applying special tax rates for my friends.");
    }
}
```

## THE KEYWORD THIS

The keyword `this` is useful when you need to refer to the instance of the class from its method. Review the code of the constructor from Listing 4-1. The names of the constructor's arguments were different from the names of the class variables. But the code in Listing 4-3 shows how you can use the same variable names, both in the arguments and in the class variables. The keyword `this` helps to resolve name conflicts. To instruct JVM to use the instance variable `grossIncome`, use the following syntax:

```
this.grossIncome = 50000;
```

If there were only one `grossIncome` variable in the class `Tax`, you could simply omit the `this` prefix. But in Listing 4-3 the absence of the `this` keyword would lead to ambiguity and the instance variable would never be initialized.

**LISTING 4-3:** Resolving name conflicts with the this keyword

```
class Tax {
    double grossIncome; // class member variables
```

```
       String state;
       int dependents;

       // Constructor
       Tax (double grossIncome, String state, int dependents){
          this.grossIncome = grossIncome;  // instance variable initialization
          this.state = state;
          this.dependents=dependents;
       }
    }
```

Consider a class called SomeOtherClass with a method defined as verifyTax( Tax t). As you can see, it expects an instance of Tax as an argument. Listing 4-4 shows how you can call it from the class Tax using the keyword this to pass a reference to the current instance of the class Tax.

**LISTING 4-4:** Calling an overloaded constructor with the keyword this

```
class  Tax {
      void verifyTax(){

          SomeOtherClass s = new SomeOtherClass();
          s.verifyTax(this);
      }
   }
```

Here's another use case — a class has several overloaded constructors with different numbers of arguments. You can use the this() notation to call a specific version of the constructor. In Listing 4-5 the second constructor invokes the first one.

**LISTING 4-5:** Calling an overloaded constructor with the keyword this

```
class Tax {
      double grossIncome; // class member variables
      String state;
      int dependents;

      // First Constructor
      Tax (double grossIncome, String state, int dependents){
         this.grossIncome = grossIncome;  // instance variable initialization
         this.state = state;
         this.dependents=dependents;
      }

      // Second Constructor
      Tax (double grossIncome, int dependents){
         this(grossIncome, "NY", dependents);
      }

   }
```

## PASSING BY VALUE OR BY REFERENCE

Calling a method with arguments enables you to pass some required data to the method. The question is how JVM passes these values to the method. Does it create a copy of a variable in a calling program and give it to the method?

The primitive values are passed by value (meaning that an extra copy will be created in memory for each variable). If you create an instance of Tax as in Listing 4-6, there will be two copies of grossIncome and two copies of the variable dependents — one in TestTax and the other one in Tax.

**LISTING 4-6:** The TestTax class

Available for
download on
Wrox.com

```
class TestTax{
    public static void main(String[] args){
            double grossIncome; // local variables
            String state;
            int dependents;

            grossIncome= 50000;
            dependents= 2;
            state= "NJ";

            Tax   t = new Tax(grossIncome, state, dependents);

            double yourTax = t.calcTax(); //calculating tax

            // Printing the result
            System.out.println("Your tax is " + yourTax);
    }
}
```

In the preceding example, if you'll be changing the value of grossIncome or dependents in the constructor of the class Tax, it won't affect the values in the corresponding variables of the class TestTax because there will be two copies of these primitives.

Now consider another example. I'll declare another variable of type Tax and will assign the value of t to it:

```
    Tax   t2 = t;
```

The variable t is pointing to an instance of the object Tax in memory. In other words, the variable t holds the reference (the address in memory) to an object. The code line above will not create another copy of the Tax object in memory, but will copy its address to the variable t2. Now we still have a single instance of the Tax object, but now two reference variables — t and t2 — are pointing at it. Until both of these variables will go out of scope (explained in the next section), the object Tax will not be removed from memory.

The process of removal of unused objects from memory is called garbage collection (GC). JVM runs GC automatically.

The code in Listing 4-4 passes the argument's value differently. It seems that it passes the entire instance of the object `Tax` to the method `verifyTax()`. In reality, though, another copy of just the reference variable pointing at the `Tax` instance will be created in `SomeOtherClass`, but the instance of the class `Tax` will remain the same.

This means that if the code in `SomeOtherClass` will be changing some properties of the `Tax` instance, the changes will be applied to the only copy of the `Tax` instance and will be visible from both `Tax` and `SomeOtherClass`.

## VARIABLE SCOPES

Variable scope defines how long the variable will live and remain usable. If you declared the variable inside a method, it's a local variable that will go out of scope (become unavailable) as soon as the method finishes its execution. For example, variables `t`, `grossIncome`, `dependents`, and `state` from Listing 4-6 are local.

If variables have been declared outside the method (such as `grossIncome`, `dependents`, and `state` in Listing 4-1) they are *class variables* and can be used by any method of this class. On the other hand, the variables `grossIncome`, `dependents`, and `state` in Listing 4-1 are also *instance variables* and store instance-specific data.

You can create more than one instance of the class `Tax`, and each instance can have different values in its instance variables. For example, the following lines of code will create two instances of `Tax`, with different values for `grossIncome`, `dependents`, and `state` (these instance variables are initialized in the constructor):

```
Tax    t1 = new Tax(50000, "NY", 3 );
Tax    t2 = new Tax(65000, "TX", 4 );
```

## THE KEYWORD STATIC

Java has a special keyword, `static`, that indicates that the class variable will be shared by all instances of the same class. If the class `Tax` had the declaration `static double grossIncome;` then this variable's value would be shared by all instances of the class `Tax`, which doesn't make sense. Besides, after the creation of two instances (`t1` and `t2`), as in the preceding code, the first value of the variable (`50000`) would be overwritten with the second one (`65000`).

But if you introduce in `Tax` a class variable to count the number of its instances (think the number of customers whose taxes have been calculated), such a variable has to be declared as `static`, so its only version can be incremented by each instance on creation, as in Listing 4-7.

**LISTING 4-7:** The Tax class with the keyword static

```
class Tax {
    double grossIncome; // class member variables
    String state;
```

*continues*

**LISTING 4-7** *(continued)*

```
        int dependents;
        static int customerCounter;

        // Constructor
        Tax (double gi, String st, int depen){
            grossIncome = gi;  // member variable initialization
            state = st;
            dependents=depen;
            customerCounter++;   // increment the counter by one
        }
    }
```

You can also declare methods with the `static` qualifier. Such methods can be called without the need to instantiate the class first. This is usually done for utility methods that don't use any instance variables, but rather get input via the argument and return the result.

The following function converts Fahrenheit to Celsius and returns the result:

```
class WeatherReport{
        static double convertToCelsius(double far){
            return ((far - 32) * 5 / 9);
        }
    }
```

You can call this function from another class without the need to instantiate `WeatherReport` first:

```
    double centigrees=WeatherReport.convertToCelsius(98.7);
```

## TRY IT

In this section you create yet another version of the `Tax` class with a three-argument constructor and add a utility function to convert the tax value from dollars to euros, assuming the dollar-to-euro conversion rate is 1.25.

## Lesson Requirements

For this lesson you should have Eclipse IDE installed. If you prefer to use a plain text editor to code your Java programs, that's fine too.

> *You can download the code and resources for this Try It from the book's web page at* www.wrox.com. *You can find them in the Lesson4 folder in the download.*

## Step-by-Step

1.  In Eclipse IDE, create a new project named Lesson 4.

2.  Create a new class called `Tax` (File ➪ New ➪ Class). Enter the code shown in Listing 4-7.

3.  Add the following statement as the last line of the constructor of the class `Tax`:

    ```java
    System.out.println("Preparing the tax data for customer #" + customerCounter);
    ```

4.  Add the method `calcTax()` to the class `Tax` and calculate tax by multiplying the gross income by 0.33 and deducting the number of dependents multiplied by one hundred:

    ```java
    return (grossIncome*0.33 - dependents*100);
    ```

5.  Add the `static` function to `Tax` to convert the calculated tax to euros, applying the currency-conversion rate of 1.25. Print the calculated tax in euros using the function `System.out` `.println()`.

6.  Create a `TestTax` class and input the code from Listing 4-6. Add to this class yet another instance of the class `Tax`:

    ```java
    Tax   t2 = new Tax(65000, "TX", 4 );
    ```

    Calculate the tax using the second instance of the class `Tax`:

    ```java
    double hisTax = t2.calcTax();
    ```

7.  Call the method twice to convert the currency, passing the calculated tax from `t` and `t2` as an argument.

8.  Run the class `TestCalc` (right-click and select Run As ➪ Java Application). The Console view should display the two "Preparing the tax..." messages followed by the two messages with the calculated tax in euros.

To get the sample database files you can download Lesson 4 from the book's website at www.wrox.com.

 *Please select Lesson 4 on the DVD to view the video that accompanies this lesson.*

# Back to Java Basics

This tutorial didn't start with detailed coverage of basic constructs of the Java language such as the syntax of if statements, loops, and the like. You started learning Java programming with getting used to object-oriented terms and constructs of the language. This lesson is a grab bag of basic language elements, terms, and data structures.

## ARRAYS

An *array* is a data storage that's used to store multiple values of the same type. Let's say your program has to store names of 20 different girls, such as "Masha", "Matilda", "Rosa" and so on. Instead of declaring 20 different String variables, you can declare one String array with the capacity to store 20 elements:

```
String []  friends = new String [20];  // Declare and instantiate array
friends[0] = "Masha";                   //Initialize the first element
friends[1] = "Matilda";                 //Initialize the second element
friends[2] = "Rosa";

// Keep initializing the elements of the array here

friends[19] = "Natasha";                     //Initialize the last element
```

The first element of an array in Java always has an index of 0. While declaring an array you can place brackets either after the data type or after the variable name. Both of the following declarations are correct:

```
String friends[];
String[] friends;
```

You must know the size of the array before assigning values to its elements. If you want to be able to dynamically change the size of an array during the run time, consider other Java collection classes from the package java.util, such as Vector and ArrayList. Besides arrays Java has lots of collection classes that can store multiple related values, for example HashMap, List, and LinkedList. You'll have a chance to see their use in the code samples accompanying this book. Listing 5-1 contains sample code that partially populates an array.

**LISTING 5-1: Populating a simple array**

```java
public class Girlfriends1 {

public static void main(String[] args) {
        String []  friends = new String [20];  // Declare and instantiate array
        friends[0] = "Masha";                   //Initialize the first element
        friends[1] = "Matilda";                 //Initialize the second element
        friends[2] = "Rosa";
        // ...
        friends[18] = "Hillary";
        friends[19] = "Natasha";

        System.out.println("The third girl's name is " + friends[2]);
        System.out.println("The twentieth girl's name is " + friends[19]);
   }
}
```

An array has a property length that "knows" the number of elements in the array. The next line shows how you can get this number:

```java
int  totalElements = friends.length;
```

If you know all the values that will be stored in the array at the time of its declaration, you can declare and initialize an array at the same time. The following line declares, instantiates, and populates an array of four elements.

```java
String []  friends = {"Masha", "Matilda", "Rosa", "Sharon"};
```

Our array `friends` is not as practical as a Rolodex, though — it does not store girls' phone numbers. Luckily, Java supports multidimensional arrays. For example, to create a two-dimensional array (names and phone numbers), declare it with two sets of square brackets:

```java
String  friends [][] = new String [20][2];
friends[0][0] = "Masha";
friends[0][1] = "732 111-2222";
friends[1][0] = "Matilda";
friends[1][1] = "718 111-2222";
...
friends[19][0] = "Sharon";
friends[19][1] = "212 111-2222"
```

## LOOPS

*Loops* are used to repeat the same action multiple times. When you know in advance how many times you want to repeat an action, use the `for` loop. Let's print the names from the one-dimensional array `friends`.

```java
int  totalElements = friends.length;

for (int i=0; i < totalElements;i++){
   System.out.println("I love " + friends[i]);
}
```

The preceding code reads "Print the value of the element i from the array friends starting from i=0 and incrementing i by one (i++) until i reaches the value equal to the value of totalElements." Listing 5-2 adds a for loop to the program shown in Listing 5-1.

**LISTING 5-2: Looping through the array**

```java
public class Girlfriends2 {

        public static void main(String[] args) {
                String []  friends = new String [20];
                friends[0] = "Masha";
                friends[1] = "Matilda";
                friends[2] = "Rosa";
                friends[18] = "Hillary";
                friends[19] = "Natasha";

                int  totalElements = friends.length;
                int i;
                for (i=0; i<totalElements;i++){
                    System.out.println("I love " + friends[i]);
                }


        }
}
```

Since the friends array has been declared with a size of 20, Java run time has allocated memory for 20 elements. But the code in Listing 5-2 has populated only five of the 20 elements of the array, which explains why the output of this program looks as follows:

```
I love Masha
I love Matilda
I love Rosa
I love null
I love null
I love null
I love null
I love null
I love null
I love null
I love null
I love null
I love null
I love null
I love null
I love null
I love null
I love null
I love Hillary
I love Natasha
```

The keyword null represents an absence of any value in an object. Even though the size of this array is 20, only five elements were initialized.

There's another syntax of the `for` loop, known as the *for-each loop*. You simply declare a variable of the same type as the objects stored in an array and specify the array to iterate. The following code snippet declares the variable `girl`, and the colon means "in." Read this loop's condition expression as "for each `element` in `friends`." This syntax allows you to not worry about checking the size of the array, and there is no need to increment any loop variable either. This is an elegant and short loop notation:

```
for (String girl: friends){
    System.out.println("I love  " + girl);
}
```

You can rewrite the program in Listing 5-2 using the `while` loop, which is used when you do not know the exact size of the array, but just the condition of exit from the loop. Use the keyword `while`:

```
int  totalElements = friends.length;
int i=0;
while (i<totalElements){
   System.out.println("I love " + friends[i]);
        i++;    // the same as i=i+1;
}
```

Just think of a program that reads and processes the records from a database (see Lesson 22). When you write a Java program you don't know how many elements the database has, and even if you do know, this number can change in the future, so it's better to use loops with the exit condition than to use a hard-coded number of repetitions.

Use the keyword `break` to prematurely jump out of the loop on the line below the ending curly brace. For example, if you want to find the first `null` element in the `friends` array, write the following:

```
while (i<totalElements){
        if (friends[i]==null){
            System.out.println("The element " + (i+1) + " is null");
            break;
        }

        System.out.println("I love " + friends[i]);
        i++;
}  // closing curly brace for the loop
```

The `if` statement in the preceding code checks the value of each element of the array, and as soon as it finds `null`, the loop prints the message about it, stops the iteration process, and goes to the line below the closing curly brace of the loop, if any.

The keyword `continue` allows you to force the loop to jump up to its first line and retest the loop exit condition. The following code snippet will print only those values from the array that are not `null`.

```
while (i<totalElements){
    if (friends[i]==null){
        i++;
        continue;
```

```
        }
    System.out.println("I love " + friends[i]);
    i++;
                    }
    System.out.println("The iteration is over");
    }
```

The preceding code uses an `if` statement you have not seen before, which allows you to check a certain condition and redirect the program to execute one or another portion of the code accordingly. In this case, if the loop runs into a `null` value (the double equals sign means "compare the values for equality"), it increments by one the value of the variable `i` and goes to the beginning of the `while` loop, skipping the rest of the code within the loop body. (Later in this lesson there's a section explaining the syntax of the various `if` statements in greater detail.) The complete code of the program, illustrating a `while` loop with a `continue` statement, is shown in Listing 5-3.

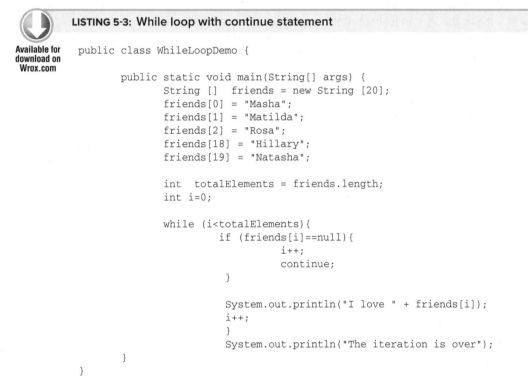

**LISTING 5-3: While loop with continue statement**

```
public class WhileLoopDemo {

    public static void main(String[] args) {
        String []  friends = new String [20];
        friends[0] = "Masha";
        friends[1] = "Matilda";
        friends[2] = "Rosa";
        friends[18] = "Hillary";
        friends[19] = "Natasha";

        int  totalElements = friends.length;
        int i=0;

        while (i<totalElements){
            if (friends[i]==null){
                i++;
                continue;
            }

            System.out.println("I love " + friends[i]);
            i++;
            }
            System.out.println("The iteration is over");
        }
    }
```

There is a rarely used `do-while` version of the `while` loop. It starts with the `do` keyword followed by the body of the loop in curly braces, and the `while` condition comes last. Such loop syntax guarantees that the code written in the body of the loop will be executed at least once, because the loop condition will be tested only after the first pass into the loop. In the following loop at the very minimum the statements about reading the array `friends` will be printed for each element of the array even if every one of them is `null`:

```
do {
    System.out.println("Reading the element" + i +" of array friends");
     if (friends[i]==null){
         i++;
         continue;
     }

     System.out.println("I love " + friends[i]);
     i++;
                         }
} while (i<totalElements);
```

The worst thing that can happen in any loop is a programmer's mistake in the loop exit condition that will always evaluate the loop condition as `true`. In programming this is known as *infinite loop*. To get a better feeling for what this term means, comment out the line that increments the value of the variable `i` inside the `if` statement, and your program will never end unless you forcefully stop it or your computer runs out of power. The reason is clear: If the program will enter the code block that just has the statement `continue`, the value of the variable `i` will never increase and the loop execution condition `i<totalElements` will hold true forever.

## DEBUGGING JAVA PROGRAMS

In programmer's lingo a *bug* is an error in a program that causes the program to work in an unexpected way. Don't confuse a bug with a syntax error in the code. The latter will be caught by the Java compiler before you even start the program, while bugs are your run-time enemies. To *debug* a program is to identify and fix the run-time errors in code.

The simplest way to debug a program is to print the value of the "suspicious variables" with `System .out.println()` or the like. You may think that a certain variable will get a particular value during the execution, but you might be wrong, and printing its value from the running program may reveal why your code produces unexpected results.

Java also comes with a logging API (application program interface) that allows you to *log* the run-time values in a file or other destination. Logging is out of the scope of this book, but you can find `Logger` and other supporting classes in the Java package `java.util.logging`.

You'll be using a debugger that comes with an IDE daily. Even though Lesson 2 was dedicated to Eclipse IDE, explaining debugging back then would have been a bit premature, as you didn't have much Java code to debug. Now you're ready to learn how the Eclipse debugger can help you.

Let's see how the `while` loop from Listing 5-3 works by running the `WhileLoopDemo` program with the Eclipse debugger. You can do it either by right-clicking the name of the program and selecting the menu option Debug As Java Application or by clicking the little icon with an image of a bug in the Eclipse toolbar. But before doing this, set a breakpoint on the line of code where you want the program to pause execution and allow you to start watching the program internals in the Eclipse Debugger's Perspective.

I'd like to pause this program right before it enters the `while` loop, so let's set the breakpoint on the following line:

```
while (i<totalElements){...}
```

Double-click the gray vertical bar located between the Package and Editor views — you should see an image of a little bullet there. This is a breakpoint, and if the program runs into the code with the set breakpoint, Eclipse IDE will switch to Debugger perspective and pause the program, highlighting the line that's about to execute. Figure 5-1 shows how the Debugger perspective may look at this point.

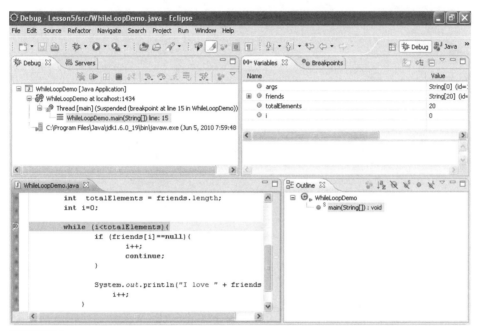

**FIGURE 5-1**

Note the little arrow in the Editor view next to the bullet — it shows you the line of code that will be executed next. The Variables view shows you the values of the program variables at this moment. The variable `i` is equal to 0; the value of `totalElements` is 20. If you click the little plus sign by the variable `friends`, it'll show the content of this array.

Now try to execute this program step-by-step, watching how the value of the variable `i` changes. You'll control program execution by clicking the buttons in the toolbar for the Debug view (see Figure 5-2).

**FIGURE 5-2**

The green play button means "Continue executing the program until it ends or hits another breakpoint." The red square button stops the debugging process. The first curvy yellow arrow (Step Into) is used if the code has been paused on a line that calls a method, and you'd like to debug the code of the method being called. The second curvy arrow (Step Over) allows you to execute the current line without stepping into any methods that may be called in this line of code.

There are other and less frequently used buttons on this toolbar, which you can study on your own, but let's enter the loop by clicking the Step Over button. Keep clicking this button and observe that the program doesn't enter the `if` statement, which is correct — the first element of the friends `array` is not `null`. Then `if` prints "I love Masha" in the console view, increments the value of the variable `i` to 1 (see the Variables view in Figure 5-3), and returns to the loop condition to check if the value of `i` is still less than the value of `totalElements`.

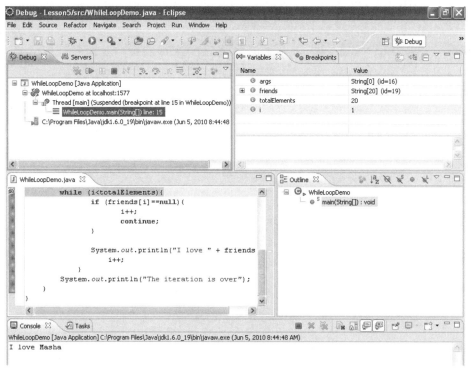

**FIGURE 5-3**

Keep clicking the Step Over button, and expand the variable `friends` in the Variables view to see its elements in order to better understand why the program skips or enters the `if` statement in the loop. Note the moment when the program exits the loop and prints the message "The iteration is over." After spending some time debugging the program you should appreciate the value of the Eclipse Debugger. In my opinion, the best way to learn a new programming language is to run someone else's code through a good debugger. The program may be bug-free, but this will help you to better understand its flow.

## MORE ABOUT IF AND SWITCH STATEMENTS

If you need to change the execution of the program based on a certain condition you can use either `if` or `switch` statements, which were introduced in Lesson 3. In this section you'll see more flavors of the conditional statements.

# The Flavors of if Statements

In Listing 5-3 you saw one version of the `if` statement:

```
if (friends[i]==null){
    i++;
    continue;
}
```

The curly braces must be used in the `if` statement to specify a block of code that has to be executed if the condition is true. Even though the curly braces are not required if there's only one statement in the code block, using them is considered a good practice — this makes the program more understandable for other people who may need to read your code (or for yourself six months from now).

```
if (friends[i]==null){
    System.out.println("I found an array element with null value");
}
// Some other code goes here
```

The code below the closing curly brace will always be executed, which may not be desirable. In this case use the `if-else` syntax:

```
if (friends[i]==null){
    System.out.println("I found an array element with null value");
} else{
    // Some other code goes here
}
```

In the preceding code snippet, the "some other code" will be executed only if the current element of the array is not `null` (or, as we put it in Java, `friends[i]!=null`). You can write an `if` statement with multiple `else` clauses. For example, the following code will print only one love confession:

```
if (friends[i]==null){
    System.out.println("I found an array element with null value");
} else if (friends[i] == "Natasha"){
    System.out.println("I love my wife so much!");
} else if (friends[i] == "Masha"){
    System.out.println("I fell in love with Masha when I was in the 8th grade.");
} else{
    System.out.println("I used to love " + friends[i] + " at some point.");
}
```

Using conditional statements can be a lot more complex than comparing two values. You can build expressions using `boolean` AND, OR, and NOT operators. The AND operation is represented as `&&`, like this:

```
if (age<20 && gender=="male") {
    // do something only for males under 20 years old
}
```

For the OR condition use `||`, for example:

```
if (age < 30 || yearsInArmy > 0) {
    // do something with people yonger than 30 or those who served
    // in the army regardless of their age
}
```

For the NOT condition (aka negation) use the `!` sign:

```
boolean hasBachelorDegree;
// Read the person record and assign the value true or false
// to the variable hasBachelorDegree
if (!hasBachelorDegree) {
      // do something with people without bachelor degree
}
```

The negation symbol can be placed either in front of a `boolean` variable, as in the preceding code snippet, or in front of the expression that returns `boolean`. The next code example shows how to use negation Note that the comparison expression was placed inside the parentheses; otherwise the Java compiler would assume that you're trying to negate a `String` value called `friends[i]`, which is not allowed.

```
if (!(friends[i]=="Hillary")){
      System.out.println("Still looking for Hillary.");
}
```

Imagine a situation in which you need to assign a value to a variable, but the value depends on the result of a certain condition. To assign the variable in a verbose way you can use a regular `if` statement and test some condition, writing one assignment operator for a result of `true`, and another in the `else` section for a result of `false`. But if you use a special construct called a *conditional operator* (`?`), the same task can be done more simply.

The conditional operator consists of the following parts: an expression that returns `boolean`, a question mark, an expression that returns some value if the first expression evaluates to `true`, a colon, and an expression that returns a value to be used if the first expression returns `false`. It sounds complicated, but it's not. The following code sample shows how to assign a $3,000 bonus if a person's salary is greater than $90,000, and only $2,000 otherwise:

```
float salary;
// Retrieve the salary of the person from some data source here
int bonus = salary>90000?3000:2000;
```

## The switch Statement

The `switch` statement is used when the program execution is defined based on multiple selections. Even though execution can be defined with a long `if-else if` construct, the `switch` statement can be more readable. In the following code fragment the bonus amount is selected based on the salary band of the worker. Imagine that this code is written in a loop that reads data from a database of employees of some firm, and that the `salaryBand` value is assigned right before the `switch` statement.

```
int salaryBand;
int bonus;
// Retrieve the salary band of the person from some data source here

switch(salaryBand){
  case 1:
        bonus=1000;
        break;
```

```
        case 2:
                bonus=2000;
                break;
        case 3:
                bonus=6000;
                break;
        case 4:
                bonus=10000;
                break;
        default:
            // wrong salary band
            System.out.println("Invalid salary band");
        }
```

At the time of this writing Java doesn't allow the use of `String` as a `switch` variable — only integer or enumerated constants are allowed. There is a proposal to support strings in Java 7, but it's not clear if this support will make it into production release.

# COMMAND-LINE ARGUMENTS

In Lesson 1 you learned how to start a Java program from a command line. After development in Eclipse or another IDE is done, Java programs are *deployed in production* and will be started from a command line — usually you get an icon to click that runs a command to start a program, but under the hood the operating system executes a command that starts your program. You can't expect an accountant to have Eclipse installed to run a tax calculation program, right? For example, to run the TestTax program from the command window you need to open a command window, change the directory to `Lesson 4` and enter the following:

```
java TestTax
```

You can run only those Java classes that have the method `main`, which takes a `String` array as an argument. This array is the means of passing some data from the command line to your program during start-up. For example, you can pass gross income, state, and number of dependents to `TestTax` by starting it from the command line as follows:

```
java TestTax 50000 NJ 2
```

The method `main(String[] args)` of the class `TestTax` receives this data as a `String` array that I decided to call `args`. This array will be automatically created by JVM, and will be large enough to accommodate all the arguments entered from the command line. This array will be populated as follows:

```
args[0] = "50000";
args[1] = "NJ";
args[2] = "2";
```

Command-line arguments are always being passed to a program as `String` arrays. It's the responsibility of the programmer to convert the data to the appropriate data type. The wrapper Java classes that were introduced in Lesson 3 can come in handy. For example, the wrapper class `Double` has the function `parseDouble` to convert `String` to `double`:

```
double grossIncome = Double.parseDouble(args[0]);
```

Review the code of the TestTax program from Listing 4-6, which has hard-coded values of gross income, state, and number of dependents. By using command-line arguments you can make the program more generic and useful not only for people from New Jersey having two dependents and an annual income of $50,000. You'll work on this assignment in the Try It section.

## TRY IT

Your assignment is to introduce command-line arguments into the program from Listing 4-6.

## Lesson Requirements

For this lesson you should have Java installed.

> You can download the code and resources for this Try It from the book's web page at www.wrox.com. You can find them in the Lesson5 folder in the download.

## Step-by-Step

1.  In Eclipse IDE, copy the `TestTax` class from the Lesson4 project to Lesson5. Also copy the `Tax` class from the project Lesson3 that has an `if` statement in the `calcTax()` method.

2.  Remove the three lines that initialize `grossIncome`, `state` and `dependents` with hard-coded values.

3.  Add the following code fragment to ensure that the program has been started with three arguments. If it has not, print the error message and exit the program.

    ```
    if (args.length != 3){
        System.out.println("Sample usage of the program:" +
                            "  java TestTax 50000 NJ 2");
        System.exit(0);
    }
    ```

4.  Add the following statements to the method `main()` to get the values passed from the command line, convert them to appropriate data types, and initialize the variables `grossIncome`, `state`, and `dependents`:

    ```
    double grossIncome = Double.parseDouble(args[0]);
    String state = args[1];
    int dependents = Integer.parseInt(args[2]);
    ```

**5.** Right-click the Lesson5 project in Eclipse IDE and select the Properties menu item (note the location of the compiled classes of your project — in my case it was `c:\practicalJava\ workspase\Lesson5\bin`).

**6.** Open the command window and change the directory to the one that contains the file `TestTax.class`.

**7.** Run your program several times, specifying different values for the command line arguments. The program should print different values for the calculated tax.

To get the sample database files you can download the content of the Lesson 5 folder from the book's website at `www.wrox.com`.

 *Please select Lesson 5 on the DVD to view the video that accompanies this lesson.*

# 6

# Packages, Interfaces, and Encapsulation

If you want to find out if a particular programming language is object-oriented, ask if it supports *inheritance*, *encapsulation*, and *polymorphism*. You know by now that Java supports inheritance, which lets you design a class by deriving it from an existing one. This feature allows you to reuse existing code without copy-pasting reusable code fragments from other classes — the class NJTax from Listing 3-5 was designed this way.

In Lessons 6 and 7 you learn what encapsulation means and continue studying coding techniques and best practices. While this lesson will show you several short code examples illustrating certain programming topics, the next one will bring all the pieces you've learned so far together in one larger practical application.

## JAVA PACKAGES

A decently size project can have hundreds of Java classes and you need to organize them in *packages* (think file directories). This will allow you to categorize files, control access to your classes (see the section "Access Levels" later in this chapter), and avoid potential naming conflicts: If both you and your colleague coincidentally decide to call a class Util, this won't be a problem as long as these classes are located in different packages.

Sometimes you'll be using third-party libraries of Java classes written in a different department or even outside your firm. To minimize the chances that package names will be the same, it's common to use so-called *reverse domain name* conventions. For example, if you work for a company called Acme, which has the website acme.com, you can prefix all package names with com.acme. To place a Java class in a certain package, add the package statement at the beginning of the class (it must be the first non-comment statement in the class). For example, if the class Tax has been developed for the Accounting department, you can declare it as follows:

```
package com.acme.accounting;
class Tax {
  // the class body goes here
}
```

If you declare the class `Tax` as shown in the preceding code, the file `Tax.java` must be stored in the corresponding directory tree:

```
Com
       Acme
             Accounting
```

Java classes are also organized into packages and the fully qualified name of a class consists of the package name followed by the class name. For example, the full name of the Java class `Double` is `java.lang.Double`, where `java.lang` is the package name. As a matter of fact, `java.lang` is the only package name that you don't have to explicitly mention in your code in order for its classes to be found, unless all classes are located in the same package.

The program documentation on all Java 6 packages is available at the following URL: `http://download.oracle.com/javase/6/docs/api/`.

Let's say your `Tax` class needs to connect to some URL on the Net with the help of the class `URL` located in the `java.net` package. You can write code containing the fully qualified name of this second class:

```
java.net.URL myURL = new java.net.URL ("http://www.acme.com");
```

But instead of using this rather long notation, include the `import` statement right above the class declaration, and then use just the name of the class:

```
import java.net.URL;
class Tax{
    URL myURL = new URL("http://www.acme.com");
    ...
}
```

If you need to import several classes from the same package, use the wild card in the `import` statement rather then listing each of the classes on a separate line:

```
import java.net.*;
```

## ENCAPSULATION

Encapsulation is the ability to hide and protect data stored in Java objects. You may ask, "Who are the bad guys who want to illegally access my data?" It's not about bad guys. When a developer creates a Java class, he or she plans for a certain use pattern of this code by other classes. For example, the variable `grossIncome` should not be modified directly, but via a method that performs some validation procedures to ensure that the value to be assigned meets application-specific rules.

A Java developer may decide to "hide" 15 out of 20 variables, say, so other classes can't access them. Imagine how many parts exist in a car and how many functions those parts can perform. Does the driver need to know about all of them? Of course not. The driver needs to know how to start and stop the car, how to indicate turns, open the windows, turn on the wipers, and do a few dozen other simple operations, which in programming jargon can be called the car's *public interface*.

## Access Levels

Java classes, methods, and member variables can have `public`, `private`, `protected`, and `package` access levels, for example:

```
public class Tax {
    private double grossIncome;
    private String state;
    private int dependents;
    protected double calcTax(...) {...}
}
```

The keyword `public` means that this element (a class, a method, or a variable) can be accessed from any other Java class. The keyword `protected` makes the element "visible" not only from the current class, but from its subclasses too.

The keyword `private` is the most restrictive one, as it makes a member variable or a method accessible only inside this class. For example, our class `Tax` may need some additional internal methods that could be called from the method `calcTax()`. The users of the class `Tax` do not need to know about these methods and they should be declared as `private`.

If you do not specify any access level, the default is `package`, which means that only classes located in the same package will have access to this method or variable. Java classes should expose only the methods that outsiders have to know, such as `calcTax()`.

If you are not sure which access level to give to methods or variables, just make them all `private`; if later on during development some other class needs to access them, you can always change the access level to be less restrictive. This will protect all the internals of your application from misuse. Think of it this way: "I want to sell my class `Tax` to various accounting firms across the country. If their software developers integrate my class with their existing systems, what are the methods that they must know about to be able to calculate tax?" If car designers did not ask themselves similar questions, drivers would need to press dozens of buttons just to start the engine.

## THE KEYWORD FINAL

The keyword `final` can have different meanings depending on the context. It's explained in the next sections.

## final Variables

You can use the keyword `final` while declaring variables, methods, and classes. A `final` variable becomes a constant (see Lesson 3) that can be initialized only once and can't change its value during the run time. Some people may argue that a constant and a variable that can get initialized only once are not the same thing, but the fact that you can't change their values makes them very similar.

Even though you can declare constants inside a method, it's more common to declare them on the class level so they can be reused by several methods of the same class. You can also declare a variable with the keyword `static` and with a proper access method so they can be used:

```
static final int BOILING_TEMP = 212; //in Fahrenheit
```

## final Methods

If you declare a class method with a `final` keyword, this method can't be overridden if someone decides to extend the class. Today it may seem obvious to you that a particular method will never ever need to be overridden. What are the chances that the formula to convert Fahrenheit to Celsius will be changed any time soon?

```
static final double convertToCelsius(double far){
        return ((far - 32) * 5 / 9);
}
```

But in many cases developers create reusable libraries of Java classes, finalizing functionality that's not written in stone. While it may seem to you that a particular method will never need to be overridden, you might have predicted all use patterns of this class. If this happens, some other developer will have to jump through hoops to create another version of your method in a subclass.

Many years ago the Java compiler optimized (inlined) final methods. It doesn't do that anymore — all methods are optimized by the Hotspot JVM. Just think twice before making a method `final`.

## final Classes

If you declare a class as `final`, no one will be able to subclass it. For example, Java's class `String` has been created as immutable and therefore declared as `final` (see http://java.sun.com/javase/6/docs/api/java/lang/String.html). If a class is declared as `final`, all its methods become implicitly `final`.

## INTERFACES

There are different approaches to how to start designing a class. Some people think of the behavior it should support. The behavior is implemented in a class in the form of methods, which can be declared in a separate entity called an *interface*. Then have your class implement this interface. Listing 6-1 shows an interface with one method declaration.

In general, you should have a reason for declaring the methods separately from the class that will implement it, and you'll see these reasons in the next lesson when you learn about polymorphism, For now, let's just get familiar with the syntax of  defining and using interfaces. The interface will not have any implementations — just declarations. (There is an exception: Marker interfaces don't even have declarations. The next section is devoted to this type of interface.)

When a class declares that it implements a certain interface, it guarantees that it contains implementation for all methods from this interface. And a class can implement more than one interface: just separate their names with commas.

Let's say you have two types of workers in your organization, employees and contractors, and that you create the classes `Employee` and `Contractor` to implement functionalities that reflect specifics of these different groups. Each person is entitled to a pay raise, though for employees this means a salary increase and for contractors it's an increase of an hourly or daily rate.

Instead of creating two different methods in these classes, it's better to define an interface called, say, `Payable` that contains the declaration of the method `increasePay()`, and to have both classes implement it, as in Listings 6-1, 6-2, and 6-3. Every method declared in the interface automatically becomes `public`.

### LISTING 6-1: Payable interface

```
public interface Payable {
        boolean increasePay(int percent);
}
```

### LISTING 6-2: Class Employee

```
public class Employee implements Payable {

        public boolean increasePay(int percent) {
                // implement salary raise here
        }

}
```

### LISTING 6-3: Class Contractor

```
public class Contractor implements Payable {
        public boolean increasePay(int percent) {
                // implement hourly rate increase here
        }
}
```

Since both `Employee` and `Contractor` contain the clause `implements Payable`, you must implement the `increasePay()` method in each of the classes, or your code won't compile. Creating classes with common interfaces leads to cleaner design of your application and makes the code more readable. But what's more important is that with the help of interfaces you can introduce polymorphic behavior to your program, and this will be illustrated in Lesson 7.

Besides method signatures, Java interfaces can contain declarations of `final` variables. For example, you can create a `final` variable in the `Payable` interface for the maximum percentage of pay increase (all variables declared in the interface automatically become `public static final`).

```
int INCREASE_CAP = 20;
```

Since both the `Employee` and `Contractor` classes implement `Payable`, they can both include `if` statements in the implementation of `increasePay()` to ensure that the provided percentage increase is less than `INCREASE_CAP`. If in the future the cap changes, you need to change it in only one place — the `Payable` interface.

Some software developers create Java interfaces that contain only `final` variables storing important application constants. Implementing such interfaces will make these constants available in the class that implements the interface(s). Not everyone approves such usage of interfaces, as it can create a messy situation when a class that implements interfaces with static constants exposes a new set of public APIs (those `final` variables) rather than just using these values internally. You can read more about this anti-pattern at the following URL: http://java.sun.com/j2se/1.5.0/docs/guide/language/static-import.html.

## Marker Interfaces

*Marker interfaces* are those that don't have any methods declared. One example of such an interface is `Serializable`, covered in Lesson 17. You don't need to write any implementation of these interfaces; the Java compiler will take care of this for you. Objects of a class that implements a marker interface will support a certain functionality. For example, if a class implements `Serializable`, JVM will be able to *serialize* it — turn into a string of bytes (in the server's JVM) in such a way that the string can be sent to another JVM (on the client's machine), which will be able to recreate the instance of the object, or *de-serialize* it.

Also, Java has an operator `instanceof` (see next section) that can check during the run time if an object is of a certain type. You can use the operator `instanceof` as shown below to check if the object implements a marker interface, or any other type of interface for that matter:

```
if (receivedFromServerObj instancef Serializable) {
    // do something
}
```

## CASTING

All Java classes form an inheritance tree with the class `Object` on top of the hierarchy — all Java classes are direct or indirect descendants of `Object`. When you declare a non-primitive variable, you are allowed to use either the exact data type of this variable or one of its ancestor data types. For example, if the class `NJTax` extends `Tax`, each of the following lines is correct.

```
NJTax myTax1    = new NJTax();
Tax myTax2      = new NJTax();   // upcasting
Object myTax3   = new NJTax();   // upcasting
```

Java is smart enough to automatically cast an instance of the class to its ancestor. When the variable has more generic type than an instance of the object this is called *upcasting*. Let's say the class object has 10 methods and class variables defined, the class `Tax` (an implicit subclass of `Object`) adds five more methods and variables (making 15), and `NJTax` adds another two (total 17). The variable `myTax1` will have access to all 17 methods and variables, `myTax2` will see only 15, and `myTax3` just 10. Why not always use exact types in variable declarations?

Let's say you need to write a program that will process data about workers of a certain company. Some of them are full-time employees and some are contractors, but you'd like to read their data from some data source and into the same array. Arrays can store only objects of the same type, remember?

Since Java can automatically upcast the objects, you can create a class called `Person` with two sub-classes, `Employee` and `Contractor`, and then read the records from a database. Based on the employment type you can then create an appropriate object instance and put it into an array of type `Person`:

```
Person workers[] = new Person [100];
workers[0] = new Employee("Yakov", "Fain");
workers[1] = new Employee("Mary", "Lou");
workers[2] = new Contractor("Bill", "Shaw");
...
```

Of course, you could've created two separate arrays, one for employees and one for contractors, but I'm laying the foundation here for explaining polymorphism — a powerful concept in object-oriented languages. You'll see a concrete example of polymorphism in Lesson 7.

At some point you'll need to process the data from the array `workers`. In a loop you can test the data type of the current element of the array with the operator `instanceof`, and then downcast the object (it can't be done automatically) to `Employee` or `Contractor` and process it accordingly.

```
for (int i; i<20; i++){
    Employee currentEmployee;
    Contractor currentContractor;

    if (workers[i] instanceof Employee){
        currentEmployee = (Employee) workers[i];
        // do some employee processing here
    } else if  (workers[i] instanceof Contractor){
        currentContractor = (Contractor) workers[i];
        // do some contractor processing here
    }
}
```

Placing a data type in parentheses in front of another object means that you want to *downcast* this object to the specified type. You can downcast an object only to one of its descendant data types. Even though the preceding code has correct syntax, it doesn't represent the best practice for processing similar objects. In the next lesson you'll see how to use polymorphism to do it in a more generic way.

If a class implements an interface, you can cast its instance to this interface. Say that a class called `Employee` implements `Payable`, `Insurable`, and `Pensionable` interfaces:

```
class Employee implements Payable, Insurable, Pensionable {
// implementation of all interfaces goes here
}
```

If you are interested in the `Insurable` behavior of your code, there's no need to cast the `Object` to type `Employee` — just cast it to the `Insurable` type as shown in the following code fragment. Keep in mind though that if you do so, the variable `currentEmployee` will expose access only to those methods that were declared in the `Insurable` interface.

```
Insurable currentEmployee;

if (workers[i] instanceof Insurable){
```

```
        currentEmployee = (Insurable) workers[i];
        // do some insurance-specific processing here
    }
```

## TRY IT

The goal of this assignment is to start using packages, protect data using private variables and define first interfaces. You create a simple program that will increase pay, which will be implemented differently for employees and contractors. After completing this assignment you'll have working but not perfect code. What can be improved will be explained in Lesson 7.

### Lesson Requirements

For this lesson you should have Java installed.

*You can download the code and resources for this Try It from the book's web page at* www.wrox.com. *You can find them in the Lesson6 folder in the download.*

## Step-by-Step

1.  In the Eclipse IDE, create a new project called Lesson6.

2.  Create the `Payable` interface as per Listing 6-1 in the package `com.practicaljava` `.lesson6` — you can enter the name of the package in the Eclipse New Java Class window. Declare a `final` variable there:

    ```
    int INCREASE_CAP = 20;
    ```

3.  Create a class called `Person`:

    ```
    package com.practicaljava.lesson6;

    public class Person {
        private String name;

        public Person(String name){
            this.name=name;
        }

        public String getName(){
            return "Person's name is " + name;
        }
    }
    ```

**4.** Create the classes `Employee` and `Contractor` in the package `com.practicaljava.lesson6`. Each class should extend `Person` and implement `Payable`. Use the Eclipse button Add to automatically include the `Payable` interface in declarations of the classes `Employee` and `Contractor`.

**5.** Check your file system to ensure that the files were created in your workspace in the directory `com/practicaljava/lesson6`.

**6.** Create a class called `TestPayIncrease` with a method called `main()`. Don't specify any package — this class will be created in a different directory.

**7.** Try to create an instance of the class `Employee` in the method `main()` of `TestPayIncrease`:

```
Employee myEmployee = new Employee();
```

You'll get an error: `Employee` can't be resolved to a type. No wonder — it's located in a different package. Move the mouse over `Employee` and Eclipse will offer you a fix — add an `import` statement:

```
import com.practicaljava.lesson6.Employee;
```

Select this fix and later add the `import` statement for all required classes.

**8.** In the `main()` method of the class `TestPayIncrease` create an array of employees and contractors and call the function `increasePay()` for each element of the array:

```
public static void main(String[] args) {

        Person workers[] = new Person[3];
            workers[0] = new Employee("John");
            workers[1] = new Contractor("Mary");
            workers[2] = new Employee("Steve");

                Employee currentEmployee;
                Contractor currentContractor;

          for (Person p: workers){
              if (p instanceof Employee){
                  currentEmployee = (Employee) p;
                  currentEmployee.increasePay(30);

              }else if  (p instanceof Contractor){
                  currentContractor = (Contractor) p;
                  currentContractor.increasePay(30);
              }
          }
    }
```

**9.** Implement the `increasePay()` method in `Employee` — don't put any restrictions on pay increases. Here's the body of `increasePay()`:

```
System.out.println("Increasing salary by " + percent + "%. "+ getName());
return true;
```

**10.** Implement the `increasePay()` method in the class `Contractor`. If the percentage of the increase is below `INCREASE_CAP`, print a message similar to the one in the preceding code. Otherwise, print a message explaining that you can't increase a contractor's rate by more than 20 percent.

**11.** Run the `TestPayIncrease` program. It should produce output similar to the following:

```
Increasing salary by 30%. Person's name is John
Sorry, can't increase hourly rate by more than 20%. Person's name is Mary
Increasing salary by 30%. Person's name is Steve
```

To get the sample database files you can download Lesson 6 from the book's website at www.wrox.com.

*Please select Lesson 6 on the DVD to view the video that accompanies this lesson.*

# 7

# Programming with Abstract Classes and Interfaces

In this lesson you learn about so-called abstract classes, and then you build a complete application that will illustrate how to design and implement programs with abstract classes and interfaces. You also learn about the notion of *polymorphism*.

## ABSTRACT CLASSES

If a class is declared *abstract* it can't be instantiated. The keyword abstract has to be placed in the declaration of a class. The abstract class may have abstract method(s). The question is "Who needs a class that can't be instantiated?"

It's easiest to answer this question by showing you how to use abstract classes while designing an application. While previous lessons ended with assignments, this lesson will start with one.

## Assignment

A company has employees and contractors. Design the classes without using interfaces to represent the people who work for this company. The classes should have the following methods:

```
changeAddress()
promote()
giveDayOff()
increasePay()
```

A one-time promotion means giving one day off and raising the salary by a specified percentage. The method increasePay() should raise the yearly salary for employees and increase the hourly rate for contractors.

## Solution with an Abstract Class

Since increasePay() has to be implemented differently for Employee and Contractor, let's declare it as abstract. The class Person will also have three concrete methods. The fact that the abstract class Person cannot be instantiated forces us, the developers, to implement abstract methods in subclasses.

Let's start by redesigning the class Person from the Try It section of Lesson 6. That version of the class didn't have the method increasePay(), which was a part of the Payable interface. As per the previous lesson's assignment, add the following concrete methods: changeAddress(), giveDayOff(), and promote() (see Listing 7-1).

This is a different approach from the one in Lesson 6, which used interfaces — here some methods are implemented in the superclass and some are not. This solution won't be using any interfaces.

**LISTING 7-1: Abstract class Person**

```java
package com.practicaljava.lesson7;

public abstract public class Person {

    private String name;

    int INCREASE_CAP = 20;  // cap on pay increase

    public Person(String name){
        this.name=name;
    }

    public String getName(){
        return "Person's name is " + name;
    }

    public void changeAddress(String address){
        System.out.println("New address is" + address);
    }

    private void giveDayOff(){
        System.out.println("Giving a day off to " + name);
    }

    public void promote(int percent){
        System.out.println(" Promoting a worker...");
        giveDayOff();

        //calling an abstract method
        increasePay(percent);
    }

    // an abstract method to be implemented in subclasses
    public abstract boolean increasePay(int percent);
}
```

Please note that even though the method increasePay() is abstract, the designer of the class Person doesn't have to know the specifics of raising pay, and subclasses may even be programmed by other developers. But he or she can write code that calls increasePay(), as in the method promote(). This is allowed because by the time the concrete class is instantiated, this method will definitely have been implemented. For simplicity, I didn't write any code that looks like actual increasing pay — this is irrelevant for understanding the concept of abstract classes.

The next step is to create the subclasses Employee and Contractor, implementing the method increasePay() in two different ways, as shown in in Listings 7-2 and 7-3.

**LISTING 7-2:** Class Employee

```
package com.practicaljava.lesson7;

public class Employee extends Person{

        public Employee(String name){
                super(name);
        }
        public boolean increasePay(int percent) {
                System.out.println("Increasing salary by " +
                        percent + "%. "+ getName());
                return true;
        }
}
```

**LISTING 7-3:** Class Contractor

```
package com.practicaljava.lesson7;

public class Contractor extends Person {

        public Contractor(String name){
                super(name);
        }
        public boolean increasePay(int percent) {
                if(percent < INCREASE_CAP){
                   System.out.println("Increasing hourly rate by " +
                                        percent + "%. "+ getName());
                   return true;
                } else {
                   System.out.println("Sorry, can't increase hourly rate by more
                        than " + INCREASE_CAP + "%. "+ getName());
                   return false;
                }
        }
}
```

Programmers writing subclasses are forced to write an implementation of increasePay() according to its signature, declared in the abstract class. If they declare a method increasing pay that has a different name or argument list, their classes will remain abstract. So they don't have a choice — they have to play by the rules dictated in the abstract class.

The class `TestPayIncrease2` in Listing 7-4 shows how to use the classes `Employee` and `Contractor` for promoting workers.

**LISTING 7-4: Class TestPayIncrease2**

```java
import com.practicaljava.lesson7.*;

public class TestPayIncrease2 {

    public static void main(String[] args) {

        Person workers[] = new Person[3];
            workers[0] = new Employee("John");
            workers[1] = new Contractor("Mary");
            workers[2] = new Employee("Steve");

            for (Person p: workers){
                    p.promote(30);
            }
    }
}
```

Compare the code of `TestPayIncrease2` to `TestPayIncrease` from the Try It section of Lesson 6. Which one do you like better? I like `TestPayIncrease2`, which exhibits polymorphic behavior, explained next.

## POLYMORPHISM

Polymorphism is easier to understand through an example. Let's look at the classes `Person`, `Employee`, and `Contractor` from a different angle. The code in Listing 7-4 populates an array, mixing up the instances of the classes `Employee` and `Contractor` with hard-coded names. In real life the data about workers usually comes from an external data source. For example, a program could get a person's work status from the database and instantiate an appropriate concrete class. The class `TestPayIncrease2` gives an additional vacation day and attempts to increase the salary or hourly rate of every worker by 30 percent.

Note that even though the loop variable `p` is of its ancestor's type `Person` in Listing 7-4, at every iteration it actually points at either an `Employee` or a `Contractor` instance. The actual object type will be evaluated only during the run time. This feature of object-oriented languages is called *run-time binding* or *late binding*.

The output of the class `TestPayIncrease2` will look as follows:

```
Promoting a worker...
Giving a day off to John
Increasing salary by 30%. Person's name is John
```

```
 Promoting a worker...
Giving a day off to Mary
Sorry, can't increase hourly rate by more than 20%. Person's name is Mary
 Promoting a worker...
Giving a day off to Steve
Increasing salary by 30%. Person's name is Steve
```

Both classes, Employee and Contractor, were inherited from the same base class, Person. Instead of having different methods for increasing the worker's compensation based on the worker's type, we give a polymorphic behavior to the method increasePay(), which applies different business logic depending on the type of the object.

Although it looks as if we're calling the same method, promote(), on every object from the array workers, this is not the case. Since the actual object type is evaluated during run time, the pay is raised properly according to this particular object's implementation of the method increasePay(). This is polymorphism in action.

The for loop in the class TestPayIncrease2 will remain the same even if we add some other types of workers inherited from the class Person. For example, to add a new category of worker — a foreign contractor — we'll have to create a class called ForeignContractor derived from the class Person and implement the method increasePay() there. The class TestPayIncrease2 will keep evaluating the actual type of Person's descendants during run time and call the proper implementation of the method increasePay().

Polymorphism allows you to avoid using switch or if statements with the expensive operator instanceof, which you used in Lesson 6. Would you agree that even though TestPayIncrease is producing the same results, its code looks pretty ugly compared to TestPayIncrease2? The code in TestPayIncrease works more slowly than the polymorphic version, and its if statement has to be modified every time a new type of worker is added.

## Making the Interface Solution Polymorphic

Could you create the polymorphic solution in the example with interfaces from Lesson 6? Yes, you could. Even though the array workers has been declared of type Person, it is populated by the objects that implement the Payable interface.

Instead of casting the objects from this array to either Employee or Contractor, you would cast these objects to Payable and call the increasePay() method without worrying too much about whether the current worker is an employee or a contractor (see Listing 7-5).

**LISTING 7-5: Class TestPayIncreasePoly**

```
import com.practicaljava.lesson6.*;

public class TestPayInceasePoly {

        public static void main(String[] args) {

            Person workers[] = new Person[3];
```

*continues*

**LISTING 7-5** *(continued)*

```
                  workers[0] = new Employee("John");
                  workers[1] = new Contractor("Mary");
                  workers[2] = new Employee("Steve");

                  for (Person p: workers){
                      ((Payable)p).increasePay(30);
                  }
              }
          }
```

Note that the variable p is cast to Payable first, and only after the method increasePay() can be called. To enforce the sequence of these operations this code has been surrounded with parentheses. The Eclipse IDE comes in handy with its context-sensitive help — when you type the period after the parentheses it readily shows you increasePay() in the list of available methods. I always use this little help: If a method name I'm about to type is not shown there, I must be doing something wrong with the types; otherwise Eclipse would have helped me out.

The other solution that would eliminate the need of casting to Payable is having the class Person implement Payable. In this case the loop from Listing 7-5 would look as follows:

```
    for (Payable p: workers){
        increasePay(30);
    }
```

What can go wrong during the execution of the code from Listing 7-5? What if a developer creates a class called ForeignContractor without implementing the Payable interface, and this error makes it into the array workers? You'll get a run-time casting error — JVM can't cast an object to Payable if it doesn't implement the Payable interface. You'll have a chance to see this error for yourself in the Try It section.

## INTERFACES VERSUS ABSTRACT CLASSES

The next question is when should you use interfaces and when should you use abstract classes. If two or more classes have lots of common functionality, but some methods should be implemented differently, you can create a common abstract ancestor and as many subclasses inheriting this common behavior as needed. Declare in the superclass as abstract those methods that subclasses should implement differently, and implement these methods in subclasses.

If several classes don't have common functionality but need to exhibit some common behavior, do not create a common ancestor, but have them implement an interface that declares the required behavior. This scenario was not presented in the "Interfaces" section of Lesson 6, but it's going to be a part of the hands-on exercise in the Try It section of this lesson.

Interfaces and abstract classes are similar in that they ensure that required methods will be implemented according to required method signatures. But they differ in how the program is designed. While abstract classes require you to provide a common ancestor for the classes, interfaces don't.

Interfaces could be your only option if a class already has an ancestor that cannot be changed. Java doesn't support multiple inheritance — a class can have only one ancestor. For example, to write

Java applets you must inherit your class from the class Applet, or in the case of Swing applets, from JApplet. Here using your own abstract ancestor is not an option.

While using abstract classes, interfaces, and polymorphism is not a must, it certainly improves the design of Java code by making it more readable and understandable to others who may need to work on programs written by you.

## TRY IT

In the first part of the assignment your goal is to break the code from Listing 7-5 to produce the run-time error ClassCastException. In the second part of the assignment you'll need to rewrite the assignment from Lesson 6 to keep the Payable interface but remove the common ancestor Person.

## Lesson Requirements

For this lesson you should have Java installed.

 *You can download the code and resources for this Try It from the book's web page at www.wrox.com. You can find them in the Lesson7 folder in the download.*

## Step-by-Step

### Part 1

1. In Eclipse open the project Lesson6 — yes, the one from the previous lesson.

2. Create a new class called ForeignContractor, as shown in the following code. Note that this class doesn't implement the Payable interface:

```
package com.practicaljava.lesson6;

public class ForeignContractor extends Person {

        public ForeignContractor(String name){
                super(name);
        }
        public boolean increasePay(int percent) {

                System.out.println("I'm just a foreign worker");
                return true;
        }
}
```

**3.**   Create the class `TestPayIncreasePolyError`, adding an instance of the `ForeignContractor` class:

```
import com.practicaljava.lesson6.*;

public class TestPayIncreasePolyError {

    public static void main(String[] args) {

            Person workers[] = new Person[3];
            workers[0] = new Employee("John");
            workers[1] = new Contractor("Mary");
            workers[2] = new ForeignContractor("Boris");


            for (Person p: workers){
                    ((Payable)p).increasePay(30);
            }
        }
    }
```

**4.**   Run the program `TestPayIncreasePolyError`. Observe the output in the console view — you'll get the run-time error `java.lang.ClassCastException` on the third element of the array. Note the number 14 — this is the line number of `TestPayIncreasePolyError` program, which casts each object to the `Payable` interface.

```
Increasing salary by 30%. Person's name is John
Sorry, can't increase hourly rate by more than 20%. Person's name is Mary
Exception in thread "main" java.lang.ClassCastException:
com.practicaljava.lesson6.ForeignContractor cannot be cast to
com.practicaljava.lesson6.Payable
        at TestPayInceasePolyError.main(TestPayInceasePolyError.java:14)
```

**5.**   Modify the code of `TestPayIncreasePolyError`, changing the type of the array from `Person` to `Payable` and changing the type of the loop variable accordingly:

```
Payable workers[] = new Payable [3];
workers[0] = new Employee("John");
workers[1] = new Contractor("Mary");
workers[2] = new ForeignContractor("Boris");

    for (Payable p: workers){
            ((Payable)p).increasePay(30);
    }
```

**6.**   Observe that now you are getting a Java compiler error preventing you from even adding to the array the instance of `ForeignContractor` because it doesn't implement `Payable`. Predicting and preventing run-time errors is a very important task for every software developer, and this subject will be covered in detail in Lesson 13.

## Part 2

**1.** In the project Lesson7 select File ⇨ New create the new package `com.practicaljava` `.lesson7.tryit`.

**2.** In Eclipse copy the `Payable` interface from Lesson6 to the package `com.practicaljava` `.lesson7.tryit`.

**3.** In the same package create the class `Employee` as follows:

```
package com.practicaljava.lesson7.tryit;

public class Employee implements Payable{
        private String name;

        public Employee(String name){
                this.name=name;
        }

        public boolean increasePay(int percent) {
                System.out.println("Increasing salary by " + percent
                + "%: " + name);
                return true;
        }
}
```

**4.** In the same package create the class `Contractor` as follows:

```
package com.practicaljava.lesson7.tryit;

public class Contractor implements Payable {

        private String name;

        public Contractor(String name){
                this.name=name;
        }
        public boolean increasePay(int percent) {
                if(percent < Payable.INCREASE_CAP){
                        System.out.println("Increasing hourly rate by " +
                                percent + "%. ");
                        return true;
                } else {
                        System.out.println("Sorry, can't increase hourly rate by
                                more than " + Payable.INCREASE_CAP + "%: " + name);
                        return false;
                }
        }
```

Note that neither `Employee` nor `Contractor` extends `Person` any longer. Both classes are free to extend any other classes now, but on the other hand each of them has to declare the variable name and the method `getName()`, which was done once in the class `Person` before.

**5.** Create a class called `TestPayIncreaseInterface`:

```
import com.practicaljava.lesson7.tryit.*;

public class TestPayIncreaseInterface {

    public static void main(String[] args) {

        Payable workers[] = new Payable [3];
            workers[0] = new Employee("John");
            workers[1] = new Contractor("Mary");
            workers[2] = new Employee("Steve");

                for (Payable p: workers){
                        ((Payable)p).increasePay(30);
                }
            }
    }
}
```

**6.** Run this program — it should produce the following output:

```
Increasing salary by 30%: John
Sorry, can't increase hourly rate by more than 20%: Mary
Increasing salary by 30%: Steve
```

To get the sample database files you can download Lesson 7 from the book's website at www.wrox.com.

*Please select Lesson 7 on the DVD to view the video that accompanies this lesson.*

# Introducing the Graphic User Interface

These days people are accustomed to working with applications that have rich user interfaces. If you develop rich Internet applications, JavaFX is the newest platform for development offered by Oracle. But Java itself offers a library of components called Swing, which is used for building graphic user interfaces (GUIs) for desktop applications, as well as a web program called *applets* (see Lesson 10). In this and the following lesson you'll learn the principles of building GUIs while developing a simple desktop calculator using the Java Swing library.

 *Eclipse Foundation offers another library of UI components called SWT, which is out of the scope of this book.*

## SWING BASICS

Originally Java offered a pretty basic library of UI-related classes called the Abstract Windowing Toolkit (AWT). A couple of years later a new widget toolkit called Swing was introduced. It offers a lighter set of UI components while keeping the main idea intact — to keep UI development independent of the specifics of the end user's operating system. Today developers are trying to create UIs that appear to be native to the OS, whether that is Windows, Mac OS, iOS, or Android. Eventually the market share of Swing-based UIs will diminish, but at the time of this writing it's still widely used by enterprises, and skilled Swing developers remain in big demand.

Swing offers you everything you need to build UIs in Java: There are controls to represent buttons, drop-downs, grids, scrollbars, trees, tab folders, and so on. Typically you'll be creating UIs by combining controls into containers (such as `JPanel`) that support various layouts that enable controls to be arranged as you or a graphic designer envision. In this lesson you use some of the Swing components while creating a UI for a simple calculator.

A complete discussion of the Swing library is out of the scope of this book, but there are plenty of books and technical articles covering this subject. The official online Swing tutorial is located at `http://java.sun.com/docs/books/tutorial/uiswing`.

Swing classes are located in the `javax.swing` package, and the process of creating a UI comes down to extending some of these classes to display the UI and respond to various user- and system-generated events. You create a top-level window with a title and border by instantiating the class `JFrame`, as in Listing 8-1.

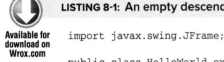

**LISTING 8-1:** An empty descendant of JFrame

```java
import javax.swing.JFrame;

public class HelloWorld extends JFrame {

    public HelloWorld(){
        setSize(200,300);
        setTitle("Hello World");
        setVisible(true);
    }
        public static void main(String[] args) {
        HelloWorld myHello = new HelloWorld();
        }

}
```

The constructor of this version of Hello World sets the size and title of the window and makes it visible. Run this program and it'll show a small empty window, as in Figure 8-1.

`JFrame` is an example of a container that can hold UI controls, which must be instantiated first and then added to the container. For example, to add a button you can include the following two lines to the constructor in Listing 8-1:

```java
JButton myButton = new JButton ("Click me");
add(myButton);
```

This code will work, but it doesn't specify the size of the button, where to put it, or whether there should be space between the components and the borders. Without layout instructions, the entire empty space in Figure 8-1 will be occupied by one huge button.

Usually `JFrame` includes some other containers, where you'll place controls such as `JButton`, `JTable`, and `JList`. Java Swing comes with *layout managers* that help you arrange all these controls appropriately. A sample coding process for creating a `JFrame` containing `JPanel` goes like this:

1. Create a `JPanel`.

2. Assign a layout manager to it.

3. Instantiate some Swing controls and add them to the panel.

**FIGURE 8-1**

**4.** Add the panel to the top-level container — JFrame — by calling the setContentPane() method.

**5.** Set the frame's size and make it visible.

You can assign different layout managers to your containers to create pretty sophisticated windows. But displaying a window with properly laid-out components is only half of the job, because these controls should know how to respond to various *events*, such as a click on a button. This lesson covers the basics of displaying UI components; the next one is about writing code for responding to events.

## LAYOUT MANAGERS

The simplest layout manager is FlowLayout, which allocates all components being added to the container horizontally. When there's no room for the next component, FlowLayout uses the next row, and the process repeats.

## A Simple Calculator with FlowLayout

The best way to learn layout management is by trying to use it in practice. Let's create a UI for a simple calculator that can accept two numbers and display the result. Create a new Eclipse project called Lesson8 and a new class called SimpleCalculator with the following code:

**LISTING 8-2:** Calculator with FlowLayout

```java
import javax.swing.*;
import java.awt.FlowLayout;

public class SimpleCalculator {
 public static void main(String[] args) {
  // Create a panel
      JPanel windowContent= new JPanel();

  // Set a layout manager for this panel
      FlowLayout fl = new FlowLayout();
      windowContent.setLayout(fl);

  // Create controls in memory
      JLabel label1 = new JLabel("Number 1:");
      JTextField field1 = new JTextField(10);
      JLabel label2 = new JLabel("Number 2:");
      JTextField field2 = new JTextField(10);
      JLabel label3 = new JLabel("Sum:");
      JTextField result = new JTextField(10);
      JButton go = new JButton("Add");

  // Add controls to the panel
      windowContent.add(label1);
```

*continues*

**LISTING 8-2** *(continued)*

```
            windowContent.add(field1);
            windowContent.add(label2);
            windowContent.add(field2);
            windowContent.add(label3);
            windowContent.add(result);
            windowContent.add(go);

        // Create the frame and add the panel to it
        JFrame frame = new JFrame("My First Calculator");

        // Add the panel to the top-level container
        frame.setContentPane(windowContent);

        // set the size and make the window visible
        frame.setSize(400,100);
        frame.setVisible(true);
    }
  }
 }
```

Compile and run this program and it'll display the window shown in Figure 8-2. This may not be the best-looking calculator, but it demonstrates the use of `FlowLayout`. In the next section you'll make it look better with the help of more suitable layout managers.

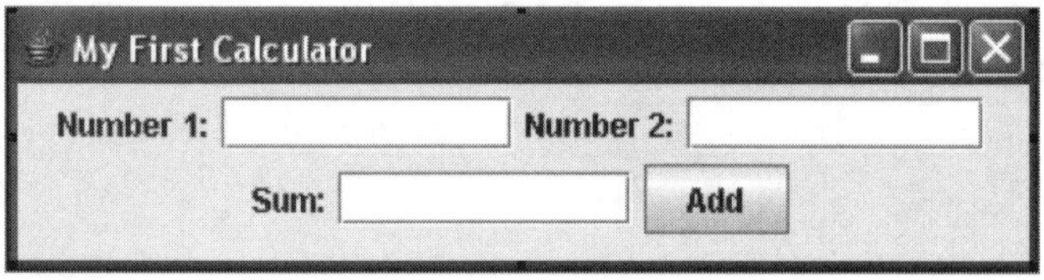

**FIGURE 8-2**

Grab the corner of the window and make it wider. You'll see how `FlowLayout` starts reallocating controls, trying to fill the new area. If you make the window wide enough, all the components will fit in one row, as in Figure 8-3.

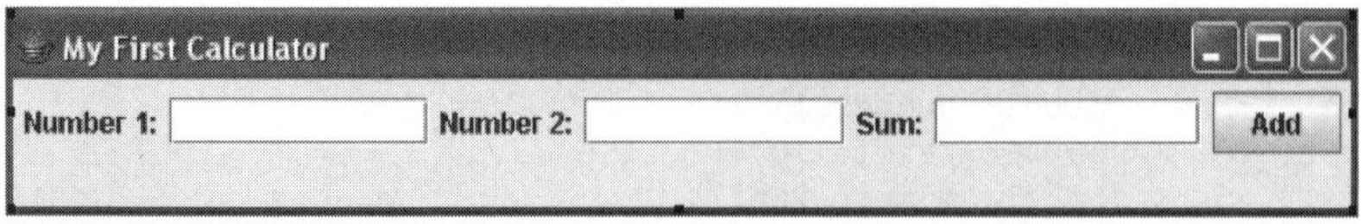

**FIGURE 8-3**

Even though you can enforce exact coordinates and sizes for each window component, Swing has layout managers that can maintain relative positions for all controls without assigning strict positions to them. Layout managers will ensure that the content of a container looks nice regardless of the current window size.

# A Brief Introduction to Layout Managers

Swing offers the following layout managers:

➤ FlowLayout

➤ GridLayout

➤ BoxLayout

➤ BorderLayout

➤ CardLayout

➤ GridBagLayout

To use any layout manager, instantiate it first and then assign this instance to a container via setLayout() as you did with the class SimpleCalculator in Listing 8-2.

## FlowLayout

This layout arranges components in a window row by row. For example, labels, text fields, and buttons will be added to the first imaginary row until there is room left in this row. When the current row is filled, the rest of the components will go to the next row, and so on. If a user changes the size of the window, it may mess up the picture, as illustrated in Figure 8-2. Indeed, FlowLayout is not the best choice for our calculator. Let's try something different.

## GridLayout

The class java.awt.GridLayout allows you to arrange components as rows and columns in a grid. You'll be adding components to imaginary cells of this grid. If the container gets resized, grid cells may become larger or smaller, but the relative positions of the components inside the container will remain the same.

So far our calculator has seven components: three labels, three text fields, and a button. You may arrange them as a grid of four rows and two columns (one cell stays empty) by creating an instance of GridLayout like this:

```
GridLayout gr = new GridLayout(4,2);
```

You can also assign some horizontal and vertical spaces of, for example, five pixels, between the cells:

```
GridLayout gr = new GridLayout(4,2,5,5);
```

Replace FlowLayout with GridLayout in Listing 8-2 and the calculator will look a little prettier. Create and compile a new class called SimpleCalculatorGrid (see Listing 8-3).

**LISTING 8-3:** Calculator with GridLayout

```
import javax.swing.*;
import java.awt.GridLayout;
public class SimpleCalculatorGrid {
```

*continues*

**LISTING 8-3** *(continued)*

```java
public static void main(String[] args) {

    JPanel windowContent= new JPanel();

    // Set the layout manager for the panel
    GridLayout gl = new GridLayout(4,2);
    windowContent.setLayout(gl);

    JLabel label1 = new JLabel("Number 1:");
    JTextField field1 = new JTextField(10);
    JLabel label2 = new JLabel("Number 2:");
    JTextField field2 = new JTextField(10);
    JLabel label3 = new JLabel("Sum:");
    JTextField result = new JTextField(10);
    JButton go = new JButton("Add");

// Add controls to the panel
    windowContent.add(label1);
    windowContent.add(field1);
    windowContent.add(label2);
    windowContent.add(field2);
    windowContent.add(label3);
    windowContent.add(result);
    windowContent.add(go);

  // Create the frame and add the panel to it
    JFrame frame = new JFrame("My First Calculator");

    frame.setContentPane(windowContent);

// set the size and display the window
    frame.setSize(400,100);
    frame.setVisible(true);
  }
}
```

Run the program `SimpleCalculatorGrid` and you'll see a much nicer calculator than before (see Figure 8-4).

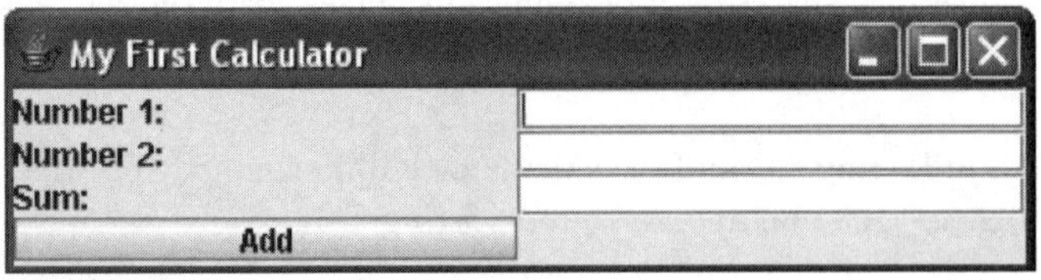

**FIGURE 8-4**

Try to resize this window — controls will grow with the window, as shown in Figure 8-5, but their relative positions won't change. Note that with `GridLayout` all cells of the grid have the same width and height.

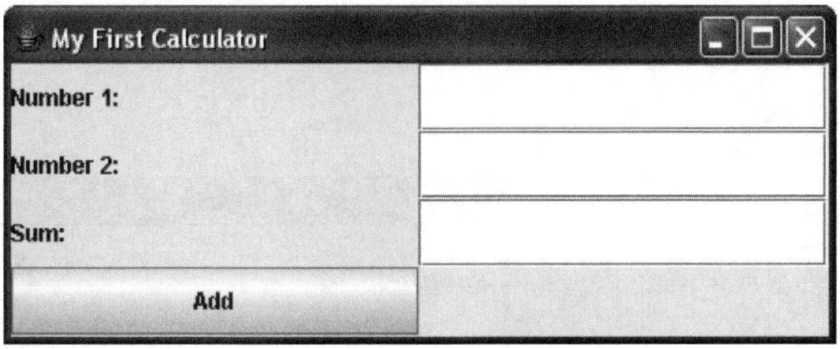

**FIGURE 8-5**

## BorderLayout

The layout manager java.awt.BorderLayout divides a container into South, West, North, East, and Center areas. The North area stays on top of the window, South at the bottom, West on the left, and East on the right. For example, in the calculator shown in Figure 8-6, a text field that displays numbers is located in the North area, and the panel p2 in the West.

You can use the following code to create a BorderLayout and place a text field there:

```
BorderLayout bl = new BorderLayout();
this.setLayoutManager(bl);

JTextField  txtDisplay = new JTextField(20);
this.add(BorderLayout.NORTH, txtDisplay);
```

You are not required to have window controls in all five areas. If you need only North, Center, and South areas, the Center area will become wider because you are not going to use the East and West areas. I'll use a BorderLayout a little later in this lesson, in the next version of our calculator: Calculator.java.

## Combining Layout Managers

Do you think that GridLayout will enable you to design a calculator that looks like the one that comes with Microsoft Windows, shown in Figure 8-6? Unfortunately it won't, because cells have different sizes there — the text field is wider than the buttons. You can, however, combine layout managers by using panels that have their own layout managers.

To combine layout managers in the new version of our calculator, do the following:

➤ Assign the border layout to the content panel of the frame.

➤ Add a JTextField to the North area of the frame to display the numbers.

➤ Create a panel, p1, with the GridLayout, add 20 buttons to it, and add it to the Center area of the content pane.

➤ Create a panel, p2, with GridLayout, add four buttons to the panel, and add p2 to the West area of the content pane.

But first start by creating a somewhat simpler version of the calculator, which will look as shown in Figure 8-7.

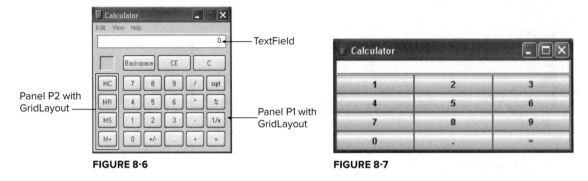

Panel P2 with GridLayout

TextField

Panel P1 with GridLayout

**FIGURE 8-6**

**FIGURE 8-7**

Create a new class, `Calculator`, as per Listing 8-4, and run the program. Read the program comments — you should be able to understand how the code works by reading the comments, shouldn't you?

**LISTING 8-4:** Calculator with combined layouts

```java
import javax.swing.*;
import java.awt.GridLayout;
import java.awt.BorderLayout;

public class Calculator {

    // Declare all calculator's components.
    JPanel windowContent;
    JTextField displayField;
    JButton button0;
    JButton button1;
    JButton button2;
    JButton button3;
    JButton button4;
    JButton button5;
    JButton button6;
    JButton button7;
    JButton button8;
    JButton button9;
    JButton buttonPoint;
    JButton buttonEqual;
    JPanel p1;

    // Constructor  creates the components
    // and adds the to the frame using combination of
    // Borderlayout and Gridlayout

    Calculator(){

        windowContent= new JPanel();

        // Set the layout manager for this panel
```

```
    BorderLayout bl = new BorderLayout();
    windowContent.setLayout(bl);

  // Create the display field and place it in the
  // North area of the window

    displayField = new JTextField(30);
    windowContent.add("North",displayField);

// Create buttons using constructor of the
// class JButton that takes the label of the
// button as a parameter

    button0=new JButton("0");
    button1=new JButton("1");
    button2=new JButton("2");
    button3=new JButton("3");
    button4=new JButton("4");
    button5=new JButton("5");
    button6=new JButton("6");
    button7=new JButton("7");
    button8=new JButton("8");
    button9=new JButton("9");
    buttonPoint = new JButton(".");
    buttonEqual=new JButton("=");

  // Create the panel with the GridLayout with 12 buttons -
  //10 numeric ones, period, and the equal sign

        p1 = new JPanel();
        GridLayout gl =new GridLayout(4,3);
        p1.setLayout(gl);

  //  Add window controls to the panel p1
        p1.add(button1);
        p1.add(button2);
        p1.add(button3);
        p1.add(button4);
        p1.add(button5);
        p1.add(button6);
        p1.add(button7);
        p1.add(button8);
        p1.add(button9);
        p1.add(button0);
        p1.add(buttonPoint);
        p1.add(buttonEqual);

  // Add the panel p1 to the center of the window
        windowContent.add("Center",p1);

//Create the frame and set its content pane
        JFrame frame = new JFrame("Calculator");
        frame.setContentPane(windowContent);

  // Set the size of the window big enough to accomodate all controls
```

*continues*

**LISTING 8-4** *(continued)*

```
    frame.pack();

                // Display the window
                frame.setVisible(true);
    }


    public static void main(String[] args) {

        Calculator calc = new Calculator();
    }
}
```

# BoxLayout

The class `javax.swing.BoxLayout` allows multiple window components to be laid out either horizontally (along the x-axis) or vertically (along the y-axis). Unlike with the `FlowLayout` manager, when the window with the `BoxLayout` is resized, its controls do not wrap. And unlike with `GridLayout`, with `BoxLayout`, window controls can have different sizes.

The next two lines of code assign `BoxLayout` with vertical alignment to `JPanel`. To make this code shorter, I have not declared a variable to store a reference to the object `BoxLayout`, but rather create an instance of this object and immediately pass it to the method `setLayout()` as an argument.

```
JPanel p1= new JPanel();
setLayout(new BoxLayout(p1, BoxLayout.Y_AXIS));
```

If you just add several buttons to the panel p1, they all display one under another.

You can use combinations of various containers implementing horizontal or vertical `BoxLayout` to build a fairly sophisticated UI. Think of a front page of a game that has to have several items next to each other on the top of the window, some controls located vertically on the left sidebar, and the rest of the window's real estate allocated for the main battlefield. You can use `BorderLayout` having a panel with a horizontal `BoxLayout` on the North, and a panel with vertical `BoxLayout` on the West. The next section shows you a sophisticated yet more verbose `GridBagLayout`, but you should always try to see if the `BoxLayout` can do the job and use it, if possible.

# GridBagLayout

In this section you'll get familiar with yet another way of designing the calculator, by using the `java.awt.GridBagLayout` manager instead of combining panels with different layouts. `GridBagLayout` is an advanced grid that allows cells of different sizes. `GridBagLayout` works with another class called `GridBagConstraints`.

Constraints are just attributes of a cell, and you have to set them for each cell separately. All constraints for a cell have to be set before you place a component in the cell. For example, one of the constraint's attributes is called `gridwidth` (see Figure 8-8). It allows you to make a cell as wide as several other cells.

When working with the grid layout you should create an instance of the constraint object first, and then set the values to its properties. Then you can add a UI component to the cell in your container.

The code sample in Listing 8-5 is heavily sprinkled with comments to help you understand how to use `GridBagLayout`. While working on this lesson's assignment you'll be using this code.

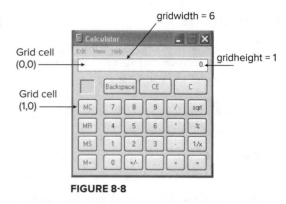

FIGURE 8-8

**LISTING 8-5: Creating constraints for GridBagLayout**

```java
// Set the GridBagLayout for the window's content pane
GridBagLayout gb = new GridBagLayout();
this.setLayout(gb);

// Create an instance of the GridBagConstraints
// You'll have to repeat these lines for each component
// that you'd like to add to the grid cell
GridBagConstraints constr = new GridBagConstraints();

//setting constraints for the Calculator's displayField:

// x coordinate in the grid
constr.x=0;
// y coordinate in the grid
constr.y=0;

// this cell has the same height as other cells
constr.gridheight =1;

// this cell is as wide as 6 other ones
constr.gridwidth= 6;

// fill all space in the cell
constr.fill= constr.BOTH;
// proportion of horizontal space  taken by  this
// component
constr.weightx = 1.0;

// proportion of  vertical space taken by  this component
constr.weighty = 1.0;
// position of the component within the cell
constr.anchor=constr.CENTER;

displayField = new JTextField();
// set constrains for this field
gb.setConstraints(displayField,constr);

// add the text field to the window
windowContent.add(displayField);
```

## CardLayout

Think of a deck of cards lying on top of each other, only the top card visible. You can use the `java` `.awt.CardLayout` manager to create a component that shows one panel at a time, such as the tabbed folder in Figure 8-9.

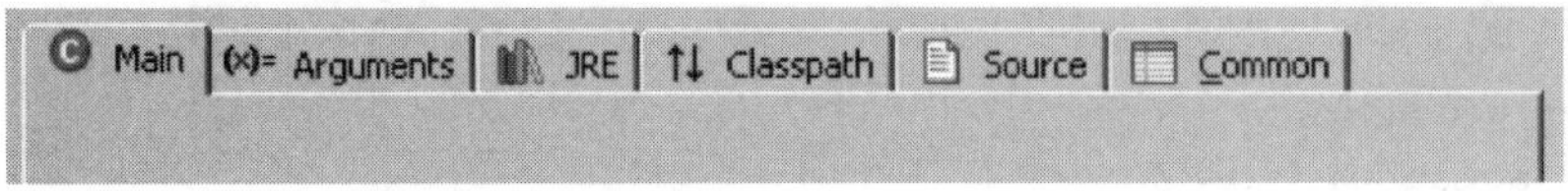

**FIGURE 8-9**

When the user clicks a tab, the content of the window changes. In fact, all the panels needed for this screen are already preloaded and lie on top of each other. When the user clicks a tab, the program just brings this "card" to the top and makes the other "cards" invisible. The tabbed folder here was used for illustration; the Swing library includes a ready-to-go component for windows with tabs, called `JTabbedPane`.

## Containers with Absolute Layout

If you want a container's content to remain the same regardless of the window's size, set the x and y coordinates, width, and height (aka the bounds) of each component while adding them to the window. Your class has to explicitly state that it won't use any layout manager by passing `null` to `setLayout()`:

```
windowContent.setLayout(null);
```

The next code snippet shows how you can set a button's width to 40 pixels and its height to 20, and place it 100 pixels to the right of and 200 pixels down from the top left corner of the window:

```
JButton myButton = new Button("New Game");
myButton.setBounds(100,200,40,20);
```

## More about Swing Widgets

It's not possible to describe all the Swing components in a short lesson — use the Swing online tutorial mentioned earlier in this lesson. Here's a list of all the Swing widgets:

| | |
|---|---|
| JButton | JScrollBar |
| JLabel | JSlider |
| JCheckBox | JProgressBar |
| JRadioButton | JComboBox |
| JToggleButton | JList |
| JScrollPane | JTabbedPane |
| JSpinner | JTable |

| | |
|---|---|
| JTextField | JToolTip |
| JTextArea | JTree |
| JPasswordField | JViewPort |
| JFormattedTextField | ImageIcon |
| JEditorPane | |

You can also create menus (JMenu and JPopupMenu), pop-up windows, and frames inside other frames (JInternalFrame), and use the standard-looking windows (JFileChooser, JColorChooser, and JOptionPane).

Java comes with an excellent demo application, SwingSet3, that shows all the available Swing components in action. You can find it in your JDK install directory. (On my computer it's in C:\Program Files\Java\jdk1.6.0_19\demo\jfc\SwingSet3.) Just open the file readme.html located in the same directory and it'll bring you to a web page containing instructions for launching the demo. The MAC OS users won't find these samples in their Java installation, but they are also available at https://swingset3.dev.java.net.

## SWING GUI BUILDERS

Java developers use various tools to speed the process of designing UIs. See what's available for the IDE that you use. For example, there is a popular plug-in called Matisse that lets you design a Swing UI in what-you-see-is-what-you-get mode. You can find its version for Eclipse-based products, called MyEclipse, at the following URL: www.myeclipseide.com/module-htmlpages-display-pid-1.html.

Matisse was originally developed for the NetBeans IDE, and you can find it here: http://netbeans.org/kb/trails/matisse.html.

Finally, consider yet another Eclipse plug-in, called Jigloo GUI Builder: http://marketplace.eclipse.org/content/jigloo-swtswing-gui-builder. You can definitely find a tool that will substantially speed up your design of UIs with the Java Swing library.

## TRY IT

Your task for today is to create another version of the calculator in Figure 8-8, using only one layout: GridBagLayout.

## Lesson Requirements

For this lesson you should have Java installed.

> You can download the code and resources for this Try It from the book's web page at www.wrox.com. You can find them in the Lesson8 folder in the download.

## Step-by-Step

This assignment comes down to creating appropriate constraints for each UI component shown in Figure 8-8. So there is just one long step in this assignment: Follow the example given in Listing 8-5 for each UI component needed for the calculator.

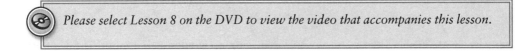

*Please select Lesson 8 on the DVD to view the video that accompanies this lesson.*

# Event Handling in UI

Java Swing, like any other UI library, is an event-driven framework. When a user interacts with a GUI program (such as by clicking a button or pressing a key) a Java Swing program receives an *event* that can initiate an appropriate reaction.

If you write the code to react to a particular event, this code will be invoked. If you haven't written such code, the event will be fired anyway, but the program won't respond to it. In this lesson you'll learn how to handle events in Java GUI programs.

## INTRODUCTION TO EVENT LISTENERS

I'm sure you've tried to click the buttons of our calculator from Lesson 8, but they were not ready to respond to your actions yet. Swing widgets can process various events, or in the programmers' jargon can *listen to events*. To listen to events, a program has to register window components with Java classes called *listeners*.

You should have components listen only to the events they are interested in. For example, when a person clicks a button, it's not important where exactly the mouse pointer is as long as it is on the button's surface. That's why you do not need to register the button with `MouseMotionListener`. On the other hand, this listener comes in handy for all kinds of drawing programs.

To process button clicks Swing provides `ActionListener`. All listeners are declared as Java interfaces and their methods have to be implemented in an object that will be listening to events.

This is how Java documentation describes the `ActionListener` interface:

> *The listener interface for receiving action events. The class that is interested in processing an action event implements this interface, and the object created with that class is registered with a component, using the component's addActionListener method. When the action event occurs, that object's actionPerformed method is invoked.*

This interface is defined in the `java.awt.event` package, as presented in Listing 9-1.

**LISTING 9-1: ActionListener interface**

```
public interface ActionListener extends EventListener
    void actionPerformed(ActionEvent e);

}
```

The `actionPerformed()` method is invoked by the JVM if the action happened. Let's use this listener in the calculator you created in Lesson 8.

## TEACHING THE CALCULATOR TO CALCULATE

The calculator's buttons should register themselves with a class that implements `ActionListener`, which means that its method `actionPerform()` contains the calculation logic. Even though you can implement `ActionListener` in the `Calculator` class itself, for better readability and code maintainability it's best to separate the code defining the UI from the code containing processing logic. Let's start writing a separate class, `CalculatorEngine`:

```
import java.awt.event.ActionListener;
public class CalculatorEngine implements ActionListener {

}
```

This class won't compile; Java will give an error message stating that the class must implement the method `actionPerformed(ActionEvent e)`. You know the rules for interfaces, right? The code in Listing 9-2 will fix this error.

**LISTING 9-2: First implementation of ActionListener interface**

```
import java.awt.event.ActionListener;
import java.awt.event.ActionEvent;
public class CalculatorEngine implements ActionListener {

    public void actionPerformed(ActionEvent e){
        // An empty method body
    }
}
```

Even though the `actionPerformed()` method doesn't contain any code yet, it's considered implemented in Listing 9-2 (the curly braces make the compiler happy). JVM calls this method on the class that implements the `ActionListener` interface whenever the user clicks the button.

The next version of `CalulatorEngine` (see Listing 9-3) will display a message box from the method `actionPerformed()`. You can display any messages using the Swing class `JOptionPane` and its method `showConfirmDialog()`.

**LISTING 9-3:** This class displays a message box

```java
import java.awt.event.ActionListener;
import java.awt.event.ActionEvent;
import javax.swing.JOptionPane;
public class CalculatorEngine implements ActionListener {

    public void actionPerformed(ActionEvent e){
        JOptionPane.showConfirmDialog(null,
                "Something happened...",
                "Just a test",
                JOptionPane.PLAIN_MESSAGE);
    }
}
```

If you register the class `CalculatorEngine` from Listing 9-3 as a listener for the class `Calculator` from Listing 8-4, it'll display the message box shown in Figure 9-1 when the user clicks inside the calculator window.

The class `JOptionPane` declares several overloaded methods named `showConfirmDialog()` — I used the version with four arguments in Listing 9-3. The first

**FIGURE 9-1**

argument is null, which means that this message box does not have a parent window. The second argument contains the title of the message box. The third contains the message itself, and the fourth argument allows you to select a button(s) to be included in the box - `PLAIN_MESSAGE` means that it needs only the button OK.

## Registering Components with ActionListener

What will call the code in the method `actionPerformed()` shown in Listing 9-3, and when? Register the calculator's buttons with the class `CalculatorEngine`, and JVM will obediently call this class every time any button is clicked. Add the following two lines at the end of the constructor of the class `Calculator` (Listing 8-4), and one button will start responding to clicks with the box from Figure 9-1.

```java
CalculatorEngine calcEngine = new CalculatorEngine();
button0.addActionListener(calcEngine);
```

The other calculator buttons remain silent because they have not been registered with our action listener yet. Keep adding similar lines to bring all the buttons to life:

```java
button1.addActionListener(calcEngine);
button2.addActionListener(calcEngine);
button3.addActionListener(calcEngine);
button4.addActionListener(calcEngine);
```

## Finding the Source of an Event

The next step is to make our listener a little smarter: It has to display message boxes with different text, depending on which button was pressed. When an action event happens, JVM calls the method `actionPerformed(ActionEvent)` on your listener class, and this method provides valuable information about the event in the argument `ActionEvent`. In particular, the method `getSource()` in the object `ActionEvent` supplied to `actionPerformed()` in Listing 9-3 will tell you what object was the reason for the action.

But according to Java documentation for `ActionEvent`, the method `getSource()` returns an instance of type `Object`, which is a superclass of all Java classes, including window components. Since in our calculator only buttons can possibly be the reason for an action event, cast the returned `Object` to the type of a `JButton`:

```
JButton clickedButton =  (JButton) evt.getSource();
```

Only after performing casting from `Object` to `JButton` can you call methods that `JButton` supports, for example `getText()`, which returns the button's label, as shown in Listing 9-4. If you press the button labeled 5, you'll see a message box that reads "You pressed 5."

**LISTING 9-4: Getting label of clicked button**

```java
import java.awt.event.ActionListener;
import java.awt.event.ActionEvent;
import javax.swing.JOptionPane;
import javax.swing.JButton;
public class CalculatorEngine implements ActionListener {
    public void actionPerformed(ActionEvent e){
        // Get the source of this action
      JButton clickedButton=(JButton) e.getSource();
      // Get the button's label
      String clickedButtonLabel =
                          clickedButton.getText();

        // Concatenate the button's label
        // to the text of the message box
        JOptionPane.showConfirmDialog(null,
                "You pressed " + clickedButtonLabel,
                "Just a test",
                JOptionPane.PLAIN_MESSAGE);
    }
}
```

What if the window events are produced not only by buttons, but by some other components as well? Then don't cast every object that has arrived with `ActionEvent` to `JButton`. Use the operator called `instanceof` to perform the proper casting. The next example first determines what type of object caused the event, and then performs casting to either `JButton` or `JTextField`:

```java
public void actionPerformed(ActionEvent evt){

    JTextField myDisplayField=null;
    JButton clickedButton=null;

    Object eventSource = evt.getSource();

    if (eventSource instanceof JButton){
        clickedButton = (JButton) eventSource;
    }else if (eventSource instanceof JTextField){
```

```
        myDisplayField = (JTextField)eventSource;
    }
}
```

Consider the buttons that perform arithmetic operations. Our calculator has to execute different code for each button:

```
public void actionPerformed(ActionEvent e){

    Object src = e.getSource();

    if (src == buttonPlus){
        // Call the method that adds numbers here
    } else if (src == buttonMinus){
        // Call the method that substracts numbers here
    }else if (src == buttonDivide){
        // Call the method that divides numbers here
    } else if (src == buttonMultiply){
        // Call the method that multiplies numbers here

    }
}
```

# How to Pass Data between Objects

When you click a numeric button on the real calculator, it does not show a message box, but rather displays the number in the text field on top. Here's a new challenge: You need to be able to reach the attribute `displayField` from the object `Calculator` from the method `actionPerformed()` defined in `CalculatorEngine`. In other words, two objects need to communicate. There are different ways of arranging this: For instance, in the class `CalculatorEngine` you can declare a variable to store a reference to the instance of the object `Calculator`.

The next version of the class `CalculatorEngine` will declare a one-argument constructor. It'll take an argument of type `Calculator`.

JVM executes the constructor of the `CalculatorEngine` instance during instantiation of this class in memory. The `Calculator` object instantiates `CalculatorEngine` and passes to the engine's constructor a reference to itself:

```
CalculatorEngine calcEngine = new CalculatorEngine (this);
```

This reference contains the location of the calculator's instance in memory. The engine's constructor can store the value from the variable `this` in its own variable, say `parent`, and eventually use it in the method `actionPerformed()` to access the calculator's display field.

## Attention, Bad Practice!

The variable parent in the following listing serves as a bridge from the object `CalculatorEngine` to `Calculator`. And the easy way to access `Calculator`'s `displayField` from `CalculatorEngine` is this:

```
parent.displayField.getText();
...
parent.displayField.setText(dispFieldText + clickedButtonLabel);
```

These two lines were taken from the code sample in Listing 9-5. This code works, but it violates one of the principles of object-oriented programming — encapsulation. The problem is that code from `CalculatorEngine` has direct knowledge of the internals of another object — `Calculator`. The engine "knows" that there is a field in `Calculator` called `displayField`, and it gets and sets its value directly.

**LISTING 9-5:** Bad execution of object communication

```
import java.awt.event.ActionListener;
import java.awt.event.ActionEvent;
import javax.swing.JButton;

public class CalculatorEngine implements ActionListener {

  Calculator parent; // a reference to the Calculator

  // Constructor stores the reference to the
  // Calculator window in  the member variable parent
  CalculatorEngine(Calculator parent){
    this.parent = parent;
  }

  public void actionPerformed(ActionEvent e){
    // Get the source of this action
    JButton clickedButton =  (JButton) e.getSource();

    // Get the existing text from the Calculator's
    // display field. Reaching inside another object is bad.
    String dispFieldText = parent.displayField.getText();

    // Get the button's label
    String clickedButtonLabel = clickedButton.getText();

    parent.displayField.setText(dispFieldText +
                                clickedButtonLabel);
  }
}
```

Imagine that for whatever reason you decide to use in `Calculator` something other than the `JTextField` widget to display the results of calculations. That other widget may not even have such APIs as `setText()` and `getText()`. Now you'll need to modify not only the `Calculator` class but also the code of the `CalculatorEngine` to replace the part that displays or reads the `displayField`. This is not the right way to design interactions between objects.

## A Better Solution with a Public API

If `Calculator` needs to communicate with other objects, it should expose a public API to get or set data, but hide details about its internals. The class `Calculator` from Listing 8-4 declares widgets without using any access level qualifiers, so default package access level is applied. Hide these UI components as shown below by using the keyword `private`:

```
private JPanel windowContent;
private JTextField displayField;
private JButton button0;
private JButton button1;
...
```

Now `CalculatorEngine` won't be able to access `displayField` directly as it did in Listing 9-5. Defining public *getter* and *setter* methods in `Calculator` will allow outsiders to access `displayField` without knowing it exists. Listing 9-6 demonstrates how a small change can protect data and enforce encapsulation.

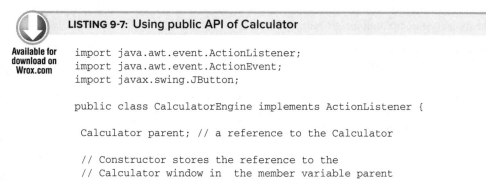

**LISTING 9-6:** Adding public API to Calculator

```
public class Calculator{
    private JTextField displayField;

    public void setDisplayValue(String val){
        displayField.setText(val);
    }

    public String getDisplayValue() {
        return displayField.getText();
    }

    // The rest of the code goes here
}
```

Now if you decide to replace the `JTextField` widget with another one, only the methods `setDisplayValue()` and `getDisplayValue()` will need a change; the `CalculatorEngine` won't need to be touched. Listing 9-7 shows the proper way to access `Calculator` from the `CalculatorEngine`.

**LISTING 9-7:** Using public API of Calculator

```
import java.awt.event.ActionListener;
import java.awt.event.ActionEvent;
import javax.swing.JButton;

public class CalculatorEngine implements ActionListener {

Calculator parent; // a reference to the Calculator

// Constructor stores the reference to the
// Calculator window in  the member variable parent
```

*continues*

**LISTING 9-7** *(continued)*

```
CalculatorEngine(Calculator parent){
  this.parent = parent;
}

public void actionPerformed(ActionEvent e){
  // Get the source of this action
  JButton clickedButton =  (JButton) e.getSource();

  // Get the existing text from the Calculator's
  // display field. Reaching inside another object is bad.
  String dispFieldText = parent.getDisplayValue();

  // Get the button's label
  String clickedButtonLabel = clickedButton.getText();

  parent.setDisplayValue(dispFieldText +
                                clickedButtonLabel);
  }
}
```

## MORE SWING LISTENERS

JDK comes with a number of event listeners located in the package `java.awt`. Here are some of them:

➤ Focus listener is notified when a widget gains or loses focus (for example, we say that a text field has focus if it has a blinking cursor).

➤ Item listener reacts to the selection of items from a list or a drop-down box.

➤ Key listener responds to user keypresses.

➤ Mouse listener responds to mouse clicks or the cursor's hovering over a widget.

➤ Mouse movement listener tells you if the mouse is being moved or dragged. To *drag* means to move the mouse while holding its left button down.

➤ Window listener gives you a chance to catch the moments when the user opens, closes, minimizes, or activates the window.

Table 9-1 shows the names of selected listener interfaces and the methods declared in these interfaces. For example, `FocusListener` declares two methods: `focusGained()` and `focusLost()`. This means that even if your class is interested only in knowing when a particular field gains focus, you also must include the empty method `focusLost()`. Java provides special adapter classes for each listener to spare you from having to manually code empty methods enforced by listener interfaces.

For more details on the listeners supported by Swing, refer to Oracle's Java tutorial at http://java.sun.com/docs/books/tutorial/uiswing/events/eventsandcomponents.html.

**TABLE 9-1:** Selected Swing Listeners

| INTERFACE | METHODS TO IMPLEMENT |
|---|---|
| FocusListener | focusGained(FocusEvent)<br>focusLost(FocusEvent) |
| ItemListener | itemStateChanged(ItemEvent) |
| KeyListener | keyPressed(KeyEvent)    keyReleased(KeyEvent)<br>keyTyped(KeyEvent) |
| MouseListener | mouseClicked(MouseEvent)<br>mouseEntered(MouseEvent)<br>mouseExited(MouseEvent)<br>mousePressed(MouseEvent)<br>mouseReleased(MouseEvent) |
| MouseMotionListener | mouseDragged(MouseEvent)<br>mouseMoved(MouseEvent) |
| WindowListener | windowActivated (WindowEvent)<br>windowClosed(WindowEvent)<br>windowClosing(WindowEvent)<br>windowDeactivated (WindowEvent)<br>windowDeiconified(WindowEvent)<br>windowIconified(WindowEvent)<br>windowOpened(WindowEvent) |

# HOW TO USE ADAPTERS

Swing adapters are classes with implemented empty functions required by listener interfaces. Let's say you need to save some data on the disk when the user closes the window. According to Table 9-1, a class that implements the `WindowListener` interface has to include seven methods. This means that you'll have to write the code that saves the data in the method `windowClosing()` and also include six empty methods.

The package `java.awt` includes a number of adapter classes that implement corresponding listener interfaces, such as `KeyAdapter` and `WindowAdapter`. Instead of implementing `WindowListener` in a class that handles the window's events, just extend a class from `WindowAdapter` and override only the methods you are interested in, for example the method `windowClosing()`:

```
class MyWindowEventProcessor extends java.awt.WindowsAdapter {

    public void windowClosing(WindowEvent e) {
        // your code that saves the data goes here.
    }
}
```

The rest is easy: Register this class as an event listener in your GUI class (e.g. `Calculator`), as shown in Listing 9-8. Java offers adapters only for those listeners that declare more than one method.

You can register multiple listeners by using adapters in `Calculator`. For example, to allow the user to enter a number by pressing numeric keys, create a class based on `KeyAdapter`, instantiate it, and register it with `Calculator` too.

**LISTING 9-8:** Registering adapter-based listener

```
MyWindowEventProcessor myWindowListener =  new MyWindowEventProcessor();
addWindowListener(myWindowListener);
```

You can achieve the same result using so-called anonymous inner classes, as explained in the next section.

# INNER CLASSES

A class defined inside another is called an *inner* class. Listing 9-9 shows an example of the class `TaxOptimizer` declared inside the class `Tax`. The class `TaxOptimizer` is a member inner class and has access to all variables of the class `Tax`. Placing one class inside another is just a way of saying that the classes belong together. After compilation, the class `Tax` file will produce two output files: `Tax.class` and `Tax$TaxOptimizer.class`.

**LISTING 9-9:** Tax class including an inner TaxOptimizer class

```
class Tax{
    double grossIncome;
    int dependents;

  double calcStateTax(){

        TaxOptimizer tOpt = new  TaxOptimizer();
        return tOpt.optimize(grossIncome, dependents);
    }

      TaxOptimizer getTaxOptimizer(){

          return new TaxOptimizer();
```

```
        }

        class TaxOptimizer{

         int taxCode;

          void setTaxCode(int tCode){
                taxCode=tCode;
          }

          int optimize(double grossIncome, int dep){
             // Some optimization code goes here
               return 0;
          }
       }
    }
  }
```

An inner class defined as static can access only static variables of the outer class. The inner class can even be defined inside a method of an outer class. In this case this local inner class is available only when the outer method is called, and it can access only static variables of the top-level class.

The method getTaxOptimizer() in Listing 9-9 returns an instance of the inner class if external classes need it. For example, if the class TestTax needs to access the method setTaxCode() from the inner class, it could do so as follows:

```
Tax t = new Tax(2, "NY", 50000);
Tax.TaxOptimizer tOptimizer = t.getTaxOptimizer();
tOptimizer.setTaxCode(12345);
```

Here's another syntax producing the same result:

```
Tax t = new Tax(2, "NY", 50000);
Tax.TaxOptimizer tOptimizer = t.new TaxOptimizer();
tOptimizer.setTaxCode(12345);
```

## Anonymous Inner Classes

If an inner class does not have a name, it's called *anonymous*. The use of anonymous inner classes is pretty easy to understand in examples of implementing Java adapters. You've learned by now that using adapters is a three-step process: Extend the adapter class, instantiate it, and register it as an event listener (see Listing 9-8). With anonymous inner classes you can perform all three steps in one shot, as in Listing 9-10.

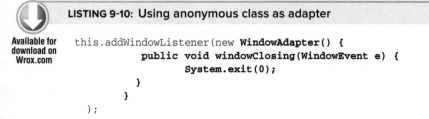

**LISTING 9-10:** Using anonymous class as adapter

```
this.addWindowListener(new WindowAdapter() {
            public void windowClosing(WindowEvent e) {
                    System.exit(0);
            }
        }
    );
```

Imagine that this code is placed in the `Calculator` class. The method `addWindowListener()` requires a subclass of `WindowAdapter` and the section in bold in Listing 9-10 demonstrates the syntax of declaring an anonymous class that extends `WindowAdapter` and overrides the method `windowClosing()`.

The `new` operator instantiates the adapter, and because this is done inside the parentheses of the method `addWindowListener()` the newly created object is used as its argument. This adapter's implementation doesn't have a name, and we don't need to know its name in this context, do we? The instance of the adapter was created and registered as an event listener, and this is all that matters.

## Closures

I've included the section on inner classes in the lesson about handling UI events just because it was easy to explain their practical use here, but inner classes were not created just for the handling of UIs. In some programming languages (such as JavaScript and ActionScript) there's a construct called *closure* — you can instantiate a method from a class, and the instantiation is done in such a way that the method can "remember" the data values from the class variables at the moment of instantiation.

At the time of this writing Java 7 has not been released yet, but there's a pretty good chance that closure will be one of the new features. Closures have simpler syntax than inner classes, and they're a long-anticipated addition to the language.

## TRY IT

The goal of this lesson is to complete the code of the calculator. It has to look as in Figure 9-2 and implement the functionality of all the buttons.

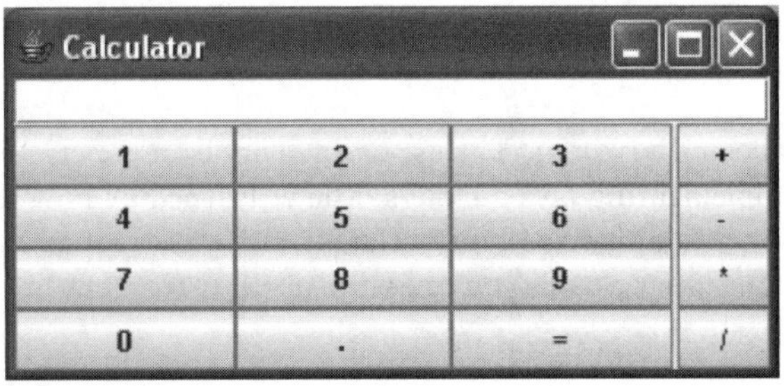

**FIGURE 9-2**

## Lesson Requirements

For this lesson you should have Java installed.

*You can download the code and resources for this Try It from the book's web page at* www.wrox.com. *You can find them in the Lesson9 folder in the download.*

## Step-by-Step

**1.** Create a new Eclipse project called Lesson9 and copy the `Calculator` from Lesson 8 into it (see Listing 8-4).

**2.** Create all missing UI components — use Figure 9-2 as a prototype.

**3.** Create the event listener `CalculatorEngine` — all event processing and calculations should be performed there.

**4.** From `Calculator`, pass to the `CalculatorEngine` engine a reference to itself.

**5.** Register with `CalculatorEngine` all GUI components that can generate events.

**6.** Implement the code for the following scenario:

    **a.** The user enters all the digits of the first number.

    **b.** If the user hits one of the action buttons (+, -, /, or *), this indicates that the first number has been entered. Store this number and selected action in class variables (declare them first) and erase the number from the display text field. You'll need to convert the `String` value to `double` with the help of class `Double`.

    **c.** The user enters the second number and hits the button =.

    **d.** Convert the `String` value from the text field into a numeric type `double` so it is able to store numbers with a decimal point. Perform the selected action using this value and the number stored in the numeric variable from Step b.

    **e.** Display the result in the display field and store this value in the variable that was used in Step b, for future calculations.

    **f.** Run the calculator. If it works, give it to your friends.

To get the sample database files you can download Lesson 9 from the book's website at www.wrox.com.

*Please select Lesson 9 on the DVD to view the video that accompanies this lesson.*

# 10

# Introduction to Java Applets

Java was born in 1995, shortly after the Internet became available to the public. The Netscape web browser enabled regular people to go online and download content from remote servers. This content was mainly some formatted text mixed with static images. But the Java programming language provided a way to incorporate downloadable applications into the web pages!

A programmer needed to write a Java application called an *applet* in a special way using GUI classes from the `java.awt` package (Swing was not invented yet). Applets were deployed on the web servers along with the HTML files that included references to the applets. Web browsers understand HTML, the markup that consists of special *tags* placed in text files so web browsers can properly format and lay out web pages. HTML has a special tag, `<applet>`, that tells the browser where to find and how to size and align a Java applet.

You can download a Java applet to your computer from the Internet as part of a web page, and web browsers use the JVM plug-in to run applets. The version of JVM included with a web browser is very important, because if you're using, say, Java Swing classes, but the user's web browser has a really old JVM, the browser won't even know how to run the code that your applet uses.

In this lesson you'll learn the basics of applet creation and the applet's life cycle. In Lesson 11 you'll build a tic-tac-toe game and will deploy it on the web server so other people can enjoy it.

## AN UNOFFICIAL HISTORY OF JAVA APPLETS

Fifteen years ago Netscape's market share was over 90 percent, but the situation changed when Microsoft introduced Internet Explorer. Back in 1998 there was an infamous lawsuit between Microsoft and Sun Microsystems — the former started quietly introducing its own class library to Java, breaking the write-once-run-anywhere principle of Sun. Sun won that lawsuit. But as the saying goes, it won the battle but lost the war.

Microsoft stopped including the current version of JVM with Internet Explorer. I'm not blaming them for this, but it hurt applets' popularity — the end user couldn't just open a web page to see an applet that required, say, JVM version 1.3. The user would need to first download the proper version of JVM, and then only the applets that were written for JVM 1.3 would work. The process of downloading the right JVM plug-in was a multi-step process.

Sun Microsystems showed a lack of competence on the client side, specifically in the area of integration of JVM into web browsers, and Adobe Flash Player, which is also a virtual machine) dominates in this area now.

High penetration of the required run-time environment and the ability to upgrade it easily are crucial for any web-based technology. Adobe Flash Player shines in this area. Flash Player is a virtual machine with a small memory footprint (1.5 Mb), and its installation takes less than 20 seconds after one button click. For years the JVM plug-in was about 16 Mb, and installation was complicated for a non-programmer — it's a lot smaller now.

This situation changed after the release of Java 6 update 10, which includes the so-called next-generation Java plug-in. Now applets don't run in the JVM packages with the web browser, but in a separate JVM launched by the Java plug-in. The applet still appears in the web browser's window, but now it doesn't depend on the willingness of the browser vendor to include the latest plug-in. You can read more about this next-generation Java plug-in at `https://jdk6.dev.java.net/plugin2`.

To control the settings of this plug-in in Microsoft Windows, use the Java Control Panel — select Start ⇨ Control Panel ⇨ Java. Under the Advanced tab find the item Java Plug-in where Enable the Next-generation Java Plug-in should be selected by default.

If you run Intel-based MAC OS X 10.6 or above, find out what Java plug-ins are installed by typing `about:plugins` into the address bar of your browser. To use the next-generation plug-in on Apple computers follow the instructions at `http://blogs.sun.com/thejavatutorials/entry/enabling_the_next_generation_java`.

The other major change introduced in the next-generation Java plug-in is the ability to launch Java applets directly from JNLP (Java Network Launch Protocol) files, which in the previous releases were used only in Java Web Start technology, which allowed local deployment of the applications over the network. As of Java 10.6.10 you can use the JNLP meta-descriptors to launch applets too. JNLP support is described in detail at `www.oracle.com/technetwork/java/javase/index-142562.html`.

What's the next step in applets' evolution? You'll be creating a UI for web-based applications with a relatively new language called JavaFX, which will be demonstrated in Lesson 37.

## RESTRICTIONS OF JAVA APPLETS

People browse the Internet without knowing if web pages contain Java applets or not, but they want to be sure that the files located in their computers will not be harmed by some bad guys who have added a nasty applet to a page. *Unsigned applets* are the ones that haven't gone through a special *signing process* to obtain a security certificate indicating that they come from a trusted source.

Unsigned (aka *untrusted*) Java applets operate inside a so-called *security sandbox* and have the following main restrictions:

➤ They can't access local files on your disk.

➤ They can connect only to the computer they were downloaded from.

➤ They can't start any other programs located in your computer.

Applets can be signed by VeriSign or Thawte and operate outside the security sandbox and be unrestricted in their ability to access the user's computer if the user accepts the applet's security. A signed applet will run outside the security sandbox. If the user refuses to accept the certificate, the applet will run within the security sandbox as unsigned.

To run an applet you'll need a Java class written in a special way, an HTML text file that contains the tag `<applet>` pointing to this class, and a web browser that supports Java. You can also test applets in Eclipse or using a special program called appletviewer. But before learning how to create applets, spend 15 minutes to get familiar with some HTML tags.

## LEARNING HTML ON THE RUN

Imagine that you've already written and compiled the game applet class called `TicTacToe`. It has to be deployed on the web servers along with the HTML wrapper — the file that includes the proper references to `TicTacToe.class`. HTML stands for Hypertext Markup Language. It defines a set of tags placed in angle brackets that can be inserted in a text file with any plain text editor, such as Notepad, TextEdit, or the editor that comes with Eclipse (select File ➪ New ➪ File). In this section I'll show you a bare minimum of HTML tags to get you going with applets, but you can find a complete HTML tutorial at www.w3schools.com/html/html_primary.asp.

Let's start with creating the text file called `TicTacToe.html`. HTML files have names that end with .html or .htm. Inside they usually have two sections: header and body. HTML tags are placed inside angle brackets and most of them have the matching closing tags that start with a forward slash, for example `<head>` and `</head>`. The content of the very basic HTML file `TicTacToe.html` is shown in Listing 10-1.

**LISTING 10-1:** The basic HTML file

```
<html>
  <head>
   <title>My First Web Page</title>
  </head>
  <body>
     My Tic-Tac-Toe game is coming soon...
  </body>
</html>
```

You can place tags either in the same line, as we did with the tags <title> and </title>, or in separate lines. Open this file in your web browser using File ➪ Open. As shown in Figure 10-1, the title bar of the window will read "My First Web Page," and inside the page you'll see the words "My Tic-Tac-Toe game is coming soon..."

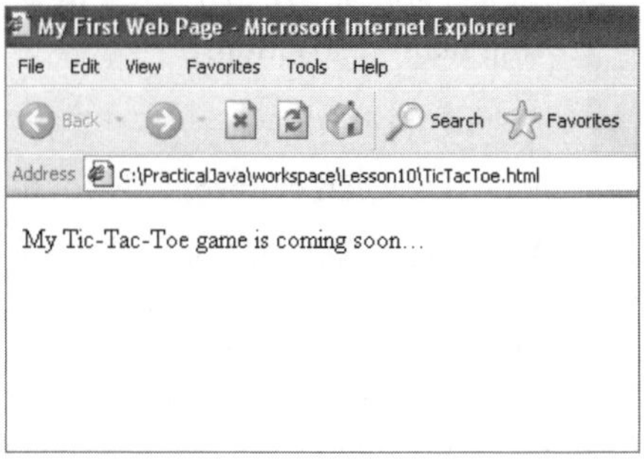

Earlier versions of the HTML standard included the tag <applet> to incorporate Java applets into an HTML page. But as of HTML 4.01 this tag has been deprecated and you should use the tag <object> for Internet Explorer or <embed> for other web browsers. But Oracle, the company behind Java, recommends using <applet> for web pages accessed through the Internet and <object> or <embed> for intranet-based websites. The main reason is that web browser vendors are infamous for being inconsistent in implementing HTML standards, and it's safer to use the tried-and-true <applet> tag to give a predictable look and feel to the web pages that host Java applets. But an intranet is a more controlled environment. You can read about embedding applets with all of these tags at http://download.oracle.com/javase/6/docs/technotes/guides/plugin/developer_guide/using_tags.html, but in this tutorial I'll stick to the <applet> tag.

**FIGURE 10-1**

The deployment options for applets have been extended as of the release of Java 6 update 10. To learn all the options for applet deployment in depth, refer to the Oracle document *Java Rich Internet Applications Deployment Advice*, available at http://download.oracle.com/javase/6/docs/technotes/guides/jweb/deployment_advice.html.

Let's add the <applet> tag to the file TicTacToe.html, as shown in Listing 10-2. With some HTML tags you can specify additional attributes. The following are the main attributes of the <applet> tag:

➤ code: Contains the name of the applet Java class.

➤ width: Contains the width in pixels of the rectangular area on the screen that will be used by the applet.

➤ height: Contains the height of the area to be used by the applet.

➤ codebase: Specifies the root directory of your applet class relative to the location of the HTML file. For example, if the applet class is located in the sub-directory bin, specify "./bin" in the codebase attribute to avoid getting FileNotFoundException.

➤ archive: Use this attribute to specify the location of the jar file if your multi-class applet has been deployed as one archive file, which can be created with the help of the jar program located in the bin directory of your Java install.

The <applet> tag from Listing 10-2 means that a compiled version of the Java class TicTacToe is located in the same directory as TicTacToe.html, and it'll occupy a screen area of 300 pixels by 250 pixels. Note that if an HTML tag doesn't have nested tags, placing a forward slash in front of the closing angle bracket is a replacement for a closing </applet> tag.

But in general, the <applet> tag may have nested elements. In particular, if you need to pass parameters to an applet you can do it via the nested element <param>.

**LISTING 10-2:** The basic HTML file

```
<html>
<body>
   Here is my Tic-Tac-Toe game:
   <applet code="TicTacToe.class" width=300 height=250 />
</body>
</html>
```

Now the screen looks different — instead of seeing the tic-tac-toe game you'll get an error message, as in Figure 10-2. No wonder: The web browser could not find `TicTacToe.class`, so it just shows a rectangle of 300 pixels by 250 pixels. You'll fix this error by creating the `TicTacToe` class a little later in this lesson.

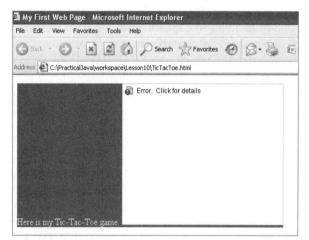

**FIGURE 10-2**

# WRITING APPLETS USING SWING

Until the Swing library came into the picture, you could create Java applets only using UI components from the `java.awt` package. Even after Swing components were introduced, using them was somewhat problematic in applets downloadable over the Internet — what if the applet had to be run in an older browser that supported only Java 1.1 and didn't know about Swing classes? But modern applets use the new plug-in and don't depend on what JDK came with the web browser. In this book I'll be writing my applets with Java Swing.

Swing applets have to be inherited from the class `javax.swing.JApplet`. For example

```
class TicTacToe extends javax.swing.JApplet {
}
```

Unlike Java applications, applets do not need a `main()` method because the web browser will download and run them as soon as it sees the `<applet>` tag in the web page. The Java plug-in will also notify the applet when some important life-cycle events happen — for example, when the applet is starting, repainting, and so on.

If your applet needs to react to these events, you should program one of the *callback methods*: `init()`, `start()`, `paint()`, `stop()`, and `destroy()`. The Java plug-in will call these methods in the following cases:

➤ `init()` is called when the applet is loaded by the Java plug-in. It's called only once, playing a role similar to that of constructors in regular Java classes.

➤ `start()` is called right after `init()`. It is also called each time a user returns to the web page with the applet after visiting another page.

➤ `paint()` is called when the applet's window needs to be displayed or refreshed after some activity on the screen, for example, when the applet is overlapping with some other window and the browser needs to repaint it. This method will get the Graphics object as an argument.

➤ `stop()` is called when the user leaves the web page containing the applet.

➤ `destroy()` is called when the browser destroys the applet. Write code in this method only if the applet uses some other resources — for example, if it holds a connection to the remote computer it was downloaded from.

Even though you do not have to program all these methods, each applet must have at least `init()` or `paint()`. For example, `init()` is the right place to get some external parameters that may be passed to the applet. Say that the HTML file has an `<applet>` tag that looks like this:

```
<applet>
        <param>name="backgroundColor" value="0xc0c0c0"</param>
</applet>
```

To get the value of the parameter `backgroundColor` just write one line in the `init()` method:

```
String backgroundColor = getParameter("backgroundColor");
```

Listing 10-3 shows the code of the applet that displays the words "Hello World." This applet has only one method, `paint()`, that receives an instance of the `Graphics` object from the Java plug-in. The class `java.awt.Graphics` has several methods for painting. Our applet uses the method `drawString()` to draw the text "Hello World."

**LISTING 10-3:** Hello World applet

Available for
download on
Wrox.com

```
import javax.swing.JApplet;
import java.awt.Graphics;

public class HelloWorld extends JApplet {

        public void paint(Graphics g){
            g.drawString("Hello World", 50, 100);
        }
}
```

Create this class in Eclipse. Then run it as a Java Applet (Eclipse will use appletviewer to display it). The window appears as shown in Figure 10-3.

To test this applet in a web browser create the file `Hello.html` as you created the file in Listing 10-2. Start your web browser and open the file `Hello.html` using the browser's File and Open menus. You'll see the same output as in Figure 10-3.

Do you think that after this simple example you are ready to write a game program? You bet! You'll do it in Lesson 11. For a more detailed tutorial on Java applets, please visit the following web page: `http://download` `.oracle.com/javase/tutorial/deployment/applet/index.html`.

**FIGURE 10-3**

## TRY IT

Turn the calculator from Lessons 8 and 9 into an applet.

## Lesson Requirements

You should have Java installed.

>  *You can download the code and resources for this Try It from the book's web page at www.wrox.com. You can find them in the Lesson10 folder in the download.*

## Step-by-Step

1. Create a new Eclipse project called Lesson10.

2. Take the `Calculator` class that you created in the Try It section of Lesson 8 and copy it into the project Lesson10. Give it an ancestor, `JApplet`.

3. Get rid of the `main()` method. Now the `Calculator` class will be instantiated for you by the Java plug-in inside the web browser.

4. Rename the `Calculator`'s constructor method into the applet's `init()` method.

5. Do not control the size of the calculator by calling `pack()`. Now the size of your `calculator` is defined by the width and height attributes of the tag `<applet>`.

6. Do not instantiate `JFrame`.

7. Add the code to perform calculations that you completed at the end of Lesson 9.

8. Don't try to control the life cycle of the calculator by processing events of the `WindowListener`, as was explained in Lesson 9. Now your window lives inside the web browser.

9. Create the file `Calculator.html` and open it in the web browser. You should see your calculator.

> *Please select Lesson 10 on the DVD to view the video that accompanies this lesson.*

# 11

# Developing a Tic-Tac-Toe Applet

Now that you're familiar with the basics of Java applets, it'll be nice to write a program a bit more useful than Hello World. In this lesson you'll program the game of tic-tac-toe as a Java Swing applet.

Every game implements some algorithm — a set of rules or a strategy that has to be applied depending on the player's actions. The algorithms for the same game can be simple or very complicated. When you hear that the world chess champion plays against a computer, he actually plays against a program. Teams of experts are trying to invent sophisticated algorithms to beat him. Let's come up with the algorithm for tic-tac-toe.

## THE STRATEGY

In the unlikely event that you aren't familiar with tic-tac-toe, or if it has a different name in your part of the world, read the following Wikipedia article: http://en.wikipedia.org/ wiki/Tic-tac-toe. Our version of the popular game will implement the following strategy:

➤  The game will be played on a two-dimensional board of three cells by three cells.

➤  Two players can play this game. One will play with the symbol X, and the other will use O.

➤  The winner must have a full row, column, or diagonal of his or her designated symbol.

➤  After each move, the program has to check if there is a winner.

➤  The game should end if there are no empty squares left.

➤  The player has to press the New Game button to play again.

➤  When the program makes a decision about where to put the next letter O, it has to try to find a row, column, or diagonal that already contains two Os, and add the third accordingly.

➤ If there is no such row, column, or diagonal, the program has to try to find two Xs in such a configuration and place an O in the free cell to block the player's winning move.

➤ If no winning or blocking move was found, the program has to try to occupy the central square, or pick the next empty square at random.

## CODING TIC-TAC-TOE

Let's implement the strategy for tic-tac-toe as an applet. First, program the UI portion, and then add event processing. I decided to use JPanel, containing nine Jbuttons, to render the three-by-three grid. Review the code in Listing 11-1. Note that the panel uses GridLayout, but with an extra row (four by three). The last row will display the player's identifier: "Player X" or "Player 0." Figure 11-1 shows how it may look.

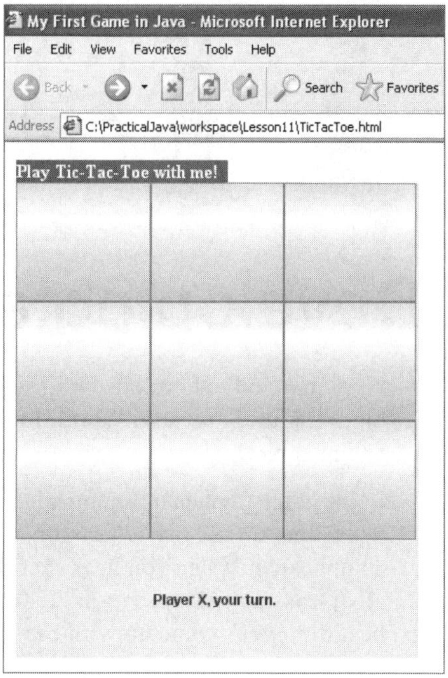

By setting the button label to X or O, on the click event, it's easy to keep track of each player's move. At the bottom of the window you'll see the name of the player who is to make the next move (see the method setPlayerName() in Listing 11-1). The method reset() will clear all the squares after the winner has been announced.

Play Tic-Tac-Toe with me!

Player X, your turn.

**FIGURE 11-1**

**Available for download on Wrox.com**

**LISTING 11-1: Coding UI for tic-tac-toe**

```java
package com.practicaljava.lesson11;

import java.awt.BorderLayout;
import java.awt.Component;
import java.awt.Font;
import java.awt.event.MouseEvent;
import java.awt.event.MouseListener;
import java.awt.GridLayout;

import javax.swing.JApplet;
import javax.swing.JButton;
import javax.swing.JLabel;
import javax.swing.JOptionPane;
import javax.swing.SwingConstants;

public class TicTacToeApplet1 extends JApplet{

    private static String PLAYERX = "Player X";
    private static String PLAYERO = "Player O";

    private String playerName = PLAYERX;

    private JButton button1;
```

```
private JButton button2;
private JButton button3;
private JButton button4;
private JButton button5;
private JButton button6;
private JButton button7;
private JButton button8;
private JButton button9;
private JLabel playerNumber;
private java.awt.Panel buttonsPanel;


public void init(){

    initComponents();
}


private void initComponents(){

    buttonsPanel = new java.awt.Panel();
    button1 = new JButton();
    button2 = new JButton();
    button3 = new JButton();
    button4 = new JButton();
    button5 = new JButton();
    button6 = new JButton();
    button7 = new JButton();
    button8 = new JButton();
    button9 = new JButton();
    playerNumber = new JLabel(playerName, SwingConstants.CENTER);

  Font buttonFont = new Font("Times New Roman", Font.PLAIN, 60);

    button1.setFont(buttonFont);
    button2.setFont(buttonFont);
    button3.setFont(buttonFont);
    button4.setFont(buttonFont);
    button5.setFont(buttonFont);
    button6.setFont(buttonFont);
    button7.setFont(buttonFont);
    button8.setFont(buttonFont);
    button9.setFont(buttonFont);

    buttonsPanel.setLayout(new GridLayout(4, 3));

    buttonsPanel.add(button1);
    buttonsPanel.add(button2);
    buttonsPanel.add(button3);
    buttonsPanel.add(button4);
    buttonsPanel.add(button5);
    buttonsPanel.add(button6);
```

*continues*

**LISTING 11-1** *(continued)*

```
        buttonsPanel.add(button7);
        buttonsPanel.add(button8);
        buttonsPanel.add(button9);

        buttonsPanel.add(new Component(){});
        setPlayeName(PLAYERX);
        buttonsPanel.add(playerNumber);

        add(buttonsPanel);
    }

    private void setPlayerName(String playerName){

        this.playerName = playerName;
        playerNumber.setText(playerName +", your turn.");
    }

    public void reset(){
        button1.setText("");
        button2.setText("");
        button3.setText("");
        button4.setText("");
        button5.setText("");
        button6.setText("");
        button7.setText("");
        button8.setText("");
        button9.setText("");
        setPlayerName(PLAYERX);
    }
}
```

As you learned in Lesson 10, the callback method `init()` will be automatically called by the Java plug-in when the applet is downloaded by the web browser. While in development mode, you can also test your applets right in Eclipse with appletviewer. Note that the code in Listing 11-1 does not set the size of the game board — that has to be done externally, either in an HTML file, as in Listing 11-2, or in Eclipse in the Run Configuration window. The width of my game board is set to 350 pixels and the height is 400.

**LISTING 11-2: HTML wrapper for the tic-tac-toe applet**

```
<HTML>
  <HEAD>
   <Title>My First Game in Java</Title>
  </HEAD>

  <BODY>

    <STRONG>Play Tic-Tac-Toe with me! </STRONG>
```

```
<BR>
<APPLET code="com.practicaljava.lesson11.TicTacToeApplet"
        codebase="./bin" width="350" height="400" />

</BODY>

</HTML>
```

---

**SWING AND GROUPLAYOUT**

The code in Listing 11-1 was written manually. But most likely, if you're developing a complex GUI, you'll use some Swing GUI builder such as Matisse that will allow you to design windows in what-you-see-is-what-you-get mode by dragging and dropping visual components onto the design area. If you look at the auto-generated code you may find GroupLayout, created by the GUI builder (but you can program this layout manually, too).

GroupLayout groups components inside a container. Imagine a shipping or billing form that contains several text labels, one under another, each having an input field next to it. Each label contains a different number of characters, which means that you'll need to align the input fields so the form looks pretty. If you can think of this UI as of two vertical groups (labels belong to one and input fields to another), you can simply set the gap between the left and right groups to 20 pixels or so.

Similarly, you can distinguish some horizontal groups in your UI. If you want to learn more about GroupLayout, follow this link: http://download-llnw.oracle .com/javase/6/docs/api/javax/swing/GroupLayout.html.

---

After the UI part is ready, let's take care of the processing logic. Our applet will be processing mouse clicks to set the label of the selected button to X or O and checking for the winner. That's why you'll need to perform these steps:

1. Add implements MouseListener to the class TicTacToeApplet.

2. Add MouseListener to each of the buttons so they properly report which player (X or O) clicked them, for example

   ```
   button1.addMouseListener(this);
   ```

3. Implement methods required by the MouseListener interface — only the mouseClicked() callback will have code in this applet.

4. Call the method checkForWinner() on each click to determine whether there are three identical symbols in a row, column, or diagonal, as shown in Listing 11-3.

**LISTING 11-3: Processing button click events**

Available for download on Wrox.com

```
public void mouseClicked(MouseEvent e) {

  JButton currentButton = (JButton)e.getComponent();
  if (currentButton.getText() == ""){
         if (playerName == PLAYERX) {
                currentButton.setText("X");
                setPlayerName(PLAYERO);

         } else if (playerName == PLAYERO){

                currentButton.setText("O");
                setPlayerName(PLAYERX);
         }
  }

        checkForWinner();
}
```

When the user clicks a button, the method `mouseClicked()` checks the name of the current player and displays X or O accordingly by calling `currentButton.SetText()`. Figure 11-2 depicts how this looks in the web browser.

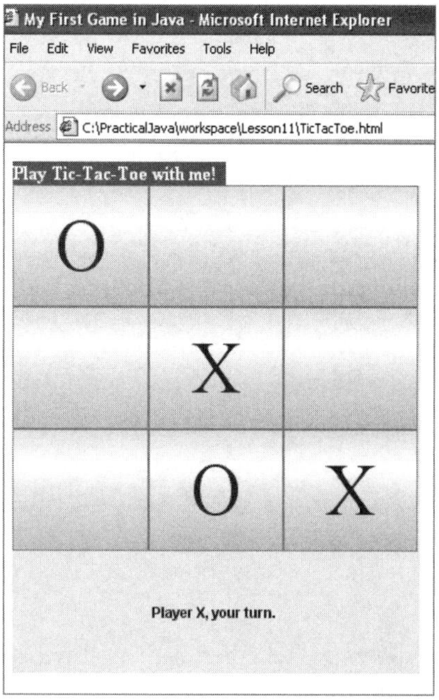


**FIGURE 11-2**

The method `checkForWinner()` will call another private method, `findThreeInARow()`. If three identical symbols are found diagonally or in any vertical or horizontal line, the method `checkForWinner()` will congratulate the winner and call `reset()` so the new game can be started. The methods `checkForWinner()` and `findThreeInARow()` are shown in Listings 11-4 and 11-5 respectively.

**LISTING 11-4:** The method checkForWinner()

```
private void checkForWinner(){

    String [] str = {"OK"};

    if(findThreeInARow()){

      String winnerName=(playerName == PLAYERX)?PLAYERO:PLAYERX;
      JOptionPane.showOptionDialog(this, winnerName.concat(
                " won!!! Congratulations!!!"), "Congratulations!",
    JOptionPane.YES_OPTION, JOptionPane.PLAIN_MESSAGE, null, str, "OK");

      reset();
    }
}
```

**LISTING 11-5:** The method findThreeInARow()

```
private boolean findThreeInARow(){

    if ((button1.getText() == button2.getText() && button2.getText() ==
      button3.getText() && button1.getText() != "") ||
    (button4.getText() == button5.getText() && button5.getText() ==
      button6.getText() && button4.getText() != "") ||
    (button7.getText() == button8.getText() && button8.getText() ==
     button9.getText() && button7.getText() != "") ||
    (button1.getText() == button4.getText() && button4.getText() ==
      button7.getText() && button1.getText() != "") ||
    (button2.getText() == button5.getText() && button5.getText() ==
      button8.getText() && button2.getText() != "") ||
    (button3.getText() == button6.getText() && button6.getText() ==
     button9.getText() && button3.getText() != "") ||
    (button1.getText() == button5.getText() && button5.getText() ==
      button9.getText() && button1.getText() != "") ||
    (button3.getText() == button5.getText() && button5.getText() ==
      button7.getText() && button3.getText() != "")
    )
      //There is a winner!
    return true;

    else
      //No three-in-a-row was found
      return false;
}
```

The complete code for this version of tic-tac-toe is included on the website and is given in Listing 11-6 for your reference.

**LISTING 11-6: Complete code for the tic-tac-toe game**

```java
package com.practicaljava.lesson11;
import java.awt.BorderLayout;
import java.awt.Component;
import java.awt.Font;
import java.awt.event.MouseEvent;
import java.awt.event.MouseListener;
import javax.swing.JApplet;
import javax.swing.JButton;
import javax.swing.JOptionPane;
import javax.swing.SwingConstants;
public class TicTacToeApplet extends JApplet
                                    implements MouseListener {

    private static String PLAYERX = "Player X";
    private static String PLAYERO = "Player O";
    private String playerName = PLAYERX;
    private JButton button1;
    private JButton button2;
    private JButton button3;
    private JButton button4;
    private JButton button5;
    private JButton button6;
    private JButton button7;
    private JButton button8;
    private JButton button9;
    private JLabel playerNumber;
    private Panel buttonsPanel;

    public void init(){
        initComponents();
    }
    private void initComponents(){
        buttonsPanel = new Panel();
        button1 = new JButton();
        button2 = new JButton();
        button3 = new JButton();
        button4 = new JButton();
        button5 = new JButton();
        button6 = new JButton();
        button7 = new JButton();
        button8 = new JButton();
        button9 = new JButton();

        playerNumber = new JLabel(playerName,
                          SwingConstants.CENTER);
        button1.addMouseListener(this);
        button2.addMouseListener(this);
        button3.addMouseListener(this);
```

```
        button4.addMouseListener(this);
        button5.addMouseListener(this);
        button6.addMouseListener(this);
        button7.addMouseListener(this);
        button8.addMouseListener(this);
        button9.addMouseListener(this);

        Font buttonFont = new Font("Times New Roman",
                                        Font.PLAIN, 60);
        button1.setFont(buttonFont);
        button2.setFont(buttonFont);
        button3.setFont(buttonFont);
        button4.setFont(buttonFont);
        button5.setFont(buttonFont);
        button6.setFont(buttonFont);
        button7.setFont(buttonFont);
        button8.setFont(buttonFont);
        button9.setFont(buttonFont);

        buttonsPanel.setLayout(new java.awt.GridLayout(4, 3));
        buttonsPanel.add(button1);
        buttonsPanel.add(button2);
        buttonsPanel.add(button3);
        buttonsPanel.add(button4);
        buttonsPanel.add(button5);
        buttonsPanel.add(button6);
        buttonsPanel.add(button7);
        buttonsPanel.add(button8);
        buttonsPanel.add(button9);
        buttonsPanel.add(new Component(){});

        setPlayerName(PLAYERX);
        buttonsPanel.add(playerNumber);
        add(buttonsPanel);
    }

    private void setPlayerName(String playerName){
        this.playerName = playerName;
        playerNumber.setText(playerName  + ", your turn. ");
    }

    private void reset(){
        button1.setText("");
        button2.setText("");
        button3.setText("");
        button4.setText("");
        button5.setText("");
        button6.setText("");
        button7.setText("");
        button8.setText("");
        button9.setText("");

        setPlayerName(PLAYERX);
```

*continues*

**LISTING 11-6** *(continued)*

```java
    }

    private void checkForWinner(){
        String [] str = {"OK"};
        if(findThreeInARow()){
          String winnerName=
          (playerName == PLAYERX)?PLAYERO:PLAYERX;

          JOptionPane.showOptionDialog(this,
          winnerName.concat(" won!!! Congratulations!!!"),
          "Congratulations!", JOptionPane.YES_OPTION,
          JOptionPane.PLAIN_MESSAGE, null, str, "OK");
            reset();
        }
    }

public void mouseClicked(MouseEvent e) {
        JButton currentButton = (JButton)e.getComponent();
        if (currentButton.getText() == ""){
            if (playerName == PLAYERX) {
                currentButton.setText("X");
                setPlayerName(PLAYERO);
            } else if (playerName == PLAYERO){
                currentButton.setText("O");
                setPlayerName(PLAYERX);
            }
        }
        checkForWinner();
    }

    public void mousePressed(MouseEvent e) {}
    public void mouseReleased(MouseEvent e) {}
    public void mouseEntered(MouseEvent e) {}
    public void mouseExited(MouseEvent e) {}

    public boolean findThreeInARow(){
        if ((button1.getText() == button2.getText() && button2.getText() ==
button3.getText() && button1.getText() != "") ||
                (button4.getText() == button5.getText() && button5.getText() ==
button6.getText() && button4.getText() != "") ||
              (button7.getText() == button8.getText() && button8.getText() ==
button9.getText() && button7.getText() != "") ||
            (button1.getText() == button4.getText() && button4.getText() ==
button7.getText() && button1.getText() != "") ||
            (button2.getText() == button5.getText() && button5.getText() ==
button8.getText() && button2.getText() != "") ||
            (button3.getText() == button6.getText() && button6.getText() ==
button9.getText() && button3.getText() != "") ||
            (button1.getText() == button5.getText() && button5.getText() ==
button9.getText() && button1.getText() != "") ||
            (button3.getText() == button5.getText() && button5.getText() ==
button7.getText() && button3.getText() != "")
        ){
```

```
            return true;
        }else {
            return false;
        }
    }

}
```

Congratulations! You've completed your first game in Java. This program uses a simple strategy because our goal is just to learn how to program Java applets. There is one more important class for working with Swing UI using the Swing Worker Thread, but it's a bit too early to explain it here because I haven't covered Java threads yet. You can read about the SwingWorker class in Lesson 20.

# TRY IT

Today's homework is to modify the code from Listing 11-6 to make it shorter and change the game — the current version of tic-tac-toe requires two human players, but I want you to replace one of them with the computer (which also has some brainpower). I also want you to highlight the winning combination rather than displaying a pop-up window with congratulations.

## Lesson Requirements

You should have Java installed.

> *You can download the code and resources for this Try It from the book's web page at* www.wrox.com. *You can find them in the Lesson11 folder in the download.*

## Step-by-Step

1. Create a new Eclipse project called Lesson11, copy TicTacToeApplet from the DVD accompanying the book into this project, and run it to ensure that you can play this two-player game.

2. The code in Listing 11-6 performs lots of repetitive actions on buttons, such as setFont(), setText(), and addMouseListener(). Create an array and store all instances of JButton there. Introduce loops to perform all repetitive actions on the buttons.

3. Get rid of the pop-up window congratulating the winner with JOptionPane .showOptionDialog(). Display this text instead at the bottom of the window (use the existing JLabel playerNumber for this).

4. Highlight the winning combination by giving the winning squares (Swing JButtons) a different color.

5. Add a new button, Play Again, at the bottom of the window for starting a new game.

**6.**   Replace the moves of Player O with randomly generated moves made by the computer right after the Player X moves. Use the method `nextInt()` from the class `java.util.Random`. If the randomly generated square is occupied, call this method again.

**7.**   Test this program and enjoy the game!

**8.**   This step is optional. If you want to make the computer's moves smarter, learn *minimax strategy* (see `http://en.wikipedia.org/wiki/Minimax`) to enable the computer to select the best move.

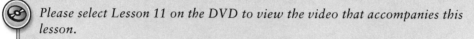

*Please select Lesson 11 on the DVD to view the video that accompanies this lesson.*

# 12

# Developing a Ping-Pong Game

The tic-tac-toe game developed in Lesson 11 was a simple one. My goal was to show you the basic layout of UI components and event processing. Now you'll learn how to draw and move such objects as ovals, rectangles, and lines in a window. You'll also learn how to process keyboard events. To add a little fun to these subjects, you'll be learning all these things while creating a ping-pong game. This game will have two players: the user and the computer.

## THE STRATEGY

Let's come up with the rules for our version of the ping-pong game:

**1.** The game lasts until one of the players (the user or the computer) reaches a score of 21. The computer's racket is on the left.

**2.** The user's racket movements will be controlled by the mouse.

**3.** The game score will be displayed at the bottom of the window.

**4.** A new game starts when a player presses the N key on the keyboard; the Q key ends the game; S serves the ball.

**5.** Only the user can serve the ball; the computer can't.

**6.** For one of the players to win a point the ball must go beyond the opponent's racket's vertical line when the racket is not blocking the ball.

**7.** When the computer bounces the ball, the ball can move only horizontally to the right.

**8.** If the ball contacts the user's racket in the upper half of the table, the ball should be moving up and left. If the ball was located in the bottom part of the table, it should move down and left.

It sounds like a very complicated task, but let's split it into a set of simple tasks and solve them one by one. The first version of the game will have only some of these rules implemented: It'll just paint the table, move the racket, and display the coordinates of the mouse pointer when you click the mouse button.

## THE CODE

From the code organization perspective, you need to decide how many classes you need to write to separate UI and functionality. This game will consist of two classes and one interface:

➤ The class `PingPongGreenTable` will take care of the visual part. During the game it'll display the table, rackets, and ball. The final version of the table is shown in Figure 12-1. This book doesn't show colors, but the table surface is green, the rackets are blue and yellow, and the ball is red.

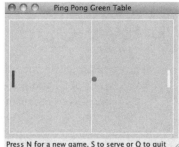

**FIGURE 12-1**

➤ The class `PingPongGameEngine` will be responsible for calculating the ball's and rackets' coordinates, starting and ending the game, and serving the ball. The engine will pass the current coordinates of the UI components to `PingPongGreenTable`, which will repaint itself accordingly.

➤ The interface `GameConstants` will contain declarations of all constants that the game needs, for example the width and height of the table, the starting positions of the rackets, and so on.

## The User Interface

The first version of the game will do only three things:

➤ Display the green ping-pong table.

➤ Display the coordinates of the mouse pointer when you click the mouse.

➤ Move the user's racket up and down according to the mouse pointer's movements.

Listing 12-1 shows the first version of the UI. The class `PingPongGreenTable1` is a subclass of the Swing `JPanel`.

**LISTING 12-1: Coding UI of the ping-pong game (version 1)**

```
public class PingPongGreenTable1 extends JPanel implements GameConstants1{

    JLabel label;
    public Point point = new Point(0,0);

    private int ComputerRacketX =15;
```

```java
private int kidRacketY =KID_RACKET_Y_START;

Dimension preferredSize = new Dimension(TABLE_WIDTH,TABLE_HEIGHT);

// This method sets the size of the frame. It's called by JVM
public Dimension getPreferredSize() {
      return preferredSize;
}

// Constructor instantiates the engine
PingPongGreenTable1(){

  PingPongGameEngine1 gameEngine = new PingPongGameEngine1(this);

   // Listen to mouse clicks to show its coordinates
     addMouseListener(gameEngine);

   // Listen to mouse movements to move the rackets
     addMouseMotionListener(gameEngine);
 }

 // Add a panel with a JLabel to the frame
 void addPaneltoFrame(Container container) {

    container.setLayout(new BoxLayout(container, BoxLayout.Y_AXIS));
    container.add(this);

     label = new JLabel("Click to see coordinates");
     container.add(label);
 }

 // Repaint the window. This method is called by the JVM
 // when it needs to refresh the screen or when a
 // method repaint() is called from PingPointGameEngine1

  public void paintComponent(Graphics g) {

    super.paintComponent(g);
    g.setColor(Color.GREEN);

    // paint the table green
    g.fillRect(0,0,TABLE_WIDTH,TABLE_HEIGHT);

    // paint the right racket
    g.setColor(Color.yellow);
    g.fillRect(KID_RACKET_X_START,kidRacketY,5,30);

   // paint the left racket
    g.setColor(Color.blue);
    g.fillRect(ComputerRacketX,100,5,30);

    //paint the ball
    g.setColor(Color.red);
```

*continues*

**LISTING 12-1** *(continued)*

```java
        g.fillOval(25,110,10,10);

        // Draw the white lines on the table
        g.setColor(Color.white);
        g.drawRect(10,10,300,200);
         g.drawLine(160,10,160,210);

        // Display the dot as a small 2x2 pixels rectangle
        if (point != null) {
            label.setText("Coordinates (x,y): " +
                          point.x + ", " + point.y);
       g.fillRect(point.x, point.y, 2, 2);
   }

     }

     // Set the current position of the kid's racket
     public void setKidRacketY(int xCoordinate){

       this.kidRacketY = xCoordinate;
     }

    // Return the current position of the kid's racket
     public int getKidRacketY(int xCoordinate){
        return kidRacketY;
     }

      public static void main(String[] args) {

        JFrame f = new JFrame("Ping Pong Green Table");

        // Ensure that the window can be closed
        // by pressing a little cross in the corner
        f.setDefaultCloseOperation(WindowConstants.EXIT_ON_CLOSE);

        PingPongGreenTable1 table = new PingPongGreenTable1();

        table.addPaneltoFrame(f.getContentPane());

        // Set the size and make the frame visible
       f.pack();
        f.setVisible(true);
      }
   }
```

At any given time the game needs to know the exact coordinates of the mouse pointer. The constructor of PingPongGreenTable1 will create an instance of the event listener class PingPongGameEngine, which will perform some actions when the user clicks the mouse button or just moves the mouse.

The method addPaneltoFrame() creates a JLabel component that will display the coordinates of the mouse.

This class is not an applet, which is why instead of the method paint() it uses the method paintComponent(). This method is called by JVM when it needs to refresh the window, or when our program calls the method repaint(). In other words, the method repaint() internally calls paintComponent() and provides our class with the object Graphics so it can paint on the window. Always call this method after recalculating the coordinates of the rackets or the ball to display them in the proper position.

To paint a racket, set the color first, and then fill a thin vertical rectangle with this paint using the method fillRect(). This method needs to know the x- and y-coordinates of the top left corner of the rectangle and its width and height in pixels.

The ball is painted with the method fillOval(), which needs to know the coordinates of the center of the oval, its height and its width. When the height and width of the oval are the same, it is a circle.

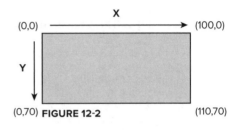

**FIGURE 12-2**

The x-coordinate in a window increases from left to right, and the y-coordinate increases from top to bottom (see Figure 12-2). For example, the width of the rectangle shown in Figure 12-1 is 100 pixels, and the height is 70.

The x- and y-coordinates of the corners of this rectangle are shown in parentheses.

Another interesting method is getPreferredSize(). The program creates an instance of the Swing class Dimension to set the size of the ping-pong table. The JVM needs to know the dimensions of the window, which is why it calls the method getPreferredSize() of the PingPongGreenTable1 object. This method returns to the JVM an object, Dimension, that is created in the code according to the size of our table.

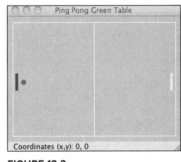

The first version of the UI is shown in Figure 12-3. You can move the mouse, and the correct racket moves along. When you click the mouse anywhere on the table, the current coordinates are displayed at the bottom.

**FIGURE 12-3**

## The Constants

Both table and engine classes use some constant values that do not change. For example, the class PingPongGreenTable1 uses the width and height of the table, and PingPongGameEngine1 needs to know the ball movement increments — the smaller the increment, the smoother the movement. It's convenient to keep all the constants (final variables) in an interface. In our game the name of the interface is GameConstants1. If a class needs these values, there are two ways of making them available in the game classes.

The first one is just adding the clause implements GameConstants1 to the class declaration and using any of the final variables from this interface as if they had been declared in the class itself. This method of adding constants has a code readability drawback — it won't be easily understood where these final variables were declared. Both the table and engine classes (see Listing 12-3) implement the GameConstants1 interface shown in Listing 12-2.

The second (and better) way of using these constants is to import the interface in the classes that need them, and use the fully qualified names of the constants, e.g. GameConstants1.TABLE_WIDTH. Changing the code of Listing 12-3 to apply this technique is one of the assignments in the Try It section.

If you decide to change the size of the table, ball, or rackets you'll need to do it in only one place — the GameConstants1 interface.

**LISTING 12-2:** The game's constants (version 1)

```
public interface GameConstants1 {

    int TABLE_WIDTH  =  320;
    int TABLE_HEIGHT = 220;
    int KID_RACKET_Y_START = 100;
    int KID_RACKET_X_START = 300;
    int TABLE_TOP = 12;
    int TABLE_BOTTOM = 180;
    int RACKET_INCREMENT = 4;
}
```

A program cannot change the values of these variables, because they were declared as final. But if, for example, you decide to increase the size of the table, you'll need to change the values of TABLE_WIDTH and TABLE_HEIGHT and then recompile the GameConstants1 interface.

## The Engine

The decision maker in this game is the class PingPongGameEngine1, which implements two mouse-related interfaces. The first version of the engine is shown in Listing 12-3.

**LISTING 12-3:** The game's engine (version 1)

```
public class PingPongGameEngine1   implements
        MouseListener, MouseMotionListener, GameConstants1{

    PingPongGreenTable1 table;
    public int kidRacketY = KID_RACKET_Y_START;

    // Constructor. Stores a reference to the UI object
    public PingPongGameEngine1(PingPongGreenTable1 greenTable){
        table = greenTable;
    }

    // Methods required by the MouseListener interface
    public void mouseClicked(MouseEvent e) {

        // Get X and Y coordinates of the mouse pointer
```

```
    // and set it to the "white point" on the table
    // Bad practice! Fix it in the Try It section
        table.point.x = e.getX();
table.point.y = e.getY();

  //The method repaint internally calls the table's
  // method paintComponent() that refreshes the window
  table.repaint();
  }

  public void mouseReleased(MouseEvent e) {};
  public void mouseEntered(MouseEvent e) {};
  public void mouseExited(MouseEvent e) {};
  public void mousePressed(MouseEvent e) {};

  // Methods required by the MouseMotionListener interface
  public void mouseDragged(MouseEvent e) {}

  public void mouseMoved(MouseEvent e) {
   int mouseY = e.getY();

   // If a mouse is above the kid's racket
   // and the racket did not go over the table top
   // move it up, otherwise move it down

   if (mouseY < kidRacketY && kidRacketY > TABLE_TOP){
kidRacketY -= RACKET_INCREMENT;
   }else if (kidRacketY < TABLE_BOTTOM) {
        kidRacketY += RACKET_INCREMENT;
   }

   // Set the new position of the racket table class
     table.setKidRacketY(kidRacketY);
     table.repaint();
   }
 }
```

The `MouseListener` will have code only in the method `mouseClicked()`. On every mouse click this method will draw a small white dot on the table and display its coordinates. This code is not very useful for our game, but I wanted to show you a simple way to get the coordinates of the mouse from the `MouseEvent` object that is given to the program by JVM.

The method `mouseClicked()` sets the coordinates of the variable `point` depending on where the mouse pointer was when the player pressed the mouse button. After coordinates are set, this method asks the JVM to repaint the table.

`MouseMotionListener` reacts to movements of the mouse over the table, and we'll use its method `mouseMoved()` to move the user's racket up or down.

The method `mouseMoved()` calculates the next position of the user's racket. If the mouse pointer is above the racket (the t-coordinate of the mouse is less than the y-coordinate of the racket) this method ensures that the racket will not go over the top of the table.

When the constructor of the table class creates the engine object, it passes to the engine a reference to the table's instance (the keyword `this` represents a reference to the memory location of the object

`PingPongGreenTable1`). Now the engine can "talk" to the table, for example by setting the new coordinates of the ball or repainting the table if needed.

I've included an example of a bad programming practice in Listing 12-3. The engine class is directly accessing the variable point declared in another class, `PingPongGreenTable1`. It would be better to make the variable `point` private and to provide a public method in the class `PingPongGreenTable1` to set the coordinates of the point. This way if you decide to rename the variable `point` you won't need to change the engine's class; the public interface will remain the same. You'll need to fix this bad practice in the "Try It" section.

In our game rackets move vertically from one position to another using the four-pixel increment defined in the interface `GameConstants1` (the engine class implements this interface). For example, the next line subtracts four from the value of the variable `kidRacketY`:

```
kidRacketY -= RACKET_INCREMENT;
```

Suppose the y-coordinate of the racket is 100: after this line it becomes 96, which means that the racket has to be moved up. You can get the same result using the following syntax:

```
kidRacketY = kidRacketY - RACKET_INCREMENT;
```

## FINISHING THE PING-PONG GAME

Well, to finish the game you need to learn about multi-threading, which will be explained in Lesson 20. If you feel a craving to finish the game right now, read the first half of Lesson 20 and then examine the code that comes on the accompanying DVD and read the following explanations. I won't include the full listing of the completed game here — just some highlights to help you in reading the code located on the disk. The class names in the completed version of the code are the same as the ones used in this lesson, but they do not end with the digit 1.

Let's start with the class `PingPongGreenTable`. You don't need to display a white dot when the user clicks the mouse; this was just an exercise to show you how to get the coordinates of the mouse pointer. That's why I'll remove the declaration of the variable `point` and the lines that paint the white dot from the method `paintComponent()`. Also, the constructor does not need to add the `MouseListener` anymore; it was there only to display the point's coordinates.

On the other hand, `PingPongGreenTable` should react to some of the keyboard buttons (N for new game, S for serving the ball, and Q for quitting the game). Adding `KeyListener` to the engine will take care of the communication with the keyboard. The declaration of the engine will look like this:

```
public class PingPongGameEngine implements Runnable,
        MouseMotionListener, KeyListener, GameConstants{...}
```

Accordingly, you'll need to add to the constructor of the class `PingPongGreenTable` the following line:

```
addKeyListener(gameEngine);
```

To make the code a little more encapsulated, I've also moved the `repaint()` calls from the engine class to `PingPongGreenTable`. Now this class will be responsible for repainting itself when needed.

I've also added methods to change the positions of the ball and the computer's racket, and to display messages. The final GameConstants interface has more variables than the one shown in Listing 12-2. You should be able to guess what they are for just by looking at their names.

Following is a summary of the changes I've made in the class PingPongGameEngine — review the code from the DVD and identify these changes:

➤   I have removed the interface MouseListener and all its methods, because we're not processing mouse clicks anymore. MouseMotionListener will take care of all mouse movements.

➤   This class now implements the Runnable interface, and you can find the decision-making code in the method run(). Look at the constructor: I create and start a new thread there. The method run() implements the game strategy rules in several steps, and all these steps are programmed inside the if statement if(ballServed), which is a short version of if(ballServed==true).

➤   Note the use of the conditional if statement that assigns a value to the variable canBounce in the code marked in the comments as Step 1. The variable will get a value of either true or false depending on the result of the following expression:

```
canBounce = (ballY >= computerRacketY &&
                    ballY < (computerRacket_Y + RACKET_LENGTH)? true: false);
```

➤   The class PingPongGameEngine implements the KeyListener interface, and the method keyPressed() checks what letter was keyed in — N to start, Q to quit, or S to serve. The code of this method enables the user to type either capital or lowercase letters, for example N or *n*.

➤   I've added several private methods like displayScore(), kidServe(), and isBallOnTheTable(). These methods are declared private because they are used within this class only, and other classes do not even have to know about them.

➤   Today's computers are too fast, and this makes the ball movements difficult to control. That's why I've slowed the game down by calling a method called Thread.sleep(). A static method, sleep(), will pause this particular thread for a number of milliseconds given as an argument of this method (see Lesson 20 for details).

➤   To make the ball movement a little more difficult to predict, when the user's racket hits the ball it moves diagonally. That's why code changes not only the x-coordinate of the ball, but the y-coordinate as well.

That's all there is to it. Run the program and enjoy the game!

# TRY IT

Your homework is to re-factor the code shown in this lesson. First split the UI, the constants, and the engine into separate Java packages. Review the code and add the proper access modifiers: Make the variables and methods that don't have to be exposed to other classes private. The code in Listing 12-3 shows an example of a bad programming practice: The engine class directly modifies the internal variable point of the UI class. Fix this.

## Lesson Requirements

You should have Java installed.

>  *You can download the code and resources for this Try It from the book's web page at* www.wrox.com. *You can find them in the Lesson12 folder in the download.*

## Hints

After learning how to work with files in Lesson 16, consider adding a new feature to the ping-pong game — that of saving the score in a file and providing a menu option to show the past scores.

## Step-by-Step

1. Create a new Eclipse project called Lesson12, copy the two classes whose names end with 1 from the DVD accompanying the book into this project, and run it to ensure that the ping-pong table is shown and the correct racket is moving up and down according to the movements of the mouse.

2. Create three packages named ui, engine, and common.

3. Move the class `PingPongGreenTable1` to ui, PingPongGameEngine1 to engine, and GameConstants1 to common.

4. Include the import statements where required.

5. Compile and run the program.

6. In the class `PingPongGreenTable1` introduce the public method `setPointCoordinates()`, which will set the x- and y-coordinates of the variable point (make this method private).

7. Browse the source code of all these classes and add the proper data access qualifiers to all variables and methods.

8. Refactor the code of `PingPongGameEngine1` to import the interface `GameConstants1` rather than implementing it.

> *Please select Lesson 12 on the DVD to view the video that accompanies this lesson.*

# 13

# Error Handling

Fixing the compiler's errors becomes trivial as you become more comfortable with the Java syntax. But you also should ensure that your programs process run-time errors that may happen regardless of your proficiency with the language itself.

Let's say a Java program that reads customers' data is deployed in production. What's going to happen if this file gets corrupted? Will the program crash with a scary geeky error message, or will it stay alive, displaying a user-friendly message such as, "There seems to be a problem with the file customers. Please make sure that the file is not corrupted"? Error processing in the Java world is called *exception handling*, which is the subject of this lesson.

## STACK TRACE

When a Java application is running, the JVM performs a number of internal and application-specific method calls. If a run-time error occurs that's not handled by the program, the program prints a *stack trace*, which reflects in the call stack the sequence of unfortunate events that caused this error. A stack trace helps software developers follow the workflow of the program that led to the error.

To illustrate what a stack trace may look like, consider the program shown in Listing 13-1, which deliberately divides by zero.

**LISTING 13-1: Generating stack trace by dividing by zero**

```
1 class TestStackTrace{
2    TestStackTrace()
3    {
4        divideByZero();
5    }
6
7    int divideByZero()
```

*continues*

**LISTING 13-1** *(continued)*

```
 8    {
 9         return 25/0;
10    }
11
12    static void main(String[]args)
13    {
14            new TestStackTrace();
15
16    }
17 }
```

Listing 13-2 depicts the output of this program, which has traced what happened in the program stack before the error occurred. Read the output from the last line upward. It shows that the program was executing the methods `main()`, `init()` for the constructor, and `divideByZero()`. The line numbers 14, 4, and 9, respectively, indicate where in the program these methods were called. After that the `ArithmeticException` was thrown — the code in line 9 tried to divide by zero. Turning the line numbers on in the Eclipse IDE helps you locate problematic code.

**LISTING 13-2:** Sample stack trace

```
c:\temp>java TestStackTrace

    Exception in thread "main"
    java.lang.ArithmeticException: / by zero
       at TestStackTrace.divideByZero(TestStackTrace.java:9)
       at TestStackTrace.<init>(TestStackTrace.java:4)
       at TestStackTrace.main(TestStackTrace.java:14)
```

Executing any Java program means running multiple threads, as explained in Lesson 20, and the stack trace output reflects what was happening in the main thread of our simple `TestStackTrace` program.

## JAVA EXCEPTIONS

In many programming languages, error processing depends on the programmer's goodwill and experience. Java forces a programmer to include the error-handling code for the majority of errors; otherwise the programs won't even compile.

Say you need to write a piece of code that reads a file containing data about customers. It's easy to foresee that unless the code includes error handling there is a chance that one day you'll see a stack trace instead of a customer list.

The creators of Java didn't want to allow this code to fail just because some programmers are too lazy to include error-handling code. Java forces you to place such code inside a `try/catch` block, as in Listing 13-3. Whenever you read or write files you have to process input/output (I/O) errors.

**LISTING 13-3:** Catching I/O errors

```
try{
    fileCustomer.read();
}
catch (IOException e){
    System.out.println("There seems to be a problem with the file customers. ");
}
```

Read the code from Listing 13-3 as follows: "Try to execute `fileCustomer.read()`, and if an error occurs, jump into the `catch` section and execute the code from there." `IOException` is a class that contains information about input/output errors.

In the case of an I/O error, the method `read()` *throws an exception* (for more details on reading files refer to Lesson 16). The `catch` block will catch this error and process it. The program won't terminate and this exception is considered handled. If the method `read()` finishes successfully, the code in the *section* `catch` won't be executed.

# EXCEPTION HIERARCHY

Errors in Java are represented as classes that can be divided into two major types: those that were caused by bad programming and those that were thrown because of some other external condition. For example, if a program declares a variable of type `Tax`, but this object was never instantiated, any attempts to call the non-static method `calcTax()` will result in `NullPointerException`:

```
Tax t;
t.calcTax();
```

This situation could have been predicted and properly handled by the programmer.

If a run-time error can be fixed, the exception is called *checked*. The method `reads()` from Listing 13-3 will throw an exception and the JVM will try to find the code that handles this error. Such an exception can be anticipated and recovered from without the need to change the code. While the program remains operational, the user can find the missing file containing the list of customers and try again to populate the GUI with this list.

All exceptions are subclasses of `Throwable`, which has two immediate descendants: `Error` and `Exception`. Subclasses of `Exception` are called *checked* exceptions and have to be handled in your code. You can declare and throw your own application-specific exception, for example `BadShipmentAddressException`.

Subclasses of the class `Error` are fatal JVM errors and are called *unchecked*. You are not required to put them in `try/catch` blocks as there is not much you can do if, say the JVM runs out of memory and crashes.

How is a programmer supposed to know in advance if some Java method may throw a particular exception and that the `try/catch` block should therefore be used? No need to memorize anything. If a method throws an exception, the Java compiler will print an error message similar to this one:

```
"Tax.java":  unreported exception: java.io.IOException; must be caught or
declared to be thrown at line 57
```

# TRY/CATCH BLOCKS

There are five Java keywords that can be used for exception handling: `try`, `catch`, `finally`, `throw`, and `throws`. One `try` block can have multiple `catch` blocks, to provide handling for more than one type of error. For example, when a program tries to read a file, the file may not be there — you must catch the `FileNotFoundException`. If the file is there, but the code tries to read past the end of file, the `catch` clause for `EOFException is necessary`. Listing 13-4 illustrates a multi-`catch` block.

**LISTING 13-4: One try with multiple catch statements**

```java
public void getCustomers(){
    try{
        fileCustomers.read();
    }catch(FileNotFoundException e){
        System.out.println("Can not find file Customers");
    }catch(EOFException e1){
        System.out.println("Done with file read");
    }catch(IOException e2){
        System.out.println("Problem reading  file " +
                                            e2.getMessage());
    }
}
```

The order of the `catch` statements may be important if the exceptions being caught belong to the same inheritance branch. For example, the class `EOFException` is a subclass of the more generic `IOException`, and you have to put the `catch` block for the subclass first. If you place the `catch` block for `IOException` before the one for `EOFException`, the latter block will never be reached — the end-of-file errors will be intercepted by the `IOException catch` block. A lazy programmer would cut corners and handle the exceptions that may happen during the reading of the file in a coarse-grained way (the compiler won't complain):

```java
public void getCustomers(){
    try{
        fileCustomers.read();
    }catch(Exception e){
        System.out.println("Problem reading  file " +
                                        e.getMessage());
    }
}
```

A `catch` block receives an instance of the `Exception` object that contains a short explanation of a problem, and the method `getMessage()` of the `Exception` object will return this info. If the description of an error returned by `getMessage()` is not clear enough, try the method `toString()` instead.

If you need more detailed information about the exception, use the method `printStackTrace()` on the received `Exception` object (see Listing 13-6). It will print all internal method calls that led to this exception, as described in the section "Stack Trace" earlier in this lesson.

# THE THROWS CLAUSE

In some cases it makes more sense to handle an exception not in the method where it happened, but in the calling one. Let's use the same example of code that reads a file. Because the method read() may throw an IOException, you should either handle it or declare that the calling method may throw it. The latter is done in Listing 13-5.

**LISTING 13-5:** Using throw clause

```
class CustomerList{

    void getAllCustomers() throws IOException{

    // Some other code goes here
    // Don't use try/catch if you are not handling exceptions here
    file.read();
    }

public static void main(String[] args){
    System.out.println("Customer List");

    // Some other code goes here

    try{
        // Since getAllCustomers()declared an exception,
        // either  handle  it over here, or re-throw it
        //(see the throw keyword explanation below)

        getAllCustomers();
    }
    catch(IOException e){
        System.out.println("Customer List is not available");
    }
    }
}
```

In Listing 13-5 IOException has been propagated from the method getAllCustomers() to the main() method, and has been handled there.

# THE FINALLY CLAUSE

The code can exit the try/catch block in several ways:

➤   The code inside the try block successfully ends and the program continues.

➤   The code inside the try block runs into a return statement.

➤   The code inside the try block throws an exception and control goes to the catch block.

As you can see, in some cases only the code from the `try` block will work; in some cases part of the code from the `try` block and all the code in `catch` will be invoked. If there is a piece of code that must be executed regardless of the success or failure of the code in the `try` block, put it under the clause `finally`.

**LISTING 13-6: Using clause finally**

```
try{
    file.read();
    //file.close();    don't close files inside try block
}
catch(Exception e){
    e.printStackTrace();
}
finally{

    file.close();

}
```

The code in Listing 13-6 will definitely close the file regardless of the success of the `read` operation, because the `close()` function is called in the `finally` block. But if you place the `close()` function inside the `try` block without writing the `finally` portion, in case of error during read the program will jump from the failed `read()` into `catch`, skipping the `close` operation. The `finally` clause is typically used for the release of system resources.

If you are not planning to handle exceptions in the current method, they will be propagated to the calling one. In this case you can use the `finally` clause without the `catch` clause:

```
void myMethod () throws IOException{
    try{
        file.read();
    }
    finally{
        file.close();
    }
}
```

# THE THROW OPERATOR

If an exception has occurred in a method, you may want to catch the exception, do partial error processing such as error logging, or throw it to the calling method again for further processing or just to make the user aware of the problem. In some cases you may want to catch an exception and handle it but throw another exception (with modified error information) to the calling method.

The `throw` statement is used to throw Java exception objects. The object that a program throws must be `Throwable` (you can throw a ball, but you can't throw a grand piano). This means that you can throw only subclasses of the `Throwable` class and that all Java exceptions are its subclasses:

```
class CustomerList{

    void getAllCustomers() throws Exception{

        // some other code goes here

        try{
                file.read(); // this line may throw an exception
        } catch (IOException e) {

          // Log this error here, and rethrow another exception
          throw new  Exception ("Customer List is not available "+
                                            e.getMessage());
            }
      }

    public static void main(String[] args){
        System.out.println("Customer List");
           ...
         try{

            // Since the  getAllCustomers() declares an exception,
            // you have  to either  handle  or re-throw it
             getAllCustomers();
         }
         catch(Exception e){
              System.out.println(e.getMessage());
         }
     }
}
```

## CREATING YOUR OWN EXCEPTIONS

Programmers can also create exceptions specific to their business applications. Such a class has to be a subclass of one of the classes from the hierarchy of `Throwable` objects.

Let's say you are in business selling bikes and need to validate a customer's order. Create a new class, `TooManyBikesException`, and throw it if someone tries to order more bikes than can fit into one container, as in the class `BikeOrder` shown in Listing 13-7.

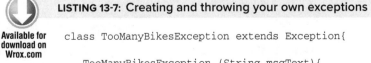

**LISTING 13-7:** Creating and throwing your own exceptions

Available for
download on
Wrox.com

```
class TooManyBikesException extends Exception{

    TooManyBikesException (String msgText){
         super(msgText);
```

*continues*

---

**LISTING 13-7** *(continued)*

```
      }
   }

   class BikeOrder{
      ...
      static  void validateOrder(String bikeModel,
              int quantity) throws TooManyBikesException{

   // perform  some data validation, and if the entered
   // the quantity or model is invalid, do  the following:

      throw new TooManyBikesException("Can not ship" +
           quantity+" bikes of the model " + bikeModel +);
    }
   }

   class OrderWindow extends JFrame{
      ...
    void actionPerformed(ActionEvent e){

      // the user clicked on the "Validate Order" button

      try{
         bikeOrder.validateOrder("Model-123", 50);

         // the next line will be skipped in case of  exception
         txtResult.setText("Order is valid");

      } catch(TooManyBikesException e){

         txtResult.setText(e.getMessage());

      }
     }
   }
```

`TooManyBikesException` shown in Listing 13-8 has a unique name and the text includes some information specific to the shipping business. But another way to provide application-specific information is to declare one or more additional variables in the custom exception. These variables carry multiple pieces of data that describe the erroneous situation and may help in fixing it.

**LISTING 13-8: Custom exception with extra property**

```
class TooManyBikesException extends Exception{

    // Declare an application-specific property
    ShippingErrorInfo shippingErrorInfo;

    TooManyBikesException (String msgText,ShippingErrorInfo shippingErrorInfo){
```

```
            super(msgText);
            this.shippingErrorInfo = shippingErrorInfo;
    }
}
```

Listing 13-8 illustrates the code that adds an application-specific object, `ShippingErrorInfo`, to the custom `TooManyBikesException`. An application can prepare the object describing a shipping error and pass it as an argument to the constructor of the exception. The latter will store it in the class variable `shippingInfo`, and whatever method catches this exception can extract the `ShippingErrorInfo` object and act accordingly.

In distributed Java EE applications an exception can travel through several tiers (such as JMS, EJB, Servlet, Swing client), and not only does having a custom property inside the exception object ensure that the valuable information won't be lost, but each tier can add more specifics to this custom property, helping in tracing the error.

There is also a class called `RemoteException`, with a field called `detail`, that's used for reporting communication errors. You can extend this class to make remote exceptions more descriptive. This subject may be more appropriate for the lessons about the server-side technologies (Lesson 26 and above), but since this is the lesson dedicated to Exceptions, I mentioned it here.

Keep in mind that a Java program can communicate with non-Java systems, and that throwing `RemoteException` or its subclass is a proper way to handle cross-language errors. For example, this technique is used for communications based on Adobe's AMF protocol between server-side Java and a rich Internet client application written with Adobe Flex.

For more details on Java exceptions refer to Oracle's tutorial at `http://java.sun.com/docs/books/tutorial/essential/exceptions`.

## TRY IT

Create a Swing application for placing bike orders. It has to have a drop-down list (`JComboBox`) containing several bike models, `JTextField` for entering quantity, and `JButton` for validating the order.

Make up several combinations of bike models and quantities that will throw an exception. Use the code snippets from Listing 13-7 as examples. The validation should start when the user clicks the button to validate the order.

## Lesson Requirements

You should have Java installed.

> *You can download the code and resources for this Try It from the book's web page at* `www.wrox.com`*. You can find them in the Lesson13 folder in the download.*

## Step-by-Step

1. Create a new Eclipse project, Lesson13.

2. Learn how to work with JComboBox at the following tutorial: `http://java.sun.com/docs/books/tutorial/uiswing/components/combobox.html`.

3. Process events and revalidate the order whenever the user selects a new bike model or changes the quantity of the order.

4. Throw and handle `TooManyBikesException` if the order can't be shipped.

> *Please select Lesson 13 on the DVD to view the video that accompanies this lesson.*

# 14

# Introduction to Collections

So far you've been introduced to only one way of storing a collection of objects — with Java arrays, which are good for storage, but fall short when you need to dynamically add or remove data, or to sort or traverse your collection. There are a number of classes and interfaces in the package java.util that are quite handy when multiple instances of some objects have to be co-located in memory. This lesson will introduce you to several of them.

You can find more collections in the java.util.concurrent package, but those will be reviewed in Lesson 21 after you become familiar with the concept of multi-threading. Together, the collection classes and interfaces located in java.util and java.util .concurrent are often called the Java Collection Framework.

## ARRAYS REVISITED

Java collection classes enable the storing of handles of related data in one place. Here a *handle* is a reference to the location of an object in memory. You were introduced to arrays in Lesson 5: Arrays let you store and access a group of variables of the same type. Let's go over the steps you follow to declare and populate an array.

First, declare a variable of the type that matches the types of the objects that will be stored in the array, and reserve enough memory to accommodate all objects. For example, to reserve memory enough for storing 10 instances of class Customer you can declare a variable cust, as follows:

```
Customer cust[] = new Customers[10];
```

At this point you've allocated enough space for the storage of 10 handles, not for the actual objects.

Next, create instances of the objects and store their handles in the array. Only the memory addresses of these instances will be stored in the array cust:

```
Customer[] cust = new Customer[10];

cust[0] = new Customer("David","Lee");
cust[1] = new Customer("Ringo","Starr");
```

```
    . . .
cust[9] = new Customer("Lucy","Mann");
```

Now let's give a 15 percent discount to all customers who spent more than $500 in our online store:

```
for (Customer c: cust){
  if (c.getTotalCharges() > 500){
      c.setDiscount(15);
  }
}
```

Note the use of the `for-each` loop here. It safely iterates through this array without trying to access elements beyond its boundaries. You could've used another syntax of the `for` loop to access array elements by index. If a programmer forgot to check the size of the array and tried to access, say, eleven's element like `cust[10].setDiscount(15)`, Java would throw a run-time `ArrayIndexOutOfBoundsException`. Remember, if an array has n elements the last element's index is n -1.

## CLASSES ARRAYLIST AND VECTOR

Arrays offer the fastest access to the collection of data, but you have to know in advance the number of elements to be stored there. Luckily Java has classes that don't have this restriction, and you can add more elements to a collection during the run time if needed. Classes `Vector` and `ArrayList` belong to this group.

Internally both collections use the array for storage, but when you keep adding elements to these collections they internally increase the size of the array (`ArrayList` increases the size by smaller increments), and as elements are deleted these collections shrink.

In both `Vector` and `ArrayList` you can store only objects — only primitives are allowed. Having said this, keep in mind that Java supports autoboxing (see Lesson 3), and if you'll try to add a primitive to a collection, it'll be automatically converted into he corresponding wrapper object.

You have to pay a price for this convenience: `ArrayList` is a little slower than the array as it needs to do internal array copying to change the collection's size, and `Vector` is even slower because it supports thread synchronization (which will be explained in Lesson 21). But after the introduction of more efficient concurrent collections, `Vector` became less popular and you can achieve its synchronized functionality by using the method `Collections.synchronizedList()` on an `ArrayList` object. All further code samples in this section use only `ArrayList`.

To create and populate an `ArrayList` object you should first instantiate it, and then add instances of other objects to the `ArrayList` by calling the method `add():`, as in Listing 14-1.

**LISTING 14-1: Populating ArrayList**

```
ArrayList customers = new ArrayList();
Customer cust1 = new Customer("David","Lee");
customers.add(cust1);
Customer cust2 = new Customer("Ringo","Starr");
customers.add(cust2);
```

The method `add()` doesn't copy the instance of the object into the `customers` collection, it just stores the memory address of the object being added. The element numbering in `ArrayList` starts with 0. If you know that an `ArrayList` will store, say, 10 objects, instantiate it with the constructor that will allocate the right amount of memory on creation:

```
ArrayList customers = new ArrayList(10);
```

You can still add more than 10 elements, but JVM will allocate additional memory as needed.

The method `get()` is used to extract a particular element from `ArrayList`. Because `ArrayList` is generic storage for any type of object, the method `get()` returns elements as `Object` data types. It's the responsibility of the programmer to provide proper casting, such as the following:

```
Customer theBestCustomer=(Customer) customers.get(1);
```

To illustrate a possible run-time error that will occur if the casting was not properly done, let's add an object of another type to our `customers` collection from Listing 14-1:

```
Order ord = new Order(123, 500, "IBM");
customers.add(ord);
```

The Java compiler will not complain because `ArrayList` can store any objects. At this point we have the elements in `customers` — two customers and one order. As a matter of fact, in Lesson 15 you'll see another way of working with a collection capable of storing objects of unspecified type aka *generics*. I may be jumping ahead here, but the proper (generic) way of declaring collection for storing customers is shown below:

```
ArrayList<Customer> customers = new ArrayList(10);
```

The following code will throw the `IllegalCastException` on the third iteration of the loop:

```
int totalElem = customers.size(); // number of elements
for (int i=0; i< totalElem;i++){
  Customer currentCust = (Customer) customers.get(i);
  currentCust.doSomething();
}
```

Listing 14-2 shows how the operator `instanceof` helps you avoid this exception. But before using `instanceof`, see if you can come up with a more elegant solution, as you learned to do in the section "Polymorphism" in Lesson 7. You'll find more samples of working with vectors in Lesson 21.

---

**LISTING 14-2: ArrayList and instanceof**

```
ArrayList customers = new ArrayList(3);

// The code to populate customers with instances of Customer and Order
// objects is omited for brevity

int totalElem = customers.size();

// Iterate through the list customers and do something with each
```

*continues*

**LISTING 14-2** *(continued)*

```
//  element of this collection

for (int i=0; i<totalElem;i++){
  Object currElement = customers.get(i);
  if (currElement instanceof Customer){
    Customer currentCust= (Customer)customers.get(i);
    currentCust.doSomething();
  }
  else if (currElement instanceof Order){
    Order currentOrder = (Order) customers.get(i);
    currentOrder.doSomething();
  }
}
```

# COLLECTION INTERFACES FROM JAVA.UTIL

A typical collection class implements several interfaces, which represent a well-designed hierarchy. For example, `ArrayList` implements the `List` interface, which extends `Collection`. Just reading the comments in the source code for `java.util` habitats can give you a good idea of what they are for.

`Collection` extends `Iterable`; there are no classes that directly implement this interface. Only its descendent interfaces are implemented. You can use a `for-each` loop (see the "Arrays Revisited" section earlier in this lesson) with classes that implement `Iterable`.

The `List` interface is defined for the ordered collections: `ArrayList`, `Vector`, and `LinkedList`. It allows duplicate elements. For example, the following code snippet will create two elements in `ArrayList`:

```
myArrayList.add("Mary");
myArrayList.add("Mary");
```

The `Set` interface is implemented by collections that don't allow duplicate elements, e.g., `HashSet` and `SortedSet`. For example, the following code snippet will create one element in `HashSet`. The second line will find out that Mary already exists, and won't change it and will return `false`:

```
myHashSet.add("Mary");
myHashSet.add("Mary");
```

The `Map` interface is for storing key/value pairs. A map can't contain duplicate keys and each key can be mapped to only one value (object). You'll see some relevant code examples in the next section.

The `Queue` interface is mainly for collections that require first-in-first-out (FIFO) operation (so-called *priority queues* are the exception). Every new element is added to the tail of the queue and the elements are retrieved from the head of the queue. You can restrict the size of the queue if need be. `LinkedList` is one of the classes that implement the `Queue` interface.

Now let's look at some of the classes that implement these interfaces.

# CLASSES HASHTABLE AND HASHMAP

The classes `Hashtable` and `HashMap` implement the `Map` interface storing key/value pairs. These classes offer a convenient way of storing and accessing the elements of a collection: by key. You can assign a key to an instance of some Java object and use it as a reference. The collections store objects as key/value pairs. Let's say we need to store instances of the classes `Customer`, `Order`, and `Portfolio` in the same collection. The code snippet from Listing 14-3 creates these instances first, and then puts them in the collection under some identifiers (keys).

**LISTING 14-3:** Hashtable for key/value pairs

```
Customer cust = new Customer("David", "Lee");
Order ord = new Order(123, 500, "IBM");
Portfolio port = new Portfolio(123);

Hashtable data = New Hashtable();
data.put("Customer", cust);
data.put("Order",ord);
data.put("Portfolio", port);
```

The values in double quotes represent keys by which the objects could be retrieved. In this example the keys are represented by the Java class `String`, but you can use any objects as keys. The keys are selected based on the application needs, e.g. the code in Listing 14-3 could be written in some order management application.

If you have an idea of how many elements you are planning to store in a `Hashtable`, use another constructor:

```
Hashtable data = new Hashtable(10); // 10-element capacity
```

The method `get()` provides access to these objects via the key. You need to either perform the proper casting as shown below or use *generics* (explained in Lesson 15):

```
Order myOrder = (Order) data.get("Order");
```

The method `size()` returns the number of elements in the `Hashtable`:

```
int totalElem = data.size();
```

Methods `containsKey()` and `containsValue()` help you to find out if the collection contains a specific key or value. You can find an example of `Hashtable` usage in Lesson 31.

The class `HashMap` is similar to `Hashtable`, but it allows `null` as a key or value and is not synchronized. If you are writing code that attempts to access the same element concurrently without using multi-threading, use `HashMap`, as it performs faster than `Hashtable`.

To speed up the table lookup, both `HashMap` and `Hashtable` index the data by applying a so-called *hash function* that (based on the contents of the object) generates a *hash code*, one number that represents a large object. There's a slight chance that two different objects will generate the same hash code, but the same object will always produce the same hash code. You can read more about hash functions in Wikipedia at http://en.wikipedia.org/wiki/Hash_function.

# Class Properties

Pretty often a desktop application offers you a way to specify and store user preferences such as fonts and colors. This is a use case in which storage of key/value pairs is exactly what's needed. You can store such preferences locally or on remote servers. In Lesson 16 you'll learn how to work with files and other data streams, but from a data structure perspective you'll be dealing with a collection of key/value pairs, such as *color=red, font=verdana*.

Windows-based applications often store some configurable parameters in the `.ini` files. In general, Java applications store their properties in plain text files, XML files, database tables, and others.

In this section you'll see some code fragments illustrating how the Java class `Properties`, which extends `Hashtable`, can be used to manipulate with properties using key/value pairs. The class `Properties` has one restriction that `Hashtable` does not: Both the key and the value have to be of type `String`. In Lesson 19 you'll see a complete application called MailMan that reads the data needed for sending emails from the `mailman.properties` file, which has the following contents:

```
SmtpServer=mail.xyz.com
to=abc@xyz.com
cc=mary@xyz.com
from=yakov @xyz.com
```

To load this file into the `Properties` object, just define an input stream on this file (see Lesson 16) and call the method `load()`, as shown in Listing 14-4. After the file has been loaded into the `Properties` object, each individual property can be obtained with the method `getProperty()`.

**LISTING 14-4:** Reading file mailman.properties into the Properties object

Available for download on Wrox.com

```
Properties prop=new Properties();
FileInputStream in =null;
try{
   new FileInputStream ("mailman.properties");
   prop.load(in);
}catch(Exception e){...}
finally{... in.close();...}

String from = prop.getPropery("from")
String mailServer=prop.getProperty("SmtpServer");
...
```

Java does not have global variables, but as a workaround you can make these properties available to any object in your application by turning them into system properties available from any class in your application:

```
System.setProperties(prop);
```

But keep in mind that the preceding line will also replace the existing system properties, which you may or may not want to do. Now you can get these values from any other class in your application, for example:

```
String mailServer = System.getProperty("SmtpServer");
```

If you decide to store properties in XML files, the class `Properties` offers you the method `loadFromXML()` to read properties and the method `storeToXML()` to store them in a simple XML format.

# ENUMERATION AND ITERATOR

In general, enumerations are sets of items that are related to each other. For example, shipment options or ice cream flavors — such enumerations are supported by the Java keyword `enum` (see Lesson 20). But because we are talking about collections, the meaning of the term *enumeration* is somewhat different. If a collection object implements the interface `Enumeration`, you can traverse its elements sequentially, without even knowing the total number. You just need to obtain the enumeration of all elements and use the methods `hasMoreElements()` and `nextElement()`. For example, to process all elements of `Vector customers` do the following:

```
Vector customers = new Vector();
...
Enumeration enum=customers.elements();//returns Enumeration

while(enum.hasMoreElements()){
    Customer currentCust = (Customer)enum.nextElement());
    currentCust.doSomething();
}
```

If you're using `ArrayList customers`, the utility class `Collections` comes in handy, as it has a method that returns enumeration:

```
Enumeration enum = Collections.enumeration(customers);
```

You can also obtain the enumeration of a `Hashtable`'s keys or elements. For example:

```
Hashtable data = new Hashtable();
...
// Get the keys
Enumeration enumKeys = data.keys();
while(enum.hasMoreElements()){
...
}
// Get the elements
Enumeration enumElements = data.elements();
...
```

In a way the `Enumeration` interface is similar to `Iterator`, which was introduced as a part of the Java Collections Framework years after. It also offers a standard way to process elements of a collection sequentially. The main difference between the two is that `Enumeration` is a read-only means of traversing a collection, while `Iterator` has a method called `remove()` that enables you to delete unwanted elements of the collection. `Enumeration` is considered a legacy interface and you should use `Iterator`. For example, you can iterate through the `ArrayList` customers as follows:

```
Iterator iCust = customers.iterator();
while (iCust.hasNext()){
   System.out.println(iCust.next())
}
```

# CLASS LINKEDLIST

Java collection classes differ in how you can retrieve and insert objects. If you need to work with a sequential list of objects and often insert the object into the list, the data structure called *linked list* can fit the bill. Java has a class called `LinkedList` that stores elements so that each contains a reference to the next (aka node). Each element in a *doubly linked list* also contains a reference to the previous element. These features of the doubly-linked class `LinkedList` allow you to create queues (FIFO), and stacks (last-in-first-out or LIFO).

Insertion of a new object inside the list comes down to a simple update of two references: The previous element of the list has to be pointed to the newly inserted object, which will have to include a reference to the next element, if any. Compare this to the complexity of lots of memory allocations and object moving in memory to increase the size of an `ArrayList` or `Vector`, and you'll appreciate the value that linked lists bring to the table. On the other hand, collections that use arrays for the underlying data storage offer random access to the data elements, while linked lists can be processed only sequentially.

You can navigate through the list using the class `ListIterator`, which supports going through the list in both directions via its methods `next()` and `previous()`. Listing 14-5 shows you an example, in which a standby passenger list is created at the boarding gate of some airline company.

**LISTING 14-5:** LinkedList example

```java
import java.util.LinkedList;
import java.util.ListIterator;

public class TestLinkedList {

 public static void main(String[] args) {

  LinkedList passengerList = new LinkedList();

  passengerList.add("Alex Smith");
  passengerList.add("Mary Lou");
  passengerList.add("Sim Monk");

  // Get the list iterator and print every element of the list
  ListIterator iterator = passengerList.listIterator();

  System.out.println(iterator.next());
  System.out.println(iterator.next());
  System.out.println(iterator.next());
 }

}
```

The code in Listing 14-5 will iterate and print all the objects from the list using `ListIterator`. You might be wondering how the `println()` method knows how to print an object returned by the iterator. It tries to find the method `toString()` defined on the object and call it. In our example the object is a string itself, but in a real-world situation you might need to print objects, and defining the `toString()` method is the right way to do so.

If you use `add()` or `remove()` while iterating through the list, the new element will be either inserted or removed at the iterator's current position.

## CLASS BITSET

The class `BitSet` stores a sequence of bits. It's a pretty efficient class when you need to pass to a program a number of flags that indicate certain conditions. Think of a financial trading application that must be extremely fast. One way to improve the performance is to represent the maximum amount of information in a minimal number of bytes.

Another use case for `BitSet` are programs that send signals with information about the state of a certain device. For example, some vending machines have smart chips that can automatically dial their owner's phone number and send a signal containing status information. Sending a set of flags (bits that are set to 1 or 0) instead of text or numbers is the most economical way to do this.

The `BitSet` class does not have a size limit and can grow as needed. Depending on which bit is set (e.g., has the value of 1) the class could indicate the following:

➤ **Bit 0:** The coin box is empty.

➤ **Bit 1:** The coin box is half full.

➤ **Bit 2:** The coin box is full.

➤ **Bit 3:** The coin box has been removed.

➤ **Bit 4:** The Coca-Cola row is empty.

One instance of a `BitSet` object carries multiple parameters describing its status. The program that receives this signal could print a nice report, and the owner of this remote machine could decide if he or she needs to send a technician to look at the machine.

The Java class `BitSet` is nothing more than a vector of bits. The following code prepares a signal indicating that the coin box is full and there are no Coca-Cola bottles left.

```
import java.util.BitSet;
class VendingMachineSender {
    public static void main(String args[]){
        BitSet report = new BitSet();
        report.set(2);    // box is full
        report.set(4);    // no Coca Cola
    }
}
```

When the phone call comes in, the callback method `phoneRings()` is invoked and the signal can be decoded like this:

```java
import java.util.BitSet;
class VendingMachineListener {
   public void phoneRings(BitSet signal)
      int size = signal.size();

      for (int i=0;i<size;i++){
         if (signal.get(i)){
            switch (i){
               case 0:
                  System.out.println("Box is empty");
                  break;
               case 1:
                  System.out.println("Box is half full");
                  break;
               case 2:
                  System.out.println("Box is full");
                  break;
               // more cases come here
            }
         }
      }
   }
}
```

## TRY IT

Modify the `LinkedList` example from Listing 14-5 to add an arbitrary object, say the VIP customer after the very first element of the list. You must do this while iterating through the list. When the program is ready it should print the following:

```
Alex Smith
VIP Customer
Mary Lou
Sim Monk
```

## Lesson Requirements

You should have Java installed.

> You can download the code and resources for this Try It from the book's web page at www.wrox.com. You can find them in the Lesson14 folder in the download.

## Step-by-Step

**1.** Create a new Eclipse project called Lesson14.

**2.** After the first call to `iterator.next()` add the following line: `iterator`
`.add("VIP Customer");`

**3.** Run the program and observe that it doesn't print "VIP Customer." This happens because
the iterator is already positioned after the newly inserted object.

**4.** Add the line `iterator.previous()` right after the "VIP Customer" to move the iterator one
element back.

**5.** Add one more print statement (otherwise the program won't reach Sim Monk). Compile and
run the program. It will print all four elements as requested.

**6.** Now break the code by changing the line that you added in Step 2 to `passengerList`
`.add("VIP Customer");`

Run the program now. It'll print the first element of the linked list and then produce a run-
time exception:

```
Alex Smith
Exception in thread "main" java.util.ConcurrentModificationException
        at java.util.LinkedList$ListItr.checkForComodification(LinkedList.
java:761)
        at java.util.LinkedList$ListItr.next(LinkedList.java:696)
        at TestLinkedList.main(TestLinkedList.java:20)
```

The reason for this concurrent modification exception is that one *thread of execution* was
iterating through a collection, and at the same time another thread was trying to modify the
underlying collection in an unsafe way. The concept of threads will be introduced in Lesson 20.

 *Please select Lesson 14 on the DVD to view the video that accompanies this lesson.*

# 15

# Introduction to Generics

In the previous lesson you saw an example of a collection that stores objects of different types (see Listing 14-2). During the run time, that program would test the actual type of each object and cast it to an appropriate type — `Customer` or `Order`. If some code adds an element of another (unexpected) data type, this will result in a casting error, `IllegalCastException`.

Starting from Java 5 you can use *generics*, which enables you to use parameterized data types — you can declare an object, collection, or method without specifying a concrete data type, shifting the definition of concrete types to the code that will be using these objects, collections, or methods. And the good part is that by using such generic notation you'll get help from Java compiler, which will not allow you to use objects of the "wrong" types that don't match the declaration. In other words, you can catch improper data types earlier, during the compilation phase.

## GENERICS WITH CLASSES

Not only Java methods can have parameters, but classes can have them as well. Consider the `ArrayList` from Listing 14-2, which is a kitchen sink–like storage that can hold pretty much any object. But if you add the parameterized type `Customer` in angle brackets to the declaration of the `customers` collection (see Listing 15-1), any attempt to place an `Order` object there will generate the following compiler error:

```
The method add(Customer) in the type ArrayList<Customer> is not applicable
for the arguments (Order).
```

Think of it this way: `ArrayList` can be used to store any objects, and using generics allows you to put a constraint on the types of objects allowed in a specific instance of `ArrayList`. This is an example of a parameterized object, which is just one use for generics.

**LISTING 15-1: Using generics in the collection**

```java
import java.util.ArrayList;
import java.util.ArrayList;

public class TestGenericCollection {

    public static void main(String[] args) {

        ArrayList<Customer> customers = new ArrayList<Customer>();
        Customer cust1 = new Customer("David","Lee");
        customers.add(cust1);
        Customer cust2 = new Customer("Ringo","Starr");
        customers.add(cust2);
        Order ord1= new Order();

        customers.add(ord1); // Compiler error

    }
}
```

Getting an error during compilation is better than getting run-time cast exceptions. What makes the `ArrayList` class capable of rejecting the unwanted data types? Open the source code of the `ArrayList` itself (pressing F3 in Eclipse shows the source code of any class or interface, if available). It starts as follows:

```java
public class ArrayList<E> extends AbstractList<E>
        implements List<E>, RandomAccess, Cloneable, java.io.Serializable
```

This magic `<E>` after the class name tells the Java compiler that some types of elements will be stored in this class, but which ones will remain unknown until a concrete instance of `ArrayList` is created. In Listing 15-1 the *type parameter* `<Customer>` replaces `<E>`, and from now on the collection `customers` will accept only instances of `Customer` objects.

I'd like to stress that this `<E>` notation is used only during the declaration of the type. The code in Listing 15-1 does not include `<E>`. The compiler replaces `<E>` with `Customer` and erases the parameterized data type. This process is known as *type erasure* — it's done for compatibility with code written in older versions of Java that didn't have generics.

Now you can simplify the code from Listing 14-2 by removing casting (see Listing 15-2). Why? Because with generics, when the compiler sees a specific type, it automatically generates the byte-code, which performs casting internally! That's why you don't even need to cast the data returned by the method `get(i)` from `Object` to `Customer` any longer. Besides, you're guaranteed that the collection `customers` will have only `Customer` instances.

**LISTING 15-2: Iterating through customers without casting**

```java
ArrayList<Customer> customers = new ArrayList<Customer>();

// The code to populate customers is omited for brevity

// Iterate through the list customers and do something with each
```

```
// element of this collection. No casting required.

for (Customer c: customers){
      c.doSomething();
}
```

# DEFINING GENERICS

If you'll be creating your own class for storing other objects, you can use any letter(s) in angle brackets to declare that your class will use parameterized types. Some developers use `<E>` for *element*; some prefer `<T>` for *type*. Such a letter will be replaced by a concrete type when used with generics' notation during concrete variable declaration. Open the source code of the Java class `Hashtable` and you'll see `<K,V>`, which stands for *key* and *value*:

```
public class Hashtable<K,V> extends Dictionary<K,V>
      implements Map<K,V>, Cloneable, java.io.Serializable {...}
```

Again, what types will be used for storing keys and values is decided when the `Hashtable` is used. You can use a parameterized type for declaring variables where you'd use regular data types. Listing 15-3 shows a fragment from the source code of the interface `java.util.List`. The interface declaration uses `<E>` as a data type.

**LISTING 15-3:** Fragment from java.util.List interface

```
package java.util;

public interface List<E> extends Collection<E> {

    Iterator<E> iterator();

    <T> T[] toArray(T[] a);

    boolean add(E e);

    boolean containsAll(Collection<?> c);

    boolean addAll(Collection<? extends E> c);

    boolean addAll(int index, Collection<? extends E> c);

    boolean removeAll(Collection<?> c);

    E set(int index, E element);

    void add(int index, E element);

    ListIterator<E> listIterator();
    ListIterator<E> listIterator(int index);

    List<E> subList(int fromIndex, int toIndex);
}
```

## WILD CARDS

Listing 15-3 contains question marks that represent unknown types. It'll be easier to explain them with an example. Let's turn the `for` loop from Listing 15-2 into a function. In Eclipse, highlight the code of the `for` loop, click the right mouse button, and select Refactor ➪ Extract Method. In the pop-up window enter the method name `processCustomers` and click OK.

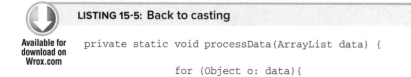

**LISTING 15-4:** Refactored class **TestGenericCollection**

```java
import java.util.ArrayList;
import java.util.Hashtable;
import java.util.List;

public class TestGenericCollection {

    public static void main(String[] args) {

        ArrayList<Customer> customers = new ArrayList<Customer>();
        Customer cust1 = new Customer("David","Lee");
        customers.add(cust1);
        Customer cust2 = new Customer("Ringo","Starr");
        customers.add(cust2);
        Order ord1= new Order();
        //customers.add(ord1); // Compiler error

        // Iterate through the list customers and do something with each
        //  element of this collection. No casting required.

        processData(customers);

    }

    private static void processData(ArrayList<Customer> customers) {
        for (Customer c: customers){
            c.doSomething();
        }
    }

}
```

What if you want to make the method `processData()` more generic and useful not only for a collection of `Customer` objects but for others too? In the pre-generics era you'd be using `instanceof` and writing something similar to Listing 15-5.

**LISTING 15-5:** Back to casting

```java
private static void processData(ArrayList data) {

    for (Object o: data){
```

```
                                ((Customer) o).doSomething();
                        }
                }
```

But now, armed with the new knowledge, you can change the signature of the method process `Data` to

```
private static void processData(ArrayList<Object> data){...}
```

Unfortunately, this solution won't work, because there is no such thing as inheritance of parameterized types. In other words, even though the class `Customer` is a subclass of `Object`, this relationship does not apply to `<Customer>` and `<Object>`. This is when the question mark that represents an unknown type becomes handy. The next step in making `processData()` more generic is to change the method signature to the following:

```
private static void processData(ArrayList<?> data){...}
```

Using such a method signature is different from simply declaring the method argument data of type `ArrayList`, which would require casting, as in Listing 15-5. With the wild-card notation you state, "At this point the type of data is not known, but whenever some code uses the method `processData()` it'll be known and properly compiled so casting won't be needed."

The next challenge you face is to compile the code calling the method `doSomething()` on the objects of unknown types.

# BOUNDED WILD CARDS

Bounded wild cards enable you to specify generic types that are not completely unknown, but rather "somewhat unknown." You can say, for example, that the method `processData()` from the previous section can work only with the objects that extend a specific class. Consider an example in Listing 15-6, which declares two classes — `Customer` and `Order` — that extend `Data`.

**LISTING 15-6: Customer and Order extending Data**

```
public abstract class Data {
        abstract void doSomething();
}

public class Customer extends Data{
        private String fName;
        private String lName;

    public Customer (String fName, String lName){
        this.fName=fName;
        this.lName=lName;
    }

        void doSomething(){
            System.out.println("Customer " + fName + " " +lName +
```

*continues*

**LISTING 15-6** *(continued)*

```
". In doSomething()");
        }
    }


public class Order extends Data{
    void doSomething(){
            // Do something specific to Order processing
        }
    }
```

You can rewrite the method `processData()` using the bounded wild card `<? extends Data>`, as in the following example:

```
private static void processData(ArrayList<? extends Data> data) {
    for (Data d: data){
        d.doSomething();
    }
}
```

If I didn't show you the code in Listing 15-6 and asked, "What does the bounded type `<? extends Data >` mean?", the right answer would have been, "It represents any subclass of the class `Data` or any class that implements the interface `Data`." The word `extends` may sound a little misleading in the latter case, but the designers of Java generics decided to keep this keyword for both classes and interfaces.

If you want to use multiple bounds, they should be separated by ampersands:

```
<? extends Data & Payable >
```

You can achieve yet another interesting effect by using the keyword `super` in the generics. For example, the next declaration means that you are allowed to use any superclass of `Data`:

```
<? super Data & Payable >
```

The `super` keyword is quite handy when you need to ensure that arguments of a method belong to the same inheritance hierarchy. For example, the method `doSomething()` can be used for processing such lists as `Person` and `RetiredEmployee` (assuming that `RetiredEmployee` is a subclass of `Employee`).

```
<T>  void doSomething(ArrayList<? super T> all, ArrayList<? extends T> best){
    //do something
}
```

## GENERIC METHODS

While declaring a method you can either predefine data types for its arguments and return values or use generics. For example, the method `toArray()` from Listing 15-3 starts with a declaration of a new parameterized type (`<T>` in that case), which has to be placed in angle brackets right before the return type in the method signature. The very fact that a method declares a new type makes it generic. the following declaration of the `toArray()` method takes an array of objects of type `T` and returns an array of `T` objects:

```
<T> T[] toArray(T[] a);
```

If you have an `ArrayList` of integers, you can declare and convert it to an array as follows:

```
ArrayList<Integer> myNumericList = new ArrayList<Integer>();
. . .
Integer myNumericArray = new Integer[myNumericList.size()];
myNumericArray = myNumericList.toArray();
```

If you need to use the same method `toArray()` with a list of customers, the data type `<T>` magically transforms (by compiler) into the `Customer` type:

```
ArrayList<Customer> myCustomerList = new ArrayList< Customer >();
. . .
Customer myCustomerArray = new Customer [myCustomerList.size()];
myCustomerArray = myCustomerList.toArray();
```

As in examples from the "Bounded Wild Cards" section, you are allowed to put constraints on the type. For example, you can restrict the `toArray()` method to work only with types that implement the `Comparable` interface:

```
<T extends Comparable> T[] toArray(T[] a);
```

## WHAT TO READ NEXT

This book is a concise tutorial that doesn't have room to cover Java generics in greater detail. If you'd like to get a deeper understanding of this topic, refer to the book *Java Generics and Collections*, 2006, written by Maurice Naftalin and Philip Wadler and published by O'Reilly, ISBN 0-596-52775-6.

Bruce Eckel devoted almost a hundred pages to generics in the fourth edition of his book *Thinking in Java*, 2006, published by Prentice Hall, ISBN 0-131-87248-6.

## TRY IT

Create a simple program that uses generics with the class `RetiredEmployee` (which extends the class `Employee`) from Listing 7-2. Write a generic method that will accept a collection of `RetiredEmployee` objects and copy it into a collection of `Employee` objects.

## Lesson Requirements

You should have Java installed.

*You can download the code and resources for this Try It from the book's web page at* www.wrox.com. *You can find them in the Lesson15 folder in the download.*

## Step-by-Step

1. Create a new Eclipse project called Lesson 15.

2. Create a class called `RetiredEmployee` that extends `Employee`.

3. Create an executable Java class, `TestGenericMethod`, that will accept a List of `RetiredEmployee` objects and copy it into a `List` of `Employee` objects. This method should print on the system console the name of each `Employee` from the resulting collection.

4. Run the `TestGenericMethod` program and observe the printed names.

> *Please select Lesson 15 on the DVD to view the video that accompanies this lesson.*

# 16

# Working with Streams

Most programs work with some kind of data, which could be stored in a local database, on a remote computer, or in a file located on your disk. Java has a concept of working with *streams of data*. You can say that a Java program reads sequences of bytes from an input stream (or writes into an output stream): byte after byte, character after character, primitive after primitive. Accordingly, Java defines various types of classes supporting streams, for example InputStream or OutputStream. There are classes specifically meant for reading character streams such as Reader and Writer. DataInputStream and DataOutputStream can read and write Java primitives, and to work with files you may consider such classes as FileInputStream and FileReader.

Classes that work with streams are located in two packages: java.io and java.nio. Classes from the former implement blocking of input/output (I/O): When bytes are being read/written by a process, they become unavailable for other threads of execution. The latter package offers non-blocking I/O with improved performance. In this lesson you'll be dealing with streams defined in java.io.

Before deciding which Java class to use for I/O in each particular case, you need to understand what kind of data is coming from the stream in question. But no matter what you select, your code will need to perform three operations:

**1.** Open a stream that points at a specific data source: a file, a socket, a URL, and so on.

**2.** Read or write data from/to this stream.

**3.** Close the stream.

If a Java program uses a third-party program, such as database management systems (DBMS), you won't need to program streams directly — the database drivers or object-relational mapping framework is all you need. In this lesson you'll see examples of performing I/O operations with different streams.

# BYTE STREAMS

A program can read or write any file one byte at a time with the help of one of the subclasses of InputStream or OutputStream respectively. The example in Listing 16-1 shows how to use the class FileInputStream to read a file named abc.dat. This code snippet reads and prints each byte's value:

**LISTING 16-1:** Using FileInputStream

```
FileInputStream myFile = null;
    try {
            myFile = new  FileInputStream("abc.dat");
            boolean eof = false;

            while (!eof) {
                int byteValue = myFile.read();
                System.out.print(byteValue + " ");
                if (byteValue  == -1){
                    eof = true;
                }
            }
            // myFile.close(); // do not do it here!!!
    } catch (IOException e) {
            System.out.println("Could not read file: " + e.toString());
    } finally{
        if (myFile !=null){
            try{
                myFile.close();
            } catch (Exception e1){
                e1.printStackTrace();
            }
        }
    }
}
```

Because the code in Listing 16-1 doesn't specify the directory where abc.dat is located, the program will try to find this file in the current directory, which is the root directory of the Eclipse project. At any given time you can easily find out the current directory programmatically by calling the method System.getProperty("user.dir").

The output of this program will be a sequence of numbers, which represents the codes of the characters located in the file. For example, if abc.dat contains the text "This is a test file," the output on the system console will look like this:

```
84 104 105 115 32 105 115 32 97 32 116 101 115 116 32 102 105 108 101 -1
```

When you are reading with FileInputStream, the end of the file  is represented by a negative one, and this is how you know when to stop. The code in Listing 16-1 checks for -1 and sets the boolean variable eof to false to finish the loop. Note that the stream is closed in the clause finally. Do not call the method close() inside the try/catch block right after the file reading is done. In case of an exception during the file read, the program will jump over the close() statement into the catch section, and the stream will never be closed!

The code fragment in Listing 16-2 writes into a file called `xyz.dat` using the class `FileOutputStream`.

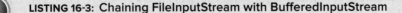

**LISTING 16-2:** Using FileOutputStream

```
// byte values are represented by integers from 0 to 255
int somedata[]= {56,230,123,43,11,37};
FileOutputStream myFile = null;
try {
    myFile = new  FileOutputStream("xyz.dat");
    for (int i = 0; i <somedata.length; i++){
       file.write(data[i]);
    }
} catch (IOException e) {
       System.out.println("Could not write to a  file: " + e.toString());
} finally{
    if (myFile !=null){
      try{
        myFile.close();
      } catch (Exception e1){
        e1.printStackTrace();
    }
   }
 }
}
```

# BUFFERED STREAMS

The code in the previous section was reading and writing one byte at a time. In general, disk access is much slower than the processing performed in memory; that's why it's not a good idea to access disk a thousand times to read a file of 1000 bytes. To minimize the number of times the disk is accessed, Java provides so-called *buffers*, which serve as reservoirs of data.

The class `BufferedInputStream` works as a middleman between `FileInputStream` and the file itself. It reads a big chunk of bytes from a file into memory in one shot, and the `FileInputStream` object then reads single bytes from there, which is memory-to-memory operations. `BufferedOutputStream` works similarly with the class `FileOutputStream`. The main idea here is to minimize disk access.

Buffered streams are not changing the type of reading — they just make reading more efficient. Think of it this way: A program performs stream chaining (or stream piping) to connect streams, just as pipes are connected in plumbing. Listing 16-3 shows an example in which a file is read so the data from `FileInputStream` will fill `BufferedInputStream` before processing.

**LISTING 16-3:** Chaining FileInputStream with BufferedInputStream

```
FileInputStream myFile = null;
BufferedInputStream buff =null;
    try {
        myFile = new  FileInputStream("abc.dat");
```

*continues*

**LISTING 16-3** *(continued)*

```
        buff = new BufferedInputStream(myFile);
            boolean eof = false;
            while (!eof) {
                int byteValue = buff.read();
                System.out.print(byteValue + " ");
                if (byteValue == -1)
                    eof = true;
            }
} catch (IOException e) { ... }
 finally{
if (myFile !=null){
        try{
            buff.close();
            myFile.close();
        } catch (Exception e1){
            e1.printStackTrace();
        }
    }
  }
```

While reading a stream with the help of `BufferedInputStream` you watch for the end-of-file character. But when you write a stream via `BufferedOutputStream` with method `write()`, you need to do one extra step: Call the method `flush()` before closing the buffered stream. This ensures that none of the buffered bytes "get stuck" and that all are written out to the underlying output stream.

You might be wondering, how large is the buffer? While the default buffer size varies depending on the OS, you can control it using a two-argument constructor. For example, to set the buffer size to 5000 bytes instantiate the buffered stream as follows:

```
BufferedInputStream buff = new BufferedInputStream(myFile, 5000);
```

## CHARACTER STREAMS

The text in Java is represented as a set of `char` values (two-byte characters), which are based on the Unicode Standard. The Java classes `FileReader` and `FileWriter` were specifically created to work with text files, but they work only with default character encoding and don't handle localization properly.

The recommended way is to pipe the class `InputStreamReader` with specified encoding and the `FileInputStream`. The class `InputStreamReader` reads bytes and decodes them into characters using a specified `CharSet`. Each JVM has a default *charset*, which can be specified during the JVM start-up and depends on the locale. Some of the standard charsets are US-ASCII, UTF-8, and UTF-16.

Listing 16-4 reads bytes from a text file and converts them from UTF-8 encoding into Unicode to return results as a `String`. For efficiency, the reading is piped with the `BufferReader`, which reads text from the stream buffering characters. Note that this code uses `StringBuffer` that usually works faster than `String` when it comes to performing text manipulations.

**LISTING 16-4:** Reading text files

```
StringBuffer buffer = new StringBuffer();
    try {
        FileInputStream myFile = new FileInputStream("abc.txt");
        InputStreamReader inputStreamReader =
                    new InputStreamReader(myFile, "UTF8");
        Reader reader = new BufferedReader(inputStreamReader);

        int ch;   // the code of one character

        while ((ch = reader.read()) > -1) {
                buffer.append((char)ch);
        }

        buffer.toString();

    } catch (IOException e) {
        ...
    }
```

For writing characters to a file, pipe `FileOutputStream` and `OutputStreamWriter`. For efficiency, use `BufferedWriter`, for example

```
try{
    String myAddress = "123 Broadway, New York, NY 10011";
    FileOutputStream myFile = new FileOutputStream("abc.txt");

    Writer out
        = new BufferedWriter(new OutputStreamWriter(myFile, "UTF8"));
    out.write(myAddress);

} catch(IOException e){
        ...
}
```

Listing 16-5 shows yet another version of the tax calculation program. This time I've added a text file, `states.txt`, that includes states that will be used to populate a drop-down box, `chStates`. My file is located in the root directory of the Eclipse project Lesson16, and it looks like this:

```
New York
New Jersey
Florida
California
```

The program in Listing 16-5 requires a class, `Tax`, that you can borrow from Lesson 4. Make sure that it has the method `calcTax()`.

**LISTING 16-5:** Bringing together Swing and streams

```java
import java.awt.event.*;
import javax.swing.*;
import java.awt.GridLayout;
import java.io.FileInputStream;
import java.io.BufferedReader;
import java.io.IOException;
import java.io.InputStreamReader;
import java.util.Vector;

public class TaxGuiFile extends JFrame implements ActionListener {
    JLabel lblGrIncome;
    JTextField txtGrossIncome = new JTextField(15);
    JLabel lblDependents=new JLabel("Number of Dependents:");
    JTextField txtDependents = new JTextField(2);
    JLabel lblState = new JLabel("State: ");

    //Define a data model for the ComboBox chState
    Vector states = new Vector(50);

    //Create a combobox to get data from the model
    JComboBox chState = new JComboBox(states);

    JLabel lblTax = new JLabel("State Tax: ");
    JTextField txtStateTax = new JTextField(10);
    JButton bGo = new JButton("Go");
    JButton bReset = new JButton("Reset");

    TaxGuiFile() {
        lblGrIncome = new JLabel("Gross Income: ");
        GridLayout gr = new GridLayout(5,2,1,1);
        setLayout(gr);

        add(lblGrIncome);
        add(txtGrossIncome);
        add(lblDependents);
        add(txtDependents);
        add(lblState);
        add(chState);
        add(lblTax);
        add(txtStateTax);
        add(bGo);
        add(bReset);

        // Populate states from a file
        populateStates();

        chState.setSelectedIndex(0);

        txtStateTax.setEditable(false);

        bGo.addActionListener(this);
```

```
        bReset.addActionListener(this);

        // Define, instantiate and register a WindowAdapter
        // to process windowClosing Event of this frame

        this.addWindowListener(new WindowAdapter() {
            public void windowClosing(WindowEvent e) {
                System.out.println("Good bye!");
                System.exit(0);
            }});
    }

    public void actionPerformed(ActionEvent evt) {
        Object source = evt.getSource();
        if (source == bGo ){
            // The Button Go processing
            try{
                int grossInc =Integer.parseInt(txtGrossIncome.getText());
                int dependents = Integer.parseInt(txtDependents.getText());
                String state = (String)chState.getSelectedItem();

                Tax tax=new Tax(dependents,state,grossInc);
                String sTax =Double.toString(tax.calcTax());
                txtStateTax.setText(sTax);
            }catch(NumberFormatException e){
                txtStateTax.setText("Non-Numeric Data");
            }catch (Exception e){
                txtStateTax.setText(e.getMessage());
            }
        }
        else if (source == bReset ){
            // The Button Reset processing
            txtGrossIncome.setText("");
            txtDependents.setText("");
        chState.setSelectedIndex(0);
            txtStateTax.setText("");
            }
    }
// The code below will read the file states.txt and
// populate the dropdown chStates
 private void populateStates(){

    states.add("Select State");

    FileInputStream myFile=null;
    InputStreamReader inputStreamReader;
    BufferedReader reader = null;

    try {
     myFile = new FileInputStream("states.txt");
     inputStreamReader =
                new InputStreamReader(myFile, "UTF8");
```

*continues*

**LISTING 16-5** *(continued)*

```
            reader = new BufferedReader(inputStreamReader);

            String nextLine;
            boolean eof = false;
            while (!eof) {
                nextLine = reader.readLine();
                 if (nextLine == null){
                    eof = true;
                } else {
                    // Populate the model
                    states.add(nextLine);
                }
            }

        }catch (IOException e){
           txtStateTax.setText("Can't read states.txt");
        }
        finally{
          // Closing the streams
          try{
              if (myFile !=null){
              reader.close();
              myFile.close();
              }
          }catch(IOException e){
              e.printStackTrace();
          }
        }
    }

    public static void main(String args[]){
        TaxGuiFile taxFrame = new TaxGuiFile();
        taxFrame.setSize(400,150);
        taxFrame.setVisible(true);
    }
}
```

The code in Listing 16-5 reads the content of the file states.txt and populates a collection — a Vector with states. This collection plays the role of a data model for the combo box states. I used a constructor of JComboBox that takes a data model as an argument. This Swing component knows how to display the content of its data model.

This is an example of the implementation of the so-called *MVC (model-view-controller)* design pattern, which promotes the separation of data and UI. JComboBox plays the role of a view, the vector is a model, and the user works as controller when she selects a particular state and the view has to be updated. The output of the program from Listing 16-5 is shown in Figure 16-1.

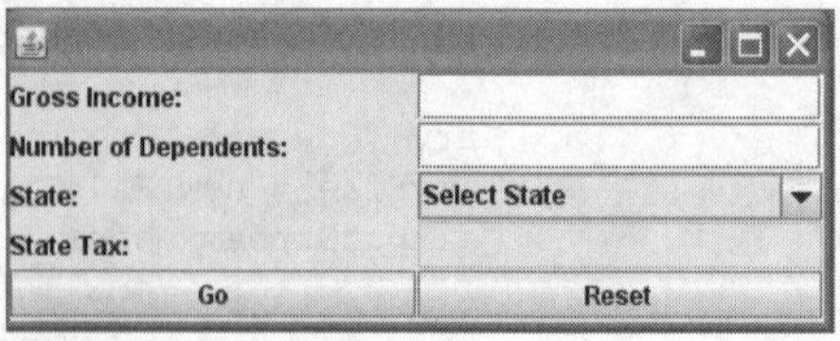

**FIGURE 16-1**

# DATA STREAMS

If you are expecting to work with a stream of a known data structure (e.g., two integers, three floats, and a double) use either `DataInputStream` for reading or `DataOutputStream` for writing. A method, `readInt()`, of `DataInputStream` will read the whole integer number (four bytes) at once, and `readLong()` will get you a long number (eight bytes).

The class `DataInputStream` is yet another filter that can be connected to another stream. Listing 16-6 has an example of how you can "build a pipe" from the following pieces:

`FileInputStream` ⇨ `BufferedInputStream` ⇨ `DataInputStream`

**LISTING 16-6:** Using DataInputStream

```
FileInputStream myFile = new FileInputStream("myData.dat");
BufferedInputStream buff = new BufferedInputStream(myFile);
DataInputStream data = new  DataInputStream(buff);

try {
    int num1 = data.readInt();
    int num2 = data.readInt();
    float num2 = data.readFloat();
    float num3 = data.readFloat();
    float num4 = data.readFloat();
    double num5 = data.readDouble();
} catch (EOFException eof) {...}
```

In this example `FileInputStream` opens the file `myData.dat` for reading, `BufferedInputStream` makes the read more efficient, and `DataInputStream` extracts from the buffer two integers, three floats, and a double. The assumption here is that the file `myData.dat` contains exactly these data types and in the specified order. Such a file could have been created with the help of `DataOutputStream`, which allows you to write primitive Java data types to a stream in a portable way. It has a variety of methods to choose from: `writeInt()`, `writeByte()`, `writeFloat()`, and so on.

# THE CLASS FILE

The class `File` allows you to rename or delete a file, perform an existence check, create a directory, and more. If you need this functionality, start by creating an instance of this class:

```
File myFile = new File("abc.txt");
```

This line does not create a file; it just creates in memory an instance of the class `File` that's ready to perform its action on the file `abc.txt`. If you want to create a physical file, use the method `createNewFile()` defined in the class `File`. Here's the list of some methods of the class `File`:

➤   `createNewFile()`: Creates a new, empty file named according to the file name used during the file instantiation. Creates a new file only if a file with this name does not exist.

➤   `delete()`: Deletes file or directory.

➤   `renameTo()`: Renames a file.

➤   `length()`: Returns the length of the file in bytes.

➤   `exists()`: Tests whether the file with the specified name exists.

➤   `list()`: Returns an array of strings containing file and directory.

➤   `lastModified()`: Returns the time that the file was last modified.

➤   `mkDir()`: Creates a directory.

The next code fragment checks for the existence of the file `customers.txt.bak`, deletes it if it is found, and then renames the file `customers.txt` to `customers.txt.bak`:

```
File file = new File("customers.txt");
File backup = new File("customers.txt.bak");
if (backup.exists()){
        backup.delete();
}
file.renameTo(backup);
```

# TRY IT

Write a program that will read a `.zip` archive file and print on the system console the list of files included in the zip archive. Do a little research about the class `java.util.zip.ZipInputStream` and use it together with `FileInputStream`. Read about the class `ZipEntry` too.

## Lesson Requirements

You should have Java installed.

> You can download the code and resources for this Try It from the book's web page at www.wrox.com. You can find them in the Lesson16 folder in the download.

## Step-by-Step

1.   Create a new Eclipse project called Lesson16.

2.   Copy any `.zip` file into its root directory.

3.   Open `FileInputStream` and connect it with `ZipInputStream`.

4.   Write a loop that will use the method `getNextEntry()` from `ZipInputStream`. This method reads the `ZipEntry`, if any, and positions the stream at the beginning of the entry data.

5.   Call the function `getName()` on each `ZipEntry` instance found.

**6.** Print the entry name on the system console.

**7.** Close the entry inside the loop.

**8.** Run the program and observe that it properly prints the file names from the selected .zip file.

**9.** If you want to learn how to create .zip files from Java, read about ZipOutputStream.

*Please select Lesson 16 on the DVD to view the video that accompanies this lesson.*

# 17

# Java Serialization

Imagine a building that, with a push of a button, can be turned into a pile of construction materials and the possessions of its residents. Push another button and the building is re-created in its original form in a different location. This is what Java serialization is about. By "pushing the serialize button" you turn an instance of an object into a pile of bytes, and "pushing the deserialize button" magically re-creates the object.

Wikipedia defines the term *serialization* as

> *the process of converting a data structure or object into a sequence of bits so that it can be stored in a file or memory buffer, or transmitted across a network connection link to be "resurrected" later in the same or another computer environment. When the resulting series of bits is reread according to the serialization format, it can be used to create a semantically identical clone of the original object... This process of serializing an object is also called deflating or marshalling an object. The opposite operation, extracting a data structure from a series of bytes, is deserialization (which is also called inflating or unmarshalling).*

In Lesson 16 you became familiar with streams that deal with single bytes, characters, Java primitives, and text. Now you'll see why and how to write objects into streams, or how to serialize Java objects.

Consider the following scenario: ClassA creates an instance of the object Employee, which has the fields firstName, lastName, address, hireDate, salary, etc. The values of these fields (that is, the object's state) have to be saved in a stream. Later on ClassB, which needs these data, somehow has to re-create the object Employee in memory. The instances of ClassA and ClassB may live in two different JVMs running on different computers.

Sure enough, you can remember the order and the data types of firstName, lastName, address, hireDate, and salary, and loop through the fields performing the output with DataOutputStream.

Here's another use case: Your application has a Preferences menu where the user can select fonts, colors, and UI controls that should be displayed on the opening view. To support such functionality, the Preferences panel creates an instance of a class, `UserPreferences`, with 50 configurable properties (some of which are of custom data types) that have to be saved in a local file. On the next start of the application the previously saved data should be read from this file with the re-creation of the `UserPreferences` object.

Writing a manual procedure that uses, say, `DataOutputStream` on each primitive property and then recursively performs the same operation for each non-primitive type is tedious. Besides, this code would need to be changed each time the properties of class `UserPreferences` change.

You can achieve the same result in a more elegant way, not one property at a time, but one object at a time, with the help of such streams as `ObjectOutputStream` and `ObjectInputStream`. This process is known as *Java serialization*, which enables you to save objects in a stream in one shot.

`ClassA` will serialize `Employee`, and `ClassB` will *deserialize* (reconstruct) this object. To support this mode the class `Employee` has to implement the `Serializable` interface, as shown in Listing 17-1.

**LISTING 17-1: Serializable class Employee**

Available for
download on
Wrox.com

```java
class Employee implements java.io.Serializable{
        String lName;
        String fName;
        double salary;

}
```

The interface `Serializable` does not define any methods, so the class `Employee` has nothing to implement. If an interface doesn't declare any methods it's called a *marker interface*.

Two use cases described in this section represent the main uses for Java serialization — distribution of the Java objects between different JVMs and object persistence for future reuse. Often serialization is implemented internally by various Java frameworks to pass objects between tiers of a distributed application that runs on multiple servers and client computers.

Some Java frameworks use serialization to load or unload objects to free the JVM's memory (these are known as *passivation* and *activation* of objects, respectively). Later in the book you'll learn about RMI and EJB, which use serialization a lot. But even in regular business application development you may need to serialize and deserialize application-specific objects. This process comes down to reading from and writing into streams, namely `java.io.ObjectInputStream` and `java.io.ObjectOutputStream`, respectively.

## THE CLASS OBJECTOUTPUTSTREAM

To serialize an object perform the following actions:

**1.** Open an output stream.

**2.** Chain it with `ObjectOutputStream`.

**3.** Call the method writeObject(), providing the instance of a Serializable object as an argument.

**4.** Close the stream.

Listing 17-2 shows a code sample that serializes an instance of the Employee object into the file c:\practicalJava\BestEmployee.ser. This code first opens FileOutputStream and then chains it with ObjectOutputStream. The method writeObject() performs the serialization of the Employee instance in one shot.

**LISTING 17-2:** Serializing an Employee object into a file

```java
import java.io.*;

class ClassA {

    public static void main(String args[]){
        Employee emp = new Employee();
        emp.lName = "John";
        emp.fName = "Smith";
        emp.salary = 50000;

        FileOutputStream fOut=null;
        ObjectOutputStream oOut=null;

    try{
      fOut = new  FileOutputStream("c:\\practicalJava\\BestEmployee.ser");

      oOut = new ObjectOutputStream(fOut);

      oOut.writeObject(emp);  //serializing employee

    } catch (IOException e){

        // close the streams
        try{
           oOut.flush();
           oOut.close();
           fOut.close();
        }catch (IOException ioe){
                    ioe.printStackTrace();
        }
    }

    System.out.println("The Employee object has been serialized into " +
                    "c:\\practicalJava\\BestEmployee.ser");

  }
 }
```

All Java primitive data types are serializable. All member variables of the serializable class must be either Java primitives or reference variables pointing to objects that are also serializable. The class

Employee from Listing 17-1 contains only serializable data types. But if a class has properties of custom data types, each of them has to be serializable. The Employee class from Listing 17-3 can be serialized only if the class PromotionHistory (and all data types it uses) was declared with implements Serializable.

**Available for download on Wrox.com**

**LISTING 17-3:** Class Employee with custom data types

```
class Employee implements java.io.Serializable{
     String lName;
     String  fName;
     double salary;

     PromotionHistory promos; // A custom data type

}
```

If you do not want to serialize some sensitive information, such as salary, declare this variable using the keyword transient. If you declare the property salary of the class Employee with the transient qualifier, its value won't be serialized.

```
transient double salary;
```

Typically, you declare a variable as transient either if it contains some sensitive information or if its value is useless in the destination stream. Suppose a Java class that runs on the server has database connectivity variables. If such a class gets serialized to the client's machine, sending database credentials may be not only useless, but unsafe. So such variables have to be declared as transient. One more reason to use the transient keyword is to serialize an object that includes properties of non-serializable types.

# THE CLASS OBJECTINPUTSTREAM

To deserialize an object perform the following steps:

1. Open an input stream.

2. Chain it with the ObjectInputStream.

3. Call the method readObject() and cast the returned object to the class that is being deserialized.

4. Close the stream.

Listing 17-4 shows a code sample that reads the previously serialized file BestEmployee.ser. This code opens a FileInputStream that points at BestEmployee.ser and then chains the FileInputStream with ObjectInputStream. The method readObject() resurrects the instance of the Employee object in memory.

**LISTING 17-4:** Deserializing Employee from file

```java
import java.io.*;
class ClassB {

    public static void main(String args[]){

        FileInputStream fIn=null;
        ObjectInputStream oIn=null;

        try{
          fIn = new  FileInputStream("c:\\practicalJava\\BestEmployee.ser");

          oIn = new ObjectInputStream(fIn);

          Employee bestEemp=(Employee)oIn.readObject();

        } catch (ClassNotFoundException cnf){
                cnf.printStackTrace();
        } catch (IOException e){

            try{
              oIn.close();
              fIn.close();
            }catch (IOException ioe){
              ioe.printStackTrace();
            }
        }

        System.out.println("The Employee  object has been deserialized from " +
                         " c:\\practicalJava\\BestEmployee.ser");
    }
}
```

Note that the class that deserializes an object has to have access to its declaration or the `ClassNotFoundException` will be thrown. During the process of deserialization all `transient` variables will be initialized with the default values for their type. For example, `int` variables will have a value of `0`.

Keep in mind that class variables with longer names produce larger footprints when the object is serialized. In time-critical applications this may be important. Imagine a Wall Street trading system in which each order is presented as an object, `TradeOrder`, with 50 properties, and you need to send a thousand of these objects over the network using serialization. Simply shortening each variable name by one character can reduce the network traffic by almost 50 KB! You'll learn how to open the network streams in Lesson 18.

## THE INTERFACE EXTERNALIZABLE

Continuing with the example of the trade order, the knowledge of the values of all 50 fields from the class `TradeOrder` may be required to support certain functionality of the application, but when the program has to send a buy or sell request to the stock exchange, only ten properties may be needed.

This raises a question — can the process of serialization be customized so only some of the object properties will be serialized?

The method `writeObject()` of `ObjectOutputStream` sends all the object's properties into a stream. But if you want to have more control over what is being serialized and decrease the footprint of your object, implement the `Externalizable` interface, which is a subclass of `Serializable`.

This interface defines two methods: `readExternal()` and `writeExternal()`. These methods have to be written by you to implement serialization of only the selected properties. Listing 17-5 shows a fragment of a class, `Employee2`, that implements `Externalizable`. It has several properties, but in a certain scenario only `id` and `salary` have to be serialized.

**LISTING 17-5:** Externalizable version of Employee

```java
class Employee2 implements java.io.Externalizable {
        String lName;
        String fName;
        String address;
        Date hireDate;
        int id;
        double salary;

    public void writeExternal(ObjectOutputStream stream)
                            throws java.io.IOException {
     // Serializing only the salary and id
     stream.writeDouble(salary);
     stream.writeInt(id);
    }

    public void readExternal(ObjectInputStream stream)
                            throws java.io.IOException {
      salary = readDouble();   // Order or reads must be the
                               // same as the order of writes
      id = readInt();
    }

}
```

Note that each property of the class is individually serialized and the methods `writeExternal()` and `readExternal()` must write and read properties, respectively, in the same order. The class `EmpProcessor` from Listing 17-6 shows how to *externalize* the object `Employee2`.

**LISTING 17-6:** Turning an object into an array of bytes

```java
import java.io.*;
import java.util.Date;

public class EmpProcessor {

        public static void main(String[] args) {

                Employee2 emp = new Employee2();
```

```
        emp.fName = "John";
        emp.lName = "Smith";
        emp.salary = 50000;
        emp.address = "12 main street";
        emp.hireDate = new Date();
        emp.id=123;

        FileOutputStream fOut=null;
        ObjectOutputStream oOut=null;

          try{
            fOut= new FileOutputStream(
                "c:\\practicalJava\\NewEmployee2.ser");

            oOut = new ObjectOutputStream(fOut);
            emp.writeExternal(oOut);  //serializing employee

          System.out.println("An employee is serialized into " +
                    " c:\\practicalJava\\NewEmployee2.ser");

          }catch(IOException e){
                    e.printStackTrace();
          }finally{
                try {
                        oOut.flush();
                        oOut.close();
                        fOut.close();
                } catch (IOException e1) {
                        e1.printStackTrace();
                }
          }
        }
     }
}
```

You had to write a little more code to implement the `Externalizable` interface than to implement the `Serializable` interface, but the size of the file `NewEmployee2.ser` will be substantially smaller. First of all, you serialized the values of only two properties, and files created with the `Externalizable` interface contain only data, while files created with `Serializable` also contain class metadata that includes properties' names. The code snippet in Listing 17-7 shows you how to re-create the externalized object `Employee2`.

**LISTING 17-7:** Re-creating externalized object

```
fIn= new FileInputStream("c:\\practicalJava\\NewEmployee2.ser");
oIn = new ObjectInputStream(fIn);

Employee2 emp = new Employee2();
emp.readExternal(oIn);
```

# CLASS VERSIONING

Imagine that a program, ClassA, serializes the `Employee` object from Listing 17-1 into a file on Mary's computer. Two days later Mary starts another program, ClassB, that offers a download of its new version with long-awaited features. After upgrade, ClassB starts generating errors, which are caused by the fact that the new upgrade includes a modified version of the class `Employee` that now has one property with a different data type than what exists in memory. The upgrade also includes one new property that wasn't in the previous version of the `Employee` object.

Now the deserialization process will try to ignore the new property but will fail because of the mismatched property types between the serialized and in-memory versions of `Employee`. Serialization may also fail because of a change in the inheritance tree of `Employee`.

During serialization, JVM automatically calculates a special value: the *serial version unique ID*, which is based on the properties of the serializable object, the class name, the implemented interfaces, and the signatures of non-private methods. If you are curious to see how this number looks for your class, run the program serialver (it's located in the `bin` directory of your Java install), providing the name of your class as a command-line argument.

But if your class explicitly defines and initializes a `static final` variable called `serialVersionUID`, Java will use your value instead of trying to generate one. For example,

```
Public static final  serialVersionUID = 123;
```

Now, if you keep the value of this variable in the new version of `Employee` the same as in the old one, you'll have some freedom to add more methods to this class, and JVM will assume that both classes have the same version. If a new version has added a public field, the deserialization process will ignore it. If a new version has removed a field, the deserialized version will still have it initialized with a default value. But if you change the data type for the public field, the deserialization process will fail anyway.

# SERIALIZING INTO BYTE ARRAYS

An interesting effect will be produced if you serialize your objects into an in-memory array of bytes — `byte[]`. This can be the easiest way of creating a sort of memory blob that can be exchanged among different VMs.

The syntax of such serialization is pretty straightforward. Let's assume that you have a class called XYZ that implements `Serializable` and contains all the elements of your report in the proper format. To prepare a byte array from it, write the code in Listing 17-8.

**LISTING 17-8:** Turning an object into an array of bytes

```
XYZ myXyz = new XYZ();

// Code to fill myXyz with the content goes here

//...

ByteArrayOutputStream baOut = new ByteArrayOutputStream(5000);
```

```
ObjectOutputStream oOut = new ObjectOutputStream(
                            new BufferedOutputStream(baOut));

//Here comes the serialization part

oOut.writeObject(myXyz);
oOut.flush();

// create a byte array from the stream

byte[] xyzAsByteArray = baOut.toByteArray();
oOut.close();
```

Another convenient use for serializing into a byte array is *object cloning*, which is the creation of an exact copy of an object instance. Even though the class Object, the root of all classes, includes the method clone(), it works only with objects that implement the Cloneable marker interface; otherwise the cloning will fail. Things may get more complicated when an object contains instances of other objects: You need to program a *deep copy* of the object.

Serialization into a byte array with immediate deserialization creates a deep copy of the object in no time. After executing the code from Listing 17-9 you'll get two identical objects in memory. The variable bestEmployee points at one of them, and the variable cloneOfBestEmployee points at another.

**LISTING 17-9: Object cloning with serialization**

Available for
download on
Wrox.com

```
Employee bestEmployee = new Employee();

//Serialize into byte array
ByteArrayOutputStream baOut = new ByteArrayOutputStream();
ObjectOutputStream oOut = new ObjectOutputStream(baOut);
oos.writeObject(bestEmployee);

//Deserialize from byte array
ByteArrayInputStream baIn = new ByteArrayInputStream(baOut.toByteArray());
ObjectInputStream oIn = new ObjectInputStream(baIn);
Employee cloneOfBestEmployee = (Employee) oin.readObject();
```

# TRY IT

Create a Java Swing program called MyCustomizableGUI that will enable the user to specify her preferences, such as background color, font family, and size. Selected values should be assigned to properties of the serializable class UserPreferences and stored in the file preferences.ser. Each time MyCustomizableGUI is started it should determine if the file preferences.ser exists. If the file does exist, MyCustomizableGUI should deserialize it and apply previously saved preferences to the GUI.

## Lesson Requirements

You should have Java installed.

*You can download the code and resources for this Try It from the book's web page at* www.wrox.com. *You can find them in the Lesson17 folder in the download.*

## Step-by-Step

1. Create a new Eclipse project and name it Lesson17.

2. Create an executable Swing class called MyCustomizableGUI with a text field and a User Preferences button.

3. Program the button to open a new window Preferences (based on JDialog), that has three drop-downs (aka JComboBox), and Save and Cancel buttons. The first drop-down will allow the user to select a color, the second a font, and the third a font size.

4. Create a serializable class, UserPreferences, that will remember the user's selections. When the user has made her choices, the Save button has to serialize the instance of UserPreferences into a file named preferences.ser.

5. Each time MyCustomizableGUI starts it has to determine if the file preferences.ser exists, deserialize it if so, and apply the appropriate color as the background color of the window MyCustomizableGUI. The font preferences should be applied to the text field.

6. Run the program to ensure that you can change and save the preferences and that they are properly applied to the GUI.

*Please select Lesson 17 on the DVD to view the video that accompanies this lesson.*

# 18

# Network Programming

Computers connected to a network can communicate with each other only if they agree on the rules of communication, called *protocols,* that define how to request the data, if the data should be sent in pieces, how to acknowledge received data, if the connection between two computers should remain open, and so on. TCP/IP, UDP/IP, FTP, and HTTP are some examples of network protocols.

*Local area network (LAN)* refers to a computer network connecting devices in a small area — the same office or house, or a rack. Interconnected computers located farther apart or that belong to different companies are part of a *wide area network (WAN).* The Internet consists of millions of networks and individual devices. When connected networks belong to the same organization it is referred to as an *intranet.* For security reasons intranets are shielded from the rest of the world by special software called *firewalls.*

The World Wide Web (WWW) uses *uniform resource locators (URLs)* to identify online resources. For example, the following URL says that there is (or will be generated on the fly) a file called `training.html` located at the remote host known as `mycompany.com`, and that the program should use the HTTP protocol to request this file. It also states that this request has to be sent via port 80.

```
www.mycompany.com:80/training.html
```

The hostname must be unique and it is automatically converted to the IP address of the physical server by your *Internet service provider (ISP),* aka your hosting company. The IP address is a group of four numbers, for example `122.65.98.11`. Most of the individuals connected to the Internet are getting so-called *dynamic* (not *permanent*) IP addresses assigned to their home computers, but for a small extra fee you can request a static IP address that can be assigned to any server located in your basement, office, or garage. In the enterprises, network computers usually get static (permanent) IP addresses. For individual use, it's sufficient to have a dynamically assigned IP address as long as your ISP can find your server by resolving a domain name to the current IP address.

Finding a resource online is somewhat similar to finding a person by his or her address. The role of an IP address is similar to the role of a street number of a building, and a port plays the role of an apartment number in that building. Many people can live in the same building, just as many programs can run on the same server. A port is simply a unique number assigned to a server program running on the machine.

Multiple Java technologies exist for providing data exchange among computers in a network. Java provides classes for network programming in the package `java.net`. This lesson shows you how to read data from the Internet using the class URL as well as direct socket-to-socket programming. Lesson 19 is about sending e-mails with JavaMail API. Lessons 26 through 37 introduce you to other technologies that you can use over the network: Java Servlets, RMI, EJB, and JMS.

## READING DATA FROM THE INTERNET

You learned in Lesson 16 that to read local file streams, a program has to specify the file's location, such as `c:\practice\training.html`. The same holds true for reading remote files — the only difference is that you open the stream over the network. Java has a class, `java.net.URL`, that will help you to connect to a remote computer on the Internet and get access to a resource there, provided that it's not protected from the public. First, create an instance of the URL of your resource:

```
try{
   URL xyz = new URL("http://www.xyz.com:80/training.html");
     ...
}
catch(MalformedURLException e){
     e.printStackTrace();
}
```

The `MalformedURLException` will be thrown if an invalid URL has been specified, for example if you typed `htp` instead of `http` or included extra spaces. If the `MalformedURLException` is thrown, it does not indicate that the remote machine has problems — just check the spelling of your URL.

Creation of the URL object does not establish a connection with the remote machine; you'll still need to open a stream and read it. Perform the following steps to read a file from the Internet:

**1.** Create an instance of the class URL.

**2.** Create an instance of the `URLConnection` class and open a connection using the URL from Step 1.

**3.** Get a reference to an input stream of this object by calling the method `URLConnection.getInputStream()`.

**4.** Read the data from the stream. Use a buffered reader to speed up the reading process.

While using streams over the networks you'll have to handle possible I/O exceptions the way you did while reading the local files. The server you are trying to connect to has to be up-and-running and, if you're using HTTP-based protocols, a special software — web server — has to be "listening to" the specified port on the server. By default, web servers are listening to all HTTP requests on port 80 and to secure HTTPS requests directed to port 443.

The program in Listing 18-1 reads the content of the existing or generated file index.html from google.com and prints this content on the system console. For you to test this program your computer has to be connected to the Internet. The program may not work properly if your connection goes through a firewall.

**LISTING 18-1:** Reading the content of index.html from google.com

```java
import java.net.*;
import java.io.*;

public class WebSiteReader {

    public static void main(String args[]){

        String nextLine;
        URL url = null;
        URLConnection urlConn = null;

        InputStreamReader  inStream = null;
        BufferedReader buff = null;

        try{

            // index.html is a default URL's  file name
            url  = new URL("http://www.google.com" );
            urlConn = url.openConnection();

            inStream = new InputStreamReader(urlConn.getInputStream(), "UTF8");

            buff  = new BufferedReader(inStream);


            // Read and print the lines from index.html
            while (true){

                nextLine =buff.readLine();

                if (nextLine !=null){
                    System.out.println(nextLine);
                }else{
                    break;
                }
            }

        } catch(MalformedURLException e){
            System.out.println("Please check the URL:" + e.toString() );
        } catch(IOException  e1){

            System.out.println("Can't read  from the Internet: "+ e1.toString() );
        } finally{
            if (inStream != null){
```

*continues*

**LISTING 18-1** *(continued)*

```
                try{
                    inStream.close();
                    buff.close();
                } catch(IOException e1){
                    System.out.println("Can't close the streams: "+ e1.getMessage());
                }
            }
        }
    }
}
```

The code in Listing 18-1 creates an instance of the class URL, then gets a reference to an instance of URLConnection to open a connection with the stream, and, finally, opens InputStreamReader, which is chained with BufferedReader. Run this program and you'll see the output shown in Listing 18-2.

**LISTING 18-2:** The fragment of console output shown after google.com is read

```
<!doctype html><html><head><meta http-equiv="content-type" content="text/html;
  charset=ISO-8859-1"><title>Google</title><script>
window.google={kEI:"BHVpTNWrGoGclgeNrczDBA",kEXPI:"25976,26060",
kCSI:{e:"25976,26060",ei:"BHVpTNWrGoGclgeNrczDBA",expi:"25976,26060"},
ml:function(){},kHL:"en",time:function(){return(new Date).
getTime()},log:function(b,d,c){var a=new Image,e=google,g=e.lc,f=e.li;
a.onerror=(a.onload=(a.onabort=function(){delete g[f]}));g[f]=a;c=c||"/gen_204?atyp
=i&ct="+b+"&cad="+d+"&zx="+google.time();
a.src=c;e.li=f+1},lc:[],li:0,Toolbelt:{}};

window.google.sn="webhp";window.google.timers={load:{t:{start:(new Date)
.getTime()}}};try{}catch(u){}window.google.jsrt_kill=1;
...
</scri
pt>
```

The class WebSiteReader explicitly creates the object URLConnection. Strictly speaking, you could achieve the same result by using the class URL:

```
URL url = new URL("http://www.google.com");
InputStream in = url.getInputStream();
Buff= new BufferedReader(new InputStreamReader(in));
```

The reason you may consider using the URLConnection class is that it could give you some additional control over the I/O process. For example, by calling its method setDoOutput(true) you specify that this Java program is intended to write to the remote URL too. In the case of HTTP connections, this will also implicitly set the type of request to POST (see Lesson 27). The method useCaches() of URLConnection also allows you to specify whether the protocol can use a cached object or should always request a fresh copy. In general, if you are planning to write Java programs that will work using HTTP protocol, use the class `HttpURLConnection`, which supports HTTP-specific features, such as processing header fields, getting HTTP response codes, setting request properties, and so on.

## CONNECTING THROUGH HTTP PROXY SERVERS

For security reasons, most enterprises use *firewalls* (see `http://en.wikipedia.org/wiki/Firewall_%28computing%29`) to block unauthorized access to their internal networks. As a result their employees can't directly reach the outside Internet world (or even some internal servers), but go through HTTP proxy servers. Check the settings of your Internet browser to see if you are also sitting behind a firewall, and find out the hostname and port number of the proxy server if you are. Usually, web browsers store proxy parameters under the Advanced tabs of their Settings or Preferences menus.

If your browser has downloaded a page containing a Java applet, the latter knows the parameters of the proxy servers and can make requests to the remote servers through the firewall. But a regular Java application should specify the `http.proxyHost` and `http.proxyPort` parameters to "drill a hole" in the firewall. For example, if the name of your proxy server is `proxy.mycompany.com` and it runs on port 8080, the following two lines should be added to your Java application that needs to connect to the Internet:

```
System.setProperty("http.proxyHost","http://proxy.mycompany.com");
System.setProperty("http.proxyPort", 8080);
```

If you do not want to hardcode these values, pass them to your program from the command line:

*java -Dhttp.proxyHost=http://proxy.mycompany.com*

*–Dhttp.proxyPort=8080  WebSiteReader*

The other option for programmatically specifying proxy parameters is to do it via the class `java.net.Proxy`. The code for the same proxy server parameter would look like this (you can replace the name of the server with an IP address):

```
Proxy myProxy = new Proxy(Proxy.Type.HTTP,
                new InetSocketAddress ("http://proxy.mycompany.com", 8080);
url  = new URL("http://www.google.com/index.html" );
urlConn = url.openConnection(myProxy);
```

## HOW TO DOWNLOAD FILES FROM THE INTERNET

Combine the class URL with the reading files techniques and you should be able to download practically any unprotected file (such as images, music, and binary files) from the Internet. The trick is in opening the file stream properly. Listing 18-3 shows the code of a Java class, `FileDownload`, which takes the URL and the destination (local) file name as command-line arguments, connects to this resource, and downloads it into a local file.

**LISTING 18-3: Downloading an arbitrary file from the Internet**

```java
import java.io.FileOutputStream;
import java.io.InputStream;
import java.net.URL;
import java.net.URLConnection;

class FileDownload{
   public static void main(String args[]){
     if (args.length!=2){
       System.out.println(
         "Proper Usage: java FileDownload URL OutputFileName");
       System.exit(0);
     }

    InputStream in=null;
    FileOutputStream fOut=null;
    try{
      URL remoteFile=new URL(args[0]);
      URLConnection fileStream=remoteFile.openConnection();
    // Open output and input streams
      fOut=new FileOutputStream(args[1]);
      in=fileStream.getInputStream();

   // Save the file
      int data;
      while((data=in.read())!=-1){
          fOut.write(data);
      }
 } catch (Exception e){
   e.printStackTrace();
   } finally{
       System.out.println("The file " + args[0] +
           " has been downloaded successfully as " + args[1]);
     try{
       in.close();
       fOut.flush();
       fOut.close();
     } catch(Exception e){e.printStackTrace();}
   }
  }
 }
```

Note how this `FileDownload` program starts by checking the number of provided command parameters: If the number is anything but two, the program prints an error message and quits. Here's an example of how you can run this program to download a W-4 tax form from the Internal Revenue Service website:

*java FileDownload* `http://www.irs.gov/pub/irs-pdf/fw4.pdf w4form.pdf`

# THE STOCK QUOTE PROGRAM

In this section you'll learn how to write a program that can read stock market price quotes from the Internet. There are many Internet sites providing such quotes; the Internet portal Yahoo! is one of them.

Visit `http://finance.yahoo.com`, enter the symbol of any stock, MOT for example, and press the Get Quotes button. You'll see the pricing information about Motorola, Inc. — a fragment of this web page is depicted on Figure 18-1.

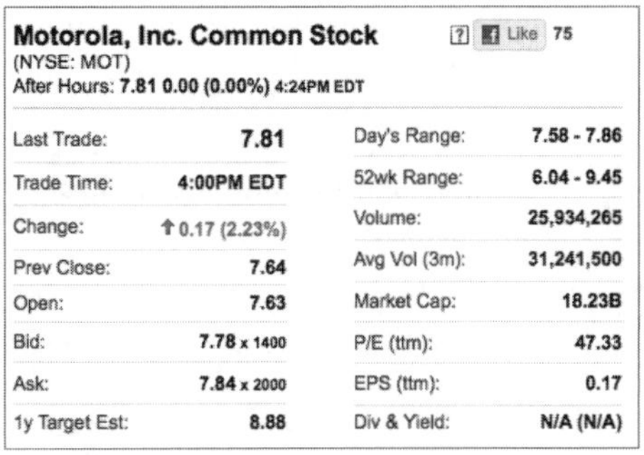
Motorola, Inc. Common Stock ? Like 75
(NYSE: MOT)
After Hours: 7.81 0.00 (0.00%) 4:24PM EDT

| | | | |
|---|---|---|---|
| Last Trade: | 7.81 | Day's Range: | 7.58 - 7.86 |
| Trade Time: | 4:00PM EDT | 52wk Range: | 6.04 - 9.45 |
| Change: | ↑0.17 (2.23%) | Volume: | 25,934,265 |
| Prev Close: | 7.64 | Avg Vol (3m): | 31,241,500 |
| Open: | 7.63 | Market Cap: | 18.23B |
| Bid: | 7.78 x 1400 | P/E (ttm): | 47.33 |
| Ask: | 7.84 x 2000 | EPS (ttm): | 0.17 |
| 1y Target Est: | 8.88 | Div & Yield: | N/A (N/A) |

**FIGURE 18-1**

But what's more interesting for our goal is the URL that is displayed in the Web browser:

```
http://finance.yahoo.com/q?s=MOT
```

Right-click this web page and select View Source from the pop-up menu to see the HTML contents of this page; you'll see lots of HTML tags, and the information about MOT will be buried somewhere deep inside. Modify the line in the class `WebSiteReader` from Listing 18-1 to have it print the content of this page on the system console:

```
url  = new URL("http://finance.yahoo.com/q?s=MOT");
```

You can also store the whole page in a Java `String` variable instead of printing the lines. Just modify the `while` loop in Listing 18-1:

```
String theWholePage;
String txt;
while (txt =buff.readLine() != null ){
     theWholePage=theWholePage + txt;
 }
```

If you add some smart tokenizing (splitting into parts based on the specified tokens as in Listing 18-4) of `theWholePage`, to get rid of all HTML tags and everything but Last Trade info, you can create your own little Stock Quote program. While this approach is useful to sharpen your tokenizing skills, it may not be the best solution, especially if Yahoo! changes the wording it uses on this page. That's why we'll be using another URL that provides stock quotes in a cleaner *comma-separated values (CSV)* format. Here's the URL that should be used for the symbol MOT:

```
http://quote.yahoo.com/d/quotes.csv?s=MOT&f=sl1d1t1c1ohgv&e=.csv
```

This URL produces a string that includes the stock symbol, last trade, date and time of the price quote, earning per share (EPS), opening price, day's range, and volume. Compare the CSB line below with the data shown in Figure 18-1 — they are the same (the date is not shown on Figure 18-1).

```
"MOT",7.81,"8/16/2010","4:00PM",0.17,7.63,7.86,7.58,25934265
```

Now the task of tokenizing the entire web page comes down to parsing a short CSV line. The `StockQuote` class from Listing 18-4 does exactly this: It accepts the stock symbol from the command line, gets the data from Yahoo!, tokenizes the received CSV line, and prints the price quote on the console.

---

**LISTING 18-4:** Printing stock quotes

```java
import java.net.*;
import java.io.*;
import java.util.StringTokenizer;

public class StockQuote {

    static void printStockQuote(String symbol){

        String csvString;
        URL url = null;
        URLConnection urlConn = null;
        InputStreamReader  inStream = null;
        BufferedReader buff = null;

        try{
            url  = new URL("http://quote.yahoo.com/d/quotes.csv?s="
                    + symbol + "&f=sl1d1t1c1ohgv&e=.csv" );

            urlConn = url.openConnection();
            inStream = new InputStreamReader(urlConn.getInputStream());

            buff  = new BufferedReader(inStream);

            // get the quote as a csv string
            csvString =buff.readLine();

            // parse the csv string
            StringTokenizer tokenizer = new StringTokenizer(csvString, ",");

            String ticker = tokenizer.nextToken();
            String price  = tokenizer.nextToken();
            String tradeDate = tokenizer.nextToken();
            String tradeTime = tokenizer.nextToken();

            System.out.println("Symbol: " + ticker +
                " Price: " + price + " Date: "  + tradeDate
                + " Time: " + tradeTime);

        } catch(MalformedURLException e){
            System.out.println("Please check the spelling of "
                            + "the URL: " + e.toString() );
        } catch(IOException   e1){
```

```
        System.out.println("Can't read from the Internet: " + e1.toString() );
      }finally{
        try{
          inStream.close();
          buff.close();
        }catch(Exception e){
          System.out.println("StockQuote: can't close streams" +
                                              e.getMessage());
        }
      }
    }

    public static void main(String args[]){

      if (args.length==0){
        System.out.println("Sample Usage: java StockQuote IBM");
        System.exit(0);
      }

      printStockQuote(args[0]);
    }


  }
```

If you've gone through all the previous lessons in this book, reading and understanding the code in Listing 18-4 should be a piece of cake for you. Test the StockQuote program by running it from Eclipse (enter MOT as an argument in the Run Configuration window) or run it from a command window as follows:

*java StockQuote MOT*

## SOCKET PROGRAMMING

Java-based technologies offer many options for network communications, and one of the technologies to consider is *sockets*. In this section you learn how to use the Java classes Socket and ServerSocket from the package java.net. A socket is a connection end point in IP networking. *TCP/IP protocol* maintains a socket connection for the whole period of communication, while *UDP* is a connectionless protocol, which sends data in small chunks called *datagrams*.

The socket address is a pair: IP address and port. When a Java program creates an instance of the ServerSocket class, this instance becomes a server that just runs in memory and listens on the specified port for other program requests. The following lines create a server that is listening to port 3000:

```
ServerSocket  serverSocket = new ServerSocket(3000);
client = serverSocket.accept();
```

The client program should create a client socket — an instance of the class `Socket` — pointing at the computer/port on which the `ServerSocket` is running. The client program can connect to the server using hostnames or IP addresses too, for example:

```
clientSocket = new Socket("124.67.98,101", 3000);
clientSocket = new Socket("localhost", 3000);
clientSocket = new Socket("127.0.0.1", 3000);
```

While deciding which port number to use for the `ServerSocket`, avoid using port numbers below 1024 to avoid conflicts with other system programs. For example, port 80 is typically used by HTTP servers; port 443 is reserved for HTTPS; port 21 is typically used for FTP communications; port 389 is for LDAP servers, and so on. After creating a socket-based connection, both client and server should obtain references to its input/output streams and use them for data exchange.

## Why Use Sockets?

Why even use manual socket programming if you can easily establish inter-computer communication with, say, HTTP-based protocol (it uses sockets internally), start one of many open-source or commercial web servers, and have clients connect to the server as shown in the preceding sample programs in this lesson? Because a socket connection has a lot less overhead than any standard protocol.

You can create your own very compact protocol that will allow you to send only the data you need, with no or minimal headers. Socket communication provides a duplex byte stream, whereon the data travels simultaneously in both directions, unlike protocols based on the request-response model. Think of financial trading systems: Speed is the king there, and the ability to send data up and down at the same time saves milliseconds, which makes a difference.

On the other hand, if you design your application to use sockets, the live connection will be maintained for each user connected to `ServerSocket`. If your program has to maintain several thousand concurrent connections it will require more powerful servers than programs using the request-response system, with which a connection is maintained only during the time of the client's request.

## The Stock Quote Server with Sockets

Let's build a socket-based client/server application that emulates both a server providing fake price quotes for requested stocks and a client consuming this data.

The server will start and listen to requests on port 3000 (see Listing 18-5). The method `accept()` of the `SocketServer` class is the one that waits for the client's requests. As soon as it starts you'll see the message "Waiting for a quote request" on the system console, and nothing else will happen until the request comes in from the client. Creating a `SocketServer` instance binds it to the specified port, but if this port is already in use by another process you'll get a `BindException`.

**LISTING 18-5:** The server generating stock quotes

```
import java.io.*;
import java.net.*;
public class StockQuoteServer {
```

```java
public static void main(java.lang.String[] args) {
    ServerSocket serverSocket = null;
    Socket client = null;

    BufferedReader inbound = null;
    OutputStream outbound = null;

    try
                    {
                    // Create a server socket
                    serverSocket = new ServerSocket(3000);

                     System.out.println("Waiting for a quote request");
                    while (true)
                    {
                      // Wait for a  request
                      client = serverSocket.accept();

         // Get the streams
                    inbound=new BufferedReader(new
            InputStreamReader(client.getInputStream()));
                    outbound =
                              client.getOutputStream();

            String symbol = inbound.readLine();

         //Generete a random price
         String price= (new
                    Double(Math.random()*100)).toString();

        outbound.write(("\n The price of "+symbol+
                    " is " + price + "\n").getBytes());

                        System.out.println("Request for " + symbol +
             " has been processed. The price is " + price);
         outbound.write("End\n".getBytes());
                        }
    }
    catch (IOException ioe)
    {
                    System.out.println("Error in Server: " + ioe);
    } finally{
        try{
            inbound.close();
            outbound.close();
        }catch(Exception e){
            System.out.println("StockQuoteServer: can't close streams"
                                    + e.getMessage());
        }
    }
    }
    }
}
```

When a client connects to the socket, the server gets references to its I/O streams and sends randomly generated quotes for the requested stock. In the real world this server would have to be connected to another program providing real-time market data, but for our purposes generating random numbers as "price quotes" will suffice. The client program shown in Listing 18-6 has to be started with a command-line parameter such as IBM or MSFT to produce a price quote.

**LISTING 18-6:** The client sending requests for stock quotes

```java
import java.io.*;
import java.net.*;


public class Client {

public static void main(java.lang.String[] args) {

  if (args.length==0){

    System.out.println("Usage: java Client Symbol");
          System.exit(0);
  }

  OutputStream outbound = null;
  BufferedReader inbound = null;

  Socket clientSocket = null;

    try {

        // Open a client socket connection
        clientSocket = new Socket("localhost", 3000);

        System.out.println("Client: " + clientSocket);

        // Get the streams

          outbound = clientSocket.getOutputStream();
          inbound=new  BufferedReader(new
          InputStreamReader(clientSocket.getInputStream()));

        // Send stock symbol to the server
        outbound.write((args[0]+"\n").getBytes());
        outbound.write("End\n".getBytes());

        String quote;
        while (true){
          quote = inbound.readLine();
          if (quote.equals("End")){
                break;
          }
          System.out.println("Got the quote for " + args[0]+":" + quote);
        }
```

```
}catch (UnknownHostException uhe){

    System.out.println("UnknownHostException: " + uhe);

} catch (IOException ioe){

    System.err.println("IOException: " + ioe);
} finally{

    // Close the streams
    try{
        outbound.close();
        inbound.close();
        clientSocket.close();
    } catch(IOException e){
        System.out.println("Can not close streams..." +
                                    e.getMessage());
    }
  }
 }

}
```

Have you noticed that `StockQuoteServer` appends the word `End` to indicate that the price quote has ended? The class `Client` also checks for this word. This is an example of a very simple custom-made networking protocol.

## TRY IT

The goal of this exercise is to test the socket communication in action, even if you have only one computer.

## Lesson Requirements

You should have Java installed.

> You can download the code and resources for this Try It from the book's web page at www.wrox.com. You can find them in the Lesson18 folder in the download.

## Hints

In this exercise you'll be using two separate command windows to run the client and the server. But Eclipse IDE also enables you to have more than one Console view. Find a little icon that looks like a monitor in the Console view toolbar and click the little triangle next to it to switch between toolbars.

## Step-by-Step

1. Create a new Eclipse project called Lesson18. Copy into this project and compile the classes `StockQuoteServer` and `Client` from the DVD accompanying the book.

2. Even though you can run both programs from Eclipse, it's easier to observe the entire process if you run them from separate command windows. Open two command windows and imagine that they belong to different computers.

3. In each command window, go to the bin directory of the Lesson 18. In one of them start the server and in the other start the client — for example

   ```
   java StockQuoteServer
   java Client IBM
   ```

4. Observe that the server generates prices, and that both client and server print the same price. By starting client and server in different command windows you are starting two separate JVM's, emulating network communication between computers.

5. Open a couple more command windows and start the client program in them, providing different stock symbols as arguments. Observe that the same server can handle multiple clients' requests. If you have access to a real network in which each computer has Java run time installed, run the client and server programs on different computers — just replace the `localhost` in the class `Client` with the network name or IP address of the server's computer.

> *Please select Lesson 18 on the DVD to view the video that accompanies this lesson.*

# 19

# Processing E-Mails with Java

People send and receive e-mails using e-mail client programs such as Microsoft Outlook and Gmail. Can you write your own program to send and receive e-mails? The chances are slim that you'll need to develop a client to compete with Gmail, but enterprise Java applications often need the ability to send or receive e-mails in certain conditions.

For example, an application that processes credit card transactions suspects a fraudulent activity and needs to send an e-mail to the account owner. Such an application becomes an e-mail client. A Java application provided by your bank can run on your Android smartphone and have an integrated e-mail inbox that accumulates all messages sent to you by the bank.

Another good example involves the forgotten-password functionality. A user clicks the Forgot Your Password? hyperlink and enters a valid e-mail address in a text input field. A couple of seconds later an e-mail containing instructions for resetting the password arrives in her e-mail inbox. The server-side Java program sent this e-mail automatically using JavaMail's *application program interface (API)*.

In this lesson you'll learn how to write a Java program that can send e-mails reminding you about your friends' birthdays.

## PROTOCOLS AND SERVERS

For e-mail messaging you'll be using standard protocols: *Simple Mail Transfer Protocol (SMTP)* for sending e-mails and *Post Office Protocol (POP)* or *Internet Message Access Protocol (IMAP)* for retrieving e-mails. The third version of this protocol is called *POP3*; IMAP is a more advanced alternative to POP3. The format of the message body and its attachments, if any, is defined by the *Multipurpose Internet Mail Extensions (MIME)* protocol.

Some vendors use proprietary protocols for e-mails, but we'll stick to standards. For Java SE, JavaMail API is an optional package that has to be downloaded separately, but it is included with Java EE. The API is simple to use — it takes only a few lines of code to send an e-mail from a Java program.

To test a client program that sends e-mails you'll need to know the hostname and port of some SMTP server and have an account with the service provider. Typically such servers use port 25 or 587 for e-mails encrypted using *Transport Layer Security (TLS)* protocol and port 465 for *Secure Sockets Layer (SSL)* encryption. Some ISPs may block these ports though.

Apart from an SMTP server hosted by your ISP, you can use the free public server `smtp.gmail.com` offered by Google. For the parameters of this server refer to the following Web page: `http://mail .google.com/support/bin/answer.py?hl=en&answer=13287`. Yahoo! also offers a free public SMTP server at `smtp.mail.yahoo.com`.

Here's a word of caution: After you learn how easy it is to write a Java program that sends e-mails, you might have an urge to start sending mass e-mails to large lists of recipients to promote your business or share the latest jokes you've found online. Unsolicited e-mail is called spam, and if you write a program that sends dozens of e-mails per minute your ISP will probably notice it and give you a warning or even terminate your Internet access.

## CREATING BIRTHDAY MAILER

Because I'll be writing a birthday mailer program using Java SE, I need to download the *jars* (libraries) with JavaMail classes. At the time of this writing JavaMail API 1.4.3 is the latest release, and you can download it from `www.oracle.com/technetwork/java/index-138643.html`.

Unzip the JavaMail archive — it includes all required jar files, demos, and documentation. Create an Eclipse project called Lesson19, right-click the project name, and select Properties ⇨ Java Build Path. Go to the Libraries tab, click Add External JARs, and add `mailapi.jar` and `smtp.jar` to the project from the `lib` directory of the extracted archive. These jars contain all the classes from the `javax.mail` package required to send e-mails. If you are using a really old version of Java (prior to version 6) you'll also need to download and add to your project the JavaBeans Activation Framework (JAF).

## Required Supporting Classes

At a minimum you have to use the following classes to send an e-mail:

➤ `javax.mail.Session`: This class knows important characteristics of your environment, such as the name of the mail server.

➤ `javax.mail.Message`: This class represents your message, containing recipients, subject, content, and so on.

➤ `javax.mail.internet.InternetAddress`: The recipient of your message will be represented by this class.

➤ `javax.mail.Transport`: This class will pass your message for the delivery to a protocol-specific transport.

# Writing the Mail Sender

Now you'll learn how to write a program to send e-mail messages. I'll be using the publicly available SMTP server from Yahoo!, but if you decide to use the server provided by your ISP you can find out its hostname and port from the settings of your current e-mail client program. For example, Microsoft Outlook has this information in the menu Tools ⇨ Accounts ⇨ Mail ⇨ Properties.

Typically SMTP servers require you to provide a valid e-mail address and password for authentication. Because your JavaMail program won't use a log-on window, you can hard-code e-mail credentials in a subclass of JavaMail's `Authenticator`, as shown in Listing 19-1.

**LISTING 19-1: Authenticator class**

```
package com.practicaljava.lesson19;

import javax.mail.Authenticator;

import javax.mail.PasswordAuthentication;

class MyMailAuthenticator extends Authenticator {

    protected PasswordAuthentication getPasswordAuthentication() {

        return new PasswordAuthentication ("test@yahoo.com", "password123");

    }
}
```

If `MyMailAuthenticator` isn't able to authenticate using the provided e-mail/password combination, it'll throw the `AuthenticationFailedException` with the error message "Access Denied." If you'll specify a nonexistent sender's e-mail address, the program will throw `SMTPSendFailedException` with the error "From address not verified." If authentication is not required, the class `MyMailAuthenticator` is not needed.

A sample file that stores the birthdays of your e-mail contacts is shown in Listing 19-2. It's a file in a CSV format, where each line contains the birthday, name, and e-mail address of a contact.

**LISTING 19-2: The file birthday.txt**

```
Aug-9,Mary Lou,mlou@gmail.com
Mar-31,John Smith,jsmith@gmail.com
Aug-9,David Lee,dlee@yahoo.com
```

The `Mailer` program (see Listing 19-3) will read this file into an array, and if the birthday's date is the same as the current date, it'll send a "happy birthday" e-mail to this person. The program starts by creating an object with the properties of the SMTP server at Yahoo! Then it creates an instance of the `MyMailAuthenticator` class and gives both of them to the `Session` instance.

When this is done the method `main()` invokes the method `readBirthdayFile()`, which populates `ArrayList friends` with the data from the file `birthday.txt`. Then the method `iterateThroughBirthdays()` parses only those lines in which the birthday date is the same as the current date. This program uses the class `java.util.Scanner`, which parses the content of the String (the friend's data) based on specified delimiters.

The `setPropsAndSendEmail()` method has the code for sending e-mails. First it creates an instance of the `Message` object and populates it with all the familiar parameters: from, recipient(s), subject, data, and the text of the message. The call to `Transport.send()` performs the actual process of sending this message.

**LISTING 19-3: The Mailer class**

```java
package com.practicaljava.lesson19;

import java.io.*;
import java.text.*;
import java.util.*;
import javax.mail.*;
import javax.mail.internet.*;

public class Mailer        {

    private Session session = null;

    private static  String emailSenderAddress = "yfain11@yahoo.com";
    private static  String emailSubject = "Happy Birthday!!!";
    private String emailText = "Happy birthday dear %s!!!";

    ArrayList<String> friends = new ArrayList<String>();

    Mailer() {

        Properties sessionProperties = new Properties();
        sessionProperties.put("mail.smtp.host", "smtp.mail.yahoo.com");
        sessionProperties.put("mail.smtp.user", emailSenderAddress);
        sessionProperties.put("mail.smtp.port", "25");
        sessionProperties.put("mail.smtp.auth", "true");

        MyMailAuthenticator authentificatorForMessage =
                                    new MyMailAuthenticator();

        session = Session.getInstance(sessionProperties,
                                    authentificatorForMessage);
    }


    private void setPropsAndSendEmail(String emailRecipient, String emailText){

        try{

            Message emailMessage = new MimeMessage(session);

            emailMessage.setFrom(new InternetAddress(emailSenderAddress));
```

```java
            emailMessage.setRecipients(Message.RecipientType.TO,
                            InternetAddress.parse(emailRecipient, false));
            emailMessage.setSubject(emailSubject);
            emailMessage.setSentDate(new Date());
            emailMessage.setText(emailText);
            Transport.send(emailMessage);
            System.out.println("Your email to " + emailRecipient +
                                    " has been sent successfully");
        }catch(Exception e){

            System.out.println("Your email to " + emailRecipient +
                            "  has not been sent: " + e.getMessage());
            e.printStackTrace();
        }
    }


    private void readBirthdayFile() throws IOException {

        FileInputStream birthdayFile = new FileInputStream("birthday.txt");

        BufferedReader birthdayFileReader = new BufferedReader(
                            new InputStreamReader(birthdayFile));

        String friendInfo;

        while ((friendInfo = birthdayFileReader.readLine()) != null){
            friends.add(friendInfo);
        }

        birthdayFileReader.close();

        birthdayFile.close();
    }


    private void iterateThroughBirthdays(){

        Iterator<String> iterator = friends.iterator();

        while (iterator.hasNext()){

            scanForManInfoAndSendEmail(iterator.next());

        }
    }


    private void scanForManInfoAndSendEmail(String stringFromArray){

        Scanner scannerOfLines = new
```

*continues*

**LISTING 19-3** *(continued)*

```
                        Scanner(stringFromArray).useDelimiter("[,\n]");

        if (scannerOfLines.next().equals(getCurrentDateMMMd())) {

            String emailAddressee = scannerOfLines.next();
            String emailAddress = scannerOfLines.next();
            setPropsAndSendEmail(emailAddress,
                        String.format(emailText, emailAddressee));
        }
    }

    private static String getCurrentDateMMMd(){

        return new SimpleDateFormat("MMM-d", Locale.US).format(new
                            GregorianCalendar().getTime());

    }


    public static void main(String[] args){

        Mailer mm = new Mailer();

        try {

            mm.readBirthdayFile();
            mm.iterateThroughBirthdays();

        } catch (IOException e) {

            e.printStackTrace();
        }
    }
}
```

## HOW TO RETRIEVE E-MAILS

Even though more often than not the receivers of the messages sent by a Java application will use one of the popular e-mail clients already available, you may need to incorporate message-retrieving functionality into your application. In this section I'll just give an overview of the process of retrieving e-mails programmatically, and in the "Try It" section you'll write such a program on your own.

As in your local post office, incoming mail should be stored somewhere. The POP3 or IMAP mail server provides such storage. POP3 is an older protocol that retrieves messages from a single mailbox. IMAP is newer and more advanced: It allows the organization of messages in folders with filtering support.

To get access to the user's incoming e-mails the Java program needs to connect to the mail server and get an instance of the Store object by calling the method getStore() on the Session object.

You'll need to know the hostname of your mail server, the protocol it uses, and the relevant user ID and password in order to get the `Store` instance.

The next step is establishing a connection with `Store` by calling its method `connect()`. After this is done, get `store`'s default root folder and then a specific sub-folder, such as `INBOX`.

Folders in JavaMail are represented by the class `Folder`. Its method `open()` will open the specified folder for `READ_ONLY` or `READ_WRITE`. Finally, the `getMessages()` method returns an array of `Message` objects. Iterating through this array will allow you to retrieve message data by calling `getSubject()`, `getFrom()`, `getContent()`, and so on.

Listing 19-4 shows a fragment of the code for retrieving messages from a Gmail account. To enable or disable the IMAP or POP protocol, go to Setting ⇨ Forwarding POP/IMAP in your Gmail client.

**LISTING 19-4:** Fragment of code for e-mail retrieval from Gmail

```
Properties properties = System.getProperties();
Session session = Session.getDefaultInstance(properties);

String host = "pop.gmail.com"; // or "imap.gmail.com"
String username = "yakov";
String password = "mypasswd";
Store store = session.getStore("pop3s"); // or "imap"
store.connect(host, username, password);

Folder rootFolder = popStore.getDefaultFolder();
defaultPopFolder = defaultPopFolder.getFolder("INBOX");
defaultPopFolder.open(Folder.READ_ONLY);


Message[] message = folder.getMessages();

for (int i = 0; i < message.length; i++) {

    // get message parts here
}
```

JavaMail has full support for multipart messages with attachments (see the `Multipart`, `MimeMultipart`, and `MimeBodyPart` classes), but multipart message support is beyond the scope of this book. The description of these classes is available in the Java help system. Look for these class descriptions in the package `javax.mail`.

## USEFUL OPEN-SOURCE COMPONENTS

Apache Commons is a community project that offers a number of open-source reusable components. One of the libraries contains classes for sending and receiving e-mails form Java. You can read about this project at `http://commons.apache.org/email/userguide.html`.

The process of sending a simple e-mail with this library comes down to creating an instance of one class, `SimpleEmail`. Then you need to set the properties of this object: host, port, from, to, authenticator, subject, and message body. When this is done, just call the `send()` method.

If all you need is to send simple e-mails, the benefits of using the Apache Commons e-mail library may not be so obvious. But if your program needs to send multipart e-mails with attachments, or HTML-formatted e-mails, consider using this library. One useful feature of this library is that it gives you the ability to specify an alternative recipient for bounced e-mails.

There is one more community project to consider: Apache Velocity (`http://velocity.apache.org/`). Imagine that you need to write a program that will perform mass mailing of pre-formatted letters, inserting customer-specific information (such as name and address) into each one. The Apache Velocity project would be quite handy for this purpose. It is also useful if you want to send automatic account registrations or password-change e-mails. Instead of hard-coding the letter text into your Java program, you can create text files (templates) containing special markup to be substituted with real values by your Java program during run time.

For further details, read the user guide at the following URL: `http://velocity.apache.org/engine/devel/user-guide.html`.

Third-party libraries (e.g. Spring Framework, discussed in Lesson 35) hide specifics of the use of JavaMail API. Check out the documentation on using e-mails with the Spring Framework at the following URL: `http://static.springsource.org/spring/docs/2.0.x/reference/mail.html`.

## TRY IT

Write a Java program that will retrieve messages from your mail inbox and print their subjects on the system console.

## Lesson Requirements

You should have Java installed. For this section I assume that you've created Eclipse project Lesson19 and that it contains a working version of the `Mailer` program.

> *You can download the code and resources for this Try It from the book's web page at* www.wrox.com. *You can find them in the Lesson19 folder in the download.*

## Step-by-Step

1. Add JavaMail libraries `pop.jar` and `imap.jar` to the project.

2. Read the chapter on message storage and retrieval in the document "JavaMail Design Specification" and code sample "Showing the message" from Listing B-X in Appendix B of "JavaMail Design Specification." This document is located in the `doc` folder of the JavaMail distribution.

**3.** Write the Java program MailReader to retrieve and print on the system console the subjects of messages located in your inbox.

**4.** Run MailReader and compare the printed message subjects with the ones displayed by the mail client you use regularly.

*Please select Lesson 19 on the DVD to view the video that accompanies this lesson.*

# 20

# Introduction to Multi-Threading

In March of 2010 I was interviewed by Janice Heiss from Oracle (http://java.sun.com/ developer/technicalArticles/Interviews/community/yakov_qa_2010.html), and she asked me to name the Java class I couldn't live without. I didn't think twice: Thread. This is where the power of Java resides. There are books devoted to Java threads, which give you amazing power and flexibility when it comes to building highly available, scalable, and responsive applications capable of processing thousands of concurrent requests of various types.

Up until now you've been creating Java programs that were executing code sequentially. But the main power of Java lies in its ability to do things in parallel, or, as they say, to run *multiple threads of execution*. As always, going through a practical use case is the best way to understand this feature.

Let's discuss a program that should display market news and information about the user's stock portfolio in the same window. While the market news feed is coming from a remote computer, stock portfolio data are retrieved from the database and may be located on the local machine.

Suppose it takes five seconds to get the market news and only three seconds to get the portfolio data. If you run these two tasks sequentially (one after another), you need eight seconds to complete the job.

But market news doesn't depend on your portfolio data and these two tasks can run in parallel. They run on different computers and use different processors. If you can implement parallel processing, the total time should be less than eight seconds (close to five seconds in our use case — the time it takes for the longer task to complete).

A Java program can start multiple threads of execution that will run in parallel. Even if you have only one processor in your computer, it still could be a good idea to run some tasks in parallel. Think of a web browser that allows you to download a file and perform page browsing at the same time. Web browsers maintain two or more connections to any website, and can download multiple resources (text, images, videos, music) at the same time. Any web browser works in a multi-threaded mode.

If these jobs ran sequentially, the browser's window would be frozen until the download was complete. On a multiprocessor computer, parallel threads can run on different CPUs. On a single-processor computer, threads will take turns getting "slices" of the processor's time. Because switching CPU cycles between threads happens fast, a user won't notice the tiny delays in each thread's execution, and browsing will feel smooth.

In many cases, especially on single CPU computers, the benefit of many threads comes about because there's a lot of idle time in most operations. In particular, if an operation is I/O bound instead of CPU bound using multiple threads helps take advantage of those otherwise unused blocks of time.

People also can work in a multi-threaded mode. For example, they can drink coffee while talking on a cell phone and driving a car. In the airport you can see people walking on the moving belt — they will reach their gate faster than by standing still.

## THE CLASS THREAD

If class A needs to initiate some executions in classes B and C, the latter two must declare multi-threading support from the get-go. Each of the classes B and C must either be inherited from the Java class Thread or implement one of the following interfaces: Runnable or Callable (the latter is covered in Lesson 21). If a class is inherited from the class Thread it has to override the method run().

The first version of the market-portfolio example has three classes (see Listings 20-1, -2, and -3). Two of them are subclasses of the class Thread (MarketNews and Portfolio), and the third (TestThreads) is just a testing program that instantiates them and starts the execution of some code in each of them. You must initiate the code that has to work as a thread in the method run().

**LISTING 20-1: Class MarketNews**

```java
public class MarketNews extends Thread {
  public MarketNews (String threadName) {
        super(threadName);  // name your thread
    }

   public void run() {
      System.out.println( "The stock market is improving!");
      }
  }
```

**LISTING 20-2: Class Portfolio**

```java
public class Portfolio extends Thread {
    public Portfolio (String threadName) {
        super(threadName);
    }

    public void run() {
       System.out.println( "You have 500 shares of IBM ");
      }
   }
```

**LISTING 20-3: Class TestThreads starts MarketNews and Portfolio**

```java
public class TestThreads {
    public static void main(String args[]){
        MarketNews mn = new MarketNews("Market News");
        mn.start();

        Portfolio p = new Portfolio("Portfolio data");
        p.start();

        System.out.println( "TestThreads is finished");
    }
}
```

The method `main()` in Listing 20-3 instantiates each thread, passing the name for the thread as a constructor argument, and then calls its `start()` method. Each thread itself invokes internally the code located in its method `run()`. After calling `mn.start()`, the program `TestThread` does not wait for its completion but immediately executes the lines that follow, creating and starting the thread `Portfolio`. Even if `MarketNews` will take time, the `Portfolio` thread will start immediately.

If you run the `TestThread` program it'll print the output from threads `MarketNews` and `Portfolio` almost simultaneously — there is no lengthy and time-consuming code in their `run()` methods. A bit later, in the section "Sleeping Threads," I'll show you how to emulate a lengthy execution. The output of the `TestThread` program can vary — it all depends on which thread will finish first.

## THE INTERFACE RUNNABLE

The second way to create threads is to implement a `Runnable` interface. In this case your class also has to have business logic in the method `run()`. The second version of our market-portfolio example (Listings 20-4, -5, and -6) also has three classes, but `MarketNew2` and `Portfolio2` are not inherited from the class `Thread` — they implement the `Runnable` interface.

Creation of a thread in this case is a two-step process: create an instance of a class that implements `Runnable` and then give it as a constructor argument during instantiation of the class `Thread`.

**LISTING 20-4: Class MarketNews2**

```java
public class MarketNews2 implements Runnable {
    public void run() {
        System.out.println( "The stock market is improving!");
    }
}
```

**LISTING 20-5: Class Portfolio2**

```java
public class Portfolio2 implements Runnable {
    public void run() {
        System.out.println( "You have 500 shares of IBM ");
    }
}
```

**LISTING 20-6:** Class TestThreads2

```java
public class TestThreads2 {
    public static void main(String args[]){

        MarketNews2 mn2 = new MarketNews2();
        Thread mn = new Thread(mn2,"Market News");
        mn.start();

        Runnable port2 = new Portfolio2();
        Thread p = new Thread(port2, "Portfolio Data");
        p.start();

        System.out.println( "TestThreads2 is finished");
    }
}
```

Note that I've declared the variable `port2` in Listing 20-6 to be not of type `Portfolio2`, but of type `Runnable`. I did it for illustration purposes and to encourage you to use what you've learned about casting to interfaces in Lesson 7 (see Listing 7-5). It takes three lines of code in Listing 20-6 to instantiate and start a thread. You can do this in one line, but this syntax won't give you a reference to the thread object should you need to call any methods on this object in the future (see variables `mn` and `p` in Listing 20-6):

```java
(new Thread(new MarketNews2("Market News"))).start();
```

The `Runnable` interface provides a more flexible way to use threads, because it allows a class to be inherited from any other class, while having all the features of a thread. For example, a Swing applet must be a subclass of a `javax.swing.JApplet`, and, because Java doesn't support multiple inheritance, it should implement `Runnable` to support multi-threading.

## SLEEPING THREADS

One of the ways to make the processor available to other threads is by using `Thread`'s method `sleep()`, which enables you to specify in milliseconds (and nanoseconds) how long the thread has to sleep. For example, the thread `MarketNews3` in Listing 20-7 puts itself to sleep for a thousand milliseconds (one second) after each output of the message about market improvements.

**LISTING 20-7:** Class MarketNews3

```java
public class MarketNews3 extends Thread {
    public MarketNews3 (String str) {
        super(str);
    }

    public void run() {
        try{
            for (int i=0; i<10;i++){
```

```
         sleep (1000);  // sleep for 1 second
         System.out.println( "The market is improving " + i);
      }
    }catch(InterruptedException e ){
      System.out.println(Thread.currentThread().getName()
                                      + e.toString());
    }
  }
}
```

When `MarketNews3` goes to sleep, the thread `Portfolio` from Listing 20-8 gets the CPU and will print its message and then sleep for 700 milliseconds on each loop iteration. Every second `MarketNews3` wakes up and does its job.

---

**LISTING 20-8:** Class Portfolio3

```
public class Portfolio3 extends Thread {
    public Portfolio3 (String str) {
          super(str);
    }

    public void run() {
      try{
        for (int i=0; i<10;i++){
        sleep (700);     // Sleep for 700 milliseconds
        System.out.println( "You have " +  (500 + i) +
                                    " shares of IBM");
        }
      }catch(InterruptedException e ){
        System.out.println(Thread.currentThread().getName()
                                      + e.toString());
      }
    }
}
```

After adding the sleeping part to our thread, the program TestThreads3 (see Listing 20-9) will generate mixed console output about market and portfolio from both threads — this proves that they are taking turns even with the single-processor machine.

---

**LISTING 20-9:** Class TestThreads3

```
public class TestThreads3 {

    public static void main(String args[]){

        MarketNews3 mn = new MarketNews3("Market News");
        mn.start();

        Portfolio3 p = new Portfolio3("Portfolio data");
```

*continues*

**LISTING 20-9** *(continued)*

```
        p.start();

        System.out.println( "The main method of TestThreads3 is finished");
    }
}
```

If you need to "wake up" a sleeping thread before its sleeping time is up, use the method `interrupt()`. Just add `mn.interrupt()` to the class `TestThreads3` right after starting the `MarketNews` thread. This will trigger `InterruptedException`, and `MarketNews3` will wake up and continue its execution from the operator located below the `sleep()` method call. The class `Thread` has a method `interrupted()` that returns `true` if the current thread has been interrupted. The output of the program `TestThreads3` can look as follows:

```
The main method of TestThreads3 is finished
You have 500 shares of IBM
The market is improving 0
You have 501 shares of IBM
The market is improving 1
You have 502 shares of IBM
You have 503 shares of IBM
The market is improving 2
You have 504 shares of IBM
The market is improving 3
You have 505 shares of IBM
You have 506 shares of IBM
The market is improving 4
You have 507 shares of IBM
The market is improving 5
You have 508 shares of IBM
The market is improving 6
You have 509 shares of IBM
The market is improving 7
The market is improving 8
The market is improving 9
```

These days it's hard to find a single-CPU server machine. Most of the readers of this book have dual-core CPUs — these have two processors in the same chip. Modern JVMs use multiple cores for multi-threaded applications, but you shouldn't assume that your program will run twice as fast on such hardware. JVM optimization is a complex subject and is out of the scope of this tutorial. You may boost the performance of your system by increasing the number of threads running in parallel, but you should define the right ratio between the number of threads and the number of processors during the performance-tuning phase of application development.

## HOW TO KILL A THREAD

The class `Thread` has a method, `stop()`, that was supposed to know how to kill the current thread. But it was deprecated many years ago because it could bring some of the objects in your program into an inconsistent state caused by improper locking and unlocking of the object instances.

There are different approaches to killing threads. One of them involves creating your own method on the thread, say `stopMe()`, in which you set your own `boolean` variable, say `stopMe`, to `false` and test its value periodically inside the thread's method `run()`. If application code will set the value of `stopMe` to `true`, just exit the code execution in the method `run()`. In Listing 20-10, the loop in the method `run` checks the value of the variable `stopMe`, which is initialized with the reference to the current `Thread` object. As soon as it is changed (set to `null` in this case), the processing will complete.

**LISTING 20-10:** Killing a thread

```
class KillTheThread{
        public static void main(String args[]){
          Portfolio4 p = new Portfolio4("Portfolio data");
        p.start();

        // Some other code goes here,
        // and now it's time to kill the thread
        p.stopMe();

          }
}

class Portfolio4 extends Thread{

private volatile Thread stopMe = Thread.currentThread();

    public void stopMe() {
        stopMe = null;
    }

    public void run() {
        while (stopMe == Thread.currentThread()) {
          try{
            //Do some portfolio processing here
          }catch(InterruptedException e ){
            System.out.println(Thread.currentThread().getName()
                                    + e.toString());
        }

        }
    }
}
```

The variable `stopMe` has been declared with a `volatile` keyword, which warns the Java compiler that another thread can modify it and that this variable shouldn't be cached in registers, so that all threads must always see its fresh value. The class Portfolio4 could be written differently — the variable `stopMe` could be declared as `boolean`.

Not every thread can be killed using the code shown in Listing 20-10. What if a thread is not doing any processing at the moment, but is waiting for the user's input? Call the method `interrupt()` on such a thread. Killing a thread by interrupting it may be the only technique you need to use in such cases.

If you need to kill a thread that's busy doing some blocking I/O operations and the preceding methods of killing such a thread don't work, try closing I/O streams — this will cause IOException during the current read/write operation and the thread will be over.

If you'd like to read more comprehensive coverage of this subject, see Dr. Heinz Kabutz the Java Specialist's newsletter Issue #56, available at www.javaspecialists.co.za/archive/Issue056.html.

## THREAD PRIORITIES

Single-processor computers use a special scheduling algorithm that allocates processor time slices to the running threads based on their priorities. If Thread1 is using the processor and the higher-priority Thread2 wakes up, Thread1 is pushed aside and Thread2 gets the CPU. It is said that Thread2 *preempts* Thread1.

The class Thread has a method, setPriority(), that allows you to control its priority. There are 10 different priorities, which are final integer variables defined in the class Thread. Some of them are named constants MIN_PRIORITY, NORM_PRIORITY, and MAX_PRIORITY. Here's an example of their usage:

```
Thread myThread = new Thread("Portfolio");
myThread.setPriority(Thread.NORM_PRIORITY + 1);
```

If two threads with the same priority need the processor, it'll be given to one of them using an algorithm specific to the computer's OS.

## THREAD SYNCHRONIZATION AND RACE CONDITIONS

During the design stage of a multi-threaded application's development you should consider the possibility of a so-called *race condition*, which happens when multiple threads need to modify the same program resource at the same time (*concurrently*). The classic example is when a husband and wife are trying to withdraw cash from different ATMs at the same time.

Suppose the balance on their joint account is $120. If a Thread class is responsible for the validation and update of the balance of their bank account, there is a slight chance that the husband's thread will enable him to withdraw $100, but that before the actual withdrawal the wife's thread will come in trying to validate a $50 withdrawal. She is also enabled to make her withdrawal, because $120 is still there! The couple would successfully withdraw a total of $150, leaving a negative balance in their account. This is an example of a race condition.

A special keyword, synchronized, prevents race conditions from happening. This keyword places a *lock* (a monitor) on an important object or piece of code to make sure that only one thread at a time will have access. The code in Listing 20-11 locks the entire method withdrawCash() so no other thread will get access to the specified portion of code until the current (locking) thread has finished its execution of withdrawCash().

**LISTING 20-11:** Declaring a synchronized method

```
class ATMProcessor extends Thread{
  ...
  synchronized withdrawCash(int accountID, int amount){
    // Some thread-safe code goes here, i.e. reading from
    // a file or a database
    ...
    boolean allowTransaction = validateWithdrawal(accountID,
                                                  amount);
    if (allowTransaction){
      updateBalance(accountID, amount, "Withdraw");
    }
    else {
      System.out.println("Not enough money on the account");
    }
  }
}
```

The locks should be placed for the shortest possible time to avoid slowing down the program: That's why synchronizing short blocks of code is preferable to synchronizing whole methods. Listing 20-12 shows how to synchronize only the portion of the code that may cause the race condition, rather then locking the entire method `withdrawCash()`.

**LISTING 20-12:** Declaring a synchronized block

```
class ATMProcessor extends Thread{
  ...
  withdrawCash(int accountID, int amount){
    // Some thread-safe code goes here, i.e. reading from
    // a file or a database
    ...
    synchronized(this) {
    if (allowTransaction){
      updateBalance(accountID, amount, "Withdraw");
    }
    else {
      System.out.println("Not  enough money on the account");
    }
    }
  }
}
```

When a `synchronized` block is executed, the section of the code in parentheses is locked and can't be used by any other thread that's locked on the same section of the code until the lock is released. Listing 20-12 locks the current instance of the class `ATMProcessor` (represented by the `this` keyword) only for the duration of the `updateBalance()` method, which is a shorter period of time than locking `withdrawCash()` would take.

## JAVA ENUMERATIONS

The `enum` construct is not related to the thread concept and can be used for a variety of reasons, but because this lesson refers to enumerations for the first time in this book, a little sidebar explanation seems appropriate.

If you need to define a group of predefined constants, you can use the `final` keyword. For example, to define various categories of products in a store you can declare the following constants:

```
public static final int CATEGORY_BOOKS  = 1;
public static final int CATEGORY _VIDEOS = 2;
public static final int CATEGORY _ELECTRONICS  = 3;
public static final int CATEGORY _TOYS = 4;
```

But Java offers a special keyword, `enum`, that enables you to define such constants in a more elegant way:

```
enum Category {BOOKS,VIDEOS,ELECTRONICS,TOYS}
```

Not only is this notation more compact, but it also prevents the programmers from having to prefix each constant with `CATEGORY_` to stress that these values represent a group, but you can define variables to represent the entire group, pass `enum` as an argument to a method, and return `enum` from a method. For example, if you need to write a program that will redirect the store customer to the proper representative, you can write something similar to what's shown in Listing 20-13.

**LISTING 20-13: enum example**

Available for download on Wrox.com

```
enum Category {BOOKS,VIDEOS,ELECTRONICS,TOYS}

public class EnumExample {
    ...
    public static void redirectToRepresentative(Category cat){

        switch(os) {
          case BOOKS:
              System.out.println("Get Mary on the phone");
              break;
          case VIDEOS:
              System.out.println("Call Raj");
              break;
          case ELECTRONICS:
              System.out.println("Find Boris");
              break;
          case TOYS:
              System.out.println("Email David");
              break;
```

```
                default:
                    System.out.println("We don't sell such
    products.");
                    break;
            }
        }
    }
```

All `enums` implicitly extend `java.lang.Enum` and implement `Comparable` and `Serializable` interfaces. On top of that you can declare `enum` variables that implement other interfaces, and declare additional methods, for example:

```
enum Category implements Sellable {
    BOOKS,VIDEOS,ELECTRONICS,TOYS;

    printSalesData(int region){
        // Calculate sales here
    }

}
```

## THREAD STATES

A thread goes through various states during its life span. The class `Thread` has a method, `getState()`, that will return one of the values defined in the enumeration `Thread.State`.

➤ `BLOCKED`: Thread state for a thread that is blocked and waiting to enter or reenter a synchronized method or block of code

➤ `NEW`: Thread state for a thread that has been instantiated but not started yet

➤ `RUNNABLE`: Thread state for a runnable thread

➤ `TERMINATED`: Thread state for a terminated thread

➤ `TIMED_WAITING`: Thread state for a waiting thread with a specified waiting time

➤ `WAITING`: Thread state for a waiting thread

The class `Thread` has a method, `isAlive()`, that can help you to find out the status of the thread. If it returns `true`, the thread has been started and hasn't died yet. If it returns `false`, the thread is either new or already dead.

## WAIT AND NOTIFY

The class `Object` also has some methods relevant to threads: `wait()`, `notify()`, and `notifyAll()`. Because every Java class is inherited from the class `Object`, these methods can be called on any object.

Let's revisit our class `TestThreads3`, which spawns the threads `MarketNews3` and `Portfolio3`. It has the following line at the end of the `main()` method:

```
System.out.println("The main method TestThreads3 is finished");
```

Run the program `TestThreads3` and it'll print on the system console something like this:

```
The stock market is improving 1
You have  500  shares of IBM
The main method of TestThreads3 is finished
The stock market is improving 2
You have  501  shares of IBM
The stock market is improving! 3
You have  502  shares of IBM
...
```

Note that the method `main()` did not wait for the portfolio and market news threads' completion! But if the `main` class needs to wait until the threads complete their actions, you can use the method `wait()`:

```
public static void main(String args[]){
  ...
  mn.start();
  ...
  p.start();

  synchronized (this) {
    try{
      wait(10000);
    } catch (InterruptedException e){  ...}
  }
    System.out.println("The main method of TestThreads3 is finished");
}
```

The method call `wait(10000)` means "wait for up to 10 seconds." The last `println` statement will be executed either after 10 seconds or when this thread receives notification of some important event, whichever comes first. Examples of important events are a price drop on the auction for items you're interested in, the reopening of the airport after freezing rain, and the execution of your order to purchase 100 shares of IBM stock. A thread can notify other thread(s) by calling the method `notify()` or `notifyAll()`.

Calling `sleep(10000)` puts a thread into a not-runnable state for exactly 10 seconds, although `wait(10000)` may mean that it will come back to a runnable state earlier. If the method `wait()` is called without any arguments, the calling program will wait indefinitely until it receives a notification. The call to `wait()` makes the current thread give up its lock to another one and puts it to sleep until either the specified time has elapsed or the thread gets a notification from another object. Let's consider one of the use cases illustrating this.

`ClassA` spawns a thread, `ClassB`, and starts waiting. `ClassB` retrieves some data, and then sends a notification back to the instance of `ClassA`. The `ClassA` resumes its processing after notification has been received. Listing 20-14 shows implementation of this scenario. Note that the ClassB gets the reference to the object ClassA so it knows who to notify.

**LISTING 20-14: Notification example**

```
class ClassA  {
 String marketNews = null;

 void  someMethod(){

    // The ClassB needs a reference to the locked object
    // to be able to notify it

    ClassB myB=new ClassB(this);
    myB.start();
    synchronized(this) {
     wait();
    }

    // Some further processing of the MarketData goes here...
  }

  public void setData (String news){
    marketNews = news;
  }
}

class ClassB extends Thread{

  ClassA parent = null;

  ClassB(ClassA caller){
    parent = caller; // store the reference to the caller
  }

  run(){
    // Get some data, and, when done, notify the parent
    parent.setData("Economy is recovering...");
    ...
    synchronized (parent){
     parent.notify();  //notification of the caller
    }
  }
}
```

The method notifyAll() notifies and wakes up *all* threads waiting for the lock to be released on this object. If several threads are waiting, those that have the highest priority will run first. If several waiting threads have the same priority, the order of awakening is decided by the JVM. While notify() can work a tiny bit faster than notifyAll(), the latter is able to create objects that are *loosely coupled* — meaning that they don't know about each other.

In Listing 20-14 simple replacement of `parent.notify()` with `notifyAll()` is not enough because `ClassB` also passes the data about the economy back to `ClassA`. But if `ClassB` just needs to notify you about some important application event, `notifyAll()` can be a better choice.

## TRY IT

Implement and test the example from Listing 20-14 and then rewrite it to reduce the tight object coupling of the objects. `ClassB` shouldn't know the exact type of the object to notify (`ClassA`) — this makes `ClassB` useful with other objects, too. You'll need to introduce a new interface, say `Updatable`, that declares one method, `setData()`, to make `ClassB` work not only with `ClassA`, but with any class that implements `Updatable`.

## Lesson Requirements

You should have Java installed.

*You can download the code and resources for this Try It from the book's web page at* www.wrox.com. *You can find them in the Lesson20 folder in the download.*

## Step-by-Step

1. Create `ClassA` as in the code shown in Listing 20-14, and add the method `main()` to it.

2. Create `ClassB` and test the application to see that `ClassA` receives the notification about the economy.

3. Declare the new interface, `Updatable`.

4. Modify the constructor of `ClassB` to accept any `Updatable` object.

5. Run and test the new version of the application.

*Please select Lesson 20 on the DVD to view the video that accompanies this lesson.*

# 21

# Digging Deeper into Concurrent Execution

Even in such a concise tutorial as this one, Java threads deserve two dedicated lessons. Let's continue delving deeper into the world of multi-threaded applications.

## JOINING THREADS

In Lesson 20 you learned that a thread can wait for a fixed period or for a notification on some event. Now let's consider a scenario in which you need to start multiple threads and continue program execution only when all threads are complete. The Thread class has a method, join(), that you can use in this case.

Revisit the TestThreads3 program shown in Listing 20-9. If you run this program the system console will show the message "The main method of TestThreads3 is finished"; after that will it show the output of the portfolio and market news threads, which keep running for a while. If you want to make sure that the main method is waiting until the other two threads are finished, you can use the method join(), as shown in Listing 21-1.

**LISTING 21-1:** Joining threads

```java
public class TestThreadJoin {

    public static void main(String args[]){

        MarketNews3 mn = new MarketNews3("Market News");
        mn.start();

        Portfolio3 p = new Portfolio3("Portfolio data");
        p.start();

        try{
```

*continues*

**LISTING 20-1** *(continued)*

```
                mn.join();
                p.join();

            }catch (InterruptedException e){
                e.printStackTrace();
            }

            System.out.println( "The main method of TestThreadJoin is finished");

        }
    }
```

The output of the program from Listing 21-1 is shown next. Both `Portfolio3` and `MarketNews3` are joined with the main application thread, which prints its message that the main method is finished only after the other two are done.

```
You have 500 shares of IBM
The market is improving 0
You have 501 shares of IBM
The market is improving 1
You have 502 shares of IBM
You have 503 shares of IBM
The market is improving 2
You have 504 shares of IBM
The market is improving 3
You have 505 shares of IBM
You have 506 shares of IBM
The market is improving 4
You have 507 shares of IBM
The market is improving 5
You have 508 shares of IBM
The market is improving 6
You have 509 shares of IBM
The market is improving 7
The market is improving 8
The market is improving 9
The main method of TestThreadJoin is finished
```

Make a small change in the code and place `mn.join()` before the start of the portfolio thread, and you'll see different output — the ten messages about the market improving will be printed first, followed by the ten messages about your shares of IBM.

## GOODIES FROM JAVA.UTIL.CONCURRENT

Java 5 introduced lots of goodies that make thread programming a lot more robust and flexible, and most importantly that increase the performance of multi-threaded applications. In this section I'll just highlight some of the must-know techniques, classes, and interfaces from this package. For detailed coverage of this subject get the book *Java Concurrency in Practice*, Brian Goetz et al., 2006 Addison-Wesley, ISBN: 0321349601.

## ReentrantLock versus Synchronized

The package `java.util.concurrent.locks` includes the class `ReentrantLock`, which can be used as a replacement for the `synchronized` keyword. Using it may improve the performance of your code. The idea is to place a lock before the section of your program that may cause a race condition, and to remove the lock afterward. The next code snippet is a revision of the code shown in Listing 20-12:

```
private Lock accountLock = new ReentrantLock();

witdrawCash(int accountID, int amount){
    // Some thread-safe code goes here, i.e. reading from
    // a file or a database
    ...

    accountLock.lock(); // place a lock when this thread enters the code

    try{
    if (allowTransaction){
     updateBalance(accountID, amount, "Withdraw");
    }
    else {
     System.out.println("Not  enough money on the account");
    }
    }finally {
       accountLock.unlock(); // allow other threads to update balance
    }
}
```

Note that the lock has to be removed in the `finally` section to ensure that unlocking always gets executed, even if there is an exception thrown from the `try` block. When the code is unlocked it can be given to one of the waiting threads. The class `ReentrantLock` has an overloaded constructor with a `boolean` argument — if you specify `true` while creating the lock, the control will be given to the longest-waiting thread.

There is another useful class, `Condition`, that can be associated with the lock. This object enables a locked block of code to suspend its execution until other threads notify the current one that some condition has become `true`, e.g., the bank account has enough funds now for you to make a withdrawal.

If you don't need the flexibility offered by the `ReentrantLock/Condition` combo, just use the `synchronized` keyword with `notify()/notifyAll()` methods to control thread locking. Or, even better, see if using one of the concurrent collections (reviewed in the section "A Brief Introduction to Concurrent Collections") can take care of all your locking needs so you don't need to create explicit locks in your code.

## Executor Framework

Creating threads by subclassing `Thread` or implementing `Runnable` works, but there are certain shortcomings to these approaches. First, the method `run()` cannot return a value. Second, an application may spawn so many threads that it can take up all the system resources, and if this happens the application will stop functioning. In other words, you need to control the number of threads allowed for each application.

You can overcome the first shortcoming by using the Callable interface, and the second one by using classes from the *Executor framework*. The Executors class spawns the threads from Runnable objects, ExecutorService knows how to create Callable threads, and ScheduledExecutorService allows you to schedule threads for future execution.

The utility class Executors has static methods that will enable you to create an appropriate executor. In particular, its method newFixedThreadPool() creates a pool of threads of a specified size. For example, Executors.newFixedThreadPool(5) gives you an instance of ExecutorService that automatically supports a pool of not more than five threads. If all five threads are busy when a request to create a new thread comes in, that request will wait until one of the running threads completes. Using thread pools ensures that you can control system resources better.

If you need a thread to return some data on completion, create a class that implements the Callable interface and defines a method call() that plays the same role as run() in Runnable. In this case you'll need to create threads differently; the class Thread won't take a Callable object as an argument. The class Executors comes to the rescue: it offers a number of static methods that will create a thread from your Callable class and return the result of its execution packaged inside the special object implementing the interface Future.

The method call() is defined with a parameterized value (remember generics?):

```
public interface Callable <V>{
   V call() throws Exception;
}
```

Accordingly, if some method needs to create a thread using Callable, the code should instantiate the Callable thread with a specific data type in place of <V>. For example, the thread Portfolio may return an Integer as a result of some processing in its call() method:

```
public class Portfolio implements Callable<Integer>{

    public Integer call() {
       // Perform some actions
       return someInteger;

    }
}

public class MarketData implements Callable<Integer>{

    public Integer call() {
       // Perform some actions
       return someInteger;

    }
}
```

One way to create a `Future` object is by submitting an instance of the `Callable` thread to the `Executor`. Call the function `get()` on the `Future` instance, and it'll block on the thread until its `call()` method returns the result:

```
//Threads' results can be stored in the collection of Futures
List<Future<Integer>>  threadResults= new ArrayList<Future<Integer>>();

// Submit Callables for execution
threadResults.add(myExecutorService.submit(new Portfolio()));
threadResults.add(myExecutorService.submit(new MarketData()));

for (Future<Integer> future : threadResults) {
        future.get();
}
```

Calling methods `get()` on several instances of the `Future` objects is equivalent to joining threads.

The process of spawning threads using `Executors`, `Callable`, and `Future` may go like this:

1. Declare and instantiate a class that implements the `Callable` interface, and program the business logic in its method `call()`.

2. Create an instance of the `Future` object.

3. Create an instance of an `ExecutorService` using `Executors.newFixedThreadPool()`.

4. Call the function `submit()` on the `ExecutorService`, providing an instance of the `Callable` object as an argument.

5. Call the function `get()` on the `Future` object from Step 2. This function will wait until the thread returns the result (or throws an exception).

6. Accept the result of the thread execution into a variable of the data type used in Step 1.

7. Call the function `shutdown()` on the `ExecutorService` from Step 3.

The code in Listings 21-2 to 21-4 demonstrates the spawning of the familiar threads portfolio and market news using the classes from the Executor Framework. In this example each `Callable` thread performs some dummy actions and returns an integer as a result.

**LISTING 21-2: Portfolio that implements Callable**

```
class PortfolioCallable implements Callable<Integer> {

    public Integer call() throws Exception {
      for (int i=0; i<5;i++){
          Thread.sleep (700);     // Sleep for 700 milliseconds
          System.out.println( "You have " +  (500 + i) +
                                      " shares of IBM");
      }

      // Just return some number as a result
```

*continues*

**LISTING 21-2** *(continued)*

```
        return 10;
    }
}
```

**LISTING 21-3: MarketNews that implements Callable**

```
class MarketNewsCallable implements Callable<Integer> {

    public Integer call() throws Exception {

            for (int i=0; i<5;i++){
                Thread.sleep (1000);   // sleep for 1 second
                 System.out.println( "The market is improving " + i);
                }
        // Just return some number as a result
        return 12345;
        }
    }
```

The `TestCallableThreads` class creates a collection of `Future` objects — one per thread. Executor creates a pool of two threads and each thread is submitted for execution. The method `get()` waits for the completion of each thread, and the result of each `call()` method is stored in the collection results.

**LISTING 21-4: Spawning threads with the Executor framework**

```
public class TestCallableThreads {

    public static void main(String[] args)
      throws InterruptedException, ExecutionException {

      //A placeholder for Future objects
          List<Future<Integer>> futures =
        new ArrayList<Future<Integer>>();

       // A placeholder for results
          List<Integer> results = new ArrayList<Integer>();

      final ExecutorService service =
        Executors.newFixedThreadPool(2); // pool of 2 threads

      try {

        futures.add(service.submit(new PortfolioCallable()));
        futures.add(service.submit(new MarketNewsCallable()));

        for (Future<Integer> future : futures) {
         results.add(future.get());
```

```
        }

    } finally {
     service.shutdown();
    }

    for (Integer res: results){
        System.out.println("\nGot the result: " + res);
    }
  }
}
```

The output of this program is shown next. But if you change the number of threads in the pool from two to one, the program will first print all messages from the portfolio thread and only after that print all messages from the market news.

```
You have 500 shares of IBM
The market is improving 0
You have 501 shares of IBM
The market is improving 1
You have 502 shares of IBM
You have 503 shares of IBM
The market is improving 2
You have 504 shares of IBM
The market is improving 3
The market is improving 4

Got the result: 10
Got the result: 12345
```

# A Brief Introduction to Concurrent Collections

The package `java.util.concurrent` offers a number of data structures that simplify programming with threads. I'll just briefly name some of them in this section.

## Queues

The concept of a *queue* (First In First Out or FIFO) fits well in any process that involves asynchronous intra-object communications. Instead of object A trying to place a direct lock on object B, the former (aka the *producer*) can place some data objects in a queue, and the latter (aka the *consumer*) will retrieve (*dequeue*) them from the queue asynchronously. Most importantly, the queues from the `java.util.concurrent` package are *thread-safe*, which means that you can add an object to a queue without worrying about race conditions.

If the queue is blocking, the thread will also block while trying to add an object to a full queue or remove an object from an empty one. The following classes implement the `BlockingQueue` interface: `LinkedBlockingQueue`, `ArrayBlockingQueue`, `SynchronousQueue`, `PriorityBlockingQueue`, and `DelayQueue`. To add an object to a queue you can use such methods as `add()`, `put()`, and `offer()`. To retrieve an object from a queue use `poll()`, `remove()`, `take()`, or `peek()`.

*Unbound* queues don't place limitations on the number of elements. `ConcurrentLinkedQueue` is an example of such a queue.

Java 6 has introduced a `Deque` interface for inserting and removing elements from both ends of the queue. The class `LinkedBlockingDeque` is a concurrent implementation of this interface.

## Collections

Using concurrent collections is a recommended way of creating thread-safe data structures. Such collections include `ConcurrentHashMap`, `ConcurrentSkipListMap`, `ConcurrentSkipListSet`, `CopyOnWriteArrayList`, and `CopyOnWriteArraySet`. Java documentation describes when to use each of these collections. For example, a `CopyOnWriteArrayList` is preferable to a synchronized `ArrayList` when the expected number of reads and traversals is much greater than the number of updates to a list. These collections were written to minimize the time during which data is locked.

The utility class `java.util.Collections` has a number of static methods that create thread-safe collections. Their method names start with the word *synchronized*. For example, `synchronizedList()` takes a regular `List` (such as `ArrayList`) as an argument and makes it thread-safe. You can read more about Java collections at `http://java.sun.com/javase/6/docs/technotes/guides/collections/index.html`.

Finding a ready-to-use synchronized collection is better than writing `synchronized` blocks on your own — the chances are slim that you'll write more efficient synchronization code than already exists in Java.

# SWINGWORKER THREAD

Any Java Swing application spawns a number of threads. At the very minimum it runs the main application thread, the second one captures system events, and the third communicates with the GUI. The application itself may spawn additional threads. But if more than one thread will need to update the UI components, the changes may not be rendered properly, because Swing components were not made thread-safe to minimize the number of locks that hurt performance.

To avoid this problem, UI updates shouldn't be made directly, but rather submitted to an *event dispatch thread*. Swing uses a single-threaded model, which means that all UI updates are rendered via a single thread.

Suppose your GUI application is written with Java Swing, and a click on `JButton` initiates some server-side data request that takes about 10 seconds to complete. You should never execute long requests in the event dispatch thread. If you do, then the UI will become frozen, as no updates can be made until the long running process releases the lock on the thread. Therefore, you need to start a separate thread for such a long process, and when it finishes, the program has to modify the GUI via the event dispatch thread.

For example, if the result of a button click has to update a `JTextField`, you may create a new thread in the button's `actionPerformed()` method and, from within the `run()` method of this thread, update the text field. This will work...most of the time, if there are no conflicts with other threads running in your application.

All UI-related Swing events (such as button clicks and window repaints) are placed in a special queue, and the object `java.awt.EventQueue` retrieves them from this queue. You should direct modification of the UI (the `JTextField` in our example) to this queue.

In the older version of Java, to ensure that all application-specific data would modify the GUI via this queue, developers used the method invokeLater() to ensure that UI changes were placed in the EventQueue:

```
SwingUtilities.invokeLater()
    new Runnable(){
     public void run(){
       // Do some processing here
       //... and then update the UI
       myTextField.setText(someData);
     }
   }
);
```

While this technique still works, it clogs the code with anonymous Runnable classes. The class javax.swing.SwingWorker gives you a cleaner (though not necessarily simpler) means of dealing with the event dispatch thread. This thread class implements Runnable and Future, and so can be submitted to the Executor for execution and return a result.

Let's say a Swing application needs to make a request to the server to get the market news information, which may take a couple of seconds. So that the UI won't be frozen for these seconds, this request has to be performed in a background thread, and when the result is ready the UI has to be updated. To arrange this, create a subclass of SwingWorker and override its doInBackground() method, then instantiate it and call its execute() method, as in Listing 21-5.

**LISTING 21-5: Basic use of SwingWorker**

```
class MarketNewsWorker extends SwingWorker <List<String>, String>{

    @Override public List<String> doInBackground(){
        // Make a request to the server and return a result,
        // i.e. a list of Strings
       return myListOfTextData;
   }
     // method method overides go here
  }

class TestMarketNews{
    ...
    public static void main(String[] args){
        new MarketNewsWorker().execute();
    }
 }
```

This code gives you a high-level picture, but there is more to executing the thread with SwingWorker. First, you probably noticed the unknown syntax element @Override, which is Java *annotation* stating that the method doInBackground() is being overridden. Adding the @Override annotation is not required here; it's just an example of an annotation. You'll learn about annotations in Lesson 24.

Second, the class `MarketNewsWorker` uses generics and has two parameters, `<List<String>` and `String>`. The reason for this is that the overridden method `doInBackground()` *might* call the `SwingWorker`'s `process()` method, and *will* call its `done()` method on completion — this is where the UI is being updated. Two parameters indicate what types of data will be returned by `doInBackground()` and given to `process()` respectively.

Why might you consider calling the method `process()` during your thread execution? You might do it to support some kind of progress meter or other means of reporting the progress of long-running processes. If, for example, a long-running thread is reading a large file or performing some lengthy calculations, you might want to calculate the percentage of completion and report it to the calling Swing application.

You are not allowed to call the `process()` method directly, but have to call a method called `publish()`, which will internally call `process()`. Override `process()` to add some messages to the log file or update the progress meter. The code to display the result of the calculations on the UI should be written in the method `done()`.

Listing 21-6 shows you a typical way to program with `SwingWorker`. I left out the details on purpose so you'd have something to do for today's homework.

**LISTING 21-6: A typical way to use SwingWorker**

```
class MarketNewsWorker extends SwingWorker <List<String>, String>{

    @Override public List<String> doInBackground(){
        // Make a request to the server and return a result,
        // i.e. a list of Strings
        for (String news: someNewsCollection){
            //process each news and report the progress
            ...
            publish("Processed the news " + news); //this calls process()
        }
        return myListOfTextData;
    }

    @Override protected void process(String progressMessage){
        // display the progress information here
    }

    @Override protected void done(){
        // modify UI components here by calling get()
        // Future's get() gives you the result of
        // the thread execution
    }
}

class TestMarketNews{
    ...
    public static void main(String[] args){
        new MarketNewsWorker().execute();
    }
}
```

You just completed a rather advanced lesson of this book. The subject definitely requires more research and practice. Some good content to read next is the lesson on concurrency in Oracle's Java tutorial, which you'll find here: http://download-llnw.oracle.com/javase/tutorial/essential/concurrency/. As always, trying it hands-on will deepen your understanding.

## TRY IT

Create a Swing application with the UI that consists of two JTextArea controls and one JButton with the label "Get the News." Prepare two text files with some text information (the news), and write the code that reads them to the left and right text areas respectively. File reading has to be implemented concurrently using two SwingWorker threads.

## Lesson Requirements

You should have Java installed.

> *You can download the code and resources for this Try It from the book's web page at* www.wrox.com. *You can find them in the Lesson21 folder in the download.*

## Step-by-Step

1. Create a new Eclipse project called Lesson21.

2. Create a class called NewsReader as a subclass of SwingWorker. This class should have a constructor that takes one argument of type File.

3. Prepare two text files with some news in each.

4. Create a Swing application with two text areas and a button.

5. On the click of the button instantiate two NewsReader threads. Each thread should get an instance of the File object pointing to the corresponding news file.

6. Override the NewsReader's methods doInBackground() and done() to read the files and populate the Swing view.

7. Test this program.

8. This step is optional. Override the method process() and make sure that it updates the view with progress information about the reading process. The progress should be displayed as a percentage: The percentage formula is progressToDisplay=readBytes/FileSize*100.

 *Please select Lesson 21 on the DVD to view the video that accompanies this lesson.*

# Working with Databases Using JDBC

Business applications usually store data in the databases. In most of the enterprise applications, Relational Database Management Systems (RDBMSes) are used as data storage. They store the data records in *tables*. Each record (such as that of an employee) is represented by a table row, which consists of one or more columns or *record fields* (e.g., name, address, hire date). RDBMSes understand the SQL language.

The most popular RDBMSes are Oracle, DB2, Sybase, Microsoft SQL Server, and MySQL Server. All samples from this lesson will use JavaDB, which is included with your JDK installation.

Java includes two packages that contain classes required for work with DBMSes: java.sql and javax.sql. The former contains commonly used classes such as Connection, Statement, and ResultSet. The latter is used for supporting database connectivity on the server side, containing classes such as DataSource, and RowSet.

The JDBC API is not DBMS-specific — if you write a program that uses JDBC classes to retrieve/update data in Oracle, you'll be using the same classes to work with MySQL Server or DB2. You just need the JDBC drivers from the corresponding DBMS vendor — the drivers hide their database specifics behind the same public JDBC API.

JDBC drivers either pass SQL statements from Java to a DBMS for execution or simply execute a program stored inside a DBMS (called a *stored procedure*). If some data has been retrieved as the result of these actions, your Java program will handle it by making appropriate calls to the JDBC API. Over the past 15 years the JDBC specification has been evolving and, at the time of this writing, most drivers comply with JDBC version 4.0.

In this lesson all communications with the DBMS are made by supplying SQL statements to the JDBC API. There is an alternative way of working with data, by using one of the object-relational mapping (ORM) frameworks. In Lesson 36 you'll get familiar with a popular ORM framework called Hibernate.

## JDBC DRIVER TYPES

A JDBC driver plays the role of the middleman between a Java program and a DBMS. Drivers are available from database vendors, from Oracle, and from third-party vendors of Java application servers.

There are four general types of JDBC drivers.

A Type 1 driver is a JDBC-ODBC bridge that enables Java programs to work with the database using ODBC drivers from Microsoft. The drawbacks of ODBC drivers are that they are slower than the others, must be installed and configured on each user's machine, and work only on Windows machines. The Type 1 JDBC drivers are rarely used.

A Type 2 driver consists of Java classes that work in conjunction with the non-Java native drivers provided by the DBMS vendor. These drivers work much faster than Type 1, but also require installation and configuration on the machine on which Java programs run.

A Type 3 driver is called a *middleware driver* and can be provided by vendors of application servers. It consists of two parts: the *client* portion performs a DBMS-independent SQL call, which is then translated to a specific DBMS protocol by the *server* portion of the driver.

A Type 4 driver is a pure Java driver, which usually comes as a `.jar` file and performs direct calls to the database server. It does not need any configuration on the client's machine, other than including the name of the main driver's class in your Java code. That's why it's also known as the *thin driver*. For example, Java applets can be packaged with this type of driver, which can be automatically downloaded to the user's machine along with the applets themselves.

For simplicity I'll be using JDBC drivers of Type 4 in this lesson, but many production systems can deploy Type 3 drivers to provide better performance.

## CREATING A DATABASE WITH DERBY

In this lesson I'll be using an open-source DBMS called JavaDB (also known as Derby), which is packaged with Java 6. It's a small DBMS that you wouldn't use for serious production systems, but it's great for learning JDBC or to use for many small systems. If you've installed Java SDK as instructed in Lesson 1 (see Figure 1-2), you already have JavaDB installed in the folder `c:\Program Files\Sun\JavaDB`. Modify your system variable PATH so it starts with the following code:

```
c:\Program Files\Sun\JavaDB\bin;
```

To make sure that you change PATH properly, open a command window and enter `sysinfo`. This command should print information about your Java environment, and you should find a reference to Derby and JDBC 4.0, as shown in Figure 22-1.

If you don't have JavaDB installed, download and install it from `http://db.apache.org/derby`. Derby is well documented and if you haven't had a chance to work with relational DBMSes, download and read the "Getting Started with Derby" manual.

Derby has an interactive command-line utility called ij that you can use to create databases and tables and populate them with data, among other actions. I'll show you how to create a sample database and a table to store data about employees. First open a command window and issue the command `startNetworkServer`. Figure 22-2 shows the message that Derby has started and is ready to accept connections on port 1527.

**FIGURE 22-1**

**FIGURE 22-2**

Open another command window and start ij. First, connect to the database Lesson22 by issuing the following command:

```
connect 'jdbc:derby://localhost:1527/Lesson22;create=true';
```

This command will try to connect to the database Lesson22, and will create it if no such database is found. The next command will create a database table, Employee, to store records that consist of three fields: EMPNO, ENAME, and JOB_TITLE. The first field will be stored as an integer, and the other two as simple text (varchars) allowing 50 and 150 characters respectively.

```
CREATE TABLE Employee (
    EMPNO int NOT NULL,
    ENAME varchar (50) NOT NULL,
    JOB_TITLE varchar (150) NOT NULL
);
```

Finally, to populate the table with some data, issue the INSERT command in ij:

```
INSERT INTO Employee values (7369,'John Smith', 'Clerk'), (7499,
'Joe Allen','Salesman'), (7521,'Mary Lou','Director');
```

Figure 22-3 is a snapshot of the command window after the database Lesson22 and the table Employee have been created, and the three records have been inserted there.

**FIGURE 22-3**

If you want to ensure that the records were successfully created in the database, issue the SELECT SQL statement to retrieve the data:

```
Select * from Employee;
```

You'll see the output of the above SQL statement in the next section. If you are not familiar with the syntax of SQL, refer to the tutorial at www.w3schools.com/sql/default.asp.

## SAMPLE JDBC PROGRAM

In this section I'll show you the steps that you can perform to retrieve the data in any Java program that works with a relational database using JDBC. A sample program will implement all of these steps to display the list of employees from the database table Employee.

**1.** Load the JDBC driver using the method forName() of the Java class Class. You have to find out the name of the class to load from the JDBC driver's documentation. If you work with Oracle DBMSes, you can load a Type 4 JDBC driver with the following command:

```
Class.forName("oracle.jdbc.driver.OracleDriver");
```

In the case of JavaDB, which was installed and registered with your JDK, you can skip this step.

**2.** Obtain the database connection to the database Lesson22 by calling

```
DriverManager.getConnection(url, user, password);
```

In the case of Derby DB you don't have to supply the user and the password; simply provide the URL of your database, for example

```
DriverManager.getConnection("jdbc:derby:Lesson22");
```

**3.** Create an instance of the Java class `Statement`:

```
Connection.createStatement();
```

As an alternative, you can create `PreparedStatement` or `CallableStatement`, explained later in this lesson in "The PreparedStatement Class" and "The CallableStatement Class" sections later in this lesson.

**4.** For SQL `Select` execute the following command:

```
Statement.executeQuery("Select ...");
```

For SQL queries, which produce more than one result, use the method `execute()`.

For `Insert`, `Update`, and `Delete` SQL statements use the following:

```
Statement.updateQuery("Insert ...");
```

**5.** Write a loop to process the database result set, if any:

```
while (ResultSet.next()) {...}
```

**6.** Free system resources by closing the `ResultSet`, `Statement`, and `Connection` objects.

All these steps are implemented in the class `EmployeeList`, shown in Listing 22-1, which prints the records from the table Employee. Even though you don't need to explicitly load the driver for Derby with `Class.forName()`, the location of the driver class has to be known to your program, otherwise you'll get a "No suitable driver" error. Either add `derbyclient.jar` to the `CLASSPATH` system variable, or just add it as an external `.jar` to your Eclipse project (see the Java Build Panel, available from the Eclipse project Properties menu).

**LISTING 22-1: The EmployeeList program**

```
package com.practicaljava.lesson22;

import java.sql.*;
class EmployeeList {
public static void main(String argv[]) {

   Connection conn=null;
   Statement stmt=null;
   ResultSet rs=null;

  try {

     // Load the JDBC driver - Class
     // This can be skipped for Derby, but derbyclient.jar
```

*continues*

**LISTING 22-1** *(continued)*

```java
    //has to be in the CLASSPATH

    // Class.forName("org.apache.derby.jdbc.ClientDriver");

    conn = DriverManager.getConnection("jdbc:derby://localhost:1527/Lesson22");


    // Create an SQL query
    String sqlQuery = "SELECT * from Employee";

    // Create an instance of the Statement object
    stmt = conn.createStatement();

    // Execute SQL and get obtain the ResultSet object
    rs = stmt.executeQuery(sqlQuery);


    // Process the result set - print Employees
    while (rs.next()){
    int empNo = rs.getInt("EMPNO");
        String eName = rs.getString("ENAME");
        String job = rs.getString("JOB_TITLE");

System.out.println(""+ empNo + ", " + eName + ", " + job );
    }
    } catch( SQLException se ) {
      System.out.println ("SQLError: " + se.getMessage ()
          + " code: " + se.getErrorCode());
    } catch( Exception e ) {

      System.out.println(e.getMessage());
      e.printStackTrace();
    } finally{

        // clean up the system resources
        try{
rs.close();
stmt.close();
conn.close();
        } catch(Exception e){
            e.printStackTrace();
        }
    }
  }
}
```

The output of the program EmployeeList should look like this:

```
7369, John Smith, CLERK
7499, Joe Allen, SALESMAN
7521, Mary Lou, Director
```

When you execute any SQL statements, always include processing of errors that may be returned by the DBMS. Catching the SQLException is the right way to get the error message. Note that the code in Listing 22-1 calls the method getErrorCode() to extract the database-specific error code from the SQLException object.

# PROCESSING RESULT SETS

Let's take a closer look at the code in Listing 22-1. After rs = stmt.executeQuery(sqlQuery), the cursor rs points at the very first record (row) of the result set in memory. Each row contains as many fields (columns) as were specified in the SQL Select statement. Each of the values is extracted by an appropriate method based on the data type of the field. The names of these methods are self-explanatory: rs.getString(), rs.getInt(), and so on. If you know the name of a column from the result, use it as a method argument:

```
int empNo = rs.getInt("EMPNO");
String eName = rs.getString("ENAME");
```

JDBC drivers are smart enough to convert the data from the database types to the corresponding Java types: For example, Derby's varchar will become Java's String.

You could have gotten the values of each field by specifying the relative position of the column from the result set:

```
int empNo = rs.getInt(1);
String eName = rs.getString(2);
```

Besides having names, columns in the result set are numbered starting with 1. In some cases numbers are your only choice; for example, the following SQL query does not list column names to select (the asterisk means "all"):

```
stmt.executeQuery("Select count(*) from EMP");
```

The class EmployeeList just prints the retrieved data in a loop. You can also place the result set in a Java collection object for further processing. The ResultSet object holds the database connection and is not serializable. That's why common practice for programming server-side operations with DBMSes is to create a class representing a row from the result set and populate, say, an ArrayList or other Java collection with its instances.

Listing 22-2 shows an example of such a class, which can represent one employee record. Classes that hold only the value of some data are often called *value objects*. Because in distributed applications such objects may need to be transferred between different computers, they are also known as *Data Transfer Objects (DTOs)*.

**LISTING 22-2:** The EmployeeDTO

```
class EmployeeDTO{

    //private properties
    private int empNo;
    private String eName;
    private String jobTitle;

    //setters
    public void setEmpNo(int val){empNo=val;}
    public void setEName(String val){eName=val;}
    public void setJobTitle(String val){jobTitle=val;}

    // getters
    public int getEmpNo(){return empNo;}
    public String getEName(){return eName;}
    public String getJob(){return jobTitle;}
}
```

EmployeeDTO declares private variables to store the data but access to this data is performed via public *setters* and *getters*, the methods that allow external code to set and get the appropriate values. This technique can be useful when some application-specific logic has to be applied at the moment when some code needs to get or modify the properties of the class EmployeeDTO.

For example, you can place some authorization code inside the setter to ensure that the external object has enough permissions to change the property jobTitle. If the business logic of obtaining such authorization changes in the future, you need to modify only the code inside the setter, but the external code will remain unchanged.

The next code snippet shows how the class EmployeeList can prepare a collection of EmployeeDTO objects while processing the result set retrieved by the SQL Select statement.

```
class EmployeeList {
...
 // Create an object for collection of employees
 ArrayList<EmployeeDTO> employees = new ArrayList<EmployeeDTO>();

 // Process ResultSet and populate the collection


 while (rs.next()){
  EmployeeDTO currentEmp = new EmployeeDTO();
  currentEmp.setEmpNo(rs.getInt("EMPNO"));
  currentEmp.setEName(rs.getString("ENAME"));
  currentEmp.setJob(rs.getString("JOB_TITLE"));

  employees.add(currEmp);
 }
...
}
```

If this code is deployed on the server's JVM and you need to send the data to another computer that runs, say, a Swing client, you can consider applying Java serialization here for sending a collection of employees to the front. But make sure that the class `EmployeeDTO` implements the `Serializable` interface.

# THE PREPAREDSTATEMENT CLASS

Listing 22-1 uses the class `Statement` to create an object capable of executing SQL. But this is not the only way to supply SQL to the JDBC API. The class `PreparedStatement` is a subclass of `Statement`, but it pre-compiles the SQL statement before executing it.

With `PreparedStatement` you can create SQL with parameters that are dynamically passed by the program. Suppose you need to execute the query `"SELECT * from EMP WHERE empno=..."` multiple times, providing the `empno` values from the array `empNumbers[]`. If you use the class `Statement`, the variable `sqlQuery` will have to be pre-compiled on each iteration of the loop:

```
for (int i=0;i<empNumbers.length; i++){
  sqlQuery="SELECT * from Employee WHERE empno=" + employees[i];
  stmt.executeQuery(sqlQuery);
}
```

The class `PreparedStatement` offers a more efficient solution:

```
PreparedStatement stmt=conn.prepareStatement(
                     " SELECT * from Employee WHERE empno=?");

for (int i=0;i<empNumbers.length; i++){

  // pass the array's value that substitutes the question mark
  stmt.setInt(1,employees[i];)
  stmt.executeQuery(sqlQuery);
}
```

In this case the SQL statement is compiled only once and parameters are provided by the appropriate `setXXX()` method depending on the data type. The SQL statement may have several parameters (question marks), and the first argument of the setter enables you to specify each parameter's number. For example:

```
PreparedStatement stmt=conn.prepareStatement(
     "SELECT * from Employee WHERE empno=? and ename=?");

for (int i=0;i<empNumbers.length; i++){
  stmt.setInt(1,empNumbers[i];)
  stmt.setString(2,empNames[i];)
  stmt.executeQuery(sqlQuery);
}
```

If you need to pass a NULL value as a parameter, use the method `setNull()`.

# THE CALLABLESTATEMENT CLASS

This class extends `PreparedStatement` and is used for executing stored procedures from Java. Let's say there is a stored procedure entitled `changeEmpTitle` that takes two parameters: `empno` and `title`. Here's the code to execute this stored procedure:

```
CallableStatement stmt = conn.prepareCall("{call changeEmpTitle(?,?)}");

stmt.setInt(1,7566);
stmt.setString (2,"Salesman");
stmt.executeUpdate();
```

If a stored procedure returns some values using output parameters, each of the OUT data types has to be registered before the statement is executed. The next code snippet shows you an example of executing a stored procedure that has two parameters: The first is an input parameter, and the second is an output parameter by which the stored procedure can return the result of its execution to the Java program:

```
CallableStatement stmt = conn.prepareCall(
                  ("{call getEmpTitle(?,?) }");
stmt.setInt(1, 7566);
stmt.registerOutParameter(2,java.sql.Types.VARCHAR);
stmt.executeQuery();
String title=stmt.getString(2);
```

# THE RESULTSETMETADATA CLASS

JDBC enables you to process result sets when the number of returned values is unknown. Imagine that you need to write a program that can accept any SQL `Select` statement, execute it, and display the retrieved data. With the class `ResultSetMetaData` you can dynamically find out how many columns there are in the result set, as well as their names and data types. The following code fragment gets the number of the database table columns in the result set and for each of them identifies and prints the column name and type:

```
String sqlQuery = "select * from Employee";
ResultSet rs = stmt.executeQuery(query);

ResultSetMetaData rsMeta = rs.getMetaData();
int colCount = rsMeta.getColumnCount();

for (int i = 1; i <= colCount; i++)  {
  System.out.println(
      " Column name: " + rsMeta.getColumnName(i) +
      " Column type: " + rsMeta.getColumnTypeName(i));
}
```

This simple but powerful technique is used internally by ORM frameworks (see Lesson 36) that can "magically" generate database models and automatically generate Java classes representing database entities.

Listing 22-3 shows a Java program called ShowAnyData that prints a result set based on any SQL Select statement passed from the command line. For example, it can be started as follows:

```
java ShowAnyData "Select * from Employee"
```

**LISTING 22-3:** Using ResultSetMetaData

```java
import java.sql.*;
class ShowAnyData {

  public static void main(String args[]) {
    Connection conn=null;
    Statement stmt=null;
    ResultSet rs=null;

  if (args.length==0){

     System.out.println("Usage: java ShowAnyData SQLSelectStatement");
     System.out.println("For example: java ShowAnyData \"Select * from Employee\"");
     System.exit(1);
   }

   try {
                    // Class.forName("org.apache.derby.jdbc.ClientDriver");
       conn = DriverManager.getConnection(
                         "jdbc:derby://localhost:1527/Lesson22");

       stmt = conn.createStatement();

       // Execute SQL query passed from command line
       rs = stmt.executeQuery(args[0]);

       // Find out the number of columns, their names and display the data
       ResultSetMetaData rsMeta = rs.getMetaData();
       int colCount = rsMeta.getColumnCount();

        for (int i = 1; i <= colCount; i++)  {
         System.out.print(rsMeta.getColumnName(i) + " ");
        }

       System.out.println();

       while (rs.next()){
          for (int i = 1; i <= colCount; i++)  {
            System.out.print(rs.getString(i) + " ");
          }
          System.out.print("\n");   // new line character
       }

     } catch( SQLException se ) {
        System.out.println ("SQLError: " + se.getMessage ()
             + " code: " + se.getErrorCode ());
     } catch( Exception e ) {
        System.out.println(e.getMessage());
```

*continues*

**LISTING 22-3** *(continued)*

```
            e.printStackTrace();
    } finally{

        // clean up the system resources
        try{
                    rs.close();
                    stmt.close();
                    conn.close();
        } catch(Exception e){
            e.printStackTrace();
        }
    }
  }
}
```

The output of the ShowAnyData program will be the same as that of EmployeeList shown in Listing 22-1. But this program can execute any SQL statement as long as you are specifying valid database objects. Note that the code in ShowAnyData first ensures that you have passed the command-line argument. If you run this program from a command line, don't forget to include the SQL statement in double quotes. In Eclipse you can specify a command-line argument by selecting the Run Configuration panel in the Arguments tab.

## SCROLLABLE RESULT SETS AND ROWSET

In all the preceding examples the code traversed the result set using the method next(), which moves only the cursor forward. Another option is to create a scrollable result set so the cursor can be moved back and forth if need be. There is a two-argument version of the method createStatement(). The first argument specifies the type of scrolling (TYPE_FORWARD_ONLY, TYPE_SCROLL_INSENSITIVE, or TYPE_SCROLL_SENSITIVE) and the second makes the result set updateable or read-only (CONCUR_READ_ONLY or CONCUR_UPDATABLE). For example,

```
Statement stmt = con.createStatement(
ResultSet.TYPE_SCROLL_INSENSITIVE, ResultSet.CONCUR_READ_ONLY);
ResultSet rs = stmt.executeQuery("SELECT * from Employee");
```

The TYPE_FORWARD_ONLY parameter allows only forward movement of the cursor. The difference between TYPE_SCROLL_INSENSITIVE and TYPE_SCROLL_SENSITIVE is in whether scrolling reflects changes that have been made to the result set. The next example sets the cursor at the end of the result set and moves the cursor backward:

```
rs.afterLast();
while (rs.previous()){
  int empNo = rs.getInt("EMPNO");
  String eName = rs.getString("ENAME");
  String job = rs.getString("JOB");
  System.out.println(""+ empNo + ", " + eName + ", " + job_title);
}
```

You can also move the cursor to a specific row by using the following self-explanatory methods:

```
rs.absolute(25);   // moves the cursor to the 25th row
rs.relative(-4);   // moves the cursor to the 21st row
rs.first();
rs.last();
rs.beforeFirst();
```

If the result set is updatable (CONCUR_UPDATABLE) you can modify the underlying database table while scrolling. For example, the following statements will update the job title of the employee based on the current cursor's position:

```
rs.updateString("JOB_TITLE","Manager");
rs.updateRow();
```

Scrollable result sets enable you to traverse the result set in both directions, but they have a drawback: They hold the database connection, which may be required by another thread or program. The package javax.sql includes the interface RowSet, which is a subclass of ResultSet. RowSet gets the data from the database, then disconnects, but still allows Java to work with the data. The package javax.sql.rowset has several concrete classes that implement RowSet, such as CachedRowSet, FilteredRowSet, and WebRowSet. The latter can turn RowSet into an XML stream to be sent to another tier in the distributed application.

## TRANSACTIONAL UPDATES

Sometimes several database modifications have to be processed as one transaction, and if one of the updates fails, the whole transaction has to be *rolled back*. These database operations have to be explicitly *committed* (finalized) in case of success. If you set the auto-commit parameter on the database connection to false, the database transaction will not be committed until the code explicitly calls the method commit(), as in the following example:

```
try{
  conn.setAutoCommit(false);

  Statement stmt = con.createStatement();

  stmt.addBatch("insert into Orders " +
              "values(123, 'Buy','IBM',200)");
  stmt.addBatch("insert into OrderDetail " +
              "values('JSmith', 'Broker131', '05/20/02')");
  stmt.executeBatch();

  conn.commit();     // Transaction succeded

}catch(SQLException e){
  conn.rollback();  // Transaction failed
  e.printStackTrace();
}
```

In the preceding code snippet two `Insert` statements have to be executed as one transaction, and if any of them fails, an exception will be thrown and the method `rollback()` will undo all the changes, including those that succeeded.

## CONNECTION POOLS AND DATASOURCES

Up until now you've been running all sample Java programs on your own computer. But imagine a distributed application in which multiple clients make requests to the same server, which has to process their SQL queries. Because obtaining a connection to the database is a slow process, it would be very inefficient to start every SQL request by obtaining a database connection and disconnecting after the request is complete. Such applications should reuse the same opened connection for multiple requests.

The package `javax.sql` includes the interface `DataSource`, which is an alternative to `DriverManager`. Vendors of JDBC drivers for servers implement this interface, and a `DataSource` is typically preconfigured for a certain number of connections (the *connection pool*). It is published in a directory using the JNDI interface. In such a setup, all clients' requests will get their database connections from this `DataSource` object, eliminating the need to open and close a new connection for each request. I'll provide an example of working with `DataSource` objects in Lesson 31 after explaining how JNDI works.

## TRY IT

In this assignment you'll modify the class `Portfolio` from Lesson 22, which was just printing some hard-coded statements. Now you'll create and populate the database table Portfolio and then read and display the data from there.

## Lesson Requirements

You should have Java installed.

> *You can download the code and resources for this Try It from the book's web page at www.wrox.com. You can find them in the Lesson22 folder in the download.*

## Hint

Obtaining a database connection is a slow operation, and doing it from inside the method `run()` every time you start a new thread is not the best solution. Consider creating a database connection up front and passing it to the thread before starting it.

## Step-by-Step

1. In the database for Lesson 22, create the table Portfolio using the following SQL statement:

```
create table Portfolio(
id NUMBER NOT NULL,
symbol VARCHAR2(10) NOT NULL,
quantity VARCHAR2(10) NOT NULL,
price NUMBER NOT NULL, PRIMARY KEY (id)
);
```

2. Populate the table Portfolio with three records, for stocks traded under the symbols IBM, AMZN, and AAPL respectively:

```
insert into Portfolio  values (1,'IBM',500,105.50),
  (2,'AMZN',1000,15.25),(3,'AAPL',2000,272.50);
```

3. Create a new Eclipse project called Lesson22.

4. Create a class called `Portfolio` that is similar to the one shown in Listing 20-5, but instead of just printing "You have 500 shares of IBM," have it connect to the database, select all the data from the table `Portfolio`, and print the symbol, quantity, and total value. (Calculate total value by multiplying price by quantity.)

5. Create a testing class called `ShowMyPortfolio` that instantiates and starts the thread `Portfolio`.

6. Test this program.

 *Please select Lesson 22 on the DVD to view the video that accompanies this lesson.*

# Swing with JTable

In this lesson you'll learn how to work with a Swing control that is advanced and popular for enterprise applications: JTable. This UI component enables you to present data in a grid with rows and columns. After learning the basics of working with JTable, in the Try It section you'll apply these new skills to display the portfolio data that, as of Lesson 22, is stored in the database.

In other words, you'll build a client-server application, where the Swing-based GUI is a client and the RDBMS is a server. Such architecture was pretty popular in the mid-nineties. Rich clients were developed in Visual Basic, PowerBuilder, Delphi, Java, or C++, and they connected directly to database servers such as Oracle, DB2, Sybase, Microsoft SQL Server, and Informix.

In the late nineties, thin clients (plain-looking HTML-based web pages with almost no code implementing business logic) became the trend. These days applications with rich UIs are coming back, but typically you'll be using an application server as a middleman between the client and the data storage. I'll describe such middlemen starting in Lesson 26, but your UI skills would be incomplete without your knowing how to program data grids.

## JTABLE AND THE MVC PARADIGM

The Swing class JTable is a powerful UI component created for displaying tabular data like a spreadsheet. The data is represented as rows and columns; that's why the JTable component is often used to display data from relational databases, which store data similarly. JTable was designed according to the *Model-View-Controller (MVC)* design pattern, according to which components responsible for presentation (or the view) are separated from components that store data (or the model) for that presentation. In general, design patterns suggest language-independent solutions for common programming tasks.

JTable is responsible for the visible portion of the grid (the V part of MVC), but the data has to be stored in a different Java class that implements the TableModel interface (the M part). Any other UI component can play the role of the controller (the C part) and initiate some actions that will move the data from model to view or vice versa. For example, a click on the JButton can initiate the population of the table model from the database and display the data in JTable.

# THE MODEL

Swing includes the classes `DefaultTableModel` and `AbstractTableModel`, which implement the `TableModel` interface and have methods to notify a `JTable` when the data is changing.

A programmer usually creates a model as a subclass of `AbstractTableModel`, and this class has to contain the data in some collection, for example `ArrayList`. When `JTable` needs to be populated, it requests the data from a class that implements `TableModel`, invoking such callback methods as `getColumnCount()` and `getValueAt()`. When a Swing program creates an instance of `JTable` it has to assign to it a corresponding table model class. Listing 23-1 shows how the class `MyTableModel` (created by you) is given to the constructor of `JTable`.

Typically, the UI class that creates `JTable` defines one or more listeners that are notified of any changes in the table's data. The incomplete class `MyFrame` in Listing 23-1 implements the `TableModelListener` interface that defines just one method - `tableChanged()`. This method should contain the code performing data modifications, for example code to save the data in the database.

**LISTING 23-1:** A window with JTable

```java
package com.practicaljava.lesson23;

import javax.swing.*;
import javax.swing.table.AbstractTableModel;
import javax.swing.event.TableModelEvent;
import javax.swing.event.TableModelListener;

public class MyFrame  extends JFrame implements TableModelListener{

  private MyTableModel myTableModel;
  private JTable myTable;

  MyFrame (String winTitle){
  super(winTitle);

  myTableModel = new MyTableModel();
  myTable = new JTable(myTableModel );

  //Add the JTable to frame and enable scrolling
  add(new JScrollPane( myTable));

  // Register an event listener
   myTableModel.addTableModelListener(this);
  }

  public void tableChanged(TableModelEvent e) {
   // Code to process data changes goes here
  }

  public static void main(String args[]){
```

```
    MyFrame myFrame = new MyFrame( "My Test Window" );

    myFrame.pack();
    myFrame.setVisible( true );

}

    class MyTableModel extends AbstractTableModel {
      // The data for JTable should be here
    }

}
```

In very simple cases you can create a JTable without declaring a table model class (JTable has a no-argument constructor), but Java will internally use its DefaultTableModel class anyway. My sample class MyFrame, though, will use the data model that's a subclass of the AbstractTableModel.

Note that the class MyTableModel is an inner class declared inside the class MyFrame. Having a model as an inner class is not a must, but if the data model will be used with only one specific JTable, its model might as well be declared inside the same class.

The code in Listing 23-1 is not complete; it doesn't include any data yet, and the table model must include the mandatory callbacks described in the next section.

## Mandatory Callbacks of Table Models

The class that implements the TableModel interface and feeds data to JTable must include at least three callback methods: getColumnCount(), getRowCount(), and getValueAt().

The method getColumnCount() must return an integer value — the number of columns in this JTable. This method will be called once by a JTable. For example, if you are planning to display orders, each of which consists of four fields — order ID, stock symbol, quantity, and price — just put one line in this method:

```
    return 4;
```

The method getRowCount() must return an integer — it will also be called only once. The data has to be placed into an array or a data collection (such as ArrayList MyData) before it appears on the screen, and the code for this method could look like this:

```
    return myData.size(); //myData is an ArrayList in this sample
```

The method getValueAt(int row, int col) returns an Object and will be called once for each cell (each intersection of a row and a column). You have to write the code that will return the value for the requested row and column.

Let's say you have a class called Order, as shown in Listing 23-2, and you want to store instances of this class in ArrayList myData. This is going to be your data storage.

**LISTING 23-2:** The Order class

```java
public class Order {
  private int orderID;
  private String stockSymbol;
  private int quantity;
  private float price;

    public Order(int id, String stockSymbol, int quantity, float price){
        orderID=id;
        this.stockSymbol=stockSymbol;
        this.quantity=quantity;
        this.price=price;
    }
}
```

Whenever the callback getValueAt(int row, int col) is called on the model, you have to return
the cell value based on the passed row and column. The inner class MyTableModel from Listing 23-3
includes the method getValueAt() working with myData, which is an ArrayList of Order objects.

**LISTING 23-3:** The JFrame window with implemented table model

```java
public class MyFrame  extends JFrame implements TableModelListener{

        MyTableModel myTableModel;
        JTable myTable;

  MyFrame (String winTitle){
   super(winTitle);

   myTableModel = new MyTableModel();
   myTable = new JTable(myTableModel );

   //Add the JTable to frame and enable scrolling
   add(new JScrollPane( myTable));

   // Register an event listener
    myTableModel.addTableModelListener(this);
  }

  public void tableChanged(TableModelEvent e) {
   // Code to process data changes goes here
  }

  public static void main(String args[]){
   MyFrame myFrame = new MyFrame( "My Test Window" );

   myFrame.pack();
   myFrame.setVisible( true );

  }

  // Inner class for data model
```

```java
class MyTableModel extends AbstractTableModel {

 ArrayList<Order> myData = new ArrayList<Order>();

MyTableModel(){

     myData.add(new Order(1,"IBM", 100, 135.5f));
     myData.add(new Order(2,"AAPL", 300, 290.12f));
     myData.add(new Order(3,"MOT", 2000, 8.32f));
     myData.add(new Order(4,"ORCL", 500, 27.8f));
}

public int getColumnCount() {
 return 4;
}

public int getRowCount() {
 return myData.size();
}

public Object getValueAt(int row, int col) {

     switch (col) {
       case 0:    // col 1
         return myData.get(row).orderID;
       case 1:    // col 2
           return myData.get(row).stockSymbol;
       case 2:    // col 3
           return myData.get(row).quantity;
       case 3:    // col 4
           return myData.get(row).price;
       default:
         return "";
     }
 }
 }
 }
```

Note the use of generics in the declaration of the myData collection. Another Java feature not to be missed here is *autoboxing* — the primitive Order fields int and float are automatically converted into the corresponding wrapper objects Integer and Float.

Running the program from Listing 23-3 will display the window shown in Figure 23-1. Have you noticed that the window looks a bit unusual? The reason is that I decided to run this program on my MacBook laptop under the Mac OS. Java is a cross-platform language and this code will run without changes under Windows too — the look and feel will be different, though.

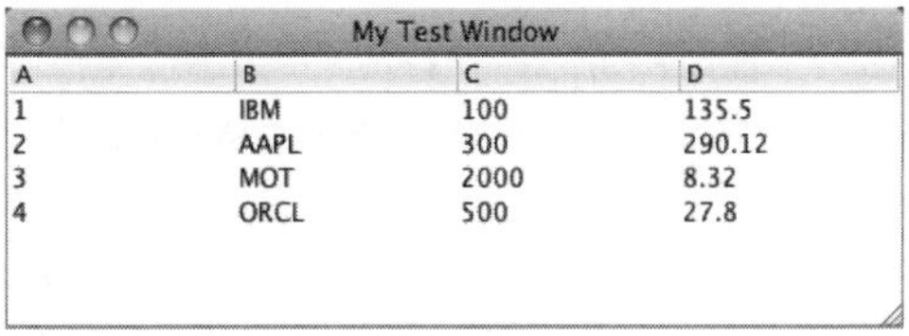

| A | B | C | D |
|---|---|---|---|
| 1 | IBM | 100 | 135.5 |
| 2 | AAPL | 300 | 290.12 |
| 3 | MOT | 2000 | 8.32 |
| 4 | ORCL | 500 | 27.8 |

My Test Window

**FIGURE 23-1**

## Optional Callbacks of Table Models

The JTable shown in Figure 23-1 doesn't show the proper titles of the columns — the auto-generated A, B, C, and D don't count. You can fix this easily by overriding the getColumnName() method in the table model class. This callback, if present, will be called (once for each column) to render the column titles. Add the following code to the class MyTableModel and the window will look as it does in Figure 23-2:

| Order ID | Symbol | Quantity | Price |
|----------|--------|----------|-------|
| 1 | IBM | 100 | 135.5 |
| 2 | AAPL | 300 | 290.12 |
| 3 | MOT | 2000 | 8.32 |
| 4 | ORCL | 500 | 27.8 |

**FIGURE 23-2**

```
String[] orderColNames = { "Order ID",  "Symbol", "Quantity", "Price"};

public String getColumnName(int col) {
    return orderColNames[col];
}
```

If you want to make some of the columns or cells editable, just override the isCellEditable() method and return true from this callback for the editable columns. Here's how to make the third column of our JTable editable:

```
public boolean isCellEditable(int row, int col) {

  if (col ==2){
      return true;
  } else {
    return false;
  }
}
```

If your table has editable columns you need to override the method setValueAt(Object value, int row, int col) and include the code that will copy the data from the UI component — JTable — to the appropriate field in its model objects. This method is called automatically when the user changes the value in a table cell and moves the cursor out of that cell by pressing the Enter or Tab key or by clicking a different cell.

The following method, setValueAt(), will take the modified order quantity and set the new value for the quantity field in the appropriate Order in the model. By default, all the data shown in JTable's cell has the String data type, and it's your responsibility to do proper casting.

```
public void setValueAt(Object value, int row, int col){

  if (col== 2){
  myData.get(row).quantity=(Integer.valueOf(value.toString()));
  }

  //Notify listeners about the data change
  TableModelEvent event = new TableModelEvent(this, row, row, col);
  fireTableChanged(event);
}
```

The `fireTableChanged()` method has been placed in the `setValueAt()` method to notify any listener(s) who want to know about the data changes. For example, if the quantity on any order has been changed and has gone over a certain threshold, the application may need to immediately perform some actions to report this to some authority.

Review the code in Listing 23-3. The class `MyFrame` implements `TableModelListener`, so the method `tableChanged()` will be invoked as a result of the `fireTableChanged()` method call. Add the following line to the `tableChanged()` method:

```
System.out.println("Someone modified the data in JTable!");
```

Now run the program and modify the quantity in any row of `JTable`. The message will be printed on the system console. But JVM fires a table changed event with a payload — `TableModelEvent` — that carries useful information about what exactly has changed in the table model.

`TableModelEvent` has several constructors; I've chosen the one that takes modified rows and columns as arguments. For example, if you change the quantity in the last row, as shown in Figure 23-2, the method `tableChanged()` will receive an instance of `TableModelEvent` that will encapsulate the reference to the entire model encapsulating the following values describing the change:

```
column=2    //  the third column
firstRow=3  //  starting from the row #4
lastRow=3   //  ending with the row #4
```

Based on this information you can implement any further processing required by the functional specification of your application. If you need to apply the UI changes to the database, the method `tableChanged()` can be the right place to use the JDBC API or other communication with the server-side code to persist the changes.

There are several functions with names that start with the word `fire`. For example, to apply each cell's change to the database, call the method `fireTableCellUpdated()`. To apply all changes at once, call the method `fireTableDataChanged()`. Refer to the documentation of the class `AbstractTableModel` to decide which method fits your needs.

## INTRODUCTION TO RENDERERS

The process of transferring data from the table model to `JTable` is performed by *cell renderers*. When the user is modifying the content of the cell, the *cell editor* is engaged. By default, the content of each cell in a `JTable` is rendered using one of three default renderers, based on the type of data in the column. Boolean values are rendered as checkboxes, `javax.swing.Icon` is rendered as an image, and any other object is rendered as a string of characters.

To change the default rendering (for example, if you don't want to see checkboxes for Boolean values) you can either override the callback `getColumnClass()` or define a *custom cell renderer*. The latter option gives you a lot more flexibility. For example, you may need to display a photo of a person and his or her name in each cell. Or you may need to show cell values that meet certain criteria in a different color. To do something like one of these, you need to create a custom renderer.

The UI portion of each column is represented by the class `TableColumn`, which has a property, `cellRenderer`, of type `TableCellRenderer`, which defines the only method: `getTableCellRendererComponent()`. This method prepares the content for each column's cells of `JTable` and returns an instance of the `Component` class to be used for the cell rendering. This process will use `DefaultTableCellRenderer` unless you create a custom renderer. Custom renderers give you full control over how the cell is displayed.

The class `DefaultTableCellRenderer` extends `JLabel` and is Swing's implementation of the `TableCellRenderer` interface. Let's look at an example that formats the text in the Price column shown in Figure 23-2 to be right-justified and to display in red all prices greater than $100.

First the code fragment from Listing 23-4 gets a reference to the fourth column of `JTable` (remember, column numbering is zero-based). Then it needs to call the method `setCellRenderer()` on this column, provided that the custom renderer class was defined and instantiated. But you can define, instantiate, and set the custom renderer in one shot by using the mechanism of *anonymous inner classes*.

The anonymous inner class in Listing 23-4 extends the class `DefaultTableCellRenderer` and overrides the callback method `getTableCellRendererComponent()`. The latter sets the cell value to be right-justified and to be red if it is greater than 100. At the end, the method `getTableCellRendererComponent()` returns a `JLabel` object to be rendered in the current cell of `JTable`.

---

**LISTING 23-4: Custom rendering of the Price value**

```
//Assign custom cell renderer to the Price column
// Get the reference to the fourth column - Price

TableColumn column = myTable.getColumnModel().getColumn(3);

// Create a new cell renderer as an anonymous inner
// class and assign it to the column price

column.setCellRenderer(
      new DefaultTableCellRenderer(){
    public Component  getTableCellRendererComponent(
          JTable table, Object value, boolean isSelected,
                    boolean hasFocus, int row, int col) {

        JLabel label = (JLabel) super.getTableCellRendererComponent(
              table, value, isSelected, hasFocus, row, col);

        // right-align the price value
        label.setHorizontalAlignment(JLabel.RIGHT);

        // display stocks that cost more than $100 in red
        if (((Float) value)>100){
           label.setForeground(Color.RED);
        } else{
```

```
        label.setForeground(Color.BLACK);
    }

    return label;

    } // end of getTableCellRendererComponent
  } // end of new DefaultTableCellRenderer
); // end of setCellRenderer(...)
```

Add this code fragment at the end of the constructor in the class `MyFrame` from Listing 23-3 and run the application. The screen will show the text in the Price column right-justified and the first two prices printed in red (see Figure 23-3).

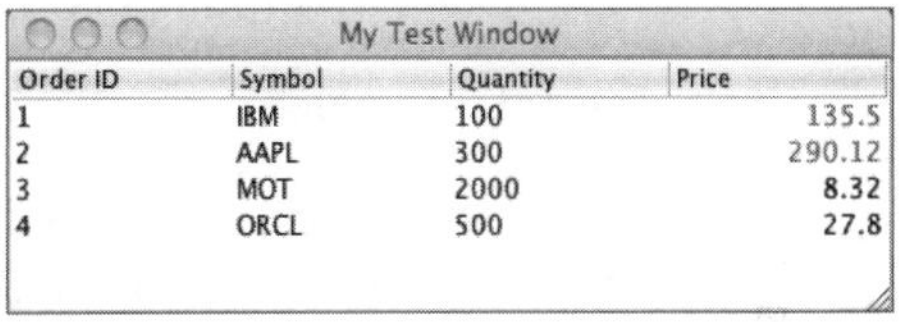

| Order ID | Symbol | Quantity | Price |
|---|---|---|---|
| My Test Window | | | |
| 1 | IBM | 100 | 135.5 |
| 2 | AAPL | 300 | 290.12 |
| 3 | MOT | 2000 | 8.32 |
| 4 | ORCL | 500 | 27.8 |

**FIGURE 23-3**

## SUMMARY

This lesson was a high-level overview of the `JTable` component, which is probably the most advanced UI component that deserves serious study if you are planning to develop Java Swing applications. You can continue studying all the features of `JTable` by following the official Oracle tutorial at `http://download.oracle.com/javase/tutorial/uiswing/components/table.html`.

## TRY IT

Create an application that will display your portfolio, stored in the database table. You'll need to use the database and the Portfolio table you created in the Try It section of Lesson 22.

## Lesson Requirements

You should have Java installed.

> *You can download the code and resources for this Try It from the book's web page at* `www.wrox.com`. *You can find them in the Lesson23 folder in the download.*

## Hint

In Windows, the Java installation directory includes several examples of `JTable`, which can serve as good complementary material to this lesson. Just go to the folder `demo\jfc\TableExample` and follow the instructions in the `Readme` document.

## Step-by-Step

1. Create the Eclipse project Lesson23. Copy there the classes `MyFrame` and `Order` from the accompanying DVD. Compile and run the program to ensure that it displays hard-coded portfolio data, as shown in Figure 23-2.

2. Replace the hard-coded table model `ArrayCollection myData` with the JDBC code to connect to the database Lesson22, run the appropriate SQL `Select` statement, and populate `myData` with data from the received result set.

3. Test this program.

*Please select Lesson 23 on the DVD to view the video that accompanies this lesson.*

# 24

# Annotations and Reflection

In general, *metadata* is data about your data. In the context of DBMSes, metadata can be information describing the way you store data, such as the table and field names or primary keys. Program code metadata is data about your code. Any Java class has its metadata embedded, and you can write a program that "asks" another class, "What methods do you have?" or similar questions about class fields, constructors and ancestors.

If you've ever looked at the source code of any Java class, you can easily identify Javadoc-style comments for classes, interfaces, variables, and methods. These comments may include specially formatted words.

In Eclipse you can select any Java class and press F3 to open the source code of this class. Because the previous lesson was about working with JTable, let's open the source code of this class. In the top part of the code you'll find a description similar to the one that follows (I removed a large portion of the text for brevity):

```
/**
 * The <code>JTable</code> is used to display and edit regular two-dimensional
 * tables of cells.
 * To enable sorting and filtering of rows, use a
 * {@code RowSorter}.
 *  * As for all <code>JComponent</code> classes, you can use
 * {@link InputMap} and {@link ActionMap} to associate an
 * {@link Action} object with a {@link KeyStroke} and execute the
 * action under specified conditions.
 * <p>
 * <strong>Warning:</strong> Swing is not thread safe. For more
 * information see <a
 * href="package-summary.html#threading">Swing's Threading
 * Policy</a>.
 * <p>
 *
 * @version 1.292 05/30/08
```

```
 * @author Philip Milne
 * @author Shannon Hickey (printing support)
 * @see javax.swing.table.DefaultTableModel
 * @see javax.swing.table.TableRowSorter
 */
```

The special words marked with an @ sign are Javadoc metadata describing links, version, author, and related classes to see in Java documentation. If you run the source code of this class through the Javadoc utility the utility will generate HTML output that can be opened by any web browser. It's a good practice to include Javadoc comments in your classes.

Javadoc acts as a processing tool that extracts from the source code all comment blocks that start with /** and end with */. It then formats this text using HTML tags and embedded annotations to generate program documentation. The preceding text is an example of the use of specific tags that are predefined, and understood by Javadoc. This was an example of metadata that are understood by just one utility — Javadoc.

But Java allows you to declare your own custom annotations and define your own processing rules that will route the execution of your program and produce configuration files, additional code, deployment descriptors, and more. No matter what your goals, when you create annotations you also need to create or use an *annotation processor* to get the expected output.

Starting in Lesson 27 you'll learn about annotations defined by the creators of Java EE technologies. But in this lesson you'll get familiar with Java SE annotations, which you will eventually use in your projects.

## JAVA ANNOTATIONS BASICS

The Java annotation model enables you to add custom annotations anywhere in your code, not just in the comments section. You can apply custom annotations to a class, a method, or a variable — just specify allowed *targets* when the annotation is being defined. Java annotations start with the @ sign and may optionally have one or more parameters. Some of the annotations are built into Java SE and are used by the javac compiler, but most of them are consumed by some kind of processing program or tool.

There are about a dozen of predefined annotations already included with Java SE. You can find them, along with their supporting classes, in the packages java.lang, java.lang.annotation, and javax.annotation. You can check the Annotations section of the latest online documentation on the Java SE API, which at the time of this writing is located at http://download.oracle.com/javase/7/docs/api/overview-summary.html.

Some of these annotations are used by the compiler (@Override, @SuppressWarning, @Deprecated, @Target, @Retention, @Documented, and @Inherited); some are used by the Java SE run time or third-party run times and indicate methods that have to be invoked in a certain order (@PostConstruct, @PreDestroy), or mark code that was generated by third-party tools (@Generated). I'm not going to give you a detailed description of how to use each of these annotations, but I will give you selected examples that will help you get started with annotations.

# @Override

In the Try It section of Lesson 3 you overrode the method `public double calcTax()` in the class `NJTax`. The method signature of `calcTax()` was the same in both `NJTax` and its superclass `Tax`. Now deliberately add an argument to `calcTax()` in NJTax, as if you had done so by accident. The code will compile with no errors. But you could have done this by mistake, and instead of overriding the method as planned, you've overloaded it. This won't happen if you use the annotation `@Override` whenever you are planning to override a method:

```
@Override public double calcTax(String something)
```

Now the compiler will complain with the following error:

```
The method calcTax(String) of type NJTax must override or implement a supertype
method
```

The annotation `@Override` signals the compiler that overriding is expected, and that it has to fail if an override does not occur.

# @SuppressWarning

The compiler can generate warning messages that won't stop your program from running, but that do indicate potential problems. In some cases, though, you want to suppress some or all warnings so the output of the project build looks clean. For example,`-Xlint:none` disables all warnings, while `-Xlint:fallthrough` instructs the compiler to warn you about if you forget to add the `break` statement to the `switch` statement (see Lesson 5). In Eclipse IDE, to set the compiler's options you right-click the project and select Properties ➪ Java Compiler ➪ Errors/Warnings ➪ Potential Programming Problems.

But what if you want to omit the `break` keyword in the `switch` statement on purpose? You still want to get warned in all other cases about missing `break`, but not in this particular method. This is where the `@SupressWarnings` annotation becomes quite handy and Listing 24-1 illustrates it. To see this example at work, turn on the compiler's option that warns you about the `switch case` fall-throughs.

**LISTING 24-1:** Custom rendering of the Price value

```
package com.practicaljava.lesson24;

public class SuppressWarningDemo {

    @SuppressWarnings("fallthrough")
    public static void main(String[] args) {
        int salaryBand=3;
      int bonus;
     // Retrieve the salary band of the person from some data source here
        switch(salaryBand){
         case 1:
             bonus=1000;
             System.out.println("Giving bonus " + bonus);
             break;
```

*continues*

**LISTING 24-1** *(continued)*

```
            case 2:
                bonus=2000;
                System.out.println("Giving bonus " + bonus);
                break;
            case 3:
                bonus=6000;
                System.out.println("Giving bonus " + bonus);
            case 4:
                bonus=10000;
                System.out.println("Giving bonus " + bonus);
                break;
            default:
                // wrong salary band
                 System.out.println("Invalid salary band");
        }
    }
}
```

Note that the `break` keyword is missing in the `case 3` section. In this code it's done on purpose: All employees in `salaryBand` 3 are entitled to two bonuses — six thousand dollars in addition to ten thousand dollars. The compiler's annotation `@SuppressWarnings("fallthrough")` suppresses compiler warnings only for this method. In all other classes or methods that may have `switch` statements, the warning will be generated.

## @Deprecated

If you are developing classes that are going to be used by someone else, mark as `@Deprecated` any classes or methods that may be removed in future versions of your code. Other developers will still be able to use this code, but they'll be warned that switching to newer versions is highly recommended.

## @Inherited

This annotation simply means that the annotation has to be inherited by descendants of the class in which it is used. You'll see an example of its use in the next section.

## @Documented

If you want an annotation to be included in the Javadoc utility, mark it as `@Documented`. You'll see an example of this annotation in the next section.

## CUSTOM ANNOTATIONS

Creating your own annotations is more interesting than using core Java or third-party annotations. First of all, you have to decide what you need an annotation for and what properties it should have. Then you need to specify the allowed *targets* for this annotation (for example, class, method, or variable). Finally, you have to define your *retention policy* — how long and where this annotation will live. Let's go through an example to illustrate all these steps.

Suppose you need to create an annotation that will allow the user to mark class methods with a SQL statement to be executed during the run time. These classes will be loaded dynamically. The goal is to declare your own annotation to be used by other Java classes, and to write the annotation processor that will read these Java classes, identify and parse annotations and the values of their parameters, if any, and do whatever is required accordingly.

Declaring annotations is very similar to declaring interfaces, but don't forget to add the @ sign at the beginning. I'll name my annotation MyJDBCExecutor:

```
public @interface MyJDBCExecutor{

}
```

If metadata is data about data, then *meta-annotations* are annotations about annotations. This is not as confusing as it sounds. To specify where you can use this newborn annotation, define the meta-annotation @Target. The enumeration ElementType defines possible target values: METHOD, TYPE, CONSTRUCTOR, FIELD, PARAMETER, PACKAGE, LOCAL_VARIABLE, and ANNOTATION_TYPE. If you don't use @Target, the annotation can be used anywhere. For example, this is how you can allow use of the annotation only with methods and constructors:

```
import java.lang.annotation.*;

@Inherited
@Documented
@Target({ ElementType.METHOD, ElementType.CONSTRUCTOR })
@Retention(RetentionPolicy.SOURCE)
public @interface MyJDBCExecutor {

}
```

The retention policy in the preceding code snippet is set to SOURCE, which means that this annotation will be used for processing only during the compilation of your program. The other two allowed values for retention policy are RUNTIME and CLASS.

Annotations with the CLASS retention policy stay in the compiled class, but are not loaded during run time. The CLASS retention policy is used by default if a retention policy is not explicitly specified.

Annotations with the RUNTIME retention policy have to be processed by a custom processing tool when the compiled code is running.

Annotations may have parameters. Say we want to add a single parameter that will allow us to specify an SQL statement to be processed. Our MyJDBCExecutor has to be declared as follows (omitting the import statement):

```
@Target({ ElementType.METHOD, ElementType.CONSTRUCTOR })
@Retention(RetentionPolicy.SOURCE)
public @interface MyJDBCExecutor {
    String value();
}
```

A sample Java class, `HRBrowser`, may use this annotation like this:

```
class HRBrowser{

  @MyJDBCExecutor (value="Select * from Employee")
  public List getEmployees(){
     // add calls to some JDBC executing engine here
  }

}
```

If the annotation has only one parameter named `value`, the "value=" part in the preceding code snippet is not required. But I'd like this annotation to have three parameters: SQL to execute, transactional support, and a notification flag to inform other users of the application about any database modifications. Let's add more parameters to our annotation:

```
package com.practicaljava.lesson24;

import java.lang.annotation.*;

@Target({ ElementType.METHOD})
@Retention(RetentionPolicy.SOURCE)
public @interface MyJDBCExecutor {
        String sqlStatement();
        boolean transactionRequired() default false;
        boolean notifyOnUpdates() default false;

}
```

I've replaced the parameter `value` with a more meaningful `sqlStatement`, and added two more: `transactionRequired` and `notifyOnUpdates`. I gave the latter two default values. If a Java class won't need to support transactions and notify other applications about updates, why force software developers to provide values for these parameters?

If we don't specify default values the Java compiler will generate compilation errors if the values for `transactionRequired` and `notifyOnUpdates` are missing in classes that use `@MyJDBCExecutor`. Here's an example of a class, `HRBrowser`, that's annotated only with a `select` statement — no other actions are needed here:

```
class HRBrowser{

  @MyJDBCExecutor (sqlStatement="Select * from Employee")
  public List<Employee> getEmployees(){
     // The code to get the the data from DBMS goes here,
     // result set goes in ArrayList, which is returned to the
     // caller of the method getEmployees()
     ...
     return myEmployeeList;
  }
}
```

The code sample in Listing 24-2 adds the method `updateData()` and uses all three annotation parameters.

**LISTING 24-2:** Using the annotation MyJDBCExecutor

```
class HRBrowser{

@MyJDBCExecutor (sqlStatement="Select * from Employee")
public List<Employee> getEmployees(){
        // Generate the code to get the the data from DBMS,
        // place them in ArrayList and return them to the
        // caller of my getEmployees
           ...
              return myEmployeeList;
}

@MyJDBCExecutor (
          sqlStatement="Update Employee set bonus=1000",
          transactionRequired=true,
          notifyOnUpdates=true)
public void updateData(){
    // JDBC code to perform transactional updates  and
    // notifications goes here
  }
}
```

The annotations with the SOURCE retention policy can be processed by the Annotation Processing Tool (APT) located in the bin directory of your Java installation. As a result of such processing, the new source code may be generated for further compilation. (The use of APT is an advanced subject and is out of the scope of this tutorial. Refer to the following web page for more information: http://download.oracle.com/javase/1.5.0/docs/guide/apt/GettingStarted.html.)

I was involved in the development of an open-source code generator called Clear Data Builder (CDB) (available at http://sourceforge.net/projects/cleartoolkit/). The CDB allows the user to write a simple Java class that has an abstract method annotated with an SQL statement and several other parameters, and within seconds to generate complete code for the functional application that has Adobe Flex code on the client side talking to Java at the server, which is accessing data stored in any relational DBMS via JDBC. In this project we used only the annotations with the SOURCE retention policy, and before compiling classes would generate additional code according to specified annotations.

If CDB would be processing the annotation @MyJDBCExecutor, it would engage additional tools and generate and compile all JDBC code for the methods getEmployees() and updateData() automatically.

For the annotations with the RUNTIME retention policy you should know how to write an annotation processor, however, as it has to "extract" the values from the annotations during run time, and, based on those values, engage the appropriate code. But there is one Java feature, *reflection*, that you must understand before you can write your own annotation-processing class.

## REFLECTION

Strictly speaking the subject of Java reflection doesn't belong to the lesson on annotations — reflection is used widely in various areas of Java development. But because this subject has to be covered before you can proceed with annotation processing, I decided to include it here.

Reflection enables you to find out about the internals of a Java class (its methods, constructors, and fields) during the run time, and to invoke the discovered methods or access public member variables. A special class called `Class` can load the class in memory, and then you can explore the content of the class by using classes from the package `java.lang.reflect`. Consider the class `Employee`, shown in Listing 24-3.

**LISTING 24-3:** Class Employee extends Person

```
abstract public class Person {
   abstract public void raiseSalary();
}

public class Employee extends Person{
 public void raiseSalary() {
    System.out.println("Raising salary for Employee...");
  }
}
```

The `ReflectionSample` class in Listing 24-4 loads the class `Employee`, prints its method signatures, and finds its superclass and methods. The process of querying an object about its content during run time is called *introspection*.

**LISTING 24-4:** Introspecting Employee

```
import java.lang.reflect.*;
public class ReflectionSample {
   public static void main(String args[]) {
       try {
          Class c = Class.forName("Employee");
          Method methods[] = c.getDeclaredMethods();
          System.out.println("The  Employee methods:");

          for (int i = 0; i < methods.length; i++){
              System.out.println("*** Method Signature:" +
                                  methods[i].toString());
          }

          Class superClass = c.getSuperclass();
          System.out.println("The name of the superclass is "
                              + superClass.getName());

          Method superMethods[] = superClass.getDeclaredMethods();
          System.out.println("The superclass has:");

          for (int i = 0; i < superMethods.length; i++){
              System.out.println("*** Method Signature:" +
                                  superMethods[i].toString());
              System.out.println("      Return type: " +
                  superMethods[i].getReturnType().getName());
```

```
        }

    } catch (Exception e) {
        e.printStackTrace();
    }
  }
}
```

Here's the output of the program ReflectionSample:

```
The  Employee methods:
*** Method Signature:public void Employee.raiseSalary()
The name of the superclass is Person
The superclass has:
*** Method Signature:public abstract void Person.raiseSalary()
      Return type: void
```

Some other useful methods of the class Class are getInterfaces(), getConstructors(), getFields(), and isAnnotationPresent(). The following code snippet shows how to get the names, types, and values of the public member variables of the loaded class:

```
Class c = Class.forName("Employee");

Field[] fields = c.getFields();
for (int i = 0; i < fields.length; i++)   {
   String name = fields[i].getName();
   String type = fields[i].getType().getName();

   System.out.println("Creating an instance of Employee");
   Object obj = c.newInstance();
   Object value = fields[i].get(obj);
   System.out.println("Field Name: " + name + ", Type: "
                  + type + " Value: " + value.toString());
}
```

The process of reflection uses introspection to find out during run time what the methods (or properties) are, but it also can call these methods (or modify these properties). The method invoke() will let you call methods that were discovered during run time:

```
Class c= Class.forName("Employee");
Method raiseSalary = c.getMethod( "raiseSalary", null);
raiseSalary.invoke(c.newInstance(),null);
```

The first argument of the method invoke() represents an instance of the object Employee, and null means that this method doesn't have arguments. With reflection, the arguments are supplied as an array of objects. You can find out what the method arguments are by calling the method Method .getParameterTypes(), or create and populate them on your own, as in the following example. Add the following method to the class Employee:

```
public void  changeAddress(String newAddress) {
    System.out.println("The new address is "+ newAddress);
}
```

Note the `public` qualifier: it's needed for proper introspection, otherwise the `NoSuchMethodException` will be thrown by the following code snippet. The `ReflectionSample` class can invoke `changeAddress()` as follows:

```
Class c= Class.forName("Employee");
Class parameterTypes[]= new Class[] {String.class};
Method myMethod = c.getMethod( "changeAddress", parameterTypes);

Object arguments[] = new Object[1];
arguments[0] = "250 Broadway";
myMethod.invoke(c.newInstance(),arguments);
```

Reflection helps in building dynamic component-based applications that can load different classes based on certain business logic and invoke this logic during run time. Many third-party Java frameworks read configuration files and then instantiate and use required objects.

## RUN-TIME ANNOTATION PROCESSING

The author of a custom run-time annotation usually gives it to other developers along with the processing tool. They will add the annotation to their classes and compile them, and the processing tool will consume these classes during run time. Reuse the code example from Listing 24-2, but this time imagine that `@MyJDBCExecutor` becomes the annotation with `RUNTIME` retention policy and that there is no need to generate additional source code for the compilation time. Suppose this annotation will be used in `HRBrowser`, and another class will have to analyze the annotation parameters and route the execution accordingly.

Now I'll write the annotation processor class called `MyJDBCAnnotationProcessor`, and the class `HRBrowser` in Listing 24-2 can serve as a command-line argument to that processor:

```
c:/>java MyJDBCAnnotationProcessor HRBrowser
```

The class `MyJDBCAnnotationProcessor` has to load the class `HRBrowser`, introspect its content, find the annotations and their values, and process them accordingly. I'll show you how to write such a processor, or rather its annotation-discovery part.

Listing 24-5 shows `MyJDBCAnnotationProcessor`, which starts by loading another class, whose name was supplied in the command line. After that it introspects the loaded class and places all references to its method definitions into an array called `methods`. Finally, it loops through this array, and for each method that has annotations it finds and prints the values of the parameters `sqlStatement`, `notifyOnUpdates`, and `transactionRequired`.

**LISTING 24-5: MyJDBCAnnotationProcessor**

```
import java.lang.reflect.*;
import com.practicaljava.lesson24.MyJDBCExecutor;

public class MyJDBCAnnotationProcessor {

  public static void main(String[] args) {
    // TODO add a check for the number of command line arguments
```

```
        // has to be the name of the class to load.

    String classWithAnnotation = args[0];

      try {
         //Load provided on the command line class
        Class loadedClass = Class.forName(classWithAnnotation);

        // Get references to class methods
        Method[] methods = loadedClass.getMethods();

        // Check every method of the class.If the annotation is present,
        // print the values of its parameters

         for (Method m: methods){
          if (m.isAnnotationPresent(MyJDBCExecutor.class)){
                MyJDBCExecutor jdbcAnnotation =
                            m.getAnnotation(MyJDBCExecutor.class);

           System.out.println("Method: " + m.getName() +
             ". Parameters of MyJDBCExecutor are: " +
             "sqlStatement="+ jdbcAnnotation.sqlStatement() +
             ", notifyOnUpdates="+ jdbcAnnotation.notifyOnUpdates() +
             ", transactionRequired="+ jdbcAnnotation.transactionRequired());
          }
        }

    } catch (ClassNotFoundException e) {

                e.printStackTrace();
      }

    }
    }
```

After running this processor with the class HRBrowser, the former correctly identifies the annotated methods and prints the values of their parameters:

```
Method: getEmployees. Parameters of MyJDBCExecutor are: sqlStatement=Select * from
Employee, notifyOnUpdates=false, transactionRequired=false

Method: updateData. Parameters of MyJDBCExecutor are: sqlStatement=Update Employee set
bonus=1000, notifyOnUpdates=true, transactionRequired=true
```

Any class can use more than one annotation. In this case the annotation processor would need to start by getting all annotations of the loaded class using loadedClass.getAnnotations(). It would then process these annotations in a loop.

## SUMMARY

In real-world applications you wouldn't simply be printing the values of the annotation parameters, but rather would be executing different branches of your code based on these values. This is the point of run-time annotation processing. You may ask, "OK, now I know the annotations and their values, so what do I do with them?" The big idea is that you've written a generic processor that can work with any classes that include your annotations. It's a pretty powerful mechanism for all software developers who are creating tools for other people to use.

You'll probably be using annotations and run-time processors written by other people rather than ones you write yourself. You'll see lots of examples of using annotations starting from Lesson 27, while you're learning about Java EE development. But now that you know what's going on under the hood in annotation processors, learning about Java EE annotation will be a lot easier.

## TRY IT

Create a class-level run-time annotation called @DBParams that will enable you to specify the name of the database, the user ID, and the password. Write a processor for this annotation.

## Lesson Requirements

You should have Java installed.

> You can download the code and resources for this Try It from the book's web page at www.wrox.com. You can find them in the Lesson24 folder in the download.

## Step-by-Step

1. Create the Eclipse project Lesson24.

2. Declare there the annotation DBParams with the retention policy RUNTIME targeted to TYPE.

3. Define three parameters in this annotation: dbName, uid, and password.

4. Create the class MyDBWorker and annotate it with @DBParms populated with some initial values.

5. Write an annotation processor class called DBParamProcessor to find and print the annotation values in the class MyDBWorker.

6. Run and test DBParamProcessor.

> Please select Lesson 24 on the DVD to view the video that accompanies this lesson.

# 25

# Remote Method Invocation

So far most of the Java programs in this tutorial have been running in one JVM. There were two exceptions: In Lesson 18 you used two JVMs while learning about socket programming, and your JDBC programs from Lesson 22 communicated with another JVM running database server. The application running on the user's computer isn't always allowed to access remote data directly — that's one of the reasons *distributed Java applications* came into the picture. (The word distributed means having parts of the applications running on several computers.) The other reason was to provide a centralized server catering to multiple lightweight clients.

There are lots of ways to create Java distributed applications that run on more than one JVM, and Remote Method Invocation (RMI) is one of them even though it's being used seldom these days. For example, a client Java application (JVM1) connects to a server Java application (JVM2), which connects to the DBMS that runs on a third computer. The client application knows nothing about the DBMS; it gets the data, an `ArrayList` of `Employee` objects, from the server's application that runs in JVM2. RMI uses object serialization for the data exchange between JVM1 and JVM2.

But unlike with socket programming, where the client explicitly connects to the server, with RMI one Java class can invoke methods on Java objects that live in another (remote) JVM. Although from a syntax perspective it looks as if the caller and the server's class are located in the same JVM, they may be thousands of miles away. The RMI client won't have a copy of the server-side method; it'll just have the method's local representative — a *proxy*, or, using the RMI terminology, a *stub*.

Any RMI application consists of an RMI server, a client, and the *registry* (a naming service). These three components could run on three different JVMs running on different networked computers. The RMI server creates Java objects that implement business logic, registers them with the naming service, and waits for remote clients to invoke methods on them.

A client application gets a reference to a remote server object or objects from the registry and then invokes methods on this remote object. The main concept of RMI is that even though the methods are called in the client's JVM, they are executed on the server's! RMI supporting classes and the registry tool are included with the Java SE.

## DEVELOPING APPLICATIONS WITH RMI

This lesson is written as an illustration of a sample RMI application with a minimum theory. For a more detailed description of RMI please refer to the following website: `http://download.oracle` `.com/javase/6/docs/technotes/guides/rmi/index.html`.

Writing distributed RMI applications involves the following steps:

**1.** Declaring the remote interface.

**2.** Implementing the remote interface.

**3.** Writing a Java client that connects to the remote server and calls remote methods.

**4.** Starting the registry and registering the RMI server with it.

**5.** Starting the server and the client applications.

Let's perform each of these steps by developing the RMI version of the Stock Quotes Server (see its version with sockets in Lesson 18), which will provide a client with price quotes for a specified stock. Some of the following steps could be combined, but for simplicity's sake I'll write a separate class for each required action.

## Defining Remote Interfaces

The Java classes that you are planning to deploy on the server side have to implement *remote interfaces*, which declare business method(s) to be invoked remotely by RMI clients. The client's code will look as if it's calling local methods, but these calls will be redirected to a remote server via the RMI protocol. Following are the rules for creating remote interfaces:

➤ The remote interface must declare public methods to allow clients to perform remote method invocation.

➤ The remote interface must extend `java.rmi.Remote`.

➤ Each method must declare `java.rmi.RemoteException`.

➤ Because method arguments and returned data will be traveling across the network by means of Java serialization, their data type must be `Serializable`.

You start developing the server side of any distributed Java application by answering the question "What business methods have to be exposed to the client applications and what should their signatures be?" When you know the answer, define remote interfaces that declare those methods.

Listing 25-1 shows the code of the `StockServer` remote interface that will be implemented on the server but must exist on the client side too. This interface declares two business methods: `getQuote()` and `getNasdaqSymbols()`. The first will generate a random price quote for the specified symbol, and the second will return the list of valid stock symbols.

**LISTING 25-1:** StockServer interface

```java
package com.practicaljava.lesson25;
import java.rmi.Remote;
import java.rmi.RemoteException;
import java.util.List;

public interface StockServer extends Remote {
    public String getQuote(String symbol) throws RemoteException;

    public List<String> getNasdaqSymbols()throws RemoteException;
}
```

# Implementing Remote Interfaces

Although the remote interface just declares the methods, you need to create a class that will run on the server side and provide implementation for those methods. There is a special requirement to *export* such a class to the Java RMI run time to enable the class to receive remote calls. This is somewhat similar to binding to a port in the case of `ServerSocket` (see Listing 18-5), but in the case of Java RMI the server also creates a stub — a dummy class (for the client side) that contains proxies of each implemented method from remote interfaces.

The easiest way to export an RMI server instance is by extending it from `java.rmi.server` `.UnicastRemoteObject`, as in Listing 25-2. If your server has to be extended from another class you can explicitly export the server object by calling `UnicastRemoteObject.export()`.

Listing 25-2 shows an implementation of the class `StockServerImpl`, which will process the client's requests. This class generates random price quotes for the stocks located in `ArrayList nasdaqSymbols`.

**LISTING 25-2:** StockServerImpl class

```java
package com.practicaljava.lesson25;

import java.rmi.*;
import java.rmi.server.*;
import java.util.ArrayList;

public class StockServerImpl extends UnicastRemoteObject  implements StockServer {
    private String price=null;
    private ArrayList<String> nasdaqSymbols = new ArrayList<String>();

    public StockServerImpl() throws RemoteException {
        super();

        // Define some hard-coded NASDAQ symbols
        nasdaqSymbols.add("AAPL");
        nasdaqSymbols.add("MSFT");
        nasdaqSymbols.add("YHOO");
        nasdaqSymbols.add("AMZN");
```

*continues*

**LISTING 25-2** *(continued)*

```
        nasdaqSymbols.add("MOT");
    }

    public String getQuote(String symbol)
                        throws RemoteException {

        if(nasdaqSymbols.indexOf(symbol.toUpperCase()) != -1) {

            // Generate a random price for valid symbols
            price = (new Double(Math.random()*100)).toString();
        }
        return price;
    }

    public ArrayList<String> getNasdaqSymbols()throws RemoteException {
        return nasdaqSymbols;
    }
}
```

## Registering Remote Objects

To make a remote object available to clients, you need to bind it to some name in a registry, a naming service that knows where exactly in the network your RMI server StockServerImpl is running. This will allow Java clients to look up the object on the host machine by name.

Listing 25-3 depicts the code that binds the instance of StockServerImpl to port 1099 on the host machine, which is the local computer in my example. To the rest of the world this server will be known as QuoteService.

**LISTING 25-3: Starting the server and binding it to a registry**

```
package com.practicaljava.lesson25;

import java.rmi.Naming;
import java.rmi.RMISecurityManager;
import java.net.MalformedURLException;
import java.rmi.RemoteException;

public class StartServer {

    public static void main (String args[]) {

        try {

            StockServerImpl ssi = new StockServerImpl();
            Naming.rebind("rmi://localhost:1099/QuoteService",ssi);

        }catch (MalformedURLException e1){
                System.out.println(e1.getMessage());
```

```
        }catch(RemoteException ex) {
            ex.printStackTrace();
        }
    }
}
```

There are two methods in the class `java.rmi.Naming` that can bind an object in the registry. The method `bind()` binds an RMI server to a name. It throws `AlreadyBoundException` if the binding already exists. The method `rebind()` replaces any preexisting binding with the new one. In addition to binding a server to a name, this also ensures that the clients requesting such services as `getQuotes()` or `getNasdaqSymbols()` receive their stubs — the local proxies of the remote methods.

The registry must be up and running by the time you start the program in Listing 25-3. One way to start the registry is by entering `start rmiregistry` in the Windows command window or `rmiregistry` in Mac OS.

Instead of starting the registry manually, you can start it from within the StartServer program itself by calling the following method:

```
LocateRegistry.createRegistry(1099);
```

If you know that another process has already pre-created the registry, just get its reference and bind the server to it. The `getRegistry()` method can be called without arguments if the RMI registry runs on the default port 1099. If this is not the case, specify the port number (5048 in the following example). The variable `registry` in the following code fragment is a stub to the remote object `StockServerImpl`:

```
StockServerImpl ssi = new StockServerImpl();
Registry registry = LocateRegistry.getRegistry(5048);
registry.bind("QuoteService", ssi);
```

# Writing RMI Clients

The client program, running anywhere on the Internet, performs a lookup in the registry on the host machine (using the host machine's domain name or IP address) and obtains a reference to the remote object. Listing 25-4 shows a sample client program. Notice the casting to the `StockServer` type of the data returned by the method `lookup()`.

Even though the class `StockServerImpl` has been bound to the name `QuoteService`, because this class implements the `StockServer` interface we can cast the returned object to it. The variable `myServer` will see only the methods defined in this interface, while the class `StockSertverImpl` may have other public methods too.

**LISTING 25-4: RMI client**

```
package client;

import java.rmi.*;
```

*continues*

**LISTING 25-4** *(continued)*

```java
import com.practicaljava.lesson25.StockServer;

public class Client {

  public static void main (String args[]) {

    if (args.length == 0) {
      System.out.println("\n Sample usage: java client.Client AAPL");
      System.exit(0);
    }


    try {
        StockServer myServer = (StockServer)
        Naming.lookup("rmi://localhost:1099/QuoteService");

      String price = myServer.getQuote(args[0]);
        if  (price != null){
          System.out.println("The price of " + args[0] +
                            " is: $" + price);
        }
        else{
           System.out.println("Invalid Nasdaq symbol. " +
              "Please use one of these:" +
              myServer.getNasdaqSymbols().toString());
        }

  } catch (MalformedURLException ex) {
        System.out.println(ex.getMessage());
      }catch (RemoteException ex2) {
        System.out.println(ex2.getMessage());
      }
    }
  }
}
```

# Security Considerations

Can any RMI client restrict the actions that remotely loaded code can perform on the local computer? Can the server restrict access? You can specify a security policy file containing access restrictions. For example, in the code in Listings 25-3 and 25-4 you can start the `main()` method with the following:

```java
if (System.getSecurityManager() == null) {
     System.setSecurityManager(new  RMISecurityManager());
  }
```

The class `java.rmi.RMISecurityManager` extends the class `java.lang.SecurityManager` and provides a security context under which the RMI application executes. In RMI clients the goal is to prevent remotely loaded stub code from downloading unsecured code via remote method invocation.

The RMI client uses a file in which security policies are defined. You can use the default security file, `java.policy`, located in your JDK or JRE installation directory under `lib/security`. The default policy file gives all permissions to the code, but you can create your own file and supply it either via the command-line parameter or in the code before the security manager is set:

```
System.setProperty("java.security.policy", "mypolicyfile");
```

For a more detailed description of security policy files refer to the documentation at http://download.oracle.com/javase/1.3/docs/guide/security/PolicyFiles.html.

Java applets can also serve as RMI clients, but they don't need RMI security managers. The only restriction on them is that they can connect only to the RMI server running on the same host on which they were deployed.

## Finding Remote Objects

RMI clients find remote services by using a *naming* or *directory service*. A naming service runs on a known host and port number. The subject of naming and directory services will be covered in more detail in Lesson 31.

By now you know that an RMI server can start its own registry that offers naming services for RMI clients. The behavior of the registry is defined by the interface java.rmi.registry.Registry, and you saw an example of binding to the registry in the section "Registering Remote Objects."

By default the RMI registry runs on port 1099, unless another port number is specified. When the client wants to invoke methods on a remote object it obtains a reference to that object by looking up the name. The lookup returns to the client a remote reference, aka *stub*.

The method lookup() takes the object name's URL as an argument in the following format:

```
rmi://<host_name>[:<name_service_port>]/<service_name>
```

host_name stands for the name of a computer on the local area network (LAN), or the name of a domain name system (DNS) on the Internet. name_service_port has to be specified only if the naming service is running on a port other than the default. service_name stands for the name of the remote object that should be bound to the registry.

Figure 25-1 illustrates the architecture of an RMI application. In the Try It section you'll implement this architecture for our sample stock quote service.

## TRY IT

In this exercise your goal is to start and test all the parts of the distributed Stock Server application, and you'll run all these parts on the same computer. To emulate multiple computers you'll open three command windows: one for the RMI client, one for the

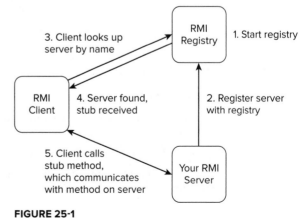

**FIGURE 25-1**

registry, and one for the server. If everything is done properly you should be able to start the RMI client with one of the stock symbols known to the server, and get a price quote back.

## Lesson Requirements

You should have Java installed.

> You can download the code and resources for this Try It from the book's web page at www.wrox.com. You can find them in the Lesson25 folder in the download.

## Hints

There is an RMI plug-in for the Eclipse RMI that may be handy for developing RMI-based distributed applications. It contains a useful utility called RMI Spy that shows all outgoing and incoming method calls, and measures execution times. Another useful utility in this plug-in is Registry Inspector, which displays information about objects in the registry. The RMI plug-in is available from www.genady.net/rmi/index.html.

## Step-by-Step

1. Create an Eclipse project called Lesson25 with two packages: `client` and `com.practicaljava.lesson25`.

2. In `com.practicaljava.lesson25` create the interface `StockServer` that extends `java.rmi.Remote`, as in Listing 25-1.

3. In `com.practicaljava.lesson25` create the class `StockServerImpl` that extends `UnicastRemoteObject` and implements the interface `StockServer`, as in Listing 25-2.

4. In `com.practicaljava.lesson25` create the class `StartServer` from Listing 25-3 to start the server and bind it to the naming service.

5. In `client` create the class `Client` that will access the remote server. Follow the code from Listing 25-4.

6. Compile all the classes.

7. Open three command windows.

8. Start the RMI registry from the first command window. The naming service will listen to default port 1099. If you are running this program in Windows, use the command `start rmiregistry`. If you are running Mac OS, use the command `rmiregistry`.

    Don't expect to see any confirmations that the registry has successfully started. The absence of error messages is your confirmation.

**9.** In the second command window, start and register `StockServer` with the naming service (registry) that you just started. In the command line specify the system property `java.rmi` `.server.codebase` — this is where your `StockServer` compiled class is located. I created this example on my MacBook with the user name yfain11, and my Eclipse workspace was located in the directory `practicalJava`. The `codebase` command-line option starts with `-D` and is shown in bold.

```
java -classpath /Users/yfain11/practicalJava/workspace/Lesson25/bin
-Djava.rmi.server.codebase=
file:/Users/yfain11/practicalJava/workspace/Lesson25/bin/ com.practicaljava.
lesson25.StartServer
```

After you enter a command similar to the preceding, the server will start and bind to the registry, printing the following message in the command window:

```
<QuoteService> server is ready.
```

**10.** Open the third command window and switch to the `bin` directory — the `client` sub-directory should be there, as you created it in Step 1. Run the `Client` program, passing the stock symbol as a command line argument, and the `Client` will connect to your "remote" server and receive the price quote, for example:

```
java client.Client AAPL
```

Figure 25-2 shows how the three command windows look on my MacBook. They will look similar in Windows.

**FIGURE 25-2**

*Please select Lesson 25 on the DVD to view the video that accompanies this lesson.*

# 26

# Java EE 6 Overview

Starting from this lesson you'll be learning about Java Enterprise Edition (Java EE or formerly J2EE), which is a powerful, mature, and widely used platform for development of distributed applications. The word *enterprise* here doesn't imply that it is only for large-scale applications. Java EE components are used for the development of everything from an application for a local pizza parlor's website running on a five-hundred-dollar computer to a super-powerful Wall Street trading application that runs on a *cluster* of hundreds of interconnected servers.

This lesson is an overview of the Java EE architecture, concepts, components, and terms that will be covered in detail in the remaining lessons of this book. The goal of these lessons is to give you an understanding of how to approach the development of Java EE applications by showing you how to build small applications rather than making you read the thousand-page manuscript that would otherwise be required for detailed coverage of this subject.

There are an abundance of online materials and books published on the subject of Java EE, and when you will figure out which components are a good fit for your project, finding materials on the selected topic will not be difficult at all. My task is to help you in making that decision and getting you started in the quickest possible way. The Oracle website Java EE at a Glance is a good complement for this lesson: `www.oracle.com/technetwork/java/javaee/overview/index.html`.

If you start browsing the Internet trying to find more information on Java EE, you can easily get confused by trying to compare the features of different versions of Java EE components. I highly recommend that you stay focused on the features of Java EE 6, which is the most current platform and the easiest to use. It was released in December 2009.

## THE BIG PICTURE

Go to your favorite online job search engine and search for job listings with the keyword *J2EE*. Even though J2EE was re-branded into Java EE many years ago, recruiters and job agencies keep referring to this platform as J2EE. Here's one of many job descriptions I found on a major Internet job board:

**Title:** Java/J2EE Engineer with Core Java, Hibernate

**Skills:** J2EE, JMS, Spring, MQ, EJB, J2EE, Servlets, JDK, Core Java, Websphere, Junit, log4j, Apache, Oracle, SQL

The candidate should know:

* Core Java 6

* Expertise in EJB, J2EE, Servlets

* Expertise in Web Services, JAX-WS, JAX-RPC

* Working knowledge of Hibernate, JDBC, JPA (Oracle)

* Java Frameworks: JUnit, Log4j

* Oracle 11, SQL

* Expertise in Development IDEs: Eclipse/RAD

* Knowledge of Spring framework

* WebSphere Application Server v6/7

* JMS and WebSphere MQ v6/7

How many items from this list of skills did you recognize after mastering the first 25 lessons of this book? You know Core Java 6, JDBC, Eclipse, and SQL. After studying the remaining lessons you'll understand what other skills are required in this ad, why they are required, and how they all fit together. You'll also have technical knowledge of many of the buzzwords listed there.

## JCP, JSR, and Other Acronyms

The Java community is accustomed to lots of acronyms. Initially these acronyms might sound intimidating and confusing, but with a little effort they will make perfect sense and explain the way the Java ecosystem lives and functions.

Each version of Java EE includes a set of specifications for various technologies, such as Servlets, JavaServer Pages (JSP), Enterprise Java Beans (EJB), and Java Messaging Service (JMS). Each of these specifications has been defined by an organization called the Java Community Process (JCP). If a person or a group of people decides to propose a specification for some future technology, it will create a Java Specification Request (JSR) and form a group of experts to work on this specification. JSRs are numbered. For example, the specification for Servlets 3.0 was described in JSR 315.

If you decide to get familiar with any specific JSR, visit the website `http://jcp.org`. Currently Java EE includes 45 JSRs, Java SE has 44, and Java ME (Micro Edition covers small devices) has 85. In other words, Java EE is based on standards. If you'd like to get hold of the 33 specifications that were included in Java EE 6, they are described in JSR 316 and are available at `http://jcp.org/aboutJava/communityprocess/final/jsr316/index.html`.

## Tiers of Java EE Applications

A typical distributed Java application can be divided into three or four logical tiers. (If the application is getting data directly from a DBMS, as described in Lesson 22, it has a two-tier client-server architecture, and Java EE components are not needed.) Figure 26-1 shows selected technologies and possible ways of building a distributed application that includes Java EE tiers or layers.

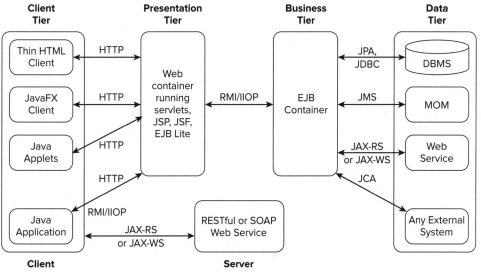

**FIGURE 26-1**

The client tier can be implemented on a user's desktop, notebook, or mobile phone, or any other device that has JRE or can connect with Java on the web server. You can create a client as an independent Java application, an applet, or a *thin client* (an HTML/JavaScript file running in a web browser). The word *thin* refers to the fact that no business processing is being done on the client side, so the server has to work hard processing all application logic for all clients.

If you're building a web application, the web tier (aka the *presentation tier*) comes into the picture. You have your choice of JSP, JavaServer Face (JSF), Servlets, or web services. These components are responsible for the look of your thin client. Java Swing and JavaFX are typically (but not necessarily) used as *fat clients* of web applications. The word *fat* here refers to the fact that the client can contain some business logic, which minimizes the load on the server.

The business logic of your application is placed in the business tier, which is represented by EJBs. In the past EJBs were pretty heavy components and third-party frameworks such as Spring (see Lesson 35) became a popular choice for implementing the business tier. But Java EE 6 will regain its market share in this department because it's a light POJO- and annotation-based technology that incorporates the best features of the third-party framework. POJO stands for *plain old Java object* — a Java class that can be written any way you want and doesn't have to extend any framework class or implement mandatory interfaces. This term is easily understood by people who witnessed the evolution of EJBs, which were Java classes that had to be written and deployed in a certain convoluted way and accompanied by heavy XML configuration files. Things changed drastically, and now EJBs have turned into POJOs marked with annotations. If for some reason you skipped Lesson 24 on annotations, you should go back and study it; otherwise you won't understand most of the remaining material in this book.

While drawing the diagram for Figure 26-1, I moved the Web Services box a couple of times between the presentation and business tiers. On one hand, Web Services (see Lesson 34) are based on web communication protocols; on the other hand they can serve as a façade hiding anything, including an entire legacy application written in COBOL on mainframes. In the final version of my diagram, Web Services span both tiers and exist as a separate box in the data tier.

Using DBMSes remains the most popular but not the only way to store data in enterprise Java EE applications. The data can be served by an external web service or arrive as a real-time feed from some messaging infrastructure. MOM stands for *message-oriented middleware*, and you'll learn what it is in Lesson 30.

Without some practical example, all these new buzzwords may not make much sense to you. You'll see examples in the upcoming lessons, but let's just briefly discuss how you can rebuild the Stock Market application that you already started developed using sockets and RMI.

➤ Have an applet to connect to `StockQuoteServlet`, which creates what is known as a *session EJB* called `StockMarketQuote`, which connects to external stock exchange software and requests a price quote on the specified symbol(s). This session bean has a timer that updates the quotes every second.

➤ Do as described in the previous bullet, but replace the applet with a thin HTML client.

➤ The same as before, but replace the Servlet with a JSP.

➤ The same as before, but replace the JSP with a JSF.

➤ The same as before, but replace the session bean with a timer with a message-driven bean (MDB) that subscribes via MOM to the external stock exchange application that sends back new prices only when they change.

➤ The same as before, but add a session bean with business that will process every price quote received by MDB and apply a secret modeling algorithm, and on certain conditions send a message to buy or sell a specific number of shares of the suggested stock to a third-party trading system via a call to a web service.

Is this enough? I can keep going. As you can see, there are many ways to design a distributed Java EE application. This is what Java architects do for a living.

# Containers versus Application Servers

Java EE tiers are implemented in *containers*. It's easy to guess that containers were created to contain something. In the Java EE world containers not only contain, but also control the birth, life, and death of Java components. For example, you don't need to write the `new` statement to create a new instance of an EJB; the container will create a pool of them based on configuration parameters. Even on the client side, while reading about applets you might have noticed that applets' life cycles are controlled by the JRE, which can be called an applet container. Basically, a container is an area inside JVM that can support a lifecycle of certain types of Java objects, such as applets, servlet, EJB, etc.

Containers can take care of various functions, and one of them is thread safety. It's great that multiple clients can connect and make requests to the same server, but can you be sure that a thread initiated by Mary won't interfere with John's thread? An EJB container implements a single-threaded model ensuring that each client's request operates in a dedicated thread. Containers may offer transactional support with Java Transaction API (JTA) and persist data for you with Java Persistence API (JPA).

In the first few lessons I used a blueprint analogy to explain the relationship between Java classes and objects. I'll use this analogy again, but this time to explain the relationship between the Java EE specification and application servers. The Java EE is a specification, and when a release is published, vendors who want to implement it in their software products create application servers that support this specification.

Multiple vendors offer their versions of a Java EE application server. The question is what version of the Java EE specification they support. Currently the application servers GlassFish (Oracle) and JBoss (Red Hat) support Java EE 6. At the time of this writing WebLogic (Oracle) and WebSphere (IBM) are still on Java EE 5, but should offer support of the latest specification soon.

Java EE application servers have to support multiple containers, for example a Servlet container and an EJB container. Some vendors prefer to create products supporting only certain technologies defined in the Java EE specification. For example, Tomcat (Apache), Jetty (Eclipse Foundation), and Resin (Caucho) offer support for selected technologies (such as Servlets and JSP), which makes them suitable for implementing web applications, but if you are planning to create web applications based on one of these products, you'll need to figure out what other tools or frameworks will be needed to support transactions, the business tier, data persistence, and more.

In this book I'll be using GlassFish 3 from Oracle, which is fully compliant with Java EE 6. I have selected the most widely used technologies in Java EE development today. In particular you'll be learning about the following:

➤ Java Servlets 3.0

➤ JSP 2.2

➤ EJB 3.1

➤ JPA 2.0

➤ JTA 1.1

➤ CDI 1.0

➤ JMS 1.1

➤ JAX-RS 1.1

Two of the acronyms in this list have not been spelled out yet in this book. CDI stands for Context and Dependency Injection and JAX-RS is Java API for RESTful Web Services. You may feel overwhelmed with all these terms, but I'll try to explain them in easy-to-understand language.

## PROFILES AND PRUNING

Although Java EE 6 offers a full stack of server technologies, most of the real-world applications don't need all of them. In the past, to get Java EE certified, a vendor of an application server had to implement all JSRs that were listed in the Java EE specification. But most of the applications don't use all technologies included in full Java EE specification. This is how that concept of a profile came about. A profile is a preconfigured subset of Java technologies geared toward solving a specific type of application. Currently, besides the Full Profile, there is the Web Profile, which is designed specifically for the development of web applications. Web profiles include Servlets JSF, JSP, CDI, EJB Lite, JPA, JTA, Interceptors, Managed Beans, and Bean validation.

In the future new profiles may be created to address specific needs of developers. For example, chances are that a new profile will be created for developers for small devices. In general, the mechanism of lightweight profiles should encourage vendors of web containers to expand their support of Java EE by implementing web profile components. For example, creators of the Resin container are focusing on the implementation of a web profile.

*Pruning* is a way to reduce the size of the Java EE platform. The pruning process starts with marking in JavaDoc the technologies that are candidates for removal. Then, based on the reaction of the Java community, they will be either removed from the future specifications or not. As an example, some of the Java EE components (such as EJB 2.x) will be removed in Java EE 7.

## MISCELLANEOUS CONCEPTS

You may say, "I want my RMI-based stock server application back. Why make things so complex?" The reason is that the only instance of `UnicastRemoteObject` in our RMI `StockServer` may need to process thousands of concurrent user requests, and because of this you'll need to write code ensuring that such concurrent processing is thread safe.

Servlet and EJB containers are scalable and they take care of all multi-threading issues, enabling you to write application code as if the application were the only user! This alone should be a good reason for using the Java EE stack as opposed to RMI. Without going into a detailed comparison between RMI and Java EE, I'll just add that if you need to deploy your StockServer application on the Web, corporate firewalls won't allow clients that use the JRMP communication protocol required by RMI.

Java EE is a very robust, reliable, and scalable platform and you will appreciate what its container will do for your code. I'll just mention a couple of concepts here.

If you want Java EE containers to help you, help them by providing configuration parameters (annotations) that specify how many instances of the same session bean `StockMarketQuote` you want pre-created for you by the EJB container. Each of these session beans may be "rented" from a pool to the client's request, and then put back. How many beans do you need? I don't know. I don't have enough information at this point, as it depends on the load on your system — the number of concurrent (simultaneous) requests for price quotes that have to be supported by your system.

Java EE implements *dependency injection*. An object doesn't have to reach out to get the resources it needs, because the container injects the resources into the object using annotations. you'll see examples of CDI later in the book.

Interceptors offer a mechanism by which containers can intercept method invoked on your session beans. When the call is intercepted you can specify additional code to be called before or after the method is executed. For example, imagine that you need to add logging before certain methods are called. Adding interceptors is an easy way to do this.

Integration of Java EE 6 with third-party web frameworks like Spring and Hibernate is made easy by *web fragments*.

Starting in the next lesson you'll have a chance to apply all these concepts and features.

# TRY IT

This lesson was a high-level overview of the Java EE 6 platform. The hands-on exercises starting from the next lesson will require that you have an application server installed, and installing the GlassFish v3 server is your next assignment.

## Lesson Requirements

You should have Java installed.

## Hints

NetBeans IDE has very good support for Java EE 6. By now switching from one IDE to another should be as easy for you as switching from one bicycle to another. If you'd like to experiment with NetBeans 7 IDE instead of Eclipse, download the Java bundle from `http://netbeans.org/downloads/index .html` — it includes NetBeans 7 IDE with the GlassFish v3 server packaged and preconfigured.

## Step-by-Step

1.  Download GlassFish Server Open Source Edition. At the time of this writing the latest version, GlassFish 3.0.1, is available at the following URL: `https://glassfish.dev.java .net/public/downloadsindex.html#top`.

2.  Click the Download button, and the next web page will offer downloads for Windows, Linux, and Mac OS. You will have your choice of two profiles: full platform and web profile. Get the full platform distribution for your OS and follow the installation instructions.

3.  If you are using Windows, just run `glassfish-3.0.1-windows.exe`.

**4.** Mac OS users should use the Unix distribution called `glassfish-3.0.1-unix.sh`. In the Terminal window set the executable permissions and then run the installer:

```
chmod +x glassfish-3.0.1-unix.sh

./ glassfish-3.0.1-unix.sh
```

**5.** During the installation process you'll be asked to select the directory where GlassFish Server will be installed. In my case, on Mac OS, it's `/Users/yfain11/glassfishv3`.

**6.** Select and enter the password on the next screen, shown in Figure 26-2. Note that by default GlassFish Server will run on port 8080 and the port for server administration is 4848.

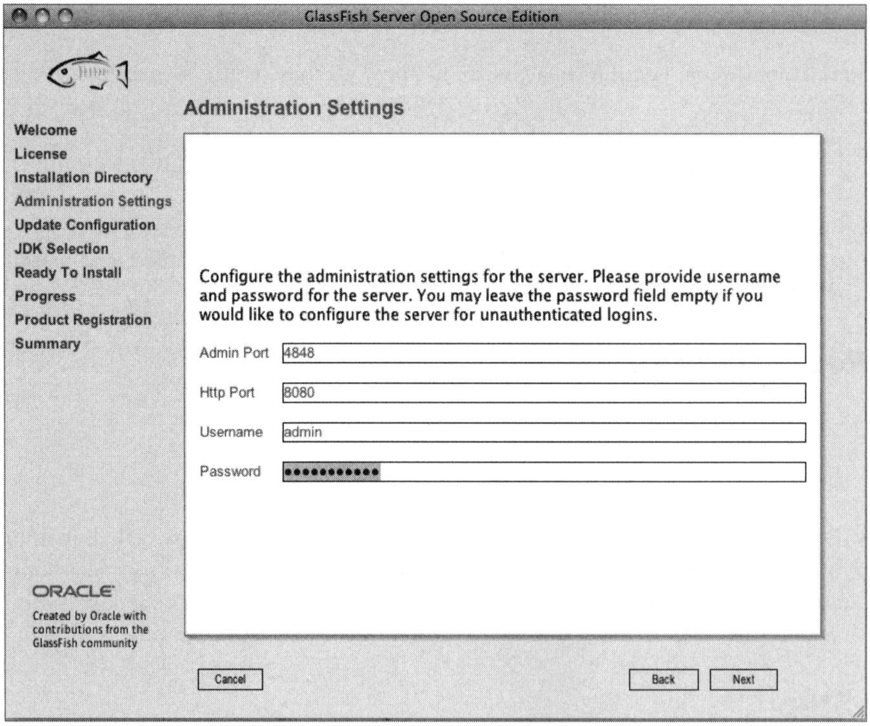

**FIGURE 26-2**

**7.** Click Next and Install on the next two pop-ups. The installation process will start and at the end you may optionally register your newly installed copy of GlassFish Server. Your installation process is complete.

**8.** Download the Oracle GlassFish Server 3.0.1 Quick Start Guide from `http://docs.sun .com/app/docs/doc/821-1757` and test your server by starting and stopping the default domain as described in this document. For reference, here's the output in my Terminal window after I start GlassFish on my Mac:

```
yakov-fains-macbook-pro-2:bin yfain11$ ./asadmin start-domain
Waiting for DAS to start ..........
Started domain: domain1
Domain location: /Users/yfain11/glassfishv3/glassfish/domains/domain1
Log file: /Users/yfain11/glassfishv3/glassfish/domains/domain1/logs/server.log
Admin port for the domain: 4848
Command start-domain executed successfully.
```

After the server has successfully started, open your web browser and enter `http://localhost:8080/` — you should see the GlassFish welcome page.

> *Please select Lesson 26 on the DVD to view the video that accompanies this lesson.*

# 27

# Programming with Servlets

Web applications can serve static or dynamic content. Some examples of static content are text files with HTML markup, images, and video. Dynamic content is formed on the fly. Think of a web application that enables you to browse the inventory of an online store. The content you see on your screen is being created based on your queries — in other words, dynamically.

In the Java EE world, web content is served either by a program running in a container with deployed servlets, JSP, JSF, or a third-party framework, or it's a SOAP or RESTful Web Service. Servlets, JSP, and JSF not only return the data, but also present it as formatted HTML pages, hence the term *presentation layer* (refer to Figure 26-1). Web Services, on the other hand, return just the data (see Lesson 34).

A servlet is a Java program written by certain rules and deployed in a Java EE–compliant servlet container of your choice. The client program can be a lightweight HTML, JavaScript, applet, or JavaFX program. In this lesson I'll be explaining the most widely used means of web communication: HTTP requests and responses. HTTP stands for *Hypertext Transfer Protocol*.

All examples in this lesson will work in any Java EE container supporting the Servlet 3.0 specification. I use GlassFish v3.

Figure 27-1 shows a web browser making HTTP requests to `MyServlet`, a servlet written by you or another developer, and receiving HTTP responses that `MyServlet` sends back.

## THE BIG PICTURE

Before you even learn how to create servlets, let's look at the components and the workflow of an imaginary online store, `www.MyBooks.com`, developed with Java servlets.

> ➤ The client's machine just needs a web browser. The bookstore will consist of a number of HTML web pages for getting user input. The Web browser sends it to the server with the name `MyBooks.com` in the form of an `HTTPRequest` object.

> ➤ The `MyBooks.com` computer has to run some web server software, usually on port 80. For secure communication with HTTPS (HyperText Transfer Protocol Secure) the port 443 is used. The web server will "listen to" the users' requests. If a web server receives a simple request for static HTML content, the web server will process the request

without needing to engage any additional software, and it'll send back `HTTPResponse` with the requested static content.

➤ The website `MyBooks.com` will also run a servlet container with deployed servlet(s). If the web server receives a user request to find books based on some criteria, it'll create and pass `HttpServletRequest` to the appropriate servlet, `FindBooks`, which is deployed and running in the servlet container. The next section shows sample HTML containing a form that explicitly lists `FindBooks`.

➤ The servlet creates (on the fly) the HTML page listing the found books that meet the requested search criteria, and sends it to the web server in `HttpServletResponse`, which wraps it inside the `HttpResponse` object and sends it back to the user's web browser.

➤ The user's browser displays the received page without knowing if it is an old static HTML page or a freshly baked one.

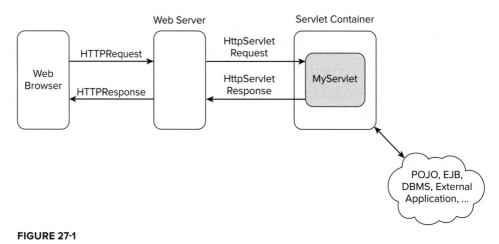

**FIGURE 27-1**

## THE THIN CLIENT

Listing 27-1 shows a simple HTML file with a form containing a text input field and a Submit button, which users can use to find a book by its title.

**LISTING 27-1: HTML that gives 404**

```html
<html>
  <head>
   <title>Find a book</title>
  </head>

  <body>
    Enter a word from the book title:
    <form action=http://www.MyBooks.com/servlet/FindBooks method=Get>
      <input type=Text name=booktitle>
```

```
            <input type=Submit value="Search">
        </form>
    </body>
</html>
```

Create a file called **BookSearch.html** containing the code from Listing 27-1. Open this file in a web browser (File ⇨ Open), enter any text in the input field, and press Search. You'll get an error message because there is neither a server nor a servlet called FindBooks at this address. But now you see what the thinnest client can look like.

Clients communicate with servlets using HTTP protocol, and when no requested network resource is found, the HTTPResponse object comes back with an error. If the server responds, but the requested resource (the FindBooks servlet) is not there, the error code 404 is returned. If the server doesn't respond, the web client will show an appropriate error code. If the client's request successfully received the needed resource from the server, the HTTPResponse contains the status code 200. The list of all possible HTTP status codes is available at www.w3.org/Protocols/rfc2616/rfc2616-sec10.html.

# HOW TO WRITE A SERVLET

To create a servlet, write a class that extends from HTTPServlet and annotate it with the @WebServlet annotation. The class HTTPServlet extends GenericServlet, which defines the method service(). The method service() receives the client's response and directs it to one of the methods of your class that's a descendant of HTTPServlet. You have to override either of the methods doGet() or doPost(). Which one to override? This depends on the client's request method. If the client uses the method Get (see Listing 27-1), override the callback doGet(), as in Listing 27-2.

**LISTING 27-2:** Your first servlet

```
import javax.servlet.ServletException;
import javax.servlet.annotation.WebServlet;
import javax.servlet.http.HttpServlet;
import javax.servlet.http.HttpServletRequest;
import javax.servlet.http.HttpServletResponse;
import java.io.PrintWriter;

@WebServlet(urlPatterns="/books", name="FindBooks" )
public class FindBooks extends HttpServlet {

  @Override
  public void doGet(HttpServletRequest request,
                    HttpServletResponse response) throws ServletException {
        // The code processing request goes here
        // The resulting Web page will be sent back via the
        // I/O stream that response variable contains
        PrintWriter out = response.getWriter();
        out.println("Hello from FindBooks");
  }
}
```

If you properly deploy this servlet on `MyBooks.com`, the HTML client from Listing 27-1 will get as a response a web page containing the text "Hello from FindBooks." Note that the import statements include classes from the `javax.servlet` package, which is not included with Java SE — you need Java EE 6 SDK installed. GlassFish Server comes with Java EE 6, but if you are using a different container you can get it from `www.oracle.com/technetwork/java/javaee/downloads/index.html`.

## HOW TO DEPLOY A SERVLET

The annotation `@WebServlet` is where you specify servlet deployment parameters. Prior to Java EE 6 you needed to specify deployment parameters in an XML file, but now that's optional. Our `FindBooks` servlet uses the deployment parameters `urlPatterns`, and `name`. The former is used to match one of the servlets deployed on the server to the URL. The value `/books` means that whenever the client sends a request containing the pattern `books` in its URL, the request has to be redirected to the `FindBooks` servlet. For example, the servlet container will send the request `http://localhost:8080/books` to the `FindBooks` servlet.

Each application server and servlet container has a directory known as a *document root*. It is used not only for servlet-based websites, but also for the deployment of static HTML files. For example, if you put the HTML file `TermsAndConditions.html` in the subfolder `legal` of the document root of the server `MyBooks.com`, users would need to direct their web browsers to `www.mybooks.com/legal/TermsAndConditions.html`.

In the GlassFish application server the default document root is the directory `/glassfish/domains/domain1/docroot`. In Apache Tomcat it's the directory `webapps`. If you are planning to create a servlet, its deployment directory will also be located in the document root, but it will contain the subdirectories `WEB-INF` and `META-INF`.

`WEB-INF` will have the subdirectories `classes` and `lib` and the optional file `web.xml`. The latter is optional if you can specify all deployment parameters in annotations. But if you have both annotations and `web.xml`, the values in this file will override the corresponding values in the annotations. This allows changing deployment parameters without requiring recompilation of the servlets. The `WEB-INF` directory also may have some container-specific files. For example, GlassFish has the file `sun-web.xml`, in which it stores the *context root*, which is the root directory of your Web application as well as the part of the URL that's used to access your application in the Web browser (`/Lesson27` in our case).

The directory `META-INF` may have files containing metadata about this web application, like *manifest.mf* or other data specific to a third-party framework or application server content. For example, Apache Tomcat has a file called *context.xml* where you may find information about the JDBC driver. This directory may also contain the file *web-fragments.xml*, which is a module of deployment mainly used by third-party frameworks to store their specific deployment parameters.

This is what the directory structure of the application deployed in the document root directory can look like:

```
document root dir
      WEB-INF
            Classes
                Com
```

```
        Practicaljava
           lesson27
              FindBooks.class
      Lib
   META-INF
      manifest.mf
```

The class `com.practicaljava.lesson27.FindBooks` was compiled into the directory *classes*. If you had some third-party jar files you could add them to the *lib* directory.

When your web application is complete, most likely it'll consist of multiple files, and typically the entire directory structure is deployed as one compressed file with the extension *.war*, which stands for web archive. Such files can be created manually, by your IDE plug-ins, or by one of the build tools like Ant or Maven. Later in this lesson I'll show you how to create a war file with Eclipse for Java EE Developers.

# INSTALLING THE GLASSFISH PLUG-IN FOR ECLIPSE

It's a lot more convenient to develop and deploy Web applications when you don't need to leave the IDE. Eclipse for Java EE is a good fit for the development of web projects. NetBeans IDE and IntelliJIDEA are also good tools for Java EE developers. Because I'll be using GlassFish Server, let's install the GlassFish plug-in that's available for Eclipse IDE Helios or later.

From Eclipse's Help menu select Eclipse Marketplace. A new window will pop up: Enter `GlassFish` in the Find field. This search will return several GlassFish-related plug-ins; pick the Tools Bundle for Eclipse. This is a bundle that comes as two plug-ins. Press Install and follow the instructions. At the end of the installation, Eclipse will restart showing a GlassFish welcome window; close it and switch to the Java EE perspective.

Now configure GlassFish Server. The Eclipse view will allow you to start and stop the server and deploy applications without needing to leave Eclipse. Select File ➪ New ➪ Other and pick Server in the opened window. Select the option GlassFish Open Source Edition 3 (Java EE 6).

The next pop-up will ask you about a default JRE (it must be Java 1.6 or above) and where GlassFish Server should be located. According to my installation (see Lesson 26) I specified */Users/ yfain11/glassfishv3/glassfish* and pressed Next. Accept default parameters for *domain1* in the next window and press Finish. Eclipse will start GlassFish Server, asking you for the administrator's ID and password that you specified when installing GlassFish in the previous lesson.

If you did everything right your Eclipse Servers view should look like Figure 27-2, and the Console view should show output similar to the following:

```
Waiting for DAS to start ..............
Started domain: domain1
Domain location: /Users/yfain11/glassfishv3/glassfish/domains/domain1
Log file: /Users/yfain11/glassfishv3/glassfish/domains/domain1/logs/server.log
Admin port for the domain: 4848
Command start-domain executed successfully.
```

**FIGURE 27-2**

## HOW TO CREATE A SERVLET WITH ECLIPSE

In the File ➪ New menu of Eclipse, select the option Create Dynamic Web Project. In the pop-up window name it **Lesson27**. Note that by default the GlassFish target run time has been selected (see Figure 27-3). If you have another servlet container configured in your Eclipse installation, you can deploy it under a different run time (such as Tomcat).

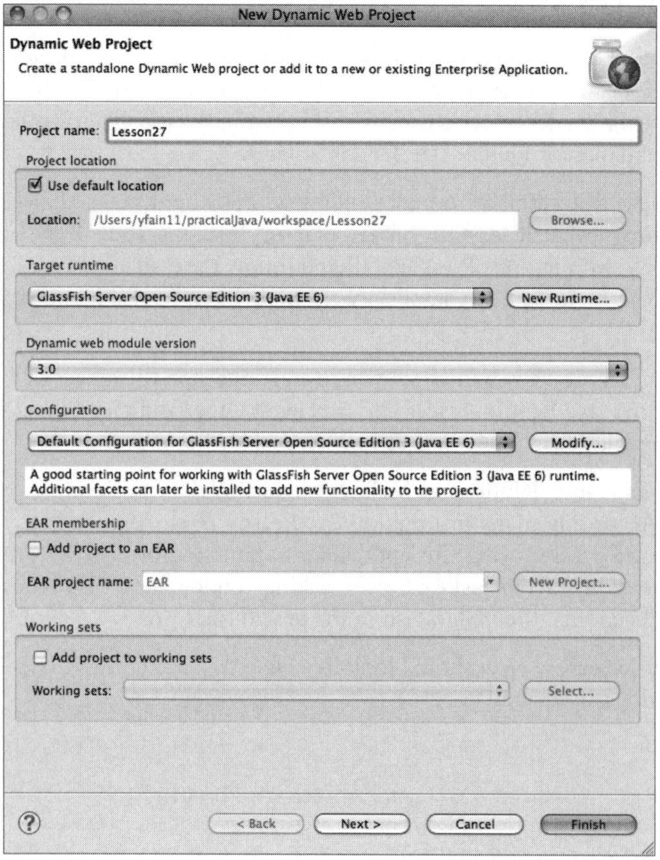

**FIGURE 27-3**

Click Finish, and it'll create a new Eclipse project, which is not the same as the projects you've been creating so far. It has a subfolder called *WebContent* that contains the *WEB-INF* and *META-INF* directories that will be used for deployment in the servlet container of your choice.

Right-click the project name and select New ⇨ Servlet, then specify com.practicaljava.lesson27 as the name of the package, and the class name as FindBooks. Click Next and edit the URL mapping field to be /book. Click Next again. The next window will ask you which method stubs you'd like to have auto-generated; keep the default doGet() and doPost(). Finally, click Finish, and the code in Listing 27-3 will be generated (I removed the comments).

**LISTING 27-3: Generated FindBooks servlet**

```java
package com.practicaljava.lesson27;

import java.io.IOException;
import javax.servlet.ServletException;
import javax.servlet.annotation.WebServlet;
import javax.servlet.http.;
import javax.servlet.http.HttpServletRequest;
import javax.servlet.http.HttpServletResponse;

@WebServlet(description = "The servlet that searches for books",
            urlPatterns = { "/books" })
public class FindBooks extends HttpServlet {
    private static final long serialVersionUID = 1L;

    public FindBooks() {
        super();
        // TODO Auto-generated constructor stub
    }

    protected void doGet(HttpServletRequest request,
        HttpServletResponse response) throws ServletException, IOException{
            // TODO Auto-generated method stub
    }

    protected void doPost(HttpServletRequest request,
        HttpServletResponse response) throws ServletException, IOException{
            // TODO Auto-generated method stub
    }
}
```

Add the following two lines in the doGet() method to get access to the output stream and send the message "Hello from FindBooks":

```java
PrintWriter out = response.getWriter();
out.println("Hello from FindBooks");
```

Don't forget to add the import statement for PrintWriter. The final step is to deploy the servlet under GlassFish Server. Open the Servers view, right-click the server, and select Add and Remove from the menu. Select the Lesson27 project in the left panel and add it to the right one (see Figure 27-4). Click Finish.

The servlet deployment is finished. Now right-click `FindBooks` in the Eclipse project, select Run on Server ⇨ GlassFish and click Finish. Eclipse will run its internal web browser and will display the message shown in Figure 27-5. Please note that the URL ends with `/books` according to the specified `urlPatterns` parameter, `http://localhost:8080/Lesson27/books`.

Because servlets belong to the presentation layer, let's change the presentation a little bit. This code in `doGet()` will show the output in a larger font and in the header <H2> style:

```
PrintWriter out = response.getWriter();
out.println("<html><body bgcolor=yellow>");
out.println("<h2>Hello from FindBooks</h2>");
```

If you want to create a war file deployable on any servlet container, find the Deployment Descriptor section in your Lesson27 project, right-click it, and select Export to WAR. In a couple of seconds you'll have `Lesson27.war`, a file that you can deploy in any Java EE 6–compliant container.

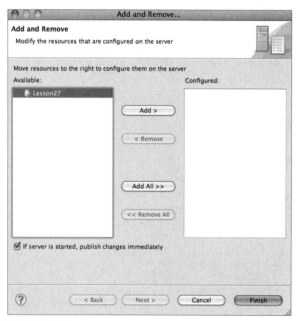

**FIGURE 27-4**

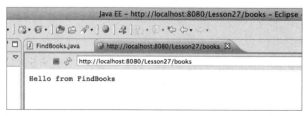

**FIGURE 27-5**

# BROWSER-SERVLET DATA FLOW

One servlet can serve multiple users, so let's review the entire process of client-servlet communication. Java Servlets run in a container, which automatically spawns a new thread for every client's request without requiring you to do any thread programming.

The web browser can use an HTML form, a link, or another program that can send, say, a Get or Post request to the server. In the very beginning, when the first user's request hits the FindBooks servlet, the container will check if this servlet is up-and-running. If not, the container will start it and call the servlet's method init() — even if you didn't override this method, it exists in the superclass HttpServlet.

Then the container calls the method service() of the servlet's superclass, which redirects the request to doGet(), doPost(), or similar doXXX(), passing the arguments HttpServletRequest and HTTPServletResponse. Your code can get the data entered by the user from the HttpServletRequest object with the method getParameter().

After you get the parameter(s), process it in the business layer, which can be implemented either as POJOs talking to some data store or as an EJB. Return the result to the client by getting the reference to the PrintWriter object — it knows how to send text data to the user. For non-textual results use the class OutputStream instead of PrintWriter. Don't forget to set the content type by calling setContentType(). For example, if you are sending an object containing PDF content and want the browser to automatically open Acrobat Reader, call the function Response .setContentType("application/pdf");.

The servlet container controls when the servlet is loaded, and when its init(), service(), and destroy() methods are called. The method destroy() is called when a server administrator decides to unload the servlet, or the server is gracefully shutting down, or the server needs to free some resources. The following code retrieves the name of the book entered by the user and responds with the price of 65 dollars:

```
public void doGet(HttpServletRequest req, HttpServletResponse res)
                   throws ServletException, IOException  {

  String title = req.getParameter("booktitle");;
  PrintWriter out = res.getWriter();
  res.setContentType("text/html");
  out.println("<html><body>");
  out.println("<h2>the book "+title+" costs only $65");
  out.println("<p>Please enter your credit card number");
  out.println("</body></html>");
}
```

# HTTP GET AND POST REQUESTS

HTTP specification defines several methods for data exchange on the Web, but Get and Post are the most widely used ones. If you don't specify the method, Get is used by default. Because the HTML tag <form> in Listing 27-1 used method=Get, the FindBooks method doGet() will be invoked by the container. In this case the web browser will append the values entered in the form to the end of the URL after the question mark. For example, if the user enters the word `Apollo` as a book title, the URL may look like this:

```
http://www.mybooks.com?booktitle=Apollo
```

If a form submits multiple values, the URL will include several key/value pairs after the question mark. With `Get` it's easy to copy and paste or bookmark the URL with parameters. On the other hand, with `Get` the data is not protected — you can see it in clear text.

The method `Post` is typically used to send larger amounts of data to the server. It's always used to send binary data to the server. Of course, the log-in forms should use `Post` because you don't want the user's ID and password to be shown in the URL. To process `Post` requests, servlets have to override the method `doPost()`.

It's common to use `Get` for data retrieval and `Post` for both data retrieval and modification.

## SESSION TRACKING

HTTP is a *stateless* protocol. If a user retrieves a web page with a list of books from the `FindBooks` servlet or any other server-side program as a result of an HTTP request, and then goes to another web page, this second page does not know what was shown on the first one. To preserve data to more than one web page, *session tracking* has to be implemented.

A session is a logical task, which the user is trying to complete by visiting a website. For example, the process of buying a book may involve several steps: book selection, input of billing and shipping information, and so on. All of these steps combined to form an example of a session. When a purchase order is placed, the session is over. To create a session, call the method `request.getsSession(true)`. Calling this method without an argument will give you either a reference to the existing session or `null`.

The session information can be stored either on the client or on the server side. On the client side the user's session data can be stored using *cookies* (defined in the next section) or URL rewriting. The server-side alternative for storing session data is a session tracking API that implements the interface `javax.servlet.http.HTTPSession`.

## Cookies

A cookie is a small piece of data that a container sends to the web client to be stored on the disk. On every subsequent request from that client, the cookie is returned to the server, uniquely associating the request with a given session. The cookies are persistent, but the user may disable them by selecting the appropriate option in the web browser. When the session is created, a special cookie, `JSESSIONID`, is sent to the client. Here's how the servlet can send a business-related cookie (`javax.servlet.http.Cookie`) to the client:

```
Cookie myCookie = new Cookie("bookName","Java Programming 24-hour trainer");
// Set the lifetime of the cookie for 24 hours
myCookie.setMaxAge(60*60*24);
response.addCookie(myCookie);
```

This is how a servlet can retrieve a client's cookies that arrive with `HttpServletRequest`:

```
Cookie[] cookies = request.getCookies();
```

```
for (i=0; i < cookies.length; i++){
  Cookie currentCookie = cookie[i];
  String name = currentCookie.getName();
  String value = currentCookie.getValue();
}
```

Even though you can store multiple cookies on the client, as in the preceding code, it's not a good idea to send the application data back and forth over the network. Typically the session data is stored in the HTTPSession object described later in the section "Server-Side HTTPSession."

# URL Rewriting

If a client disables cookies, the URL rewriting may be used for session tracking. In this case the session ID and other required session data are attached to the URL string. If you've noticed something such as jsessionid=12345 in the URL string of any website, it means that URL rewriting is being used.

# Server-Side HttpSession

You should keep the data that belong to a user's session (such as the shopping cart) inside the javax.servlet.http.HttpSession object in the servlet container, which creates one such object per client. The servlet can store there any Serializable objects. The following line creates a session object (or finds a previously created one):

```
HttpSession mySession = request.getSession(true);
```

The call getSession(true) means "find this client's session object or create a new one if no object is found." Usually the shopping process consists of a number of subsequent servlet calls (list an inventory, add an item to the shopping cart, enter shipping information, etc.). The method call getSession(true) should be used in the very first servlet that opens the business process that can be called a user session. At this moment the application server generates a unique session ID and sends it to the user's web browser using either a cookie or URL rewriting.

The call getSession(false) means "find my session object," assuming that it has been created in the previous steps of the session. If this call returns null, the session object has been destroyed and you might want to display a message saying that the session has expired, and the user has to start the process from scratch. Let's assume that the following class represents a book on the server side:

```
class Book  {
    String title;
    double price;
}
```

This is what you can do in the method doGet() of the servlet to create a session and a shopping cart:

```
HttpSession session = request.getSession(true);

// This sample uses Vector object here to store selected books.
// Try to get the shopping cart that might have been
// created during previous calls to this servlet.

Vector myShoppingCart=session.getAttribute("shoppingCart");

if (myShoppingCart == null){
```

```
    // This is the first call - instantiate the shopping cart
    myShoppingCart = new Vector();
}

// create an instance of a book object
Book selectedBook = new Book();

selectedBook.title=request.getParameter("booktitle");
selectedBook.price= Double.parseDouble(request.getParameter("price"));

// Add the book to our shopping cart
myShoppingCart.addElement(selectedBook);

// Put the shopping cart back into the session object
session.setAttribute("shoppingCart", myShoppingCart);
```

When the book order has been placed the program should close the session by making the following call:

```
session.invalidate();
```

If the session has not been invalidated explicitly, the application server will do it automatically after a specific period. This period is called *timeout* and is a configurable parameter.

## Filters

Even after a servlet is deployed you still can change the way it processes requests and responses without modifying the servlet's code. You can create *filters* — code that can be configured to process HTTP requests before they are passed to the servlet, or right after the servlet returns the request. Filters are good for adding such functionality as authentication, logging, encryption, data compression, and audit reporting.

None of these actions depend on the business logic implemented by servlets. Besides, why write code with compressed logic over and over again in each servlet if you can create one filter and apply it to all of them before the data is sent to the client? What if you need to compress and encrypt? Write two filters and chain them so both are applied to the same servlet.

To create a filter, write a class that implements the interface javax.servlet.Filter annotated with @WebFilter. There are three methods in this interface: doFilter(), init(), and destroy(). Here's a sample of a filter class to be used with two servlets, FindBooks and RemoveBook:

```
@WebFilter(servletNames={"/FindBooks", "/RemoveBook"})
public class MyAuthenticationFilter implements Filter {

    @Override
    public void doFilter(ServletRequest request, ServletResponse response,
                FilterChain chain)throws IOException, ServletException {

      // user authentication code goes here

      //Call the next filter, if any
      chain.doFilter(request, response);

    }
```

```
        }

        @Override
        public void init(FilterConfig filterConfig) throws ServletException {}

        @Override
        public void destroy() {}

    }
```

The container gives the filter both request and response objects. You can check passed parameters by the client (such as by checking ID/password), perform authentication, and, if the user is not valid, call `response.getWriter()` and send the user the message "You don't belong here" without even passing control to the servlet.

The method `destroy()` is called once before the container removes the filter; if the filter has created some resources such as DBMS connections, close them in the filter's code. The method `init()` is invoked on the filter only once during its instantiation. The filter gets the `FilterConfig` object, which gives you access to the servlet context and initialization parameters if these are specified in the `@WebFilter` annotation or in the file *web.xml*:

```
@WebFilter(servletNames={"/FindBooks", "/RemoveBook"},
           initParams={name="community", value="adults"})
```

# EVENT LISTENERS

Several important events happen to a servlet during its life cycle. You can write code reacting to these events in custom event listener classes. For example, the container fires events when the servlet context is created, and if you are interested in processing this event, create a class that implements the `ServletContextListener` interface. To catch the moment when the session has been created, invalidated, or timed out, use `HttpSessionListener`. To catch the beginning of the processing of the servlet request, create a class implementing `ServletRequestListener`.

Imagine that you need to gather statistics on the usage of the bookstore servlet and log the date and time when each user's session was created and destroyed. Listing 27-4 prints the session ID on creation and invalidation of every user's session.

**LISTING 27-4:** HttpSession listener

```
import javax.servlet.http.HttpSessionListener;
import javax.servlet.http.HttpSessionEvent;
import javax.servlet.http.HttpSession;
import javax.servlet.ServletConfig;
import javax.servlet.annotation.WebListener;

@WebListener
public class BookStoreSessionListener implements HttpSessionListener{

    public void init(ServletConfig config){
```

*continues*

**LISTING 27-4** *(continued)*

```
    }

    public void sessionCreated(HttpSessionEvent event){
      HttpSession    session = event.getSession();
      System.out.println("BookStore session created; id:"+ session.getId());
    }

    public void sessionDestroyed(HttpSessionEvent event){
      HttpSession    session = event.getSession();
      System.out.println("BookStore session destroyed; id:"+ session.getId());
    }

  }
```

To test this listener, modify the code of `doGet()` in the servlet `FindBooks` from Listing 27-4 to create and destroy the session. (In more realistic scenarios the session creation and destruction would be performed in different methods.)

```
    protected void doGet(HttpServletRequest request,
  HttpServletResponse response) throws ServletException, IOException {
            // Get or create the session
            request.getSession(true);

            PrintWriter out = response.getWriter();
            out.println("<html><body bgcolor=yellow>");
            out.println("<h2>Hello from FindBooks</h2>");

            //Destroy the session
            request.getSession(true).invalidate();
    }
```

To emulate the multiple-users scenario, make the first request to the `FindBooks` servlet from Eclipse IDE, and another one from the web browser by copying the URL `http://localhost:8080/Lesson27/books` into the address bar. You should see the creation and destruction of two sessions with different IDs in the Eclipse Console view, which runs the server:

```
INFO: BookStore session created; id:104903c1dd6a8306cb33a116257a
INFO: BookStore session destroyed; id:104903c1dd6a8306cb33a116257a

INFO: BookStore session created; id:104f16ba2e714bdd8981c7ea2e87
INFO: BookStore session destroyed; id:104f16ba2e714bdd8981c7ea2e87
```

## ASYNCHRONOUS SERVLETS

It's great that servlets automatically create and allocate a separate thread for each user's request, but each thread takes up system resources (both memory bytes and CPU cycles), and after a certain number of concurrent requests the server will simply stop responding. Imagine if thousands of users simultaneously hit the `FindBooks` servlet that has to perform a three-second DBMS search for each request. During these three seconds the container will hold the lock on each thread, doing nothing but waiting for the result of the DBMS query (running on another server!).

The idea of asynchronous servlets is to minimize the time of thread locking. If User A makes a request that takes three seconds on a DBMS server, the container's thread will be given to the request of User B, and, when User A's result comes back from the DBMS, the container will allocate this (or another) thread to return the result to User A. This architecture can substantially increase the number of concurrent requests that can be processed on the same server.

In the past, vendors of servlet containers offered their proprietary solutions for asynchronous processing. Jetty implemented its version of reusing thread via a concept called *continuations*, whereby the thread given to a request is suspended for the time required for the business logic to complete, and then is resumed when the result is ready. Apache Tomcat and GlassFish implemented technology based on the event-based model called Comet, whereby an HTTP connection to the servlet container is maintained, and the server *pushes* the data to the client via this connection.

The Servlets 3.0 specification has introduced a standard, Comet-based way of creating asynchronous Java EE web applications. In `doGet()` or `doPost()` you can instantiate the object `javax.servlet.AsyncContext`, which creates an asynchronous worker thread and doesn't lock the client's thread while preserving the client's request and response objects. Asynchronous processing is out of the scope of this tutorial, but you can find a detailed example of programming an asynchronous servlet at `http://bit.ly/b0iBcr`.

## TRY IT

Write a simple HTML client with one text input field that has a Submit button. The user will enter the stock symbol she wants to get a price quote for. Generate a random quote and return a web page with the quote. Reuse the code from `StockServerImpl` from Listing 25-2 to generate the price quotes.

## Lesson Requirements

You should have Java installed.

> *You can download the code and resources for this Try It from the book's web page at* www.wrox.com. *You can find them in the Lesson27 folder in the download.*

## Hints

You can find several examples of Servlet 3.0 web applications at www.oracle.com/technetwork/java/javaee/documentation/code-139018.html.

## Step-by-Step

1. Create an HTML client similar to the one from Listing 27-1 to allow the user to enter the stock symbol.

2. Create a servlet called `StockServerServlet` that will take one parameter, the stock symbol, and instantiate a class called `StockQuoteGenerator` that should have the code similar to Listing 25-2. There's no need to implement Remote interface though.

**3.** Pass the stock symbol received from the client to StockQuoteGenerator and get the price.

**4.** Return the dynamically created HTML page to the client via the request object.

**5.** Test the servlet in Eclipse IDE first, and then create the war file and deploy it in the document root of GlassFish Server, installed in Lesson 26.

**6.** Start GlassFish Server.

**7.** Open the HTML file you created in Step 1 in your web browser and test the servlet by entering various stock symbols.

*Please select Lesson 27 on the DVD to view the video that accompanies this lesson.*

# 28

# JavaServer Pages

JavaServer Pages (JSP) was created as a next step in servlets' evolution. JSP 2.2 is part of the Java EE 6 specification, and with it you can do everything that you can do with servlets, but more easily. Let's say you've created and deployed a servlet, which displays "Hello World." The servlet gets a hold of the output stream of the response object and executes the following line of code:

```
out.println("<html><body>Hello World </body></html>");
```

Let's say you run a small software company that employs Alex, an expensive Java developer, and Matilda, a junior Web designer who doesn't know Java but does know HTML. What if you need to change the layout of this HTML page, such as by adding several empty lines on top? It's not a big problem — Alex can modify the preceding line of code, recompile it, and redeploy the servlet. But for making small changes in the HTML-based UI it's more efficient to use Matilda. This is where JSP becomes very handy. Ask Matilda to create the following text file, *HelloWorld.jsp*:

```
<html>
 <body>
   Hello World
 </body>
</html>
```

Place this file into the document root directory (see Lesson 27) in your servlet container running at, say, MyBooks.com. Now the users can access this JSP by entering the following URL in their web browsers:

```
http://www.MyBooks.com/HelloWorld.jsp
```

Upon the first request to this page, the JSP container (vendors of servlet containers support JSP, too) will automatically generate, compile, and deploy a servlet based on the content of the file *HelloWorld.jsp*. All subsequent calls to this JSP will be processed a lot faster, because the servlet HelloWorld will already be deployed, loaded in memory, and running. As a matter of fact, JSP, as well as servlets, can be preloaded so that even the first user's request is responsive.

You might think that you could make a simple web page by creating `HelloWorld.html` without all this extra code generation. This is true, as long as your page is static and does not use any external dynamically changed data. Remember that HTML is not a programming language but a markup language — it can't even add two and two, but JSP can (see `MyCalculator.jsp` in Listing 28-1).

## EMBEDDING JAVA CODE INTO HTML

JSP defines tags that enable you to embed Java code into an HTML page. When the servlet is automatically generated behind the scenes, this Java code will also be included and executed as part of this servlet. JSP tags are included in angle brackets: for example, the `<%=...%>` tag displays the value of the variable or expression:`<%=2+2%>`. During the servlet generation process performed by the JSP engine, these tags will be replaced with the regular Java code. For example, the tag `<%=2+2%>` will automatically be replaced by a JSP container with the following Java statement:

```
out.println(2+2);
```

Listing 28-1 shows the content of the two-plus-two calculator called `MyCalculator.jsp`. `<BR>` is an HTML tag for inserting line breaks. Note that Alex, the programmer, had to write only the expression inside the JSP tag; the rest was done by Matilda. Consider this task separation an example of the designer-developer workflow.

**LISTING 28-1:** MyCalculator.jsp

```
<html>
<body>
    HTML created by Matilda goes here...
    <br>
    You may not know that 2 + 2 is  <%= 2 + 2%>
    <br>
    More    HTML created by Matilda goes here...
</body>
</html>
```

Create a Dynamic Web Project in Eclipse called Lesson 28. It'll automatically create a file called `index.jsp` — a Hello World JSP under the *WebContent* directory with the content shown in Figure 28-1. Deploying any JSP is a simple matter of copying the JSP file into the document root directory of your JSP container. Of course, if your JSPs are part of a multi-file project, most likely you'll be deploying them in a war file, as described in Lesson 27.

Right-click the name `index.jsp` and select Run on Server and you'll see the Hello World web page. Make a copy of `index.jsp` named `MyCalculator.jsp` and replace the content in the `<body>` part with the content from the `<body>` section from Listing 28-1. Run it and you'll see the web page in Eclipse, as shown in Figure 28-2. The expression `<%2 + 2%>` has been precompiled and replaced with 4. A JSP is nothing more than a servlet that is automatically generated from a file containing valid HTML and JSP tags.

```
Java EE – Lesson28/WebContent/index.jsp – Eclipse – /Users/yfain11/practicalJava/workspace
index.jsp
<%@page contentType="text/html" pageEncoding="UTF-8"%>
<!DOCTYPE HTML PUBLIC "-//W3C//DTD HTML 4.01 Transitional//EN"
                      "http://www.w3.org/TR/html4/loose.dtd">

<html>
  <head>
          <meta http-equiv="Content-Type" content="text/html; charset=UTF-8">
          <title>GlassFish JSP Page</title>
  </head>
  <body>
      <h1>Hello World!</h1>
  </body>
</html>
```

**FIGURE 28-1**

If you need to change the appearance of the page (colors, fonts, data allocation) without changing the expression (2+2), Matilda can do it easily! After the changes are applied, the JSP will be automatically regenerated into a new servlet and redeployed. Usually you do not even have to restart the server. The only exceptions are preloaded JSPs that are configured to be initialized on server startup. Any business logic changes inside the JSP tags will be programmed by Alex.

**FIGURE 28-2**

## IMPLICIT JSP OBJECTS

Because JSPs are built on top of servlets, the main concepts remain the same. Following is the list of predefined variables that you can use in JSP pages. These variables are initialized by the JSP container, and you can use them without explicit declarations.

➤ request has the same use as HttpServletRequest.

➤ response has the same use as HttpServletResponse.

➤ out represents the output write stream JspWriter. This variable points at the same object as HttpServletResponse.getWriter() in servlets. For example, a simplest JSP that returns a result from a Java class called CurrencyConverter might look like this:

```
<html>
  <body>
    <% out.println(CurrencyConverter.getDollarRate()); %>
  </body>
</html>
```

➤ session represents an instance of the user's HTTPSession object.

➤ exception represents an instance of the Throwable object and contains error information. This variable is available only from the JSP error page (described later in the section "Error Pages").

➤ `page` represents the instance of the JSP's servlet.

➤ `pageContext` represents the JSP context and is used with Tag Libraries (described later in this lesson in the section of that name).

➤ `application` provides access to web context. Its use is similar to that of `ServletContext`.

➤ `config` provides initialization information used by the JSP container. Its use is similar to that of the class `ServletConfig`.

## OVERVIEW OF THE JSP TAGS

Each JSP tag starts and ends with an angle bracket and can be included in any HTML file, but you need to save them as `.jsp` files for proper identification and processing by JSP containers. This section is a brief overview of JSP tags. For more detailed coverage refer to the JSP documentation at `http://java.sun.com/products/jsp/docs.html`.

### Directives

Directives do not generate screen output, but instruct the JSP container about the rules that have to be applied to the JSP. Some of the JSP directives are `page`, `include`, `attribute`, and `taglib`.

Page directives start with `<%@ page` and are only in effect within the current page. Directives are used with such attributes as `import`, `extends`, `session`, `errorPage`, `contentType`, and some others. For example, to import the `java.io` package use this directive:

```
<%@ page import="java.io.*" %>
```

Include directives to allow the inclusion of any text from a file or any code from another JSP, at the time when the page is compiled into a servlet, as in the following example:

```
<%@ jsp:include page="calcBankRates.jsp" %>
<%@ include file="bankRates.txt" %>
```

To use a third-party library of custom tags you need to specify where this library is located, as in the following example:

```
<%@ taglib uri="my_taglib.tld" prefix="test" %>
```

The `attribute` directive enables you to define attributes of custom tags, like this:

```
<%@ attribute name="corporate_logo_file_name" %>
```

### Declarations

Declarations are used to declare variables before they are used. You can declare a variable salary like this:

```
<%! double salary; %>
```

The variable salary is visible only inside this page. You can declare Java methods in the JSP page the same way:

```
<%! private  void myMethod(){
        ...
  }%>
```

The code contained in the declaration block turns into the Java code in the generated servlet.

# Expressions

Expressions start with `<%=` and can contain any Java expression, which will be evaluated. The result will be displayed in the HTML page, replacing the tag itself, like this:

```
<%= salary*1.2 %>
```

# Scriptlets

Initially scriptlets were created to give JSP developers a place to put any valid Java code to be included in the generated servlet's `_jspService()` method, which is an equivalent of the servlet's method `service()`, for example a scriptlet can look like this:

```
<% lastName = "Smith"; %>
```

With the creation of JSP Standard Tag Libraries (JSTL) and Expression Language (EL) there is now no need to use scriptlets, but this syntax still works.

# Comments

Comments that start with `<%--` and end with `--%>` will be visible in the JSP source code, but will not be included in the resulting HTML page.

```
<%-- Some comments --%>
```

If you'd like to keep the comments in the resulting web page, use regular HTML comment notation:

```
<!-- Some comments -->
```

# Standard Actions

Although the directive `include` adds the content of the included page during compile time, the element `jsp:include` does it during run time.

```
<jsp:include page "header.jsp" />
```

The element `forward` enables you to redirect the program flow from the current JSP to another one while preserving the `request` and `response` objects. The other way of redirecting the flow is to use `response.sendRedirect(someURL)`, but in this case new `request` and `response` objects are created, which results in a client request to the server.

```
<jsp:forward page = "someOther.jsp" />
```

The `plugin` element ensures that your JSP includes an applet or a Java bean (described later in the "JavaBeans" section). During run time the web browser replaces this tag with one of the HTML tags: `<object>` or `<embed>`.

```
<jsp:plugin type=applet code="PriceQuotes.class" >
```

The nested tag `<jsp:param>` is used to pass parameters to an applet or a bean:

```
<jsp:plugin type=applet code="Login.class">
  <jsp:params>
    <jsp:param name="userID" value="SCOTT" />
    <jsp:param name="password" value="TIGER" />
  </jsp:params>
</jsp:plugin>
```

## ERROR PAGES

Let's say we have a file called *calcTax.jsp* containing code that may throw Java exceptions. Instead of scaring users with stack trace output screens, prepare a friendly *taxErrors.jsp* explaining the problem in plain English.

*calcTax.jsp* may have an HTML `<form>` in which the user enters gross income and the number of dependents. The request for tax calculations is sent to the server's `CalcTax` Java class, which might throw an exception during its processing. Include the name of the error page that has to be shown in case of exceptions:

```
<html>
   Some code to calculate tax and other HTML stuff goes here
        ...
     <%@ page errorPage=taxErrors.jsp %>

</html>
```

Next comes the error page *taxErrors.jsp*, which illustrates how to use the JSP variable `exception`, which displays the error message in a user-friendly way, and also contains more technical error description for the technical support team:

```
<html>
 <body>
  Unfortunately there was a problem during your tax calculations. We are
  working on this issue - please try again in 10 minutes.
  If the problem persists, please contact our award winning technical support
  team at (212) 555-2222 and provide them with the following information:
 <br>
 <%=exception.toString()>

 </body>
</html>
```

# JAVABEANS

JavaBeans specification defines a bean as a Java class that implements the `Serializable` interface and that has a public no-argument constructor, private fields, and public setter and getter
methods. The similar concept of Data Transfer Objects (DTOs) was introduced in Lesson 22 (see
Listing 22-2). Java beans are used mainly for data storing and exchange. In JSP they are used to
avoid mixing Java code and HTML (see also the section "Tag Libraries" later in this lesson; they are
also helping to avoid mixing Java and HTML).

Think of the MVC pattern in JSP-based web applications. The JSP belongs to the view tier, the servlet
can play a role of a controller, and the Java bean can represent a model. Although you can mix HTML
with business logic coded in scriptlets, declarations, and expressions, you should avoid doing this and
separate presentation from business logic processing and data storage. First, this will allow you to split
the work more easily between Alex and Matilda, and second, you'll be able to have more than one presentation solution (e.g., a different UI for mobile devices) reusing the same Java code.

Using beans is the first step in separating processing logic and presentation. Listing 28-2 shows an
example of a bean, called `Student`.

**LISTING 28-2: Student bean**

Available for
download on
Wrox.com

```java
import java.io.Serializable;

class Student implements Serializable{
        private String lastName;
        private String firstName;
        private boolean undergraduate;

        Student(){
            // constructor's code goes here
        }

        public String getLastName(){
            return lastName;
        }
        public String getFirstName(){
            return firstName;
        }
        public void setLastName(String value){
                lastName = value;
        }
        public void setFirstName (String value){
                firstName = value;
        }
        public void setUndergraduate(boolean value){
                undergraduate = value;
```

*continues*

LISTING 28-2 *(continued)*

```
            }

        public boolean isUndergraduate (){
                return undergraduate;
        }
    }
```

Don't confuse JavaBeans with Enterprise Java Beans (EJB), which is a different concept and will be covered in Lesson 32.

## Using JavaBeans in JSP

To use a bean with JSP, first you need to specify its name and location, and after that you can set or get its properties. Following are some examples of bean usage:

```
<jsp:useBean  id="Student" class="com.harward.Student" />
<jsp:getProperty name="Student" property="LastName" />
<jsp:setProperty name="Student" property="LastName" value="Smith"/>
```

The next code snippet populates the `Student` bean's properties `LastName` and `FirstName` based on the data from the HTML tag `<form>`, which has two HTML text input fields called `LName` and `FName`:

```
<jsp:setProperty name="Student" property="LastName" value=
                            "<%= request.getParameter("LName") %>" />

<jsp:setProperty name="Student" property="FirstName" value=
                            "<%=request.getParameter("FName") %>" />
```

If property names are the same in the HTML form and in the bean, mapping the HTML form's and the bean's fields becomes even simpler with the asterisk notation:

```
<jsp:setProperty name="Student" property="*" />
```

## How Long Does a Bean Live?

If a JSP variable is declared inside a scriptlet, it has a local scope. To give it an instance scope, declare the variable using the declaration `tag`. You can define a bean's scope using the `scope` attribute of the tag `jsp:useBean`. The following list defines the various scopes.

➤ `page`: The bean is available only within the current page and will be destroyed as soon as the user exits the page. This is a default scope. For example:

```
<jsp:useBean  id="Student" class="com.harward.Student" scope="page" />
```

➤ `request`: The bean is alive for as long as the `request` object is alive. Even if the control will be redirected to a different JSP by means of the tag `jsp:forward`, the bean will remain available on the new page because it'll be using the same request object, like this:

```
<jsp:useBean  id="Student" class="com.harward.Student" scope="request" />
```

➤ session: The bean is available for all pages until the user's session ends (see the section "Session Tracking" in Lesson 27).

```
<jsp:useBean  id="Student" class="com.harvard.Student" scope="session" />
```

➤ application: The bean is available for all users and all pages — this is a global bean.

```
<jsp:useBean  id="Student" class="com.harvard.Student" scope="application" />
```

# LOADING JSP FROM SERVLETS

In line with the separation of presentation and processing, JSP should have a bare minimum of any processing. When the servlet receives the data to be sent to the user, instead of sending to the client hard-coded HTML tags it should load and send the JSP page to the client. Ideally, the JSP should be laid out by a Web designer.

Let's say you have a servlet that needs to load a JSP based on the user's selection in the HTML window. If you don't need to get new copies of the request and response objects you'll need to create an instance of the RequestDispatcher class and call its method forward(), providing HttpServletRequest and HttpServletResponse as arguments, as shown in Listing 28-3. The servlet MyServlet returns to the Web browser either the JSP showing the data of the Toyota dealership or the JSP showing data about Nissan vehicles.

**LISTING 28-3:** Servlet loading JSP

```
public class MyServlet extends HttpServlet{
    public void doGet(HttpServletRequest req, HttpServletResponse res)
                              throws ServletException {

      ServletContext context = getServletContext();
      RequestDispatcher requestDisp = null;

      String make = req.getParameter("carMake");

        if (make.equals("Toyota") {
          requestDisp = context.getRequestDispatcher("Toyota.jsp");
          requestDisp.forward(req,res);
        }
        else if (make.equals("Nissan") {
          requestDisp = context.getRequestDispatcher("Nissan.jsp");
          requestDisp.forward(req,res);
        }
    }
}
```

In some cases the current servlet performs all interactions with the user, and just needs to load the code of another servlet or JSP. For this purpose use the method include() instead of forward():

```
requestDisp.include(req,res);
```

Because this redirection happens on the server side, the initial URL is still displayed in the web browser's address bar. To provide the new URL (to allow the user to bookmark the resulting page, for example), use `response.sendRedirect("/new_URL")`.

## TAG LIBRARIES

Yet another way of minimizing the amount of code in JSP is to use tag libraries containing custom and reusable tags — either your own original library or a library created by someone else. Each custom tag looks similar to a regular one, but under the hood is always supported by a Java class (or classes) written by a programmer to provide the required functionality.

If you want to create your own custom tags to be used with JSP you have to do the following:

➤ Create a tag library descriptor — an XML file with the extension `.tld`. It has to be deployed in the directory `WEB-INF/tags`.

➤ Create Java classes that provide business logic supporting the tags. Such classes are usually deployed as jars in the `WEB-INF/lib` directory.

➤ Register the tag library with the web application.

Listing 28-4 shows a sample tag library descriptor file. The tag `DowJones` should display a Dow Jones index value. The empty value in `<bodycontent>` means that this is a simple JSP tag with no content and could be used like this: `<sts:DowJones/>`.

**LISTING 28-4:** Sample .tld file

```xml
<?xml version=" 1. 0" encoding="UTF-8" ?>
<taglib xmlns=" http: / / j ava. sun. com/xml/ns/ j 2ee"
    xmlns: xsi=" http: //www. w3. org/ 2 001/XMLSchema-instance"
    xsi: schemaLocation=" http: //java. sun. com/ xml/ns/j2 ee
    http: //java. sun. com/ xml/ns/j2 ee/web-jsptaglibrary_2 _0. xsd"
    version="2 . 0" >
    <tlib-version>1.0</ tlib-version>
    <shortname>sts</shortname>
    <uri>http://www.mystockserver.com:8080/taglib</uri>
    <info>Wall Street tag library</info>

    <tag>
        <name>DowJones</name>
        <tagclass>DowJonesTag</tagclass>
        <bodycontent>empty</bodycontent>
        <info>Displays the Dow Jones index</info>
    </tag>

</taglib>
```

The class supporting a JSP tag (e.g. `DowJonesHandler`) has to implement the interface `javax .servlet.jsp.tagext.SimpleTag` or extend `SimpleTagSupport`. The JSP container will call

`DowJonesHandler`'s methods to set the JSP context — `setPageContext()` — start the execution of the tag's code — `doStartTag()`, etc. This class gives you a default implementation of the `SimpleTag` interface and initialized references to the `pageContext` and parent. Place required logic for the tag in the `doTag()` method, which is called by the container at request time.

```
import javax.servlet.jsp.*;
import javax.servlet.jsp.tagext.*;
import java.io.*;

public class DowJonesHandler extends SimpleTagSupport{

   public int doTag() throws JspException, IOException{

       String dowQuote;
       //  Obtain the DowJones quote by accessing
       //  http://finance.yahoo.com/q?d=t&s=^DJI or similar
          dowQuote=...;

       // and write it to the client
       JspWriter out = getJspContext().getOut();
       out.print("The last price is " + dowQuote);

   }
}
```

To make a tag library recognizable by your JSP container, register it by inserting the following fragment into the file *web.xml*:

```
<taglib>
     <taglib-uri>
          http://www.mystockserver.com/taglib
     </taglib-uri>
      <taglib-location>
            /WEB-INF/taglib.tld
      </taglib-location>
</taglib>
```

When you've done all this, create a simple file called *test.jsp* and start using your tag library. The sample JSP in Listing 28-5 uses the tag `<DowJones>`.

**LISTING 28-5:** Using a custom tag in a JSP

```
<html>
<head>
  <%@ taglib uri=http://www.mystockserver.com/taglib prefix="sts" %>
</head>
<body>
   Today's Dow Jones index: <sts:DowJones/>
</body>
</html>
```

If a tag requires some parameters, they should be specified in the `.tld` file with the tag `<attribute>`, for example:

```
<tag>
  ...
  <attribute>
    <name>tradeDate</name>
    <required>false</required>
  </attribute>
</tag>
```

The setter method has to be provided in the tag handler class for each parameter. Setters have to be named according to the same naming convention as Java beans:

```
public void setTradeDate(String tradeDate){
...
}
```

Custom tag libraries are created by application developers to fit the needs of a specific project(s). Third parties can also provide non-standards-based tag libraries, as with the open source implementation of JSP tag libraries in the project Apache Taglibs (`http://tomcat.apache.org/taglibs/`).

## JSTL

JSP Standard Tag Libraries (JSTL) is a standardized specification for library components that includes actions that are reusable for many JSP-based applications. Standard JSTL guarantees that any Java EE–compliant JSP container will include and support these components. There are five JSTL libraries. They contain an iterator, `if` statements, tags for XML processing, tags for executing SQL, tags for internationalization and commonly used functions.

While the JSP in Listing 28-3 had to specify the location of the tag library on your server, standardized libraries have predefined URLs. For example, to use the `forEach` iterator you'd need to specify the following URI: `http://java.sun.com/jsp/jstl/core`. XML processing tags are located at the following URI: `http://java.sun.com/jsp/jstl/xml`. Accordingly, the code fragment that uses the iterator can look like this:

```
<%@ taglib uri="http://java.sun.com/jsp/jstl/core" prefix="c" %>

<c:forEach var="item" items="${sessionScope.cart.items}">
    ...
</c:forEach>
```

Learning programming with JSTL and Expression Language is out of the scope of this tutorial; please refer to the Oracle tutorial at the following URL: `http://download.oracle.com/javaee/5/tutorial/doc/bnake.html`.

## TRY IT

Rewrite the sample stock server application that you created in the "Try It" section of Lesson 27, but this time do it using JSP and Java beans. Write a simple HTML client with one text input field and a Submit button. The user will enter the stock symbol she wants to get a price quote for. Generate a random quote and return a web page with the quote. Reuse the code of StockServerImpl from Listing 25-2 for generating the price quotes.

## Lesson Requirements

You should have Java installed.

> *You can download the code and resources for this Try It from the book's web page at* www.wrox.com. *You can find them in the Lesson28 folder in the download.*

## Step-by-Step

1. In the Eclipse project Lesson28 select the option File ➪ New. Create a new JSP file named StockQuote.jsp to allow the user to enter a stock symbol and request a price quote. Eclipse will create a file that looks like this:

    ```
    <%@ page language="java" contentType="text/html; charset=ISO-8859-1"
        pageEncoding="ISO-8859-1"%>
    <!DOCTYPE html PUBLIC "-//W3C//DTD HTML 4.01 Transitional//EN"
    "http://www.w3.org/TR/html4/loose.dtd">
    <html>
      <head>
        <meta http-equiv="Content-Type" content="text/html; charset=ISO-8859-1">
        <title>Insert title here</title>
      </head>
      <body>

      </body>
    </html>
    ```

2. Create a Java class called StockServer to contain a method with one parameter — the stock symbol — and will calculate the price quote for the specified stock with code similar to what is shown in Listing 25-2. There's no need to implement Remote interface though.

3. Use required JSP tags to include the StockServer Java class in StockQuote.jsp, and display the price quote generated by its method getQuote() as well as the list of all available stock symbols by calling getNasdaqSymbols().

4. Add an HTML <form> tag to StockQuote.jsp with one text input field and a Submit button so the user can enter the stock symbol and request the price quote.

5. Run and test StockQuote.jsp from Eclipse.

> *Please select Lesson 28 on the DVD to view the video that accompanies this lesson.*

# Developing Web Applications with JSF

In the previous lesson I mentioned that the JSP specification was created on top of servlets to simplify Web application development and as a step toward the separation of responsibilities between web designers and developers. I also said that you should minimize the use of Java code in a JSP page. But JSP doesn't enforce this practice. JavaServer Faces (JSF) does, and using it is the best way of developing Java EE web applications with a thin client.

The current version, JSF 2.0, is based on the Facelets framework that was originally an open-source product. You'll be creating JSF web pages in extensible HTML (.xhtml files), which means that the HTML has to be well-formed — every open tag should have a closing one, the values for the tags' attributes must be placed in quotes, the elements tags must respect case-sensitivity, and the document must have a single root tag.

Like JSP, the JSF framework is tag-based. But JavaServer Faces has several important advantages over JSP:

- ➤ The JSF framework comes with a set of UI components, while JSP uses standard HTML components.

- ➤ JSF is event-driven.

- ➤ You can't add Java to .xhtml files, which enforces clean code separation between Java and HTML.

- ➤ JSF offers easy navigation between web pages.

- ➤ JSF introduces configurable managed beans, which contain processing logic and navigation.

I'll give you more details on each of these bullet points later in this lesson.

## THE BIG PICTURE

The JSF framework is a part of the presentation tier and it enforces the separation of presentation and processing logic. Reiterating the MVC paradigm, the library of JSF components is responsible for the UI, the servlet FacesServlet plays the role of a controller, and managed beans are the model. The processing logic can be placed in POJO classes, in EJB, or in third-party systems, as shown in Figure 29-1.

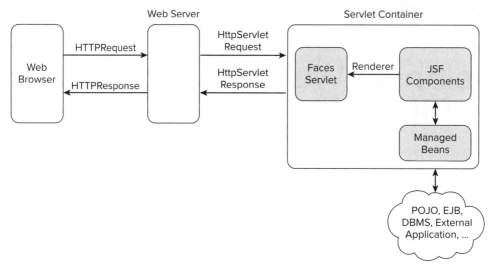

**FIGURE 29-1**

The managed beans can be linked to the UI JSF components so that when, for example, you fill out a form on a web page, the entered values are automatically assigned to the corresponding field in your Java bean. Sometimes beans that support UI components are called baking beans.

Without further ado, let's start working on a two-page web application to enroll students into classes. The first page will enable users to enter student ID, name, and course, and the second page will confirm the enrollment. The UI will be supported by managed beans, which will serve as a data model, but the data won't be saved (persisted) anywhere (you'll learn about persistence in Lesson 33).

## MANAGED BEANS

Managed JSF beans are similar to JavaBeans, introduced in Lesson 28, but the word *managed* means that they can be linked directly to JSF components. Besides storing data they may also contain information about page navigation. FacesServlet controls the managed beans.

Let's start working on the student enrollment example by creating a managed bean called Student. But first create a new dynamic web project called Lesson29 in Eclipse IDE.

Then create the Java class `Student` in the folder `com.practicaljava.Lesson29.beans` and add the annotation `@ManagedBean` right above the class name. Eclipse will mark this line with a red *x*, complaining about the missing import statement. Right-click this *x*, select the option Quick Fix, and import this annotation class from the `javax.faces.bean` package. The annotation registers the class `Student` as a JSF resource. Add the `@RequestScoped` annotation to ensure that the container creates a new instance of this bean for each user's request.

Declare three private variables: `int studentId`, `String name`, and `long classId`. Then select Source ⇨ Generate Getter and Setters and the rest of the `Student` code will be auto-generated. It will look like Listing 29-1.

**LISTING 29-1:** Managed bean Student

```
package com.practicaljava.lesson29.beans;

import java.io.Serializable;

import javax.faces.bean.ManagedBean;
import javax.faces.bean.RequestScoped;

@ManagedBean
@RequestScoped
public class Student implements Serializable{

    private long studentId;
    private String name;
     private int classId;

     public long getStudentId() {
          return studentId;
     }
     public void setStudentId(long studentId) {
          this.studentId = studentId;
     }
     public String getName() {
          return name;
     }
     public void setName(String name) {
          this.name = name;
     }
     public int getClassId() {
          return classId;
     }
     public void setClassId(int classId) {
          this.classId = classId;
     }
}
```

Configuration of the managed beans is done using annotations — no additional configuration files are required. But if you specify the file *faces-config.xml* in the WEB-INF directory, its setting will override the annotation values.

## CREATING A JSF WEBSITE

The content of the baking bean Student will have to be populated from the UI. With JSF you can either select the components that you want to put on each web page á la carte, or use a more structured and efficient approach called templating. I'll explain the creation of JSF sites with templating.

## Templating

The layout of most websites is similar: They have headers, footers, left and/or right sidebars, and content areas. This was taken into consideration by the designers of Facelets, who introduced templating. For example, you can define one template for a site that contains a header and a footer, and just change the views displayed in the content area based on the user's actions. This is what templating is all about.

You start developing the website by creating an .xhtml file containing the main layout, and then add a number of views, or *composition pages*. Each of these composition pages will declare which template it has to use, define the required components for the content area, and either reuse the headers and footers from the template or override them. You'll find the methodology of creating pages easy to understand when you create a sample template and composite page.

In Eclipse select File ➪ New ➪ XHTML page, and accept the default location, the WebContent directory. Enter StudentTemplate as the name of the file and click Next. Then select New Facelet Template in the pop-up window shown in Figure 29-2.

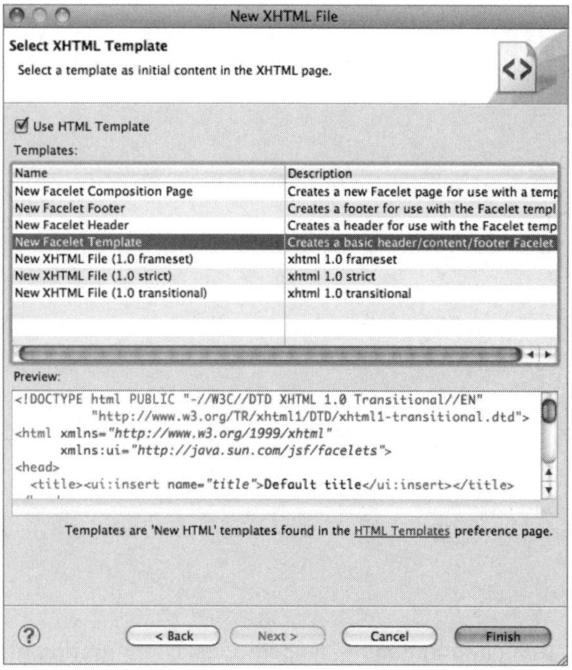

**FIGURE 29-2**

This will create a basic webpage template with three sections — header, content, and footer — as shown in Listing 29-2.

**LISTING 29-2:** Facelet template StudentTemplate.xhtml

```
<!DOCTYPE html PUBLIC "-//W3C//DTD XHTML 1.0 Transitional//EN"
          "http://www.w3.org/TR/xhtml1/DTD/xhtml1-transitional.dtd">
<html xmlns="http://www.w3.org/1999/xhtml"
      xmlns:ui="http://java.sun.com/jsf/facelets">
<head>
   <title><ui:insert name="title">Default title</ui:insert></title>
</head>

<body>

<div id="header">
    <ui:insert name="header">
          Header area.  See comments below this line in the source.
          <!--  include your header file or uncomment the include below
                  and create header.xhtml in this directory -->
          <!-- <ui:include src="header.xhtml"/> -->
    </ui:insert>
</div>

<div id="content">
  <ui:insert name="content">
          Content area.  See comments below this line in the source.
          <!--  include your content file or uncomment the include below
                  and create content.xhtml in this directory -->
<!-- <div> -->
          <!-- <ui:include src="content.xhtml"/> -->
          <!-- </div> -->
  </ui:insert>
</div>

<div id="footer">
  <ui:insert name="footer">
          Footer area.  See comments below this line in the source.
          <!--  include your header file or uncomment the include below and create
footer.xhtml in this directory -->
      <!--<ui:include src="footer.xhtml"/>  -->
  </ui:insert>
</div>

</body>

</html>
```

The three sections enclosed in the HTML `<div>` tags suggest that the web pages that will be using this template might have a header, a content area, and the footer. If you don't need this page layout just delete the appropriate `<div>`. If you need a sidebar create a `<div>` section with the ID sidebarleft or sidebarright. Notice the ui prefix inside the tags: It points at the *namespace* where all the Facelets components reside. The namespace concept (see xmlns in the code) comes from XML. You can use any prefix instead of ui, but it should uniquely identify the location of the components referred to by the prefix. Namespaces are defined in the top portion of the template in Listing 29-2. You can have more than one namespace defined in your JSF page. The h prefix is typically used for HTML JSF components, and f for the core ones:

```
xmlns:ui=http://java.sun.com/jsf/facelets
xmlns:h=http://java.sun.com/jsf/html
xmlns:f="http://java.sun.com/jsf/core"
```

I'll make a slight text edit to the code in order to have the header and the footer displayed in a large font — note the HTML tag <h1>:

```
<!DOCTYPE html PUBLIC "-//W3C//DTD XHTML 1.0 Transitional//EN"
        "http://www.w3.org/TR/xhtml1/DTD/xhtml1-transitional.dtd">
<html xmlns="http://www.w3.org/1999/xhtml"
      xmlns:ui="http://java.sun.com/jsf/facelets">
<head>
  <title><ui:insert name="title">Student Portal</ui:insert></title>
</head>

<body>

<div id="header">
    <ui:insert name="header">
        <h1>Welcome to my Students Portal</h1>
    </ui:insert>
</div>

<div id="content">
  <ui:insert name="content">
        The content of my student portal goes here  </ui:insert>
</div>

<div id="footer">
  <ui:insert name="footer">
        <h1>The footer of my portal is here</h1>
  </ui:insert>
</div>

</body>
</html>
```

You can run and test this template in Eclipse: Right-click *StudentTemplate.xhtml* and select Run as ⇨ Run on Server. If the GlassFish server is not running, Eclipse will start it for you and deploy the Lesson29 web application. Figure 29-3 shows how the internal Eclipse web browser will show this page. You can also enter the URL http://localhost:8080/Lesson29/StudentTemplate.xhtml into a regular web browser — the output will be the same.

I want to keep this well-designed header and footer on each page of my student portal that has views with changing content in the middle. Let's create a new file called *EnrollStudent.xhtml*, but this time select New Facelets Composition Page in the pop-up window shown in Figure 29-2. Eclipse will create the file shown in Listing 29-3.

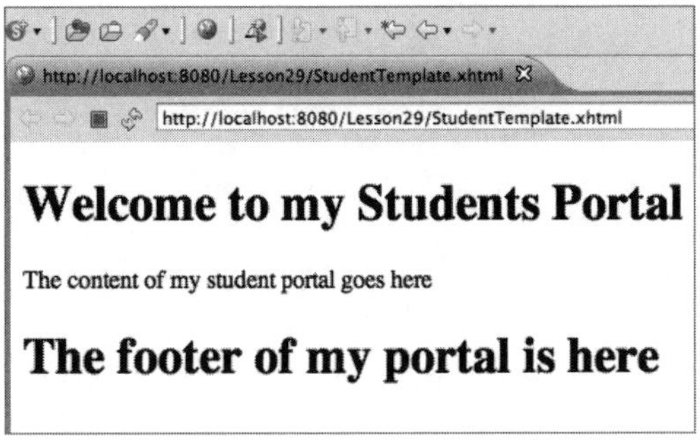

**Welcome to my Students Portal**

The content of my student portal goes here

**The footer of my portal is here**

**FIGURE 29-3**

---

**LISTING 29-3:** Default composition page in Eclipse

```
<!DOCTYPE html PUBLIC "-//W3C//DTD XHTML 1.0 Transitional//EN"
    "http://www.w3.org/TR/xhtml1/DTD/xhtml1-transitional.dtd">

<html xmlns="http://www.w3.org/1999/xhtml"
    xmlns:ui="http://java.sun.com/jsf/facelets"
    xmlns:h="http://java.sun.com/jsf/html"
    xmlns:f="http://java.sun.com/jsf/core">

<ui:composition template="">
    <ui:define name="header">
        Add your header here or delete to use the default
    </ui:define>
    <ui:define name="content">
        Add your content here or delete to use the default
    </ui:define>
    <ui:define name="footer">
        Add your footer here or delete to use the default
    </ui:define>
</ui:composition>
</html>
```

Note that this Facelet also has three sections, like the template in Listing 29-2. To link this page to a template, add *StudentTemplate.xhtml* to the `template` attribute. To reuse the header and the footer from the template, just remove the Facelets tag `<ui:define>` for the header and footer, as in Listing 29-4. When the JSF implementation can't find the definitions for these sections, it'll use the ones from the template.

---

**LISTING 29-4:** EnrollStudent.xhtml, first version

```
<!DOCTYPE html PUBLIC "-//W3C//DTD XHTML 1.0 Transitional//EN"
    "http://www.w3.org/TR/xhtml1/DTD/xhtml1-transitional.dtd">

<html xmlns="http://www.w3.org/1999/xhtml"
    xmlns:ui="http://java.sun.com/jsf/facelets"
```

*continues*

**LISTING 29-4** *(continued)*

```
        xmlns:h="http://java.sun.com/jsf/html"
        xmlns:f="http://java.sun.com/jsf/core">

    <ui:composition template="StudentTemplate.xhtml">
        <ui:define name="content">
            Add your content here or delete to use the default
        </ui:define>
    </ui:composition>
    </html>
```

Now run this page in Eclipse or in your web browser, but add /faces to the URL, like this:
http://localhost:8080/Lesson29/faces/EnrollStudent.xhtml. By default this will engage
FacesServlet, which knows how to properly interpret all JFS tags. Figure 29-4 shows the first version of the Enroll Student page.

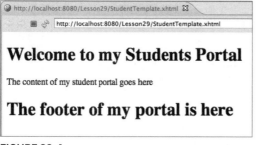

**FIGURE 29-4**

To complete the Enroll Student page, let's add several JSF tags: form, inputText, outputText, and
commandButton. Listing 29-5 shows the updated version of *EnrollStudent.xhtml*. Note that the
value attribute of each inputText tag is bound to the corresponding field of the student bean. The
first letter of the bean name starts with a lowercase letter (student, not Student). The <br/> tag is
just an HTML tag indicating a line break.

**LISTING 29-5:** EnrollStudent.xhtml, second version

```
<!DOCTYPE html PUBLIC "-//W3C//DTD XHTML 1.0 Transitional//EN"
    "http://www.w3.org/TR/xhtml1/DTD/xhtml1-transitional.dtd">

<html xmlns="http://www.w3.org/1999/xhtml"
    xmlns:ui="http://java.sun.com/jsf/facelets"
    xmlns:h="http://java.sun.com/jsf/html"
    xmlns:f="http://java.sun.com/jsf/core">

<ui:composition template="StudentTemplate.xhtml">
 <ui:define name="content">
  <h:form>

    <h:outputText value="Student Name:"/>
```

```
        <h:inputText  value="#{student.name}" title="name" id="name" /> <br/>

        <h:outputText value="Student ID:"/>
        <h:inputText value="#{student.studentId}" title="id" id="studentId"/> <br/>

        <h:outputText value="Class ID:"/>
        <h:inputText  value="#{student.Id}" title="classId" id="classId" /> <br/>
        <h:commandButton action="enrolled" value="submit" />

    </h:form>
  </ui:define>
 </ui:composition>
 </html>
```

Run `EnrollStudent.html` and you'll see the great-looking portal in Figure 29-5. Just to prove that the UI is really bound to the bean `Student`, I've hard-coded my name in this class. That's why you see it in the form. The Student ID and Class ID fields show zeros — default values for numbers.

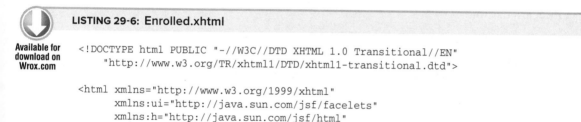

**FIGURE 29-5**

## Page Navigation

The command button in Listing 29-5 has the attribute `action="enrolled"`. This means that after this form is processed, the web application has to navigate to another JSP called `Enrolled`. Listing 29-6 shows this page.

**LISTING 29-6:** Enrolled.xhtml

```
<!DOCTYPE html PUBLIC "-//W3C//DTD XHTML 1.0 Transitional//EN"
     "http://www.w3.org/TR/xhtml1/DTD/xhtml1-transitional.dtd">

<html xmlns="http://www.w3.org/1999/xhtml"
      xmlns:ui="http://java.sun.com/jsf/facelets"
      xmlns:h="http://java.sun.com/jsf/html"
```

*continues*

**LISTING 29-6** *(continued)*

```
        xmlns:f="http://java.sun.com/jsf/core">

  <ui:composition template="StudentTemplate.xhtml">
    <ui:define name="content">

     <h:outputText value="#{student.name}"/>, thank you for enrolling in class
     <h:outputText value="#{student.classId}" />

    </ui:define>

  </ui:composition>
</html>
```

It's a pretty simple way of arranging page navigation, isn't it? I've enrolled myself into class 123 in *EnrollStudent.xhtml*. After pressing Submit, I got the confirmation shown in Figure 29-6.

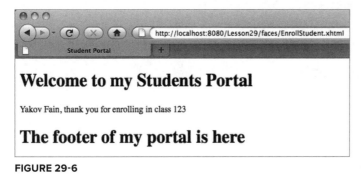

**FIGURE 29-6**

The `commandButton` button can be used for a different purpose: to call a method on a bean. You can write a bean just to serve as a data model, but nothing prevents you from writing a method that performs some business logic or performs other actions, such as getting data from a web service or saving data using EJBs. In the next code snippet the click on the button will call the method `doSomething()` on the bean `Student`.

```
    <h:commandButton value="Do Something" action="#{student.doSomething}" />
```

The method `doSomething()` can return a `String` containing the name of the next JSF page to be called, just like this:

```
    class Student{
    ...
      public String doSomething(){
          // Do something and navigate to the next page
          return "TheNextPage.xhtml";
      }
    }
```

To become familiar with other tags available in Facelets, refer to Chapter 5 of the Java EE 6 tutorial, available at `http://download.oracle.com/javaee/6/tutorial/doc/giepx.html`.

# CONVERTERS AND VALIDATORS

Managed beans can have *converters* and *validators* assigned to them. A Java class has strongly typed fields, but when the data arrives at the web page it has to be converted into Strings. JSF performs this conversion automatically for Java data types, but you can write your own converter and add some application-specific logic.

Validators enable you to put some constraints on the data in the managed beans. You can either use predefined annotations such as @NotNull, @Min, and @Max from javax.validation.constraints to specify the data validation constraints on the bean's fields, or create your own custom annotations that implement constraints specific to your application. The standard validators on the fields of the Student bean may look like this:

```
@ManagedBean
@RequestScoped
public class Student implements Serializable{

    @NotNull(message="you must enter Student ID"
    @Size(min=8, max=10,
            message="Student ID must include between 8 and 10 symbols")
    private long studentId;

    @Size(min=2, message="Name can have less than two characters")
    private String name;

    @NotNull(message="Please enter Class ID")
    private int classId;
    ...
}
```

The core JSF library has standard validators that can validate length, and ranges for long and double values. You encapsulate these validators right in the JSF file, like this:

```
<h:inputText  value="#{student.name}" title="name" id="name" >
   <f:validateLength minimum="2"/>
</h:inputText>
```

To create a custom validator (such as CreditCardValidator) you need to write a Java class that implements the javax.faces.validator.Validator interface and performs the validation in the method validate(). If the value is not valid, the method has to throw a ValidatorException. Custom validators must be registered in *faces-config.xml*.

```
<validator>
    <validator-id>CreditCardValidator</validator-id>
    <validator-class>myvalidators.CreditCardValidator</validator-class>
</validator>
```

Custom validators can be used in a JSF page with the <f: validator> tag, as in the following example:

```
<h:inputText  value="#{student.creditcad}" title="card" id="card" >
   <f:validator id="CreditCardValidator"/>
</h:inputText>
```

## TRY IT

Rewrite the sample stock server application that you created in the "Try It" section of Lesson 28, but this time do it using JSF. The JSF client should have one text input field with a Submit button. The user will enter the stock symbol she wants to get a price quote for. Generate a random quote and return a web page with the quote. Reuse the code for `StockServerImpl` from Listing 25-2 to generate the price quotes. The web page should show the list of available stocks.

The managed bean will have a method called `getQuotes()` that should be called when the user clicks the Submit button.

## Lesson Requirements

You should have Java installed.

> You can download the code and resources for this Try It from the book's web page at `www.wrox.com`. You can find them in the Lesson29 folder in the download.

## Hints

NetBeans 7 IDE supports JSF better than Eclipse does. It has a number of wizards, and in particular you can easily define the navigation of your web pages in a graphical interface. (See `http://netbeans.org/kb/docs/web/jsf20-support.html` for details.) The other popular IDE, IntelliJ IDEA 9, also offers excellent support for JSF. (Refer to `www.jetbrains.com/idea/features/javaserver_faces.html` for details.)

## Step-by-Step

1. Create a new `StockServer` bean, which will include the methods `getQuote()` and `getNasdaqSymbols()`.

2. Define a JSF template.

3. Create two JSF pages: one for making a request for a price quote for a specific stock, and the other one for showing the result. The Submit button in the first web page should call the method `getQuote()` on the managed bean.

4. Run and test this JSF application.

> *Please select Lesson 29 on the DVD to view the video that accompanies this lesson.*

# 30

# Introducing JMS and MOM

People send messages to each other via e-mail, instant messages, Twitter, Facebook, and so on. People can also communicate using more traditional methods such as the post. You just need to drop a letter in a mailbox, and the rest will be taken care of by postal service providers and logistics companies such as USPS, FedEx, UPS, and DHL.

Applications can send messages to each other using message-oriented middleware (MOM), which plays a role similar to that of the delivery services. A program "drops the message" into a message queue (think *mailbox*) using the Java Messaging Service (JMS) API, and the message is delivered to another application that reads messages off of this queue.

Although JMS is a part of the Java EE specification, you can use it with Java SE applications without needing to have any Java application server — just make a `.jar` containing JMS classes available to your program. In this lesson you'll learn how to write simple Java clients to send and receive applications with the JMS API via a MOM provider. In Lesson 31 I'll show you how to bring a Java EE application server to the messaging architecture, and why it's beneficial. Finally, in Lesson 32 you'll learn about the value that message-driven beans bring to the table.

## MESSAGING CONCEPTS AND TERMINOLOGY

You have already learned several methods of data exchange in distributed Java applications — direct socket communication, RMI, and HTTP-based interactions. But all of them were based on remote procedure calls (RPC) or the request/response model. MOM enables you to build distributed systems that communicate *asynchronously.*

JMS is an API for working with MOM. JMS itself isn't the transport for messages. JMS is to MOM what JDBC is to a relational DBMS. Java applications can use the same JMS classes with any MOM provider. Here's a list of some popular MOM software:

➤ WebSphere MQ (IBM)

➤ EMS (Tibco Software)

➤ SonicMQ (Progress Software)

➤ ActiveMQ (open source, Apache)

➤ Open MQ (open source, Oracle)

If you place an order to buy some stocks by calling the method `placeOrder()` on a remote machine, that's an example of a *synchronous* or blocking call. The calling program can't continue until the code in the `placeOrder()` method is finished or has thrown an error.

With *asynchronous* communications it's different — you can place an order but don't have to wait for its execution. Similarly, when you drop a letter in a mailbox you don't have to wait for a mail truck. The same applies to e-mail — press the Send button and continue working on other things without waiting until your message has been received. Recipients of your e-mails also don't have to be online when you send a message; they can read it later.

The process of placing a trading order comes down to putting a Java object that describes your order into a certain *message queue* of your MOM provider. After placing an order, the program may continue its execution without waiting until the processing of the order is finished. Multiple users can place orders into the same queue. Another program (not necessarily Java) should be de-queueing and processing messages. Figure 30-1 shows how a trading application can place orders (and receive executions) with another application running on a stock exchange.

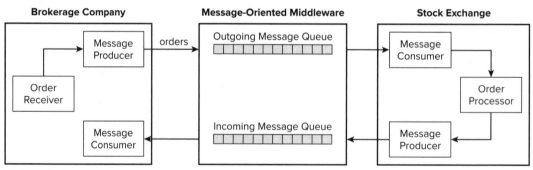

**FIGURE 30-1**

To increase the throughput of your messaging-based application, add multiple consumers reading messages off of the same queue. You can create a consumer Java program that starts multiple threads, each of them de-queuing messages from the same queue. In Lesson 32 you'll see how easy it is to configure multiple consumers using message-driven beans.

After your order has been processed, the appropriate message object will be placed into another queue and, if your application is active at that time, it will de-queue the message immediately upon its arrival. If your application is not running, but you've opted for guaranteed delivery (explained later in this lesson), the messages will be preserved in the queue by the MOM provider.

Even if the application in a brokerage company is down when the order execution arrives from the stock exchange, it'll be saved in the MOM server until the receiving program is up again.

# TWO MODES OF MESSAGE DELIVERY

A program can *send* or *publish* a message. If it sends a message to a particular queue, and another program receives the message from this queue, we call this *point-to-point (P2P)* messaging. In this mode a message is deleted from a queue as soon as it's successfully received.

If a program publishes a message to be consumed by multiple recipients, that's *publish/subscribe (pub/sub)* mode. A message is published to a particular topic and many subscribers can subscribe to receive it. The topic represents some important news for applications and/or users, for example PriceDropAlert, BreakingNews, et cetera. In pub/sub mode a message is usually deleted from a queue as soon as all subscribers receive it (read about durable subscribers in the section "How to Subscribe for a Topic").

Another good example of a pub/sub application is a chat room. A message published by one person is received by the other people present in the chat room. Developing a chat room with JMS and MOM is a pretty trivial task.

Message delivery can be guaranteed, and MOM, just like the post office, will keep the message in a queue until the receiver gets it. In this mode messages are persistent — the MOM provider stores them in its internal storage, which can be a DBMS or a file system. In a non-guaranteed mode MOM will deliver a message only to the receiving applications that are up-and-running at the moment that the message arrives.

# JMS API OVERVIEW

JMS is a pretty simple API that includes Java classes that enable you to send and receive messages. Following are the names of the major JMS interfaces and a short description of each. All of them are defined in the package `javax.jms`. All Java EE 6 JMS classes and interfaces are listed at `http://download.oracle.com/javaee/6/api/javax/jms/package-summary.html`, but I'll just give you the summary of the main ones.

➤ `Queue` is a place to put (or get) your messages. The messages will be retrieved using the first in first out (FIFO) rule. A *message producer* (sender) puts messages in a queue and a *message consumer* (receiver) de-queues them.

➤ `QueueConnection` is an interface (it extends `Connection`) that represents a particular connection to MOM (and plays a similar role to the JDBC class `Connection`).

➤ `QueueConnectionFactory` is an object that creates `Connection` objects (just the JDBC class `DataSource` does).

➤ `QueueSession` is an object that represents a particular session between the client and the MOM server. `QueueConnection` creates a session object.

➤ `QueueSender` is an object that actually sends messages.

➤ `QueueReceiver` receives messages.

➤ `TopicPublisher` publishes messages (it has a similar functionality to `QueueSender`).

➤  `TopicSubscriber` is an object that receives messages (it has a similar functionality to `QueueReceiver`).

➤  `Topic` is an object that is used in pub/sub mode to represent some important application event.

➤  `TopicPublisher` publishes messages to a topic so the `TopicSubscribers` can subscribe to it.

➤  `Message` is an object that serves as a wrapper to an application-specific object that can be placed in a JMS queue or published to a topic.

## TYPES OF MESSAGES

Every message contains a header and optional body and has facilities for providing additional properties. The header contains the message identification (unique message ID, destination, type, et cetera). The optional properties can be set by a program to tag a message with application-specific data, for example `UrgentOrder`.

The optional body contains a message that has to be delivered. Following are the types of JMS messages that you can place in a message body. All these interfaces are inherited from `javax.jms.Message`.

➤  `TextMessage` is an object that can contain any Java `String`.

➤  `ObjectMessage` can hold any `Serializable` Java object.

➤  `BytesMessage` holds an array of bytes.

➤  `StreamMessage` has a stream of Java primitives.

➤  `MapMessage` contains any key/value pairs, for example `id=123`.

## HOW TO SEND A MESSAGE

Queues have to be preconfigured in MOM and their names must be known before a program can start sending messages. In the real world a MOM server administrator manages queues and other messaging artifacts. When Java developers get to know the queue parameters, they have a choice of either creating message objects (such as `ConnectionFactory` and `Queue`) programmatically every time they need to send or receive a message, or pre-creating objects bound to some kind of naming service (you'll see examples in Lesson 31).

A program has to perform the following steps to send a message:

**1.**  Create (or get from some naming server) a `ConnectionFactory` object.

**2.**  Create a `Connection` object and call its `start()` method.

**3.**  Create a `Session` object.

**4.**  Create a `Queue` object.

**5.**  Create a `MessageProducer` object.

**6.** Create one of the `Message` objects (such as `TextMessage`) and put some data in it.

**7.** Call the `send()` method on the `QueueSender`.

**8.** Close the `QueueSender`, `Session`, and `Connection` objects to release system resources.

Listing 30-1 shows a code fragment that sends a message to a queue called `TestQueue`. Note that the method `createQueue()` just creates an instance of the `Queue` object locally — the actual destination with the name `TestQueue` has to exist in MOM.

**LISTING 30-1:** Sending a message

```
Session session=null;
ConnectionFactory factory;
QueueConnection connection=null;

try{
    //The next two lines are specific to Open MQ. Another MOM
    // provider will have their own version of creating connection
    factory = new com.sun.messaging.ConnectionFactory();
    factory.setProperty(ConnectionConfiguration.imqAddressList,
                        "mq://localhost:7677,mq://localhost:7677");

    connection = factory.createQueueConnection("admin","admin");

    connection.start();

    session = connection.createQueueSession(
                        false, Session.AUTO_ACKNOWLEDGE);
    Queue ioQueue = session.createQueue("TestQueue");
    MessageProducer queueSender = session.createProducer(ioQueue);

    // Buy 200 shares of IBM at market price
    TextMessage outMsg = session.createTextMessage("IBM 200 Mkt");

    queueSender.send(outMsg);
    queueSender.close();

    System.out.println(
"Successfully placed an order to purchase 200 shares of IBM");
    }
    catch (JMSException e){
        System.out.println("Error: " + e.getMessage());
    }
    finally{
      try{
        session.close();
        connection.close();
      } catch (Exception e) {
        System.out.println("Can't close JMS connection/session " +
                                        e.getMessage());
      }
    }
```

The code in Listing 30-1 uses an Open MQ–specific implementation of JMS's `ConnectionFactory`. After you read the section "Administering Objects in Open MQ" later in this lesson, you'll understand why these lines refer to localhost and port 7677.

## HOW TO RECEIVE A MESSAGE

The program that receives messages is called a *message consumer*. It can be a standalone Java program or a special type of enterprise Java bean called a *message-driven bean (MDB)*. You can receive messages either synchronously, using the `receive()` method, or asynchronously by implementing the `MessageListener` interface and programming a callback `onMessage()`.

Under the hood, the `receive()` method uses a polling mechanism that constantly asks for a message. It blocks program execution until the message is received or the specified time has expired:

```
QueueReceiver queueReceiver= Session.createReceiver(ioQueue);
Message myMessage = queueReceiver.receive();
```

The next line shows how to set a timeout interval of 500 milliseconds:

```
Message myMessage=queueReceiver.receive(500);
```

Using an asynchronous callback `onMessage()` is the best way to receive messages because the message consumer is not sending multiple requests to MOM just to see if the message is in the queue. The callback method `onMessage()` will be called immediately when a message is put in the queue. The listener class must perform the following steps to receive messages:

1. Create (or get from some naming server) the `QueueConnectionFactory` object.

2. Create a `Connection` object and call its `start()` method.

3. Create a `Session` object.

4. Create a `Queue` object.

5. Create a `QueueReceiver` object.

6. If your class implements `MessageListener` (see Listing 30-2) write implementation for the callback method `onMessage()`. If you want to get messages synchronously, just call the `QueueReceiver.receive()` method. In this case implementation of the `MessageListener` interface is not needed.

7. Close the `Session` and `Connection` objects to release the system resources.

The sample class `MyReceiver` in Listing 30-2 shows how to consume messages from the `TestQueue` asynchronously. Its constructor creates JMS objects and registers itself as a message listener. The callback `onMessage()` has code for processing the received messages.

**LISTING 30-2:** Receiving a message

```java
package com.practicaljava.lesson30;

import javax.jms.*;
import com.sun.messaging.ConnectionFactory;
import com.sun.messaging.ConnectionConfiguration;


public class MessageReceiver implements MessageListener{

      Session session=null;
       ConnectionFactory factory;
       QueueConnection connection=null;
       MessageConsumer consumer=null;

      MessageReceiver(){
            try{
             factory = new com.sun.messaging.ConnectionFactory();
             factory.setProperty(ConnectionConfiguration.imqAddressList,
                               "mq://localhost:7677,mq://localhost:7677");
             connection = factory.createQueueConnection("admin","admin");

             connection.start();


              Session session = connection.createQueueSession(
                               false, Session.AUTO_ACKNOWLEDGE);

            Queue ioQueue = session.createQueue( "TestQueue" );

            consumer = session.createConsumer(ioQueue);
            consumer.setMessageListener(this);

            System.out.println("Listening to the TestQueue...");

            // Don't finish -  wait for messages
            Thread.sleep(100000);

          } catch (InterruptedException e){
            System.out.println("Error: " + e.getMessage());
          }
        catch (JMSException e){
           System.out.println("Error: " + e.getMessage());
        }
        finally{
           try{
                     connection.close();
           } catch (Exception e) {
               System.out.println("Can't close JMS connection/session "
                                                   + e.getMessage());
           }
```

*continues*

**LISTING 30-2** *(continued)*

```
        }

    }

    public static void main(String[] args){
        new MessageReceiver();
    }

    public void onMessage(Message msg){
        String msgText;
        try{
            if (msg instanceof TextMessage){
                msgText = ((TextMessage) msg).getText();
                System.out.println("Got from the queue: " + msgText);
            }else{
                System.out.println("Got a non-text message");
            }
        }
        catch (JMSException e){
            System.out.println("Error while consuming a message: " +
                                            e.getMessage());

        }
    }
}
```

In this code sample the onMessage() method checks to ensure that the arrived message is of the TextMessage type. All other types of messages can be ignored.

The message acknowledgment mode is defined when the Session object is created. The createSession() method has two arguments. If the first argument is true, the session is transacted, the value of the second argument is irrelevant, and the message can be either committed or rolled back by the consumer.

If the commit() method has been called, the message is removed from the queue. The rollback() method leaves the message in the queue. If the session is non-transacted, as in our earlier example, the second argument defines the acknowledgement mode.

➤ AUTO_ACKNOWLEDGE mode sends the acknowledgment back as soon as the method onMessage() is successfully finished.

➤ CLIENT_ACKNOWLEDGE mode requires explicit acknowledgment, such as msg.acknowledge(). (This grants permission to delete the message from the queue.)

➤ DUP_OK_ACKNOWLEDGE mode is used in case the server fails; the same message may be delivered more than once. In some use cases it's acceptable — for example, receiving a price quote twice won't hurt.

If more than one message is processed by the same `Session` object, acknowledgement of one message affects all messages from the same session.

## HOW TO PUBLISH A MESSAGE

Programs publish messages to topics, which should be created in advance by the MOM system administrator. Multiple subscribers can get messages published to the same topic (this is also known as *one-to-many mode*).

Message publishing is very similar to message sending, but the program should create a `Topic` instead of a `Queue` and a `Publisher` instead of a `Sender`, and the `publish()` method should be called instead of `send()` as in Listing 30-3:

**LISTING 30-3: Publishing a message to a topic**

```
...
TopicConnection connection = connectionFactory.createTopicConnection();

TopicSession pubSession = connection.createTopicSession(false,
                                        Session.AUTO_ACKNOWLEDGE);

Topic myTopic = pubSession.createTopic ("Price_Drop_Alerts");

TopicPublisher publisher= pubSession.createPublisher(myTopic);

connection.start();

TextMessage message = pubSession.createTextMessage();
message.setText("Sale in Apple starts  tomorrow");
publisher.publish(message);
```

## HOW TO SUBSCRIBE FOR A TOPIC

Subscribers can be *durable* or *non-durable*. Durable subscribers are guaranteed to receive their messages; they do not have to be active at the time a message arrives. Non-durable subscribers will receive only those messages that come when they are active. This is similar to the way chat rooms operate — you must be online to get messages.

The code snippet in Listing 30-4 creates a non-durable subscriber. Two modifications have to be made to this code to create a durable subscriber: The client ID has to be assigned to the connection — `connection.setClientID(username)` — and the `createDurableSubscriber(topic)` method should be used instead of `createSubscriber(topic)`.

**LISTING 30-4: Subscribing to a topic**

```
TopicSession subSession =
connection.createTopicSession(false, Session.AUTO_ACKNOWLEDGE);

subSession.createTopic("Price_Drop_Alerts");

TopicSubscriber subscriber = subSession.createSubscriber(topic);

connection.start();

subscriber.setMessageListener(this);

public void onMessage(Message message) {

String msgText;
try{
    if (msg instanceof TextMessage){
            msgText = ((TextMessage) msg).getText();
            System.out.println("Got " + msgText);
    }else{
        System.out.println("Got a non-text message");
    }
}
catch (JMSException e){
    System.out.println("Error: " + e.getMessage());
}
}
```

## MESSAGE SELECTORS

If you have to share a queue with some other applications or developers from your team, use
*message selectors* (also known as *filters*) to avoid "stealing" somebody else's messages. For
example:

```
String selector = "StoreName=Apple";
session.createReceiver(queue, selector);
```

In this case the queue listener will de-queue only those messages that have the `String` property
`StoreName` with the value `Apple`. Message producers have to set this property:

```
TextMessage outMsg = session.createTextMessage();
outMsg.setText("Super sale starts tomorrow");
outMsg.setStringProperty("StoreName", "Apple");
```

Remember that message selectors slow down the process of retrieval. The messages stay in a queue
until the listener with the matching selector picks them up. Selectors really help if your team has a
limited number of queues and everyone needs to receive messages without interfering with others.
But if someone starts the queue listener without selectors, it just drains the queue.

# ADMINISTERING OBJECTS IN OPEN MQ

To test all code samples from this lesson you need a MOM provider that will transport your messages. I'll be using the open-source MOM provider Open MQ. It's well-known commercial-grade software. As a bonus, it comes with GlassFish. You already have it installed under your `glassfishv3/mq` directory. If you decide to use Open MQ with any other application server you can download it separately from `https://mq.dev.java.net/`.

As I stated earlier in this lesson, I'm not going to use Java EE server — the goal is to test standalone Java clients communicating with Open MQ directly, without the middlemen.

First, open a command (or Terminal) window to the `glassfishv3/mq/bin` directory, and start the Open MQ broker. In Mac OS I enter the following command (in Windows you'll need to run `imqbrokerd.exe`):

```
./imqbrokerd -port 7677
```

You'll see a prompt informing you that the broker is ready on port 7677. Now open another command window, change to the `glassfishv3/mq/bin` directory again, and start the admin GUI tool imqadmin to create the required messaging destinations:

```
./imqadmin
```

The window of the Open MQ administration console will open. Add a new broker and name it StockBroker, change the port to 7677, enter the password `admin`, and click OK. Figure 30-2 shows a snapshot of my screen after these steps.

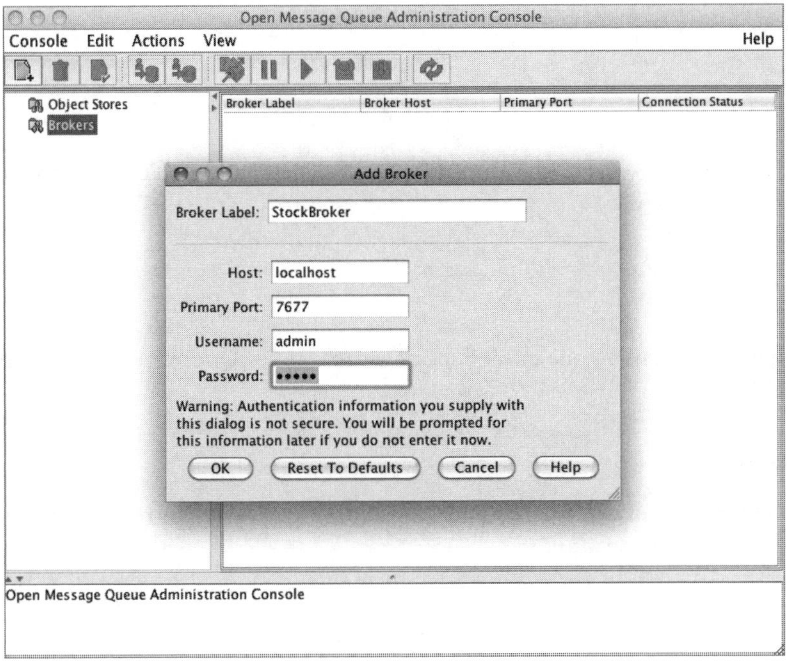

**FIGURE 30-2**

Now connect to StockBroker (using the right-click menu) and create a new destination named TestQueue to match the queue name in the code sample from Listing 30-1. I didn't change any settings in the pop-up window shown in Figure 30-3. Note the radio button on top that enables you to specify whether you need a queue or a topic.

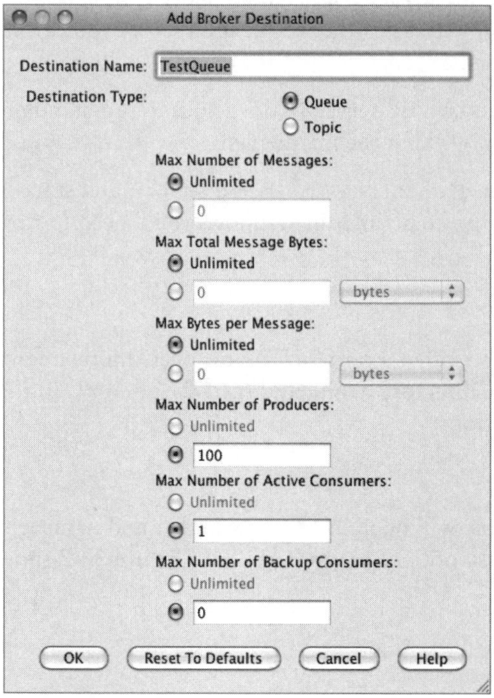

**FIGURE 30-3**

The creation of administrated MOM objects (the TestQueue) is complete; now you're ready to write and test the message sender and receiver.

## TRY IT

The goal is to write two Java programs — one to send messages to the TestQueue and the other to receive them from the TestQueue.

## Lesson Requirements

You should have Java and Open MQ installed. You'll also need the JMS classes and their implementation by Open MQ — jms.jar and imq.jar.

> *You can download the code and resources for this "Try It" section from the book's web page at* www.wrox.com. *You can find them in the Lesson30 folder in the download.*

## Hints

Open two console views by clicking the little icon with the plus sign in the lower right of Eclipse to see output of the sender and receiver in different console views. You can also use the pin feature (click the icon with the pin image) to pin each console to a specific application. You can also detach the Eclipse console to display it as a separate window.

## Step-by-Step

1. In Eclipse, go to Java perspective and select File ⇨ New ⇨ Create a New Java Project. Name it Lesson30 and click Next. Select the tab Libraries and click Add External JARs. Find `jms.jar` and `imq.jar` in `glassfishv3/mq/lib` and add them to the project. Click Finish. You've created a regular Java SE project with two extra jar files in its CLASSPATH. `jms.jar` contains the standard JMS classes and interfaces, and `imq.jar` has the Open MQ implementation of the JMS API.

2. Create a new class called `MessageSender` with a `main()` method, and add the `import` statements for all JMS classes and the Open MQ implementation of `ConnectionFactory`:

   ```
   import javax.jms.*;
   import com.sun.messaging.ConnectionFactory;
   import com.sun.messaging.ConnectionConfiguration;
   ```

3. Enter the code from Listing 30-1 into the method `main()`.

4. Compile and run the program. You should see the message "Successfully placed an order to purchase 200 shares of IBM." At this point the message is located in the TestQueue configured under the Open MQ server. It'll stay there until some program de-queues it from there.

5. Create another Java class called `MessageReceiver` to look like what is created by the code in Listing 30-2.

6. Run `MessageReceiver`. It'll print on the console the message "Listening to the TestQueue" and will be retrieving all the messages from the queue. `Thread.sleep()` will keep this program running.

7. Observe that one console displays the messages of the producer application, and that the consumer properly receives the messages and printing confirmations in another console view.

> *Please select Lesson 30 on the DVD to view the video that accompanies this lesson.*

# Introducing JNDI

Instead of having distributed Java programs instantiate lots of reusable objects over and over again, it's better if these objects are pre-created and published at a known server, where they can be easily and quickly found. The role of the Java Naming and Directory Interface (JNDI) is to make it easier to find objects in distributed applications. It plays a role similar to that of a company telephone directory assistance service. Various software vendors offer specialized directory assistance software, and JNDI provides a standard API to read from and write to such directories.

In this lesson you'll be introduced to the JNDI concepts and will see how to use JNDI for publishing (and looking up) administered JMS objects.

## JAVA NAMING AND DIRECTORY INTERFACE

A *naming service* enables you to add, change, or delete names of objects that exist in some naming hierarchy so other Java classes can look them up to find their location. One more analogy: In a library, you find the name of the physical location of the book in a directory, and then go to the shelf to pick up the book. A naming service provides a unique name for every entry that is registered (*bound to*) with the service. Every naming service will have one or more *contexts* — think of directories and subdirectories in a file system, where any directory tree with children is a context. The naming tree originates from a root node, which is also known as an *initial context* (like a root directory on the disk).

A *directory service* enables you to search the naming tree by object attributes rather than object names. One example is that of the domain name system, which is a distributed naming system that takes the domain name of a networked computer or service and returns the IP address and port number of the resource.

To allow clients to do lookups, there has to be a process that initially binds the objects to a naming tree. This can be handled by an independent program that (for example) binds employee names to a directory server of some organization. Java EE servers do a similar job (during start-up) by binding such objects as EJB, Servlets, JMS, and database connection pools to either their internal or external naming servers.

# ADMINISTERING JNDI OBJECTS IN GLASSFISH

Each Java EE application server offers a tool that allows administration of its service modules —
we are interested in binding objects to their directory names. When you start GlassFish there is
a message on the console: "Waiting for DAS to start…" DAS stands for Domain Administration
Server, which authenticates the user with administrative privileges and responds to requests from a
graphical web browser-based Admin Console. To use the console enter the following URL in your
browser: `http://localhost:4848/`. You'll be prompted for the user ID (admin) and password,
which you selected when you installed GlassFish in Lesson 26.

After a successful log-on you'll see the console, as in Figure 31-1, which enables you to administer
various Java objects, but I'll continue using the example of JMS-related ones. There are two JMS
nodes in the directory tree on the left. One is called JMS Resources, and the other Java Message
Service. The latter shows the physical queue named TestQueue that I created using the Open MQ
administrative utility in Lesson 30.

The only reason GlassFish automatically knows about the destinations in this MOM is that this
application server is integrated with Open MQ. To configure another MOM server you'd need to
create a new JMS host by filling out the form shown in Figure 31-2.

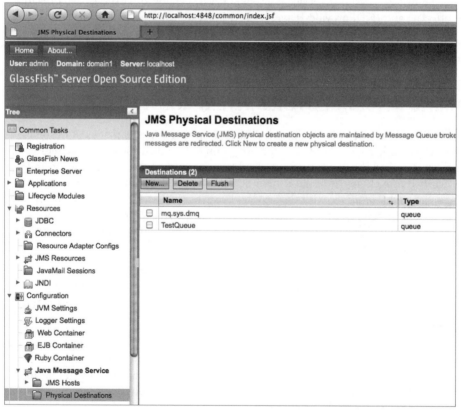

**FIGURE 31-1**

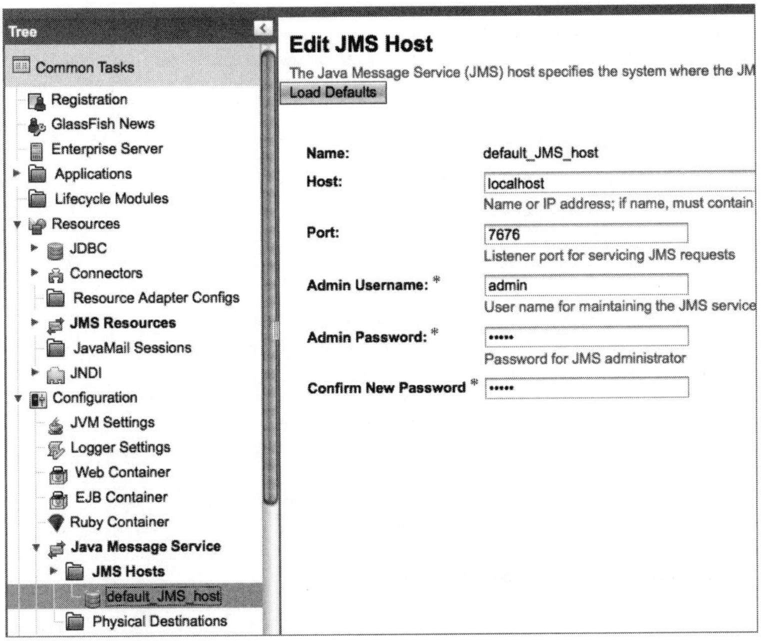

**FIGURE 31-2**

Now you need to create a GlassFish JMS entry to map to the physical MOM queue. Add the new destination resource to JMS Resources (see Figure 31-3). I called this JMS resource MyJMSTestQueue and mapped it to TestQueue, created in the previous lesson.

Now create another administered resource, a connection factory. Because the creation and closing of connections and senders are slow operations, you may want to consider writing code for JMS connection pools. Java EE servers enable you to configure such pools. In Figure 31-4 you can see that the size of the connection pool is configurable. By default, eight JMS connections will be created and, as the number of users increases, up to 32 connections will be created by GlassFish.

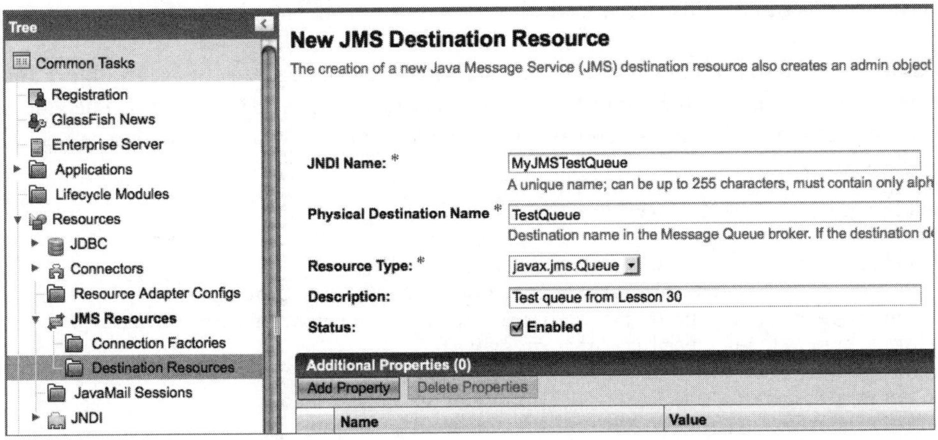

**FIGURE 31-3**

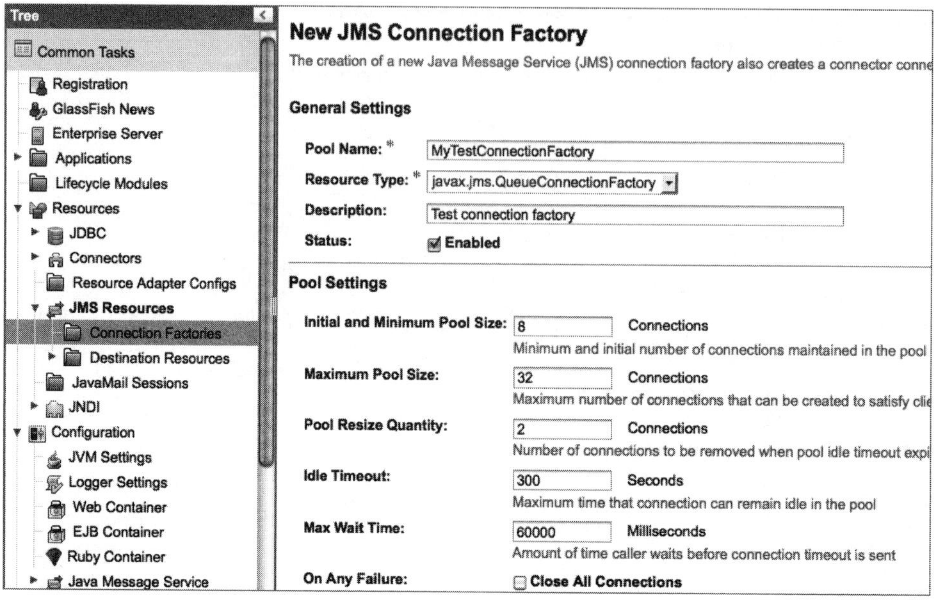

**FIGURE 31-4**

To have JMS implementation as part of a Java EE server you need to download the full profile version (see Lesson 26).

## ACCESSING THE GLASSFISH NAMING SERVICE WITH JNDI

To start searching for an object in the JNDI tree a Java program needs to get a hold of its initial node. There are two use cases to consider here:

➤ An external Java client needs to find the server that runs the naming service.

➤ A Java client is running inside the Java EE server that runs the naming service.

In the first case you need to prepare an instance of the Java `Hashtable` or `Properties` object and give it as a parameter to the constructor of the `javax.naming.InitialContext` class. The values to put in such `Properties` objects vary — consult the documentation for your application server. The following code is an example:

```
Properties props = new Properties();

props.setProperty("java.naming.factory.initial",
                  "com.sun.enterprise.naming.SerialInitContextFactory");
props.setProperty("java.naming.factory.url.pkgs","com.sun.enterprise.naming");
props.setProperty("java.naming.factory.state",
              "com.sun.corba.ee.impl.presentation.rmi.JNDIStateFactoryImpl");
props.setProperty("org.omg.CORBA.ORBInitialHost", "localhost");
props.setProperty("org.omg.CORBA.ORBInitialPort", "8080");

InitialContext ic = new InitialContext(props);
```

In the second case the Java client can just create an instance of `InitialContext` with no argument constructor — the Java EE server knows where to find its naming service:

```
InitialContext ic = new InitialContext();
```

Now you can either perform a lookup starting from the initial context node, or ask the container to inject the reference to the required resource using the syntax of Java annotations.

Revisit the code in Listing 30-1. It creates a `ConnectionFactory` object connecting to a MOM server using classes specific to Open MQ. Now, because TestQueue is known to GlassFish, a Java client wouldn't even need to know what MOM server is in use, but would just look up a standard JMS `ConnectionFactory` in the instance via the JNDI API.

The statement that a Java client is running inside the server may not sound right to you, but any program that's trying to find another object can be considered a client. For example, imagine a web application in which the web browser invokes a Servlet that needs to place an order into a message queue or invoke an EJB. In Listing 31-1 you can see a Servlet that plays the role of a Java client operating inside a Java EE container.

**LISTING 31-1: Servlet as Java client**

```java
import java.io.IOException;
import java.io.PrintWriter;

import javax.servlet.ServletException;
import javax.servlet.annotation.WebServlet;
import javax.servlet.http.HttpServlet;
import javax.servlet.http.HttpServletRequest;
import javax.servlet.http.HttpServletResponse;

@WebServlet(description = "The servlet that Sends a message to a queue",
            urlPatterns = { "/quote" }, name="QuoteService")
public class QuoteService extends HttpServlet {

    protected void doGet(HttpServletRequest request,
        HttpServletResponse response) throws ServletException, IOException {

        PrintWriter out = response.getWriter();
        out.println("<html><body bgcolor=yellow>");
        out.println("<h2>Hello from QuoteService</h2>");

        out.println("Sending a message to the TestQueue");

        MessageSender mySender=new MessageSender();
        mySender.sendMessage("IBM 200 Buy");
    }
}
```

The Servlet receives a request from the client and instantiates the Java class `MessageSender` shown in Listing 31-2. Compare the code of this class with the sender from Listing 30-1. Now this code from Listing 31-1 doesn't contain anything specific to the MOM provider.

If, say, you decide to change the MOM provider to the one that performs better, just re-create the administered JMS objects using the administration console of GlassFish and there is no need to change anything in the code of MessageSender. If you decide to switch from GlassFish to another server, just redeploy this Servlet and MessageSender in another Java EE application server.

**LISTING 31-2: Looking up JNDI object and sending message**

```java
package com.practicaljava.lesson31;

import javax.jms.*;
import javax.naming.*;

public class MessageSender {

void sendMessage(String messageToSend){
 Session session=null;
 ConnectionFactory factory=null;
 Connection connection=null;

 try{
    // Find the JNDI context
    Context jndiContext = new InitialContext();

    // Look up the factory and the queue
   factory = (ConnectionFactory) jndiContext.lookup("MyTestConnectionFactory");
   Queue ioQueue = (Queue) jndiContext.lookup("MyJMSTestQueue");

   connection = factory.createConnection();

   connection.start();

   session = connection.createSession(false, Session.AUTO_ACKNOWLEDGE);
   MessageProducer queueSender = session.createProducer(ioQueue);

   // Buy 200 shares of IBM in this example
   TextMessage outMsg = session.createTextMessage(messageToSend);

   queueSender.send(outMsg);
   queueSender.close();

   System.out.println("Successfully placed an order to purchase 200 shares of
      IBM");

 }catch (JMSException e){
                System.out.println("Error: " + e.getMessage());
 }catch (NamingException e) {

      e.printStackTrace();
 }finally{
   try{
     session.close();
     connection.close();
   } catch (Exception e) {
```

```
    System.out.println("Can't close JMS connection/session " + e.getMessage());
  }
  }
}

}
```

Run the quote Servlet in Eclipse or direct your web browser to `http://localhost:8080/Lesson31/quote` and the message to purchase 200 shares of IBM will be placed in the physical queue TestQueue in the Open MQ server. If you are not sure if this application is working the way you expect it to, see if there are error messages in the domain's log file in the directory *glassfish/domains/domain1/logs/server.log*. If this program has executed properly, at the end of the log file you'll see the following message: "Successfully placed an order to purchase 200 shares of IBM."

## INJECTION OF JNDI RESOURCES

Even though looking up the JNDI object doesn't look too difficult, there is even a cleaner and simpler way of providing these resources to your Java EE components: using the annotation `@Resource`. The application server can inject the resource so you don't need to do a JNDI lookup. For example, injection of `ConnectionFactory` and `Queue` can look like this:

```
import javax.annotation.Resource;
...
@Resource(name="MyTestConnectionFactory")
private ConnectionFactory factory;

@Resource(name="MyJMSTestQueue")
private Queue ioQueue;
```

Resources can be injected into variables, as in the preceding example, or you can put the `@Resource` annotation above the method or a class definition. Depending on its location, the time of injection varies. If you put this annotation at the class level, the resource will be injected during run time when the application looks it up. If you put this annotation above the field or setter method declaration, the resource will be injected in the component when the application is initialized.

If you need to override resources specified in annotations, you can do it in XML configuration files. You'll see more examples of using resource injection with EJB in Lesson 32.

## DATASOURCE AND JNDI

In Lesson 22, while learning JDBC, you were creating database connections before executing any database queries. Imagine that multiple clients send requests to your application server, which has to execute database queries. Creating and closing connections are slow operations, and you want to do them as infrequently as possible.

Typically the administrator of the Java EE server pre-creates the pools of database connections, and configures the minimum and maximum number of connections and some other parameters.

Figure 31-5 shows a snapshot of the GlassFish administration console, where the JNDI entry named DerbyPool represents a pool of JDBC connections. The object `javax.sql.DataSource` is a factory of database connections. The administrator configures this factory as a JNDI resource, specifying what JDBC driver to use, how many connections to create initially, and the maximum number of connections allowed.

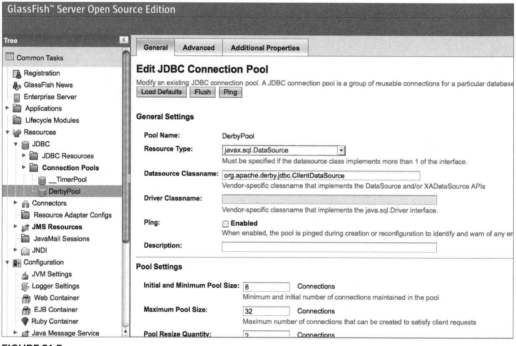

**FIGURE 31-5**

The user's request will communicate with a Java class deployed on the server, which will find the connection pool by its JNDI name (DerbyPool in this case) and make a `getConnection()` call on this resource. If there are available free connections, the Java class will immediately get an instance of the `PooledConnection` object (which works the same way as `Connection`). If many users are making concurrent requests, all connections may be taken, and there will be a slight delay until one of the busy connections is returned to the pool. Connections returned to the pool are not destroyed; they are preserved by the application server for future requests.

You can do either a JNDI lookup of the `DataSource` object or inject it to your Java code. If the name of the configured `DataSource` object is DerbyPool, the sample code to obtain a pooled database connection may look as follows:

```
InitialContext ic = new InitialContext();
DataSource ds = (DataSource) ic.lookup("DerbyPool");

Connection myConnection = ds.getConnection();
//The rest of the JDBC processing goes here as in Lesson 22

// Closing the connection just returns it back to the pool
```

```
// and makes it available for other Java clients
myConnection.close();
```

Injecting a `DataSource` using the `@Resource` syntax will look as follows:

```
@Resource(name="java:global/DerbyPool")
DataSource ds;
```

# LIGHTWEIGHT DIRECTORY ACCESS PROTOCOL

LDAP servers are specialized software products that store directory entries in hierarchical trees and are highly optimized for reading. This makes them a good choice for such directory services as employee lists or phone directories in an organization. Directories are mainly read, not changed, and this is where LDAP servers shine.

From the enterprise Java perspective you should keep LDAP solutions in mind when a really fast lookup of some Java objects is needed, such as with JMS connection factories, queues, or topics. Java developers use the JNDI API to look up and update the entries in LDAP. To use the same analogy as in the previous lesson, JNDI is to LDAP servers as JDBC is to DBMSes.

These are some popular LDAP servers:

➤ Oracle Directory Server (Oracle)

➤ Microsoft Active Directory (Microsoft)

➤ OpenLDAP (open-source, community developed)

➤ ApacheDS (open-source, Apache)

➤ OpenDS (open-source, Oracle)

The LDAP directory tree has a root entry, which consists of one or more distinguished names (unique identifiers). Typically the top of the hierarchy is an object with the prefix *o* for *organization*. One level below has the prefix *ou* for *organizational unit*, *cn* stands for *common name*, and so on. Unlike with other naming services, the search string starts from the very lowest hierarchical entry and the root entry has to be specified last. Here's an example of a distinguished name that can be used in a search:

```
cn=jsmith, ou=accounting, o=oracle.com
```

This example corresponds to the following hierarchy in an LDAP tree:

```
o = oracle.com
  ou = accounting
    cn = jsmith
```

The following code snippet prepares the JNDI properties, connects to the LDAP server, and finds the object called `CustomerHome`.

```
Hashtable env = new Hashtable();
env.put(Context.INITIAL_CONTEXT_FACTORY,
```

```
                          "com.sun.jndi.ldap.LdapCtxFactory");
env.put(Context.PROVIDER_URL, "ldap://localhost:389");
env.put(Context.SECURITY_AUTHENTICATION,"simple");
env.put(Context.SECURITY_PRINCIPAL, "cn=Directory Manager");
env.put(Context.SECURITY_CREDENTIALS,"myPassword");

DirContext ctx = new InitialDirContext(env);

CustomerHome custHome =(CustomerHome) ctx.lookup("cn=CusomerHome,
ou=RealBigProject, o=trump.com");
```

To study distributed applications you can run all the examples from this book (clients and servers) on a single computer, but real-world distributed applications can be constructed in various ways, for example:

➤ Computer #1 runs the LDAP server.

➤ Computer #2 runs an application server that has registered (published) some objects with the LDAP server on Computer #1.

➤ Computer #3 has a client program that finds object references on Computer #1 and invokes their methods on Computer #2.

➤ Computer #4 has a database management system that is being used by the application server running on Computer #2.

➤ Computer #5 publishes financial market data, and Computer #2 subscribes to this service.

...and so on, and so on.

In this lesson you've seen how to use JNDI, and some example of why you may want to use it. Comparing the code in Listing 30-1 with the one in Listing 31-1 is just one example that shows that naming and binding specific physical objects under a generic JNDI name enables you to remove these physical locations from your program code. You'll see more examples of using JNDI in Lesson 32.

## TRY IT

Create a class called `MessageReceiver` to consume messages. It has to perform a JNDI lookup and start listening to TestQueue. When the message arrives `MessageReceiver` should display it. Making a request to the Servlet from Listing 31-1 has to send a message to the queue, and `MessageReceiver` receives it and prints its content.

## Lesson Requirements

You should have Java and GlassFish v3 installed.

> *You can download the code and resources for this Try It from the book's web page at* www.wrox.com. *You can find them in the Lesson31 folder in the download.*

## Step-by-Step

1. Create a new class called `MessageReceiver` that implements `MessageListener` with the code similar to the one shown in Listing 30-2, but this time performing a JNDI lookup of MyTestConnectionFactory and MyJMSTestQueue.

2. Find out how to configure the GlassFish start-up class, and implement it to have `MessageReceiver` instantiated whenever the server starts.

3. Test a send/receive cycle by using the Servlet from Listing 31-1.

*Please select Lesson 31 on the DVD to view the video that accompanies this lesson.*

# 32

# Introduction to Enterprise JavaBeans

This lesson introduces you to one of the Java EE technologies, Enterprise JavaBeans, which can be used for implementing the business tier in a distributed application (refer to Figure 26-1). Lessons 27 and 28 were about various ways of programming the presentation tier on the Web; in Lessons 30 and 31 you learned how to organize communication between the different tiers of the application using messaging. You programmed the application business logic in POJOs.

Now you'll see how to program the business tier in EJBs, which are also POJOs, but managed by an EJB container. With the release of Java EE 6, EJB 3.1 and the Java Persistence API (JPA) 2.0 do offer you a clean and simple way to implement solutions for business logic and data persistence. The features covered in this lesson will work in application servers that support EJB 3.1. Such servers include GlassFish v3, JBoss 6, and WebSphere 8, and more vendors are working on making their application servers Java EE 6–certified. There is also the Apache TomTom bundle, which includes the open-source Apache OpenEJB project; at the time of this writing this bundle partially supports EJB 3.1.

In this lesson I'll introduce you to various types of EJBs, and the next lesson is about persisting data with JPA.

## WHO NEEDS EJB CONTAINERS?

What's wrong with POJOs? Why not just implement business logic there? You certainly can, but most likely you'd need to spend additional time manually programming a multi-threaded environment for them. The chances are that your application needs transactional support — if the business logic is located in POJO 1 and POJO 2, and the second one fails, you want to roll back whatever has been completed by the first one.

It's great that you know how to program message receivers using JMS, but how can you make this solution scalable? What if you need a couple of dozen message listeners that concurrently de-queue the messages? Don't forget about the tasks of integrating your POJOs with other tiers to perform authentication and JDBC operations.

EJB containers take care of all these infrastructure-related concerns without requiring manual programming on your side. You'll simply configure pools of *message-driven beans* (MDBs) if you need multiple message listeners. You'll turn on transactional support if need be. You don't need to worry about multi-threading problems if your beans operate in an EJB container. The configuration process is as simple as adding Java annotations in the EJB classes. Intercommunication among beans is done via dependency injection or singleton beans.

If you need to scale a distributed application, EJB containers offer clustering and failover support. Security authorization is also the container's responsibility. Without the need to manually code all these infrastructural functionalities, the code of your EJBs becomes really light.

The other interesting service offered by EJB containers is *asynchronous method invocation*, which enables asynchronous processing without the need for JMS or MOM.

EJB 3.1 supports embeddable containers: You can run EJB applications in a Java SE environment. This is a great idea for tasks such as testing because there's no need to depend on the readiness of a Java EE server — just test your EJBs locally. Creating an embeddable container is as simple as executing one line of code:

```
EJBContainer myContainer = EJBContainer.createEJBContainer();
```

If the originally selected application server doesn't deliver the performance or reliability you expected, deploy your EJBs in a different Java EE 6–compliant server without changing a line of code.

## TYPES OF EJBS

There are two major types of EJB: *session beans* and *message-driven beans*. MDBs specialize in retrieving messages from JMS queues or topics — this is all they can do. But session beans are where your application business logic will reside. There are three types of session beans:

➤ A *stateless* session bean is one that contains business logic but doesn't support state. In other words, it doesn't "remember" any data specific to the client. If the same client invokes two methods in a row on the stateless bean `FindBooks`, the container may use two separate instances of the `FindBooks` bean, as it doesn't store any intermediate data specific to the client.

➤ A *stateful* session bean is one that contains business logic and state. The EJB container allocates a specific instance of the session bean to the client and can store results between subsequent method invocations.

➤ A *singleton* session bean is one guaranteed to be the only instance of its kind in the container. Think of a singleton bean as a global repository, in which one bean can put some data to be used by another bean. Singleton session beans not only provide easy access to common data but also ensure that there are no race conditions in cases of concurrent access.

Older EJB specifications defined *entity beans* for data persistence. Formally they still exist in the EJB 3.1 specification, but they are being pruned, and most likely will disappear from future versions of Java EE releases.

An EJB container creates and maintains pools of session beans. The instances of the stateless beans are allocated to clients for much less time than stateful ones. Therefore, if you are working on a multiuser application with hundreds or thousands of concurrent requests to the EJB container, stateless beans offer a much more scalable solution, because a smaller pool can serve more users' requests.

But even with stateful session beans the EJB container is playing smart, and those instances sitting in memory without active interaction with the client are being *passivated* — removed from memory and stored on the disk. When the client issues another request to a stateful bean that has been passivated, the container will *activate* it again.

## STATELESS SESSION BEANS

I'll introduce you to stateless session beans by creating a simple example featuring an EJB that contains the business logic to return the message "Hello World."

### The Bean

Having a class that just returns "Hello World" is an obvious case for using a stateless session bean: It'll have only one method and there is no state to remember. Listing 32-1 shows you how to program such a bean.

**LISTING 32-1:** HelloWorld session bean, take 1

```
@Stateless
public class HelloWorldBean {

    public String sayHello(){
        return "Hello World!";
    }
}
```

Basically, you create a POJO and annotate it with one or more Java annotations. There are no special interfaces to be implemented to turn a POJO into an EJB. Accordingly there are @Stateful, @MessageDriven, and @Singleton annotations to mark other types of session beans. You may use the optional configuration file ejb-jar.xml in the application server's directory META-INF. This file also enables you to specify metadata for the EJB, and if you need to change the metadata on a production system without recompiling the code, make the changes in ejb-jar.xml — they will override the values specified via annotations.

### The Client's View

The bean shown in Listing 32-1 will run on the server, but the client that will invoke the sayHello() method can run either in the same JVM (e.g., a servlet or another bean) or in another one (e.g., a standalone Java SE application or Java EE class deployed in another container). Beans may or may not implement interfaces. If HelloWorldBean will be used only by clients running in the same JVM, you can mark it with a @LocalBean annotation to show that it's a no-interface bean.

If you'd like to expose certain business methods to local clients, you can create an interface and mark it with a @Local annotation. Your bean class has to implement this interface. If you'd like to expose your bean to remote clients, create an interface and mark it as @Remote. The bean has to implement this interface.

## Local No-Interface Beans

I am planning to use HelloWorldBean from the servlet running in the same JVM, so the final version of the code will look like Listing 32-2. Any EJB can use regular Java classes to implement business logic: For example, the sayHello() method can create instances of other Java classes with the new operator and invoke their business methods if need be.

**LISTING 32-2:** HelloWorld session bean, take 2

```
import javax.ejb.LocalBean;
import javax.ejb.Stateless;

@LocalBean
@Stateless
public class HelloWorldBean {

    public String sayHello(){
        return "Hello World!";
    }
}
```

Now let's do it hands-on. Create a new Dynamic Web Project in Eclipse as you did in previous lessons. Name it Lesson32. Then create a new servlet class, HelloWorldServlet, in the package com.practicaljava.lesson32.client (select the menu File ⇨ New ⇨ Servlet). This servlet will become our client, communicating with the EJB.

Next create a Java class called HelloWorldBean in the package com.practicaljava.lesson32.ejb by selecting File ⇨ New ⇨ Other ⇨ EJB ⇨ Session Bean (EJB 3.x). Do not select any local or remote business interfaces, and uncheck (when possible) the objects related to EJB 2.x. Eclipse will create a class with a default constructor. Add to this class the method sayHello() shown in Listing 32-2, and the EJB is finished.

The next step is to inject the HelloWorldBean into the servlet code with the @EJB annotation:

```
@EJB HelloWorldBean myBean;
```

Eclipse will mark this line with a red error bullet. Right-click it and select Quick Fix to automatically insert two import statements — one for the @EJB annotation and the other for HelloWorldBean.

Using JNDI remains an alternative to injecting the bean into the client. Java EE 6 supports portable JNDI names that don't depend on the application server's implementation. Instead of the @EJB annotation you could use the following code:

```
Context ctx = new InitialContext();
HelloWorldBean myBean = (HelloWorldBean)
                    ctx.lookup("java:global/Lesson32/HelloWorldBean");
```

Now add the following two lines in the `doGet()` method of the servlet to make it invoke the method `sayHello()` on the EJB:

```
PrintWriter out = response.getWriter();
out.println(myBean.sayHello());
```

That's all there is to it. The complete code of the servlet is shown in Listing 32-3.

**LISTING 32-3:** Servlet client for HelloWorldBean

```
import java.io.IOException;
import java.io.PrintWriter;

import javax.ejb.EJB;
import javax.servlet.ServletException;
import javax.servlet.annotation.WebServlet;
import javax.servlet.http.HttpServlet;
import javax.servlet.http.HttpServletRequest;
import javax.servlet.http.HttpServletResponse;

import com.practicaljava.lesson32.ejb.HelloWorldBean;

@WebServlet("/HelloWorldServlet")
public class HelloWorldServlet extends HttpServlet {

  @EJB HelloWorldBean myBean;

  protected void doGet(HttpServletRequest request,
      HttpServletResponse response) throws ServletException, IOException {

    PrintWriter out = response.getWriter();
    out.println(myBean.sayHello());
  }
}
```

## Local Beans

If you'd like to expose the business method to local clients, you can declare the interface marked with the `@Local` annotation and the bean will implement it, as in Listing 32-4.

**LISTING 32-4:** Local interface and bean

```
@Local
public interface Greeting {
    public String sayHello();
}

@Stateless
```

*continues*

**LISTING 32-4** *(continued)*

```
public class HelloWorldBeanL implements Greeting{

    public String sayHello(){
        return "Hello World!";
    }
}
```

## Remote Beans

For clients that may access the bean remotely, declare an interface marked with @Remote and have your bean class implement it. An EJB can implement both remote and local interfaces, and you can expose different methods for remote and local clients too.

**LISTING 32-5: The Greeting interface**

```
@Remote
public interface Greeting {    public String sayHello();
}

@Stateless
public class HelloWorldBeanL implements Greeting{

    public String sayHello(){
        return "Hello World!";
    }
}
```

The clients find remote beans by performing JNDI lookups. Because the client and the server may be running in different JVMs, all arguments of the remote methods must be serializable.

## The Server

Right-click the GlassFish server in the Servers view and add the project Lesson32 to deploy this Web application. You may also want to turn on automatic redeployments in GlassFish. To do this, double-click the GlassFish server in the Servers view and change the Publishing preferences to Automatically publish when resources change, as in Figure 32-1. This will eliminate the need for manual redeployment of the application every time the code changes.

Start GlassFish if it's not running and run HelloWorldServlet. You'll see the output produced by the EJB, as in Figure 32-2; you can get the same output by entering http://localhost:8080/Lesson32/HelloWorldServlet in your web browser. Even though this is a tiny application, nevertheless it demonstrates communication between objects from the presentation and business tiers. Real-world applications have more business logic, but from an architectural perspective they are the same.

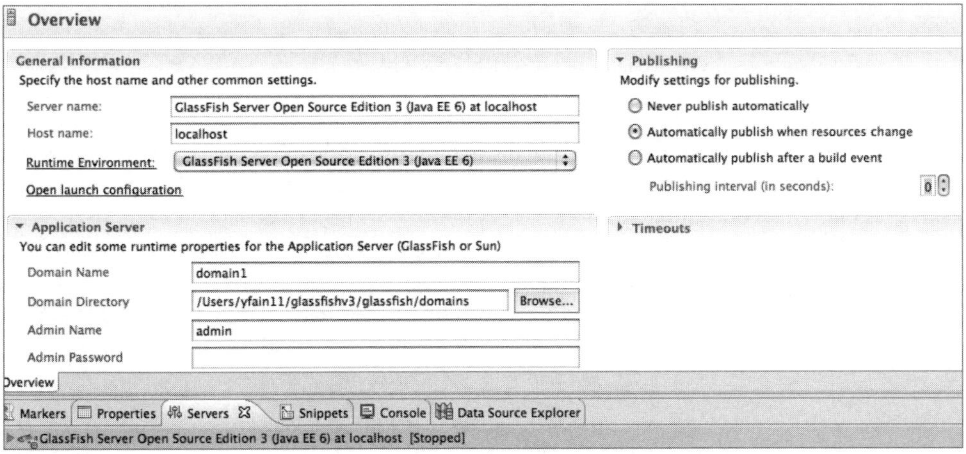

**FIGURE 32-1**

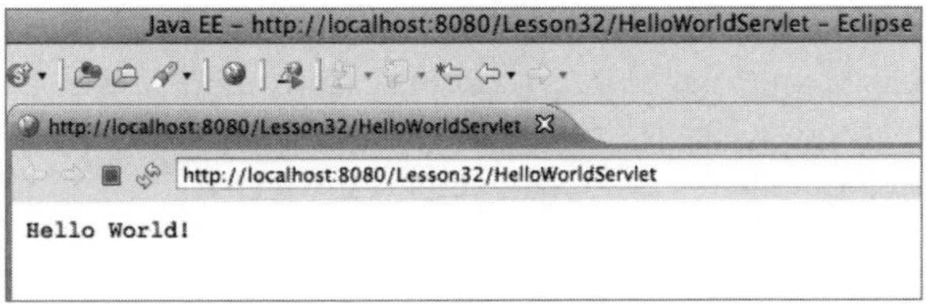

**FIGURE 32-2**

## Asynchronous Methods

There is one more feature in stateless beans that I'd like you to be aware of: *asynchronous methods*. Imagine that sayHello() is a long-running method performing some lengthy calculations and you'd like to call it and continue with other operations without waiting for it to complete. In a Core Java application you would start a thread that would eventually return the Future object, as explained in Lesson 21.

In the EJB container, however, you shouldn't create and start threads from the application code, because EJB container takes care of all multi-threading issues for you. The good news is that asynchronous methods offer a solution when you need to introduce parallel processing from EJBs.

Just mark the method with the @Asynchronous annotation and have it return an object of type javax.ejb.AsyncResult, which is an implementation of the Future interface:

```
@Asynchronous
public <Future>String sayHello(){

        // Some lengthy calculations go here
```

```
        //...

        return new AsyncResult<String>("Hello World!");
    }
```

The client would make a call to sayHello(), then execute some other code without waiting for sayHello() to complete, and at some point would request Future by making a blocking call, get(), as in the following code snippet:

```
//Asynchronous call
Future<String> myFutureGreeting = myBean.sayHello();
// Some other code that is executed immediately after the above line goes here
//...
}

// Sometime later you can make a blocking call and start
// waiting for the result of sayHello()
String myGreeting = myFutureGreeting.get();
```

You can also use asynchronous methods if a client needs to start more than one method on the EJB to run in parallel threads. The methods don't even need to return values; say one is generating large PDF files and the other prepares shipments based on today's orders. In this case you don't even need to process returned values; just declare the methods as asynchronous and invoke them from the client. They'll start immediately and will run in parallel.

## STATEFUL SESSION BEANS

Although stateless session beans are given to the client just for the time one method execution takes, stateful beans are allocated to the client for longer. They remember the results of the execution of previous method(s). For example, you can use a stateful bean to implement shopping cart functionality, enabling the user to add more than one item to the cart while browsing the company's catalog. When the client ends the session the stateful bean can be allocated to another client.

Suppose you have a stateful EJB called MyShoppingCart. The client looks up this bean using JNDI and makes the first call to the method addItem(). Then the client continues browsing and adds another item to the shopping cart. Then the client decides to check out and calls the method placeOrder(). All these method invocations are done on the same instance of the stateful bean MyShoppingCart.

```
MyShoppingCart myCart = (MyShoppingCart)
                    ctx.lookup("java:global/OnlineStore/MyShoppingCart");

// The client is browsing the catalog and finds the first item to buy
...
myCart.addItem(myFirstItem);

// The client continue browsing the catalog and finds the second item to buy
...
```

```
myCart.addItem(mySecondItem);

// The client is ready to check out
...

myCart.placeOrder();
```

To complete the shopping process and release the stateful bean for other clients you need to call one of the bean's `MyShoppingCart` methods marked with the `@Remove` annotation. In the preceding example the method `placeOrder()` should be marked with this annotation. You should also provide another `@Remove` method on the bean to allow the client to cancel the order and release the bean.

There is one more way to release a stateful bean, by using the `@StatefulTimeout` annotation, which enables you to specify how long a bean can stay allocated to the client without any activity. When this time expires the session times out and the bean is released.

# SINGLETON BEANS

Pretty often an application needs a place to keep data that is accessible to and shared by all the beans. Another use case for a singleton is to control access to some external resources. For example, if a limited number of connections are available to some external web service, you can create a singleton that will implement throttling for EJBs that need these connections. A singleton bean can be used as global storage (or a cache) for the application — the state of this bean is shared among clients.

Only one singleton bean with any given name can exist per JVM per application. If you need several singletons in an application, give them different names. An EJB container doesn't create pools of singleton beans. To create a singleton EJB just mark it with the `@Singleton` annotation:

```
@Singleton
public class MyGlobalStorage {
...
}
```

When is the singleton bean created? It's up to the EJB container to decide, unless you specifically want to request that this bean be created on application startup. This is called *eager initialization* and there is a special annotation, `@Startup`, for it:

```
@Startup
@Singleton
public class MyGlobalStorage {

    private Map<String, Object> = new HashMap<String, Object>();
...
    addToStorage(String key, Object objToStore){...}

    removeFromStorage(String key){...}
}
```

Let's say that you'd like to create a program that at certain times sends some messages into a queue. Write a singleton bean, request that the EJB container instantiate it on application start-up, and start pushing the messages immediately after the singleton has been constructed. There is another handy annotation, @PostConstruct, that will cause the container to invoke a method immediately after the bean's constructor is finished:

```
@Startup
@Singleton
public class MyStockQuoteServer {
...
 @PostConstruct
 void sendPriceQuotes(){
    // The code connecting to the stock prices feed and
    // sending messages to a queue goes here

 }
}
```

To get access to the business methods of a singleton, the client Java classes will need to call the public static method getInstance() on the specific singleton, as shown in the following code snippet. If you'll be implementing the singleton design pattern manually you need to declare a private constructor and a public static getInstance() in the class, but otherwise the EJB container will take care of this.

```
MyGlobalStorage.getInstance().addToStorage("emplOfTheMonth", bestEmployee);
```

The EJB container allows concurrent access to singleton beans, and by default it applies the *container-managed concurrency* policy, sparing the developer worry about race conditions and such. You just need to use the @Lock annotation, specifying whether you want a resource to be locked during the read or write operation. If you prefer to write thread-synchronization code by yourself, switch to *bean-managed concurrency*. You set the type of concurrency using the @ConcurrencyManagement annotation, as shown here:

```
@Singleton
@ConcurrencyManagement(ConcurrencyManagementType.BEAN)
public class MyGlobalStorage {
...
}
```

## DEPLOYING EJB

Before deployment to any application server, EJBs are usually packaged into one archive file, which could be a jar, an *Enterprise Archive* (ear), which is a jar with a .ear file name extension, or a war. Even such a simple two-class web application as our current example should be compressed and deployed as one file. If your client is a web application it's convenient to keep the EJB inside a war file. Let's create one.

Right-click the Deployment Descriptor section in the Eclipse project Lesson32 and select Export WAR file. In a second you'll get the file Lesson32.war that contains both the servlet and the EJB.

This file can be deployed in any Java EE 6–compliant application server. This war is really small: under 4 KB! Java EE 6 makes EJB components really lightweight. If you have multiple EJB classes, put them in one or more jars in the `WEB-INF/lib` directory.

If your client is not a small web application, or you want to keep EJBs deployed separately, you can package them inside a separate jar or ear file. The root directory that you'll be using to create ears has to have all compiled Java classes and, if applicable, the optional `ejb-jar.xml` file in the `META-INF` directory. As a matter of fact, you can create an ear file that will contain not only your EJBs, but also the war file.

## MESSAGE-DRIVEN BEANS

MDBs (message-driven beans) perform only one function: They retrieve messages from queues and topics via the JMS API. The clients never need to look them up or invoke their methods. The client just needs to drop a message in a queue or publish it to a topic, and the MDBs that were listening to the messages at these destinations will get invoked automatically.

MDBs must implement the `MessageListener` interface. All configuration parameters can be specified in the parameters of the `@MessageDriven` annotation, as shown in Listing 32-6.

**Available for download on Wrox.com**

**LISTING 32-6: MDB MyMessageBean**

```
@MessageDriven(mappedName="jms/testQueue", activationConfig = {
        @ActivationConfigProperty(propertyName = "acknowledgeMode",
                                  propertyValue = "Auto-acknowledge"),
        @ActivationConfigProperty(propertyName = "destinationType",
                                  propertyValue = "javax.jms.Queue")
    })
public class MyMessageBean implements MessageListener {

MessageDrivenContext ctx;

    // A no-argument  constructor is required
    public MyListener() {}

    public void onMessage(Message message){
        // The business logic is implemented here.
    }
}
```

When a message appears in the queue named `testQueue` the EJB container picks one of the MDBs from the pool and invokes its method `onMessage()`, passing the message from the queue as an argument. Unlike with the stand-alone message receivers described in Lesson 30, with MDBs the container gives you excellent freebies: distributed transaction processing, automatic pooling, co-location of receivers and other beans, and simple assignment of queues or topics to the receivers in deployment descriptors. In addition, you can easily configure the number of receivers by specifying the pool size in the deployment descriptor.

You can use any client to send a message in a queue. It can be a stand-alone client, as shown in Listing 31-2, a servlet, an EJB, etc.

# TIMER SERVICE

Many enterprise applications require the use of schedulers to perform certain repetitive tasks at certain times. Cron is a widely used scheduler for Unix-based applications. Windows also has a task scheduler (Control Panel ⇨ Scheduled Tasks). The open-source Quartz Scheduler is also popular among Java developers.

EJB 3.1 includes the `@Schedule` annotation, which takes a calendar-based expression so you can schedule the execution of required functionality in your beans. For example, you can create expressions that will invoke some business method every second, minute, hour, Monday, weekday midnight, etc.

The next code snippet shows how you can create a timer that will invoke the method `getPriceQuotes()` every second during weekdays from 9:30 A.M. to 4 P.M.:

```
@Stateless
public class MyStockQuoteFeed {

    @Schedule(second="*", minute="*", hour="9:30-16:00", dayOfWeek="Mon-Fri")
    public List getPriceQuotes(){
        // The code to connect to price quote feed goes here
        ...
    }
}
```

You can also create timers programmatically using the `TimeService` class and its methods `createTimer()`, `createSingleActionTimer()`, `createIntervalTimer()`, and `createCalendarTimer()`.

In addition to using `@Schedule` and programmatic timers, you can configure timers in the deployment descriptor `ejb-jar.xml`.

# SUMMARY

EJB 3.1 is a powerful solution for creating a scalable, easy-to-develop and -deploy, and lightweight solution for enterprise applications. Even a small-scale application can benefit from EJB 3.1. If your application doesn't need all the features mandated by the EJB specification, consider using EJB 3.1 Lite, which is a subset of the full specification.

It's not possible to cover all the features offered by EJB containers in one short lesson. I've introduced you to the main EJB concepts, but if you'd like more in-depth coverage, read Andrew Lee Rubinger and Bill Burke's *Enterprise Java Beans 3.1*, O'Reilly, 2010, ISBN: 0-596-15802-5.

# TRY IT

The assignment for this lesson is to implement the `StockServer` class as an EJB and to use the timer to automatically generate and print stock price quotes every second. The new quotes should be sent to `testQueue` via the JMS API and consumed by a message-driven bean. Reuse the code of the sample stock server application of the `StockServerImpl` from Listing 25-2 to generate the price quotes.

## Lesson Requirements

You should have Java and GlassFish v3 installed.

> *You can download the code and resources for this Try It from the book's web page at* www.wrox.com. *You can find them in the Lesson32 folder in the download.*

## Hint

If you want to push the stock prices to the end users, consider creating a JMS topic (e.g., `PriceQuotes`) to which the method `getQuote()` will publish the latest prices. The Java client should subscribe to this topic to get the fresh quotes every second.

## Step-by-Step

1.  In Eclipse project Lesson32 create a new stateless session bean, `StockServerBean`, that includes the method `getQuote()`. The initial version of the bean may look as follows:

    ```
    @Stateless
    public class StockServerBean {
      private String price=null;
      private ArrayList<String> nasdaqSymbols = new ArrayList<String>();

      public StockServerBean(){

        // Define some hard-coded NASDAQ symbols
        nasdaqSymbols.add("AAPL");
        nasdaqSymbols.add("MSFT");
        nasdaqSymbols.add("YHOO");
        nasdaqSymbols.add("AMZN");
        nasdaqSymbols.add("MOT");
      }

      public void getQuote(String symbol){

        if(nasdaqSymbols.indexOf(symbol.toUpperCase()) != -1) {

          // Generate a random price for valid symbols
          price = (new Double(Math.random()*100)).toString();
        }
        System.out.println("The price of "+ symbol + " is " + price);
      }
    }
    ```

2.  Use the `@Schedule` annotation to have the `getQuote()` method invoked every second.

3.  Replace the `println()` statement in the method `getQuote()` with the code sending a text message with the generated price quote to the queue `MyJMSTestQueue` configured in Lesson 31.

**4.** Create an MDB called `MyPriceConsumer` to retrieve and print messages from the queue `MyJMSTestQueue`.

**5.** Deploy this application in GlassFish and test it.

 *Please select Lesson 32 on the DVD to view the video that accompanies this lesson.*

# 33

# Introduction to the Java Persistence API

In the previous lesson you learned about various types of Enterprise Java Beans in which you could program the business logic of your application. Now it's time to talk about persisting data. If an online store allows users to place orders with session beans, there should be a mechanism for saving the data too. Typically, the data is persisted in DBMS.

The Java Persistence API (JPA) defines a standard way of mapping the Java classes to their relational database peers. This process is also known as *object-relational mapping (ORM)*. One of the popular third-party ORM frameworks, Hibernate, will be introduced in Lesson 36, but this lesson is a brief introduction to the standard JPA 2.0 implemented by any Java EE 6–compliant server.

## THE BIG PICTURE

In the past, J2EE specifications recommend using Entity EJB to provide all interactions with databases. Currently, entity beans are undergoing a pruning process, and you should use JPA instead to deal with your application's data querying and persistence. As a matter of fact, JPA 2.0 can be used from Java SE applications too.

JPA enables you to specify and run queries and update data without needing to write SQL statements as you did in Lesson 22 while studying JDBC.

The Java Persistence API enables you to map Java classes to database tables using metadata and perform create, retrieve, update, and delete (CRUD) operations using Java Persistence Query Language (JPQL), the Persistence Criteria API, and native database queries in SQL language. The idea is to create an application-specific domain model as a set of interrelated Java classes and map it to the corresponding data storage (the DBMS).

If a Java class marked with the `@Entity` annotation has no argument constructor you can call it an *entity*. Each entity instance corresponds to a row in a database table, as shown here:

```
@Entity
public class Employee{
 ...
}
```

If you start with an empty database, JPA tools enable you to create database tables based on Java entities. You can also map Java entities to the existing database tables. Just like database tables, Java entities can have one-to-one relationships (such as an *Employee* entity with one corresponding *OfficeAddress* entity), one-to-many relationships (such as one *Customer* with many *Orders*), many-to-one relationships (the opposite of one-to-many relationships), and many-to-many relationships (for example, a *UniversityClass* has many enrolled *Students*, but each *Student* can enroll into multiple classes).

Every entity class must define a field containing a unique value, which is the equivalent of a primary key in a database table.

The `EntityManager` class will deal with objects. Before persisting data you can validate the values using the Bean Validation API.

While JPQL provides string-based SQL-like syntax for working with entities, the newer Criteria API enables you to dynamically construct queries from strongly typed objects.

## MAPPING OBJECTS TO DATABASE TABLES

You can map Java classes to database tables via annotations, XML configuration files, or both. For example, common fields can be mapped with annotations, and DBMS-specific mapping can be done in XML files. It does not have to be one-to-one mapping; one Java entity can be mapped to a set of columns from more than one database table.

Besides having fields mapped to table columns, Java entities can have embeddable classes, like `Address` in the `Employee` entity.

Typically a database table has a *primary key* — one or more columns that uniquely identify each row. Java entities must have one or more fields making each instance unique. Such an entity ID can be marked with the `@Id` annotation, and you can request your JPA provider to auto-generate the ID by adding the annotation @GeneratedValue. Listing 33-1 shows an example of an `Employee` entity.

**LISTING 33-1: Employee entity**

```
@Entity
public class Employee{

    @Id
    @GeneratedValue(strategy=GenerationType.IDENTITY)

    @NotNull
    @Size(max=10)
```

```
    public String firstName;

    @NotNull
    @Size(min=2, max=20)
    public String lastName;

    @Column(name="boss_name")
    public String managerName;

    @OneToMany (mappedBy = "employee")
    public List<Address> addresses = new ArrayList<Address>();


}
```

If you don't specify the table name as a parameter of the annotation, JPA assumes that there is a corresponding database table with the same name as the entity class, which in our example is Employee. The specified strategy GenerationType.IDENTITY means that DBMS has an auto-generated primary key with auto-increment. Many database management systems support either identity columns or sequence objects with similar functionality.

The fields that must have values are marked as @NotNull. If an instance of the preceding Employee entity won't have values in the firstName or lastName fields, Bean Validation can catch this and generate an error. The entity fields that don't have to be persisted should be marked with the @Transient annotation.

If a table column name is not the same as the name of the entity field, you can specify the column name using @Column. According to Listing 33-1, the database column name *boss_name* corresponds to the field managerName of the entity Employee.

Not every Java class that corresponds to some data in the database has to be an entity. You can have embeddable classes that define a group of properties that belong to an entity. Let's say a company gives to each employee a smartphone identified by a phone number and model number. You can create a Java class to represent such a device and mark it with @Embeddable:

```
@Embeddable
public class SmartPhone implements Serializable{

    @Size(max=10)
    public String phoneNumber;

    public String model;
}
```

Now the Employee entity can embed the property of the SmartPhone type along with other fields:

```
@Entity
public class Employee{

    @Id
    @GeneratedValue(strategy=GenerationType.IDENTITY)

    @NotNull
```

```
    public String firstName;

  ...
  @Embedded
  public SmartPhone companyPhone;

}
```

The code in Listing 33-1 illustrates the mapping of one-to-many relations between the entities `Employee` and `Address` (not shown). One employee can have multiple addresses, so `Employee` references a collection of the `Address` entities.

## JPQL

JPQL is a SQL-like query language. The main difference is that SQL operates with the DBMS schemas, tables, and stored procedures, but JPQL manipulates with Java objects and their attributes from the domain model. You don't need to know details of the underlying data storage objects to perform JPQL queries.

If you know the queries in advance they can be precompiled; otherwise you can build them dynamically during the run time. Similarly, in JDBC you can use either `PreparedStatement` or `Statement`.

JPQL includes pretty easy-to-remember (and case-insensitive) keywords: `SELECT`, `FROM`, `WHERE`, `ORDER BY`, `GROUP BY`, and so on. Here's how you would write a JPQL query to find all managers who have subordinates with the last name Smith:

```
SELECT e.managerName,
FROM Employee AS e
WHERE e.lastName='Smith'
```

The next query finds all employees who were given iPhones by the firm. Note the dot notation to find the phone model from the embedded class.

```
SELECT e.firstName, e.lastName
FROM Employee AS e
WHERE e.companyPhone.model='iPhone'
```

To select all fields of certain entities (the equivalent of `Select *` in SQL) just specify the alias name of the entity right after the `SELECT` clause:

```
SELECT e FROM Employee AS e
```

The `Employee` and `Address` entities have a one-to-many relationship. If you'd like to find all employees who live in New York, this is the join written in JPQL:

```
SELECT DISTINCT e
FROM Employee AS e JOIN e.addresses as a
WHERE a.cityl='New York'
```

# ENTITYMANAGER

`EntityManager` is the centerpiece of persistence — it will execute all your JPA requests to read from or write into a database. Each instance of `EntityManager` is associated with a set of entities. Such a set is called a *persistence unit*. In Java EE containers the `EntityManager` can be injected as a resource, for example:

```
@PersistenceContext
EntityManager em;
```

In Java SE applications you need to instantiate `EntityManager` programmatically using `EntityManagerFactory`:

```
private EntityManagerFactory factory;

private static final String PERSISTENCE_CONTEXT_NAME = "employees";
...
factory = Persistence.createEntityManagerFactory(PERSISTENCE_CONTEXT_NAME);
EntityManager em = factory.createEntityManager();
```

The entity manager can create, update, remove, and find entities by IDs or using a query. The code to find an `Employee` entity with the ID `1234` can look like this:

```
Employee employee = em.find(Employee.class, 1234);
```

To create a new row in the `Employee` database table, create an instance of the entity `Employee` and invoke the method `persist()` on the `EntityManager`. To delete a row, call `remove()`. Your application can explicitly begin and commit transactions when the persistence is successfully completed.

```
@PersistenceContext
EntityManagerFactory factory;
EntityManager em;

@Resource
UserTransaction userTransaction;
...
em=factory.createEntityManager();


Employee newEmployee = new Employee();
newEmployee.firstName="Mary";
newEmployee.lastName="Thompson";
...
try{
  userTransaction.begin();
  em.persist(newEmployee);
  em.remove(oldEmployee);

 userTransaction.commit();

}
catch (SystemException e){ //several other exceptions can be thrown here
  e.printStackTrace();
  try{
   userTransaction.rollback();
```

```
    } catch(SystemException e1){e1.printStackTrace()}
  }
```

To select the manager name of the employee with the `firstName` Mary and the `lastName` Thompson, ask the `EntityManager` to run the following JPQL query:

```
EntityManager em;
List employees;
...employees = em.createQuery(
"SELECT e.managerName FROM Employee AS e WHERE e.firstName='Mary' "
    + " AND e.lastName='Thompson'").getResultList();
```

This static query works only for employees whose names are Mary Thompson. Note that the method `getResultList()` is invoked on the created query object. If you expect just one entity as a result, call the method `getSingleResult()` instead. To specify the first and last names dynamically, you should use parameters, for example:

```
EntityManager em;
List employees;

String firstName = "Mary";
String lastName = "Thompson";
...employees = em.createQuery(
"SELECT e.managerName FROM Employee AS e WHERE " +
  "e.firstName= :fname AND lastName= :lname")
    .setParameter("lname", lastName)
    .setParameter("fname", firstName)
    .getResultList();
```

One instance of `EntityManager` manages a *persistence unit* — a set of classes specified in the configuration file *persistence.xml*, which is located in the META-INF directory of the deployed EJB jar. If you package the application in the war file, this file has to be located either in the directory *WEB-INF/classes/META-INF* or in a jar under *WEB-INF/lib*.

The file *persistence.xml* specifies the name of the jar file that contains managed persistence classes and their names. It also contains the name of the JDBC data source (not the specific JDBC driver) used for communication with DBMS.

```
<persistence>
    <persistence-unit name="EmployeeManagement">
        <description>This unit manages Acme Employees </description>
        <jta-data-source>jdbc/HRDatabase</jta-data-source>
        <jar-file>MyEmployeeApp.jar</jar-file>
        <class>com.lesson33.Employee</class>
        <class> com.lesson33.Address</class>
    </persistence-unit>
</persistence>
```

## A BRIEF INTRODUCTION TO THE CRITERIA API

JPQL is a string-based query language, but the Criteria API allows the creation of strongly typed object-based queries. On one hand it's more verbose than JPQL, but on the other there is no need to do data-type conversion when processing query results.

These are some core interfaces in the Criteria API:

➤ `CriteriaBuilder`: A utility class that can create criteria queries.

➤ `CriteriaQuery`: This is an object that will contain all parts of the query, such as SELECT, FROM, and WHERE. It's like a memory graph, in which each node represents some clause of the query.

➤ `Root`: Represents the root of the query.

➤ `TypedQuery`: A query prepared for execution.

➤ `Join`: An object that represents a JOIN clause.

The next code fragment shows an equivalent of the JPQL query SELECT e FROM Employee AS e written using the Criteria API:

```
EntityManager em;
...
CriteriaBuilder cb = em.getCriteriaBuilder();
CriteriaQuery<Employee> crQuery = cb.createQuery(Employee.class);
Root<Employee> employee = crQuery.from(Employee.class);
crQuery.select(employee);
TypedQuery<Employee> tQuery= em.createQuery(crQuery);
List<Employee> employeess = tQuery.getResultList( );
```

Start with asking `EntityManager` to create `CriteriaBuilder`, which in turn creates the instance of `CriteriaQuery`. Note that via generics, the `CriteriaQuery` is typed based on the expected results. After that you add instances of required objects (SELECT, FROM, WHERE, and so on) to `CriteriaQuery`.

Finally, the `EntityManager` prepares the executable `TypedQuery` that produces strongly typed results by executing `getResultList()`. If you expect just one record back, use the `getSingleResult()` method. Adding several clauses to the query could look like this:

```
crQuery.select(employee).where(...).orderBy(...);
```

Because we are building the object graph, the order of the query classes in the preceding line is not important. The `Root` object can serve as a starting point for joining entities:

```
Root<Employee> employee = crQuery.from(Employee.class);
Join<Employee, Address> empJoin = employee.join(...);
```

The next example shows how to add the LIKE clause to get all employees with the last name Thompson:

```
Root<Employee> employee = crQuery.from(Employee.class);
crQuery.select(employee).where(
        cb.like(employee.<String>)get("lastName"),
        cb.parameter(String.class, "lname"));

TypedQuery<Employee> tQuery= em.createQuery(crQuery);
tQuery.setParameter("lname", "%Thompson%");
List<Employee> employeess = tQuery.getResultList( );
```

# BEAN VALIDATION

The Bean Validation framework (JSR-303) is a Java API for ensuring that the values in entities are correct. Validation can be performed at different stages of the entity life cycle. Define the constraints on your entities and the validation can be automatically initiated when you are about to create, update, or remove an entity.

Listing 33-1 includes the `@NotNull` and `@Size` constraints defined in the package `javax.validation` `.constraints`, but you can create your own validation rules as well.

The life-cycle callback methods marked with the annotations `@PrePersist` and `@PreRemove` are invoked on the entity before the `EntityManager` persists or removes this entity. Accordingly, another pair of annotations, `@PostPersist` and `@PostRemove`, are invoked after these operations.

For example, you can put the validation code in the method `transferEmployee()` to ensure that the transfer has been approved by the employee's manager. Throwing an exception invalidates the operation.

```
@PrePersist
public void validateTransfer(){
   if (!transferApproved()){
        throw new TransferException("Manager didn't approve transfer");
   }
}
```

# TRY IT

The GlassFish v3 server includes the binaries of the JPA provider EclipseLink (see www.eclipse .org/eclipselink). In this exercise you'll be using EclipseLink to auto-generate Java entities based on the existing database. This will serve as an example of object-relational mapping.

## Lesson Requirements

You should have Java, the Eclipse Java EE IDE, and GlassFish v3 installed.

> You can download the code and resources for this Try It from the book's web page at www.wrox.com. You can find them in the Lesson33 folder in the download.

## Step-by-Step

1.  Create a new JPA project in Eclipse by selecting File ➪ New ➪ Other ➪ JPA ➪ JPA project. Name it Lesson33 and keep the default settings of GlassFish Server Open Source Edition 3 as a target and Minimal JPA 2.0 Configuration as the configuration, as in Figure 33-1.

**2.** A pop-up suggesting the name of the default output folder displays. Don't change anything there; click Next.

**3.** The JPA Facet window (see Figure 33-2) will enable you to select the JPA provider — the libraries that implement JPA specification.

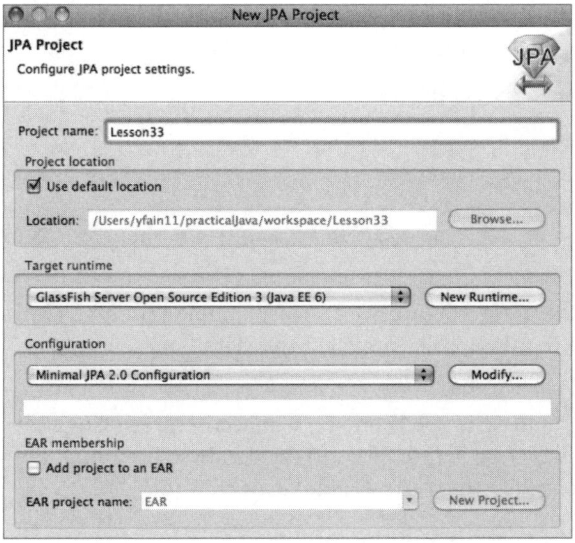

**FIGURE 33-1**

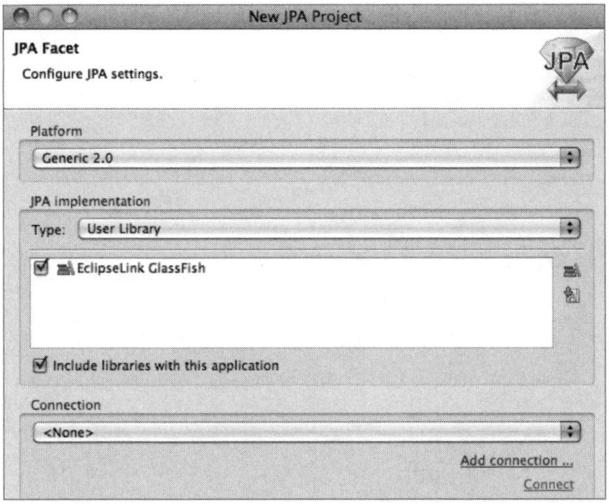

**FIGURE 33-2**

The User Library box will initially be empty. Press the little preferences icon next to it and then click New in the Preferences window. You'll need to add the following six jars from the folder *glassfishv3/glassfish/modules* to your new user library:

*org.eclipse.persistence.antlr.jar*

*org.eclipse.persistence.jpa.jar*

*org.eclipse.persistence.asm.jar*

*org.eclipse.persistence.jpa.modelgen.jar*

*org.eclipse.persistence.core.jar*

*javax.persistence.jar*

**4.** Start your Derby database server using the *startNetworkServer* command, as explained in Lesson 22.

**5.** In the connection drop-down (refer to Figure 33-2) select Sample JavaDB Database and click the Connect link. You'll see that Eclipse has opened the Data Source Explorer view showing the sample database that comes with Derby.

**6.** Right-click Sample JavaDB Database in the Database Connection view. Configure your new connection in the popup window (see Figure 33-3) to the database Lesson22 that you created in Lesson 22. Click Test Connection to ensure you did it right.

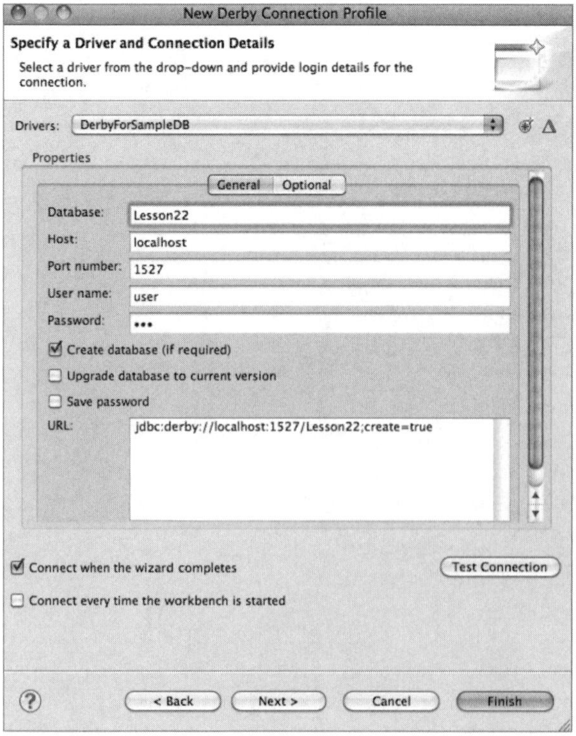

**FIGURE 33-3**

**7.** Figure 33-4 is a snapshot of Eclipse view Data Source Explorer, which shows you the table Employee from Lesson 22. It's located in the APP schema.

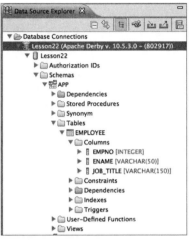

**FIGURE 33-4**

**8.** JPA requires database tables to have primary keys, but our table Employee didn't define one. You'll need to fix this by making the column empno a primary key. You can do it from the command line via the ij utility (see Lesson 22) by issuing the following command:

```
alter table APP.Employee add primary key (empno);
```

**9.** Right-click the name of project Lesson33 and select JPA Tools ⇨ Generate Entities from Tables. In the pop-up window select the table Employee and click Finish.

**10.** Open the folder *src* in your Eclipse project and you'll find there a freshly generated class called Employee that will look as follows:

```
import java.io.Serializable;
import javax.persistence.*;
/**
 * The persistent class for the EMPLOYEE database table.
 *
 */

@Entity
public class Employee implements Serializable {
    private static final long serialVersionUID = 1L;

    @Id
    private int empno;

    private String ename;

@Column(name="JOB_TITLE")
```

```java
      private String jobTitle;

      public Employee() {}

      public int getEmpno() {
        return this.empno;
      }

      public void setEmpno(int empno) {
        this.empno = empno;
      }

      public String getEname() {
        return this.ename;
      }

      public void setEname(String ename) {
        this.ename = ename;
      }

      public String getJobTitle() {
        return this.jobTitle;
      }

      public void setJobTitle(String jobTitle) {
        this.jobTitle = jobTitle;
      }
    }
```

**11.** Finally, open the folder *META-INF* and you'll find generated there the file *persistence.xml*:

```xml
<?xml version="1.0" encoding="UTF-8"?>
<persistence version="2.0"
xmlns="http://java.sun.com/xml/ns/persistence"
xmlns:xsi=http://www.w3.org/2001/XMLSchema-instance
 xsi:schemaLocation="http://java.sun.com/xml/ns/persistence
http://java.sun.com/xml/ns/persistence/persistence_2_0.xsd">

  <persistence-unit name="Lesson33">
    <class>Employee</class>
  </persistence-unit>

</persistence>
```

 *Please select Lesson 33 on the DVD to view the video that accompanies this lesson.*

# 34

# Working with RESTful Web Services

In the nineties the Web became widely used, and newly created web applications were consumed by millions of people around the world. At the same time lots of legacy applications were available for use only within corporate walls. They were written in a variety of programming languages and deployed on a plethora of types of hardware. There was a need to expose corporate data to wider audiences, which resulted in the creation of the standard interface for consuming data over the Web.

## THE SOAP WEB SERVICES

The first standard for publishing and consuming web services was the XML-based Simple Object Access Protocol (SOAP). Web clients would form HTTP requests and receive responses using the SOAP syntax.

The difference between traditional JSP/Servlet/JSF web applications and web services is that the latter offer just the data and have no interest in what the client's UI will look like. For example, an insurance company could offer information about its products, or a mutual fund could expose its data as a web service returning XML documents. Clients didn't need to know that this insurance company was running its applications using a server from Sun Microsystems or that the mutual fund was running its on mainframe computers from IBM. The clients needed to know the directory of services available from this particular organization and the address of the *endpoint* to connect to in order to consume this service.

The directory of services could be published with the XML-based Web Services Description Language (WSDL), which is pretty verbose. In the Java world, SOAP messages could be processed by means of JAX-WS without the need for a directory of services.

Even though SOAP web services are verbose, they are still widely used as a simple means of integration with the software produced by third parties. Some SOAP services are publicly available. For example, the web page www.webservicex.net offers descriptions and WSDL locations of such information and services as weather forecasts, US address verification, currency converters, and stock quotes. You can integrate these into your application, but providing a user interface for them remains your responsibility.

## THE RESTFUL WEB SERVICES

As opposed to SOAP, REST is not a protocol, but a lighter-than-SOAP means of building web services, or, to be precise, REST is an architectural style Dr. Roy Fielding identified the REST principles in his PhD dissertation. A web service built on REST principles is called a RESTful web service.

Java EE 6 specification includes the JAX-RS API for creating RESTful web services. Several Java application servers already implement JAX-RS. I'll continue using GlassFish v3, which comes with the JAX-RS implementation known as Jersey, and you won't need to download any additional libraries to run the sample code from this lesson. Other popular open-source JAX-RS implementations are Apache Wink and JBoss RESTeasy.

REST stands for *representational state of transfer*. REST defines a set of constraints that an application must comply to, and web resources that the user may need to work with.

A *resource* is anything that you can access with a hyperlink. Each resource has a uniform resource identifier (URI), such as `http://localhost:8080/StockServer` or `www.dice.com/yakovsresume.pdf`. These URIs represent the state of a stock server and Yakov's résumé, respectively.

REST resources have to support standard stateless requests. But if a typical web application uses only the HTTP methods `GET` for reading the resource and `POST` for updating it, in the RESTful world you can also use `PUT` for resource creation or updates and `DELETE` for resource removal. Web application developers often freely use both `GET` and `POST` for reading data, but REST is stricter about this.

## THE RESTFUL STOCK SERVER

In this section I'll redesign the familiar stock server example using REST. The representation of the resources (in this case stocks) can vary and is determined by media type.

With Java EE 6, creating a RESTful application is pretty straightforward — create a POJO and annotate it. For example, annotating a Java bean with `@XmlRootElement` can bring into action the JAXB framework for processing XML, which will turn the bean into an XML document before sending it to the web client. Listing 34-1 shows a Java bean called `Stock` annotated with `@XmlRootElement`.

**LISTING 34-1: Root class Stock**

```java
import javax.xml.bind.annotation.XmlRootElement;

@XmlRootElement
public class Stock {
    private String symbol;
    private Double price;
    private String currency;
    private String country;

    public Stock() {
    }

    public Stock(String symbol,Double price, String currency, String country) {
```

```
            this.symbol = symbol;
            this.price = price;
            this.currency = currency;
            this.country = country;
        }

        public String getSymbol() {
            return symbol;
        }

        public void setSymbol(String symbol) {
            this.symbol = symbol;
        }

        public Double getPrice() {
            return price;
        }

        public void setPrice(Double price) {
            this.price = price;
        }

        public String getCurrency() {
            return currency;
        }

        public void setCurrency(String currency) {
            this.currency = currency;
        }

        public String getCountry() {
            return country;
        }

        public void setCountry(String country) {
            this.country = country;
        }
    }
```

Here's an example of how a RESTful service (Listing 34-2) may return the representation of a particular stock that's identified by the URI `http://localhost:8080/Lesson34/resources/stock/IBM`:

```
<stock>
  <country>US</country>
  <currency>USD</currency>
  <price>43.12</price>
  <symbol>IBM</symbol>
</stock>
```

From the standpoint of RESTful Web service, the preceding XML code fragment is more important than the Java code in Listing 34-1. The latter is an implementation detail. It's the actual representation expressed here in XML that really matters.

Just to reiterate the concept of resources and URIs, the stock MSFT is considered another resource and can be represented by the URI `http://localhost:8080/Lesson34/resources/stock/MSFT`. The class `StockResource` is a POJO, but if you'd like to turn it into an EJB, just annotate it with the `@Stateless` annotation.

The class `StockResource` is heavily sprinkled with annotations. First comes the annotation `@Path`, which can be used with either a class or a method. JAX-RS maps client's requests to class methods. If more than one annotation `$Path` are used in a class, their values are going to be concatenated for finding the matching method.

In our example in Listing 34-2, during the client's request the class-level `@Path("/stock")` results in the routing of each request containing `/stock` in its URI to the class `StockResource`. Then the matching process continues, and if there is a stock symbol after the word `stock`, (e.g., `/stock/MSFT`), the method-level `@Path("{symbol}")` will map the `getStock()` method for processing. The `@PathParam("symbol")` will inject the stock symbol included in the URI into the `symb` argument of the method `getStock()`.

The `addStock()` method in Listing 34-2 is annotated to consume the form data and is called when the Add button in the web client (see Figure 34-1) is clicked. The `@FormParam` annotation injects the values entered in the HTML form into the method `addStock()`. If the web client isn't using a form but instead is using an HTTP GET request with parameters, you have to use the annotation `@QueryParam` instead of `@FormParam`.

---

**LISTING 34-2: REST resource StockResource**

```
import javax.ws.rs.Consumes;
import javax.ws.rs.FormParam;
import javax.ws.rs.GET;
import javax.ws.rs.POST;
import javax.ws.rs.Path;
import javax.ws.rs.PathParam;
import javax.ws.rs.Produces;
import javax.ws.rs.core.Response;

@Path("/stock")
public class StockResource {

    @Produces({"application/xml", "application/json"})
    @Path("{symbol}")
    @GET
    public Stock getStock(@PathParam("symbol") String symb) {

        Stock stock = StockService.getStock(symb);

        if (stock == null) {
            return new Stock("NOT FOUND", 0.0, "--", "--");
        }

        return stock;
    }

    @POST
```

```
@Consumes("application/x-www-form-urlencoded")
public Response addStock(@FormParam("symbol") String symb,
                         @FormParam("currency") String currency,
                         @FormParam("price") String price,
                         @FormParam("country") String country) {

    if (StockService.getStock(symb) != null)
        return Response.status(Response.Status.BAD_REQUEST).
                entity("Stock " + symb +
                " already exists").type("text/plain").build();

    double priceToUse;
    try {
        priceToUse = new Double(price);
    }
    catch (NumberFormatException e) {
        priceToUse = 0.0;
    }

    StockService.addStock(new Stock(symb, priceToUse,
                                        currency, country));

    return Response.ok().build();
    }
}
```

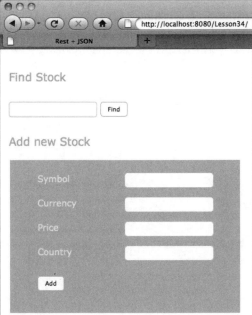

**FIGURE 34-1**

One of the methods in `StockResource` is marked with a `@GET` annotation and the other one with `@POST`. You've guessed it right — they will automatically be invoked to process the corresponding

HTTP requests. The MIME types specified in the annotation @Produces mean that the method getStock() can produce the data in either XML format or JSON format. In REST terminology, you can say that the StockResource resource supports two representations — JSON and XML. JSON stands for JavaScript Object Notation; it can be used as a lighter alternative to XML.

JSON is popular with web clients written in JavaScript (see Listing 34-5 for the sample code). There are JSON parsers for programming languages other than JavaScript languages, including Java. Here's an example of the data in JSON format, which clearly requires less overhead to represent the object Stock than XML does:

```
"stock": {
  "country": "US",
  "currency": "USD",
  "price": 43.12,
  "symbol": "IBM"
}
```

> *The public community domain* www.geonames.org *enables you to search for geographical and statistical information about countries, cities, et cetera. This website uses RESTful web services for the most part. To compare how the same data is represented in XML and in JSON, visit this web page:* www.geonames .org/export/ws-overview.html.

The class StockResource is using the helper class StockService, shown in Listing 34-3. For simplicity, this class has two hard-coded stocks, but in the real world it would be connected to one of the financial data feeds. This class uses static initializer, which calls the method generateStocks() on the first reference to StockService.

**LISTING 34-3: StockService class**

```java
import java.util.HashMap;
import java.util.Map;

public class StockService {
    public static void addStock(Stock stock) {
        stocks.put(stock.getSymbol(), stock);
    }

    public static void removeStock(String symbol) {
        stocks.remove(symbol);
    }

    public static Stock getStock(String symbol) {
        return stocks.get(symbol);
    }

    private static Map<String, Stock> stocks = new HashMap<String, Stock>();

    static {
```

```
                generateStocks();
            }

            private static void generateStocks() {
                addStock(new Stock("IBM", 43.12, "USD", "US"));
                addStock(new Stock("APPL", 320.0, "USD", "US"));
            }
        }
```

The web.xml file from Listing 34-4 is configured to redirect all HTTP requests that contain the pattern /resource to com.sun.jersey.spi.container.servlet.ServletContainer, the Jersey implementation class.

**LISTING 34-4: web.xml**

```
<?xml version="1.0" encoding="UTF-8"?>
<web-app xmlns="http://java.sun.com/xml/ns/javaee"
    xmlns:xsi="http://www.w3.org/2001/XMLSchema-instance"
    xsi:schemaLocation="http://java.sun.com/xml/ns/javaee
    http://java.sun.com/xml/ns/javaee/web-app_2_5.xsd" version="2.5">

        <servlet>
            <servlet-name>Rest</servlet-name>
            <servlet-class>
                com.sun.jersey.spi.container.servlet.ServletContainer
            </servlet-class>
            <load-on-startup>1</load-on-startup>
        </servlet>
        <servlet-mapping>
            <servlet-name>Rest</servlet-name>
            <url-pattern>/resources/*</url-pattern>
        </servlet-mapping>
    </web-app>
```

Next comes the thin web client written in HTML and JavaScript, which is not covered in this book. I'll just highlight the relevant code fragments to explain the client/server communication in the stock server example. Listing 34-5 shows the index.html file, which includes the popular JavaScript library JQuery (see the reference in the <head> section).

**LISTING 34-5: Thin web client index.html**

```
<!DOCTYPE html>
<html>

<head>
    <title>Rest + JSON</title>
    <link rel="stylesheet" type="text/css" href="css/main.css"/>

    <script src="http://code.jquery.com/jquery-1.4.4.js">
    </script>
```

*continues*

**LISTING 34-5** *(continued)*

```html
</head>

<body>

<p class="title">Find Stock</p>

<form id="get-stock" action="javascript:alert('submit')">
    <input id="get-stock-symbol" type="text"/>
    <input class="button" type="submit" value="Find"/>
</form>

<div class="result">
<table>
    <tr>
        <td>Symbol</td>
        <td id="symbol"></td>
    </tr>
    <tr>
        <td>Price</td>
        <td id="price"></td>
    </tr>
    <tr>
        <td>Currency</td>
        <td id="currency"></td>
    </tr>
    <tr>
        <td>Country</td>
        <td id="country"></td>
    </tr>
</table>
</div>

<p class="title">Add new Stock</p>

<div id="add-stock-flash-message" class="flash-message">
</div>

<form id="add-stock" action="javascript:alert('submit')">
    <fieldset>
        <ol>
            <li>
                <label for="add-stock-symbol">Symbol</label>
                <input id="add-stock-symbol" name="symbol" type="text"/>
            </li>
            <li>
                <label for="add-stock-currency">Currency</label>
                <input id="add-stock-currency" name="currency" type="text"/>
            </li>
            <li>
                <label for="add-stock-price">Price</label>
                <input id="add-stock-price" name="price" type="text"/>
            </li>
```

```
            <li>
                <label for="add-stock-country">Country</label>
                <input id="add-stock-country" name="country" type="text"/>
            </li>
            <li>
                <input class="button" type="submit" value="Add"/>
            </li>
        </ol>
    </fieldset>
</form>

<script>
    $('.result').hide();
    $('#add-stock-flash-message').hide();

    $("#get-stock").submit(function() {
        $.getJSON('resources/stock/' + $("#get-stock-symbol").val(),
      function(data) {

            $('.result').fadeOut(500, function(){
                $('#symbol').html(data.symbol);
                $('#price').html(data.price);
                $('#currency').html(data.currency);
                $('#country').html(data.country);

                $('.result').fadeIn(500)
            });
        });

        return false;
    });

    $("#add-stock").submit(function() {

        $.ajax({
            type: "POST",
            url: 'resources/stock',
            data: $("#add-stock").serialize(),

            success: function() {
                $("#add-stock-flash-message").show().html(
                        "Stock was added").fadeOut(5000);
            },

            error: function(request, textStatus, errorThrown) {
                if (textStatus == 'error') {
                    $("#add-stock-flash-message")
                        .show().html(request.responseText).fadeOut(5000);
                }
                else {
                    $("#add-stock-flash-message")
                        .show().html("Server error").fadeOut(5000);
                }
            }
```

*continues*

**LISTING 34-5** *(continued)*

```
        });

        return false;
    });
</script>

</body>
</html>
```

This HTML/JavaScript client can be invoked in such a way as to request a resource represented either as JSON or as XML. To get the data in JSON format, simply direct your web browser to `http://localhost:8080/Lesson34/index.html`. When you press the Find button on the form shown in Figure 34-1, the code in `index.html` calls the function `getJSON()`, which creates the pattern `resources/stock`, concatenates the entered stock symbol, and sends the request to the server. In the following JQuery code fragment `get-stock` is the ID of the top HTML form being submitted to the server:

```
$("#get-stock").submit(function() {
        $.getJSON('resources/stock/' + $("#get-stock-symbol").val(),
    function(data) {
...
});
```

The function `getJSON()` has requested the resource `Stock` in JSON format. Even though the Java bean `Stock` has been annotated with `@XmlRootElement`, JAXB can represent it not only as XML, but also as JSON.

To test the XML branch, enter a URL containing the pattern `/resources` that was used in the `web.xml` file from Listing 34-4. For example, the URL `http://localhost:8080/Lesson34/resources/stock/IBM` will return this REST resource as XML, as shown in Figure 34-2.

In this use case the code from the file `index.html` is not being used, and the request is redirected to the function `getStock()` of `StockResource`. The function `getStock()` is capable of producing both JSON and XML, but this time it produces plain web browser's code that knows how to consume XML only, and so JAX-RS picked up the XML format as a common denominator.

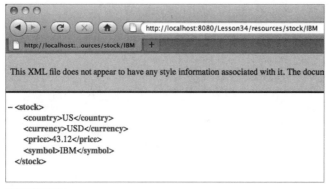

**FIGURE 34-2**

## TRY IT

Your assignment is to make the code shown in the listings work. You'll need to create an Eclipse project and copy to the proper places the code samples from the accompanying DVD (Listings 34-1 to 34-5). Then you'll need to deploy this project in GlassFish and run it.

## Lesson Requirements

You should have Java and GlassFish v3 server installed.

> *You can download the code and resources for this Try It from the book's web page* at www.wrox.com. *You can find them in the Lesson34 folder in the download.*

## Hints

Eclipse IDE for Java EE Developers has a template for the creation of REST resources. Right-click the project name, select New, and then select RESTful Web Service From Pattern (Java EE 6). Eclipse will create for you an annotated class similar to the one from Listing 34-2, which you can edit to meet your application's requirements.

## Step-by-Step

1. Create a dynamic web project called Lesson34 in Eclipse. Then create a package called com.practicaljava.lesson34.

2. Copy the classes Stock, StockResource, and StockService from the DVD into this package.

3. Copy the file web.xml shown in Listing 34-4 to the directory WebContent/WEB-INF.

4. Create the folder WebContent/css and copy to it the file main.css from the DVD — this will add some colors to the client's UI.

5. Deploy the project Lesson34 under GlassFish — right-click the server name, select Add and Remove, and in the pop-up window move Lesson34 from the left box to the right one by clicking Add. Then click Finish.

6. Open a web browser and go to http://localhost:8080/Lesson34/, which will open the file index.html from Listing 34-5. You'll see something similar to Figure 34-1.

7. Enter IBM in the search field and click Find. The pricing information (hard-coded) about this stock will be displayed as in Figure 34-3.

8. Test the Add New Stock functionality by filling out the form shown in Figure 34-3 and clicking Add. This will make a POST request to the RESTful service, which will be mapped to the method addStock() of StockResource from Listing 34-2. After the new stock has been added you can search for it by entering its name in the search field and clicking Find.

**FIGURE 34-3**

 *Please select Lesson 34 on the DVD to view the video that accompanies this lesson.*

# Introduction to Spring MVC Framework

At the beginning of the century Java EE was called J2EE, and it was a heavy and over-engineered standard. Programming EJBs was difficult and required writing a lot of boiler-plate code. Java annotations had not been invented yet. Having a Java container that would take care of multi-threading, transactions, persistence, and security was nice, but developers needed a lighter container and a simpler programming model.

Rod Johnson, a talented software engineer, wrote a book titled *Expert One-on-One J2EE Design and Development*, which was published by Wrox at the end of 2002. A year later the book's code samples and development recommendations were released as the Spring Framework.

The Spring Framework is a Java container that provides a living space for an application's objects, wired to each other in a loosely coupled way in XML configuration. This loose coupling comes at a price, though — configuration files are quite large in size.

Spring Framework was built based on the *inversion of control* (IoC) principle: The container is responsible for the instantiation and location of the objects. IoC is also known as the Hollywood principle: "Don't call us, we'll call you."

Instead of having a class called Customer reach out to some container's registry trying to find an Order, under the Spring Framework the container would use a system of callbacks to instantiate the Order and inject it into the instance of the Customer object. This is an example of the *dependency injection* pattern — the Customer gets an injection of required resources. You saw resource injection in action in the Java EE lessons.

Don't forget that even five years ago the injection of resources was not implemented in Java EE application servers. Today not only is resource injection implemented, but Java EE 6 has yet another injection mechanism known as *contexts and dependency injection* (not covered in this book), which will make future Java EE applications even lighter. But don't forget that some ideas implemented in the current Java EE specification were originally introduced by the Spring Framework.

Over the last several years the Spring Framework has served as an alternative solution for developing enterprise Java applications. It has provided an infrastructure that allows you to easily plug in third-party frameworks and components. For example, the combination of Spring and the persistence framework Hibernate (see Lesson 36) is a popular architecture for lots of production-grade applications.

Serious improvements in the Java EE 6 specification may reduce the number of applications developed with Spring/Hibernate, but as of today this duo certainly remains a nice infrastructure for developing enterprise Java applications.

## BEAN WIRING

In the Spring Framework, beans are configured in XML files, and if a class called `Customer` needs an `Order` bean you can either look for this bean by issuing `getBean("Order")` on an instance of the main Spring factory, `ApplicationContext`, or, better yet, configure injection of the `Order` into `Customer`, as in the following code:

```
<?xml version="1.0" encoding="UTF-8"?>
<beans xmlns=http://www.springframework.org/schema/beans
xmlns:xsi=http://www.w3.org/2001/XMLSchema-instance
xsi:schemaLocation="http://www.springframework.org/schema/beans
http://www.springframework.org/schema/beans/spring-beans-3.0.xsd">

    <bean id="customerBean" class="com.practicaljava.lesson35.Customer">
    <property name="order" ref="ord" />
    </bean>

    <bean id="ord" class="com.practicaljava.lesson35.Order"/>
</beans>
```

This is an example of configuring injection of one object into the field of another one in a loosely coupled way. The class `Customer` knows that someone will provide an `Order` when the time is right. This makes it easy to test the `Customer`'s functionality alone by wiring orders with hard-coded values — just change the value in the preceding XML from `com.practicaljava.lesson35.Order` to `com.practicaljava.lesson35.FakeOrder`. When the real data is available, change it back. In simple cases you can inject simpler values into Spring bean properties via setters or constructor arguments. You can provide the name of the file with configured beans to the constructor of `ApplicationContext` during instantiation.

## OVERVIEW OF SPRING MVC

The Spring Framework consists of a number of modules that can be categorized as *web*, *core*, and *data access*. And the good part is that they can be used à la carte as you need them. The web module simplifies development of web applications. The core module provides the infrastructure and wiring for Java components living in the Spring container. Data access enables you to create an abstraction layer for data access so that no Java code needs to be changed if you decide to use a different JDBC driver or DBMS.

In this lesson you'll get familiar with the Spring MVC module that was created for the development of web applications. Like Java application servers, Spring manages your Java classes, so I'll be using the term *Spring container*. The classes that are going to be managed by the Spring container can be referred to as *Spring beans*.

The Spring Framework offers a solution for building web applications. It includes a number of modules: Spring Faces, Spring Web Flow, Spring JavaScript, Spring Security, and Spring BlaseDS. And you don't have to use all these modules to build a web application — just use what you need.

There are two main models for building web applications with HTML clients:

➤ The client connects to a server-side presentation object (such as JSP) that is responsible for further routing and processing the request and for forming the next view to be returned to the client.

➤ The client connects to a server-side controller object (has no UI code) that performs the routing and processing of the request and for selection of the proper view to be returned to the client.

Building a web application in the Spring Framework represents the second model, where `DispatcherServlet` intercepts client requests and passes them to the appropriate Java controller to handle the request. The controller creates a `ModelAndView` object and gives it to a view resolver, which finds the view component to return to the client. The entire dataflow is shown in Figure 35-1.

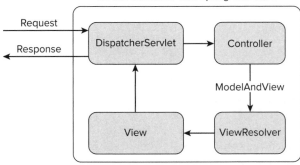

**FIGURE 35-1**

This architecture is supported by the easily extendable Spring MVC layer. Other frameworks can be plugged into the Spring infrastructure. It's popular to integrate Spring and Hibernate for data persistence, but there are other examples of framework integration. For example, Adobe's BlaseDS framework or the Apache Struts legacy framework can be plugged into Spring.

HTML forms with data validation and error processing are also supported, and you'll see how to develop such applications in the next section.

## PROCESSING HTML WITH SPRING

In this section I'll show you a simple web application using the Spring Web MVC framework. You'll see how to do the following:

➤ Configure the controller `ServletDispatcher`.

➤ Configure the `UrlBasedViewResolver` bean.

➤ Create a simple controller called `HelloWorldController` to produce data for presentation by a JSP.

➤ Handle the request of a "contact us" HTML form with the Spring JSP tag library.

## Understanding the Spring Web MVC Workflow

To start, create an Eclipse Dynamic Web Project named Lesson35. Now you'll need to download several jar files from the Spring framework and copy them to the `WebContent/WEB-INF/lib` folder. Register at the SpringSource website `www.springsource.com/download/community` and download the latest zip file of the Spring Framework. At the time of this writing it's `spring-framework-3.0.5.RELEASE.zip`.

Unzip the archive and add the following jars to the build path of your Eclipse project. Also copy these jars to the `WebContent/lib` directory so they are visible at the deployment time.

➤ `org.springframework.asm-3.0.5.RELEASE.jar`

➤ `org.springframework.beans-3.0.5.RELEASE.jar`

➤ `org.springframework.context-3.0.5.RELEASE.jar`

➤ `org.springframework.core-3.0.5.RELEASE.jar`

➤ `org.springframework.expression-3.0.5.RELEASE.jar`

➤ `org.springframework.web.servlet-3.0.5.RELEASE.jar`

➤ `org.springframework.web-3.0.5.RELEASE.jar`

For logging support you'll also need to download and add to the `lib` folder the Commons Logging API `commons-logging-api-1.1.1.jar`, which you can download from the same website — it's in `org.apache.commons` in the archive with dependencies.

Now you need to deploy the Spring Framework as a web application under GlassFish. Create the file `web.xml` with the content shown in Listing 35-1 and add it to the `WEB-INF` folder. This file instructs GlassFish to load the Spring's `DispatcherServlet` on startup and to redirect any `*.html` requests to it.

**Available for download on Wrox.com**

**LISTING 35-1: web.xml with DispatcherServlet**

```
<?xml version="1.0" encoding="UTF-8"?>
<web-app xmlns:xsi="http://www.w3.org/2001/XMLSchema-instance"
xmlns=http://java.sun.com/xml/ns/javaee
 xmlns:web=http://java.sun.com/xml/ns/javaee/web-app_2_5.xsd
 xsi:schemaLocation=
```

```
"http://java.sun.com/xml/ns/javaee
http://java.sun.com/xml/ns/javaee/web-app_2_5.xsd"
id="WebApp_ID" version="2.5">

  <display-name>Lesson35 Sample</display-name>
  <welcome-file-list>
    <welcome-file>index.jsp</welcome-file>
  </welcome-file-list>

  <servlet>
        <servlet-name>springServletDispatcher</servlet-name>
        <servlet-class>
          org.springframework.web.servlet.DispatcherServlet
        </servlet-class>
        <load-on-startup>1</load-on-startup>
  </servlet>

  <servlet-mapping>
        <servlet-name>springServletDispatcher</servlet-name>
        <url-pattern>*.html</url-pattern>
  </servlet-mapping>
</web-app>
```

In our example the MVC pattern will be represented by the following: for the model a Java class called `ContactUs`; for the view two JSP pages, `hello` and `contactUs`; and for the classes two Java controller classes, `HelloWorldController` and `ContactUsController`. Figure 35-2 shows a snapshot of my Eclipse project to give you an idea of where the files are located.

`HelloWorldController` is shown in Listing 35-2. It includes the `@RequestMapping` annotation that instructs the controller to call the method `sayHello()` for any requests with the `/hello` pattern.

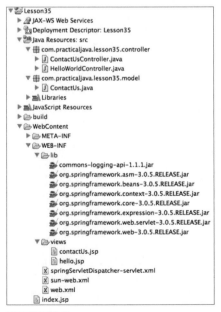

**FIGURE 35-2**

**LISTING 35-2: HelloWorldController**

```java
import org.springframework.stereotype.Controller;
import org.springframework.web.bind.annotation.RequestMapping;
import org.springframework.web.servlet.ModelAndView;

@Controller
public class HelloWorldController {

    @RequestMapping("/hello")
    public ModelAndView sayHello(){

        String greetings = "Hello people";
        return new ModelAndView("hello", "greetings", greetings);
    }
}
```

The view resolver of our application is an XML configuration file named
`springServletDispatcher-servlet.xml`, shown in Listing 35-3. Note that the prefix of this
file name matches the value in the tag `<servlet-name>` in Listing 35-1. This application uses one
of the view resolvers provided by Spring, `UrlBasedViewResolver`, which creates the appropriate
view based on the URL.

**LISTING 35-3: springServletDispatcher-servlet.xml**

```xml
<?xml version="1.0" encoding="UTF-8"?>
<beans xmlns="http://www.springframework.org/schema/beans"
        xmlns:xsi=http://www.w3.org/2001/XMLSchema-instance
    xmlns:p="http://www.springframework.org/schema/p"
        xmlns:context="http://www.springframework.org/schema/context"
        xsi:schemaLocation="http://www.springframework.org/schema/beans
            http://www.springframework.org/schema/beans/spring-beans-3.0.xsd
            http://www.springframework.org/schema/context
            http://www.springframework.org/schema/context/spring-context-3.0.xsd">

        <context:component-scan
            base-package="com.practicaljava.lesson35.controller" />

    <bean id="viewResolver" class=
"org.springframework.web.servlet.view.UrlBasedViewResolver">
        <property name="viewClass"
          value="org.springframework.web.servlet.view.JstlView"/>
        <property name="prefix" value="/WEB-INF/views/" />
        <property name="suffix" value=".jsp" />
    </bean>
</beans>
```

The preceding file is configured to add the prefix `WEB-INF/views` and the suffix `.jsp` to the value
specified in the `@RequestMapping` of the controller. As an example, for `HelloWorldController` the
URL of the view given to the response object becomes `WEB-INF/views/hello.jsp`. The source code
for `hello.jsp` is shown in Listing 35-4.

**LISTING 35-4:** hello.jsp

```jsp
<%@ page language="java" contentType="text/html; charset=ISO-8859-1"
    pageEncoding="ISO-8859-1"%>
<!DOCTYPE html PUBLIC "-//W3C//DTD HTML 4.01 Transitional//EN"
"http://www.w3.org/TR/html4/loose.dtd">
<html>
<head>
<meta http-equiv="Content-Type" content="text/html; charset=ISO-8859-1">
<title>Insert title here</title>
</head>
<body>
 ${greetings}
</body>
</html>
```

What does `${greetings}` mean? Look at the code of `HelloWorldController` in Listing 35-2. It contains the following lines:

```java
String greetings = "Hello people";
return new ModelAndView("hello", "greetings", greetings);
```

This is how the Spring controller tells the view resolver what to do with the view before it is returned to the client. The first argument of the `ModelAndView` constructor contains the name of the view, and the second one contains the name of the JSP element to be replaced with the content of the third argument. Basically, the name of the class reflects the fact that it contains elements of both the model and the view.

The class `ModelAndView` has a number of overloaded constructors (see Figure 35-3) that enable you to pass multiple values to the view object. You can also populate `ModelAndView` with data by using the method `addObject()`.

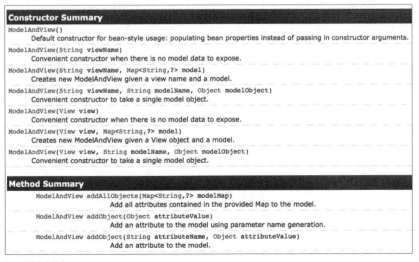

**FIGURE 35-3**

Add the project Lesson35 to GlassFish in the Eclipse Servers view and start the server. Direct your web browser to `http://localhost:8080/Lesson35/hello.html` and you'll see something like what's shown in Figure 35-4. Just to recap, because of the `*.html` mapping in `web.xml`, Spring's `ServletDispatcher` was invoked. The `.html` part was stripped off, the word `hello` was identified, and the `HelloWorldController` was instantiated and its method `sayHello()` invoked. The view resolver found `hello.jsp`, and its variable `greetings` was replaced with the text "Hello People" as per the content of the `ModelAndView` instance.

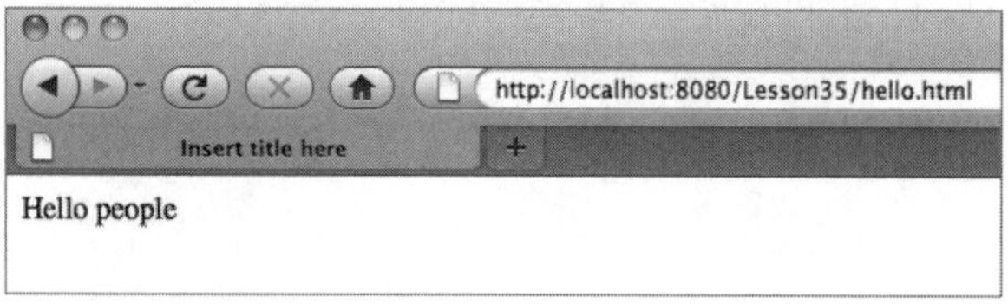

**FIGURE 35-4**

## Processing HTML Forms

Processing HTML forms with Spring is just a little bit more complex than the "Hello People" example. The Spring Framework comes with integrated tag libraries with a tag corresponding to each HTML element. In particular, there is the `form` tag library for processing HTML forms. Listing 35-5 shows `ContactUs.jsp`, which includes the appropriate `<%taglib>` directive.

**LISTING 35-5: ContactUs.jsp**

```jsp
<%@ page language="java" contentType="text/html; charset=UTF-8"
    pageEncoding="UTF-8"%>
        <%@taglib uri="http://www.springframework.org/tags/form" prefix="form"%>
<!DOCTYPE html PUBLIC "-//W3C//DTD HTML 4.01 Transitional//EN"
  "http://www.w3.org/TR/html4/loose.dtd">
<html>
<head>
<meta http-equiv="Content-Type" content="text/html; charset=ISO-8859-1">
<title>Insert title here</title>
</head>
<body>
<h2>Contact Manager</h2>

<form:form method="post" action="addQuestion.html">

    <table>
    <tr>
        <td><form:label path="author">Who are you?</form:label></td>
        <td><form:input path="author" /></td>
    </tr>
    <tr>
        <td><form:label path="subject">Subject</form:label></td>
        <td><form:input path="subject" /></td>
    </tr>
    <tr>
```

```
                    <td><form:label path="message">You Question</form:label></td>
                    <td><form:textarea path="message" /></td>
            </tr>
            <tr>
                    <td colspan="2">
                            <input type="submit" value="Submit your question"/>
                    </td>
            </tr>
    </table>

    </form:form>
    </body>
    </html>
```

When the user clicks Submit, the request is posted to the server with addQuestion.html in the
URL. Then DispatcherServlet maps addQuestion with the method addUserQuestion() in the
controller shown in Listing 35-6.

**LISTING 35-6:** ContactUsController.java

```java
package com.practicaljava.lesson35.controller;

import org.springframework.stereotype.Controller;
import org.springframework.validation.BindingResult;
import org.springframework.web.bind.annotation.ModelAttribute;
import org.springframework.web.bind.annotation.RequestMapping;
import org.springframework.web.bind.annotation.RequestMethod;
import org.springframework.web.bind.annotation.SessionAttributes;
import org.springframework.web.servlet.ModelAndView;

import com.practicaljava.lesson35.model.ContactUs;

@Controller
@SessionAttributes
public class ContactUsController {

    @RequestMapping(value="/addQuestion", method=RequestMethod.POST)
    public String addUserQuestion(@ModelAttribute("contactUs") ContactUs
                                        contactUs, BindingResult result){

        System.out.println("New message:\nSubject:"
                                        +contactUs.getSubject());
        System.out.println("Author " + contactUs.getAuthor());
        System.out.println("Message "+ contactUs.getMessage());

        return "redirect:contactUs.html";
    }

    @RequestMapping("/contactUs")
    public ModelAndView contactUs(){
        return new ModelAndView("contactUs", "command", new ContactUs());
    }
}
```

@ModelAttribute binds the method parameter to the named model attribute (see the model class in Listing 35-7). The Spring Framework maps the attributes from the model to corresponding attributes in ContactUs.jsp, shown in Listing 35-5.

**LISTING 35-7: ContactUs.java**

Available for download on Wrox.com

```
public class ContactUs {
    private String subject;
    private String message;
    private String author;

    public String getSubject() {
        return subject;
    }
    public void setSubject(String subject) {
        this.subject = subject;
    }
   public String getMessage() {
        return message;
    }
    public void setMessage(String message) {
        this.message = message;
    }
    public String getAuthor() {
        return author;
    }
    public void setAuthor(String author) {
        this.author = author;
    }
}
```

Open your web browser and enter the following URL: http://localhost:8080/Lesson35/contactUs.html. The @RequestMapping("/contactUs") annotation in Listing 35-6 responds to the client with ContactUs.jsp, which looks as in Figure 35-5.

Enter some values in the form and click Submit. This time the /addQuestion action will be matched with the method addUserQuestion() of ContactUsController. Received values from the client will be printed in the log file of GlassFish Server, located in logs/server.log under your domain directory.

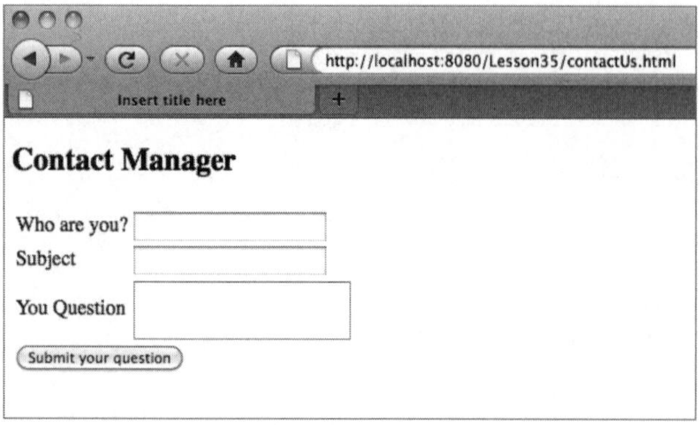


**FIGURE 35-5**

# TRY IT

Modify the code of hello.jsp to accept more than one variable. Change the code of ModelAndView so that it carries a Map of values.

## Lesson Requirements

You should have Java and GlassFish v3 installed.

 *You can download the code and resources for this Try It from the book's web page at* www.wrox.com. *You can find them in the Lesson35 folder in the download.*

## Step-by-Step

1. Modify hello.jsp to add one more variable in addition to $greetings:

2. Modify HelloWorldController to create a Map with two Strings:

   ```
   Map helloModel = new HashMap();
   helloModel.put("Hello Mary");
   helloModel.put("My name is John");
   ```

3. Use the two-argument constructor of ModelAndView and pass the Map as the second argument.

4. Direct your web browser to http://localhost:8080/Lesson35/hello.html and observe that hello.jsp shows the values from the Map.

*Please select Lesson 35 on the DVD to view the video that accompanies this lesson.*

# Introduction to Hibernate Framework

In Lesson 33 you got familiar with the Java Persistence API, which is part of Java EE 6. But JPA wasn't created from scratch. It took many ideas from Hibernate — an open-source object-relational framework started by Gavin King in 2001. Hibernate version 3.5 and above support the JPA 2.0 specification.

The official website of Hibernate is www.hibernate.org, where you can find documentation, code samples, and tools. Plenty of books and online articles are published about this popular framework. I prefer using SQL and JDBC for all data-related processing, but these days knowledge of Hibernate is required in many job postings. That's why I decided to include this brief overview of Hibernate even though it's not a part of the Java specification but a third-party framework.

If you are going to use Hibernate for work, consider using the Eclipse plug-ins available at www.hibernate.org/subprojects/tools.html.

## THE BIG PICTURE

The main idea behind any ORM framework is to replace writing SQL with manipulating the objects. In the Java world, this means putting a layer on top of JDBC that will enable you to simply create a POJO, assign values to its fields, and tell it "Persist yourself in the database." This is what Hibernate is for.

Proponents of this approach argue that removing the dependency on vendor-specific SQL syntax provides easy switching from one DBMS to another without the need to modify the Java code responsible for querying and persisting data. To me this doesn't sound like a compelling reason to move away from SQL, because it's very seldom that you need to switch from one

DBMS to another in real-world projects. Besides, if you'll be working on projects that require swift query execution, the ability to tune SQL manually and use tricks specific to DBMSes can be helpful.

On the other hand, Hibernate offers such goodies as *lazy loading* and the ability to easily configure the in-memory cache to greatly minimize disk access, which is a lot slower than memory access.

Lazy loading is easy to explain with an example. Suppose the user is presented with a list of customers, each of which may have multiple orders. With lazy loading only the list of customers is initially loaded, and only when the user selects a customer will the query to retrieve the corresponding orders be sent to data storage.

The process of retrieving data with Hibernate is very similar to what you saw in Lesson 33. You create the mapping of entities to database tables, then instantiate the `Configuration` object needed to create a `SessionFactory` and `Session`. After this is done you execute queries on these entities using Hibernate Query Language (HQL), Criteria queries, or native SQL.

The rest of this lesson is a step-by-step walkthrough that demonstrates how to write a simple application that will get the data from a DBMS using Hibernate.

## INSTALLING AND CONFIGURING HIBERNATE

In this section you'll download required jars and create the configuration file `hibernate.cfg.xml`. I'll continue using Derby, which is included with GlassFish, as our sample DBMS, but the application server GlassFish is not needed here. The idea is to look at Hibernate as an alternative persistence solution that doesn't require the Java EE application server.

Hibernate is an open-source framework hosted on the web at SourceForge (`http://sourceforge.net/ projects/hibernate/files/hibernate3/`). At the time of this writing, the latest release of Hibernate is 3.6; you need to download the file `hibernate-distribution-3.6.0.Final-dist.zip`. This distribution includes required jar files, a well-written reference manual, and a folder with libraries that might be used to support memory caching.

## Adding Hibernate Jars to an Eclipse Project

Now create a new Eclipse project called Lesson36 by selecting File ⇨ New ⇨ Other ⇨ Java Project. Note that this is a Java SE project — I'm not going to use any Java EE application server here. Make sure your Eclipse Java project includes `hibernate3.jar`, all the jars from the `required` folder, and the jar from the `jpa` folder. There is one more logging-related file, `slf4j-1.6.1.zip`, that for some licensing reason has to be downloaded from `www.slf4j.org/download.html`. You need to add to the build path just one file from there: `slf4j-simple-1.6.1.jar`.

You can add these external jars in the tab Libraries of the Java Setting window while you're creating the project, or you can add them after the project is created via Properties ⇨ Java Build Path ⇨ Libraries ⇨ Add External Jars. Figure 36-1 shows which libraries are included in the build path of my Eclipse project.

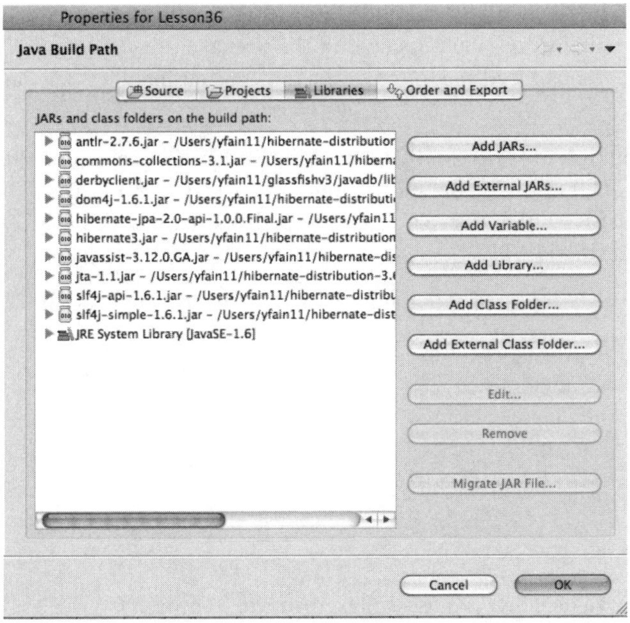

**FIGURE 36-1**

## Testing the Database Connection

In this lesson I'll keep working with the database that was initially created in Lesson 22 and then reused in Lesson 33. It contains a table called Employee and the connection is already configured (see Figure 33-4). This connection uses the Derby JDBC driver located in `derbyclient.jar`. Add this jar, located in `glassfish/javadb/lib`, to the build path of the new Eclipse project.

Now right-click the database connection Lesson22 in Eclipse and select Properties ➪ JDBC Connection Properties. Keep the user ID as `user` and change the password to `password123`. Now copy the connection URL (refer to Figure 33-3) to a text editor — you'll need the connection parameters in the next section. You can also check the properties of the selected DerbyDB driver by clicking the small button with an asterisk on it — copy the name of the JDBC driver class too.

## Configuring Hibernate with a DBMS

Now it's time to add the DBMS-related entries to the file `hibernate.cfg.xml`. You don't need to create this file from scratch; copy to the `src` folder of your Eclipse project one of the files that come with Hibernate, such as the one located in the folder `documentation/quickstart/tutorials/basic/src/test/resources`. Modify the driver class and connection URL with the values from the previous section. Make sure that this file doesn't have a setting to drop and re-create the database schema on startup. You won't need any mapping files because our entity will use annotations.

Every DBMS implements standard SQL plus some additional features meant to give it a competitive edge. To deal with these extras Hibernate includes configurable `dialects` that hide the differences from the application developer. That's why the configuration file has to specify the dialect that the current application has to support. Each dialect is a class located in the package `org.hibernate` `.dialect` inside `hibernate3.jar`, and you can find the name of the dialect that matches our database, which is `DerbyDialect`.

You might remember that the table Employee was originally created in the database schema APP. Because I specified that the connection ID is `user`, by default the queries will try to find the referenced database objects in the schema USER, which doesn't exist. To fix this situation let's specify in the configuration file that the default schema is APP.

Finally, we want Hibernate to print in the Eclipse console the underlying SQL statements that it'll use in communication with the database.

After you make all these changes your `hibernate.cfg.xml` file should look like Listing 36-1.

---

**LISTING 36-1: Hibernate.cfg.xml**

```xml
<?xml version='1.0' ?>
<!DOCTYPE hibernate-configuration PUBLIC
        "-//Hibernate/Hibernate Configuration DTD 3.0//EN"
        "http://www.hibernate.org/dtd/hibernate-configuration-3.0.dtd">

<hibernate-configuration>

    <session-factory>

        <!-- Database connection settings -->
        <property name="connection.driver_class">
            org.apache.derby.jdbc.ClientDriver
        </property>

        <property name="connection.url">
            jdbc:derby://localhost:1527/Lesson22;create=true
        </property>

        <property name="connection.username">user</property>
        <property name="connection.password">password123</property>

        <!-- Set the default schema to be APP, where table Employee was
                                                  created-->
        <property name="hibernate.default_schema">APP</property>

        <!-- JDBC connection pool (use the built-in) -->
        <property name="connection.pool_size">1</property>

        <!-- SQL dialect -->
        <property name="dialect">org.hibernate.dialect.DerbyDialect</property>

        <!--  Enable Hibernate's current session context -->
        <property name="current_session_context_class">thread</property>

        <!-- Disable the second-level cache  -->
        <property name="cache.provider_class">
```

```
                        org.hibernate.cache.NoCacheProvider
            </property>

            <!-- Echo all executed SQL to stdout -->
            <property name="show_sql">true</property>

      </session-factory>

</hibernate-configuration>
```

## RETRIEVING DATA WITH HIBERNATE

Now we need to create a Java `Employee` entity, which in this simple example corresponds to the database table Employee. The good news is that because Hibernate supports JPA 2, we can simply reuse the `Employee` entity from Lesson 33. Listing 36-2 shows this entity after we copy it into the package `com.practicaljava.lesson36`.

**LISTING 36-3: Employee entity**

```java
package com.practicaljava.lesson36;

import java.io.Serializable;
import javax.persistence.*;

@Entity
public class Employee implements Serializable {

  private static final long serialVersionUID = 1L;

  @Id
  private int empno;

  private String ename;

  @Column(name="JOB_TITLE")
  private String jobTitle;

  public Employee() {}

  public int getEmpno() {
    return this.empno;
  }

  public void setEmpno(int empno) {
    this.empno = empno;
  }

  public String getEname() {
   return this.ename;
```

*continues*

**LISTING 36-2** *(continued)*

```
      }

      public void setEname(String ename) {
        this.ename = ename;
      }

      public String getJobTitle() {
        return this.jobTitle;
      }

      public void setJobTitle(String jobTitle) {
        this.jobTitle = jobTitle;
      }
    }
```

The code to retrieve employees comes next. The program `HRManager` shown in Listing 36-3 will do this job. It starts by loading the configuration file `hibernate.cfg.xml` and creating a Hibernate session. We didn't provide any arguments to the method `configure()` — by default this method assumes that the configuration file is called `hibernate.cfg.xml`.

Then `SessionFactory` creates an instance of the `Session`. The transaction is opened, and `createQuery("from Employee")` means that we're interested in `Employee` entities. In this sample, the name of the entity and the name of the database table are the same. If this weren't the case we'd have had to specify the table name in the `@Entity` annotation in Listing 36-2.

**LISTING 36-3:** Retrieving Employee entities

```
import java.util.List;
import org.hibernate.*;
import org.hibernate.cfg.Configuration;
import com.practicaljava.lesson36.Employee;

public class HRManager {

public static void main(String[] args){

  Configuration config = new Configuration().configure();
  config.addAnnotatedClass(Employee.class);

  SessionFactory sf = config.buildSessionFactory();
  Session session = sf.getCurrentSession();

  session.beginTransaction();

  List<Employee> employee = session.createQuery("from Employee").list();

  session.getTransaction().commit();

  for (Employee emp: employee){
```

```
                  System.out.println("Got " + emp.getEmpno() + ", "
                                   + emp.getEname() + ", "+ emp.getJobTitle());
       }
     }
   }
```

The method `addAnnotatedClass(Employee.class)` tells Hibernate that there is an entity called `Employee` configured using annotations. After running, `HRManager` prints the following in Eclipse's Console view:

```
Hibernate: select employee0_.empno as empno0_, employee0_.ename as ename0_,
  employee0_.JOB_TITLE as JOB3_0_ from APP.Employee employee0_

Got 7369, John Smith, Clerk
Got 7499, Joe Allen, Salesman
Got 7521, Mary Lou, Director
```

Retrieving data with Hibernate is pretty trivial. Persisting the data in the database is not rocket science either. You'll have a chance to see such persisting for yourself when you work on the assignment in the "Try It" section.

## TRY IT

This lesson shows you how Hibernate creates database objects from Java entities. You will have to declare the Java entity `Address` and have Hibernate create and populate the corresponding table in the database.

## Lesson Requirements

You should have Java and GlassFish v3 installed.

> *You can download the code and resources for this Try It from the book's web page at* www.wrox.com. *You can find them in the Lesson36 folder in the download.*

## Hints

In the toolbar of the Data Source Explorer view is an icon that opens SQL Scrapbook. It enables you to select the DBMS and the database and to execute SQL statements. For example, enter **Select \* from APP.Employee,** then right-click and select Execute All. The SQL statement will be executed and you'll see the content of the table Employee.

# Step-by-Step

**1.** Create the following Java entity, `Address`:

```
package com.practicaljava.lesson36;

import javax.persistence.*;

@Entity
public class Address {

    private long addressID;
    private String streetAddress;
    private String city;
    private String zip;

    @Id
    public long getAddressID() {
        return addressID;
    }

    public void setAddressID(long addressID) {
        this.addressID = addressID;
    }

    public String getStreetAddress() {
        return streetAddress;
    }

    public void setStreetAddress(String streetAddress) {
        this.streetAddress = streetAddress;
    }

    public String getCity() {
        return city;
    }

    public void setCity(String city) {
        this.city = city;
    }

    public String getZip() {
        return zip;
    }

    public void setZip(String zip) {
        this.zip = zip;
    }
}
```

**2.** Create a class called `AddressCreator`. It should look like this:

```
import java.util.List;

import org.hibernate.*;
```

```
import org.hibernate.cfg.Configuration;
import org.hibernate.tool.hbm2ddl.SchemaExport;

import com.practicaljava.lesson36.Address;

public class AddressCreator {

    public static void main(String[] args){
        Configuration config = new Configuration().configure();
        config.addAnnotatedClass(Address.class);

        //Create the Address table
        new SchemaExport(config).create(true,true);

        SessionFactory sf = config.buildSessionFactory();
        Session session = sf.getCurrentSession();

        session.beginTransaction();

        // Instantiate and Populate the entity Address
        Address addr1 = new Address();
        addr1.setStreetAddress("123 Main St.");
        addr1.setAddressID(1);
        addr1.setCity("New York");
        addr1.setZip("10001");

    session.save(addr1);

    // Save the new entity in the database
        session.getTransaction().commit();

    }
}
```

**3.** Run the program AddressCreator. Observe the output in the Eclipse console. You should see the following SQL statements generated by Hibernate:

```
drop table APP.Address
create table APP.Address (addressID bigint not null, city varchar(255),
 streetAddress varchar(255),
zip varchar(255), primary key (addressID))

Hibernate: insert into APP.Address (city, streetAddress, zip, addressID)
values (?, ?, ?, ?)
```

**4.** Go to the Data Source Explorer view, reconnect to the Lesson22 database, and observe the table Address in the schema APP. Right-click the Address table and select Data ⇨ Sample Contents — you'll see one row with the New York address specified in AddressCreator.

---

*Please select Lesson 36 on the DVD to view the video that accompanies this lesson.*

# Bringing JavaFX to the Mix

JavaFX was designed to serve as a tool for creating rich Internet applications (RIAs). It is meant to compete with such RIA tools as Adobe Flex and Microsoft Silverlight. The competing technologies use two languages for creating RIAs — one for declarative definition of the UI components, and another for the coding of processing logic. Adobe Flex uses MXML for UI components and ActionScript for processing logic. Microsoft Silverlight uses XAML for UI components and one of the .NET languages (such as C#) for processing.

JavaFX was originally designed to use JavaFX Script for UI components and Java for processing logic. But recently things changed, and up to the last minute I wasn't sure if this lesson should be included in the book. Oracle has announced that JavaFX will be undergoing a major redesign in 2011. JavaFX 1.3 includes the JavaFX Script language, but JavaFX 2.0 will be completely Java-based.

Currently, no pre-release version of JavaFX 2.0 is available, and there is a chance that whatever you read about the client portion of this lesson's application will be outdated. But no matter what changes in JavaFX 2.0, the deployed application will run in JVM with the installed JavaFX run time. There is also hope that the Java community will continue supporting the open-source version of JavaFX Script.

This lesson is not an introduction to JavaFX programming, but rather an overview of an application that uses multiple technologies you are already familiar with, plus a client created with JavaFX 1.3.

## CONSUMING STOCK QUOTES WITH JAVAFX

In this lesson you'll see how a web client written in JavaFX can subscribe to price quotes published from the server side via messaging. Multiple technologies used in this version of the Stock Server example are depicted in Figure 37-1.

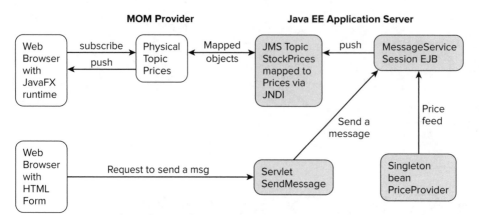

**FIGURE 37-1**

These are the players that provide the generation and processing of the price quote feed:

1. The singleton session bean `PriceProvider` (see the source code in Listing 37-1) knows how to generate random price quotes. It gets instantiated on startup of the GlassFish application server.

2. A stateless session bean called `MessageService` (Listing 37-2) gets the references to JMS-administered objects via resource injection and publishes the price quote to the JMS topic known as `jms/StockPrices`, which is mapped to the physical topic `Prices` in the Open MQ messaging server.

3. The Java client subscribes to the topic `Prices`. Listing 37-3 shows the Java classes `Messages` and `JMSListener`, and the interface `MessageHandler`. These client classes do not have any presentation logic.

4. The presentation client `Main.fx` (Listing 37-4) is written in JavaFX Script. It wraps the Java client messaging classes and gets the price quotes from them. As soon as the new quote comes in, the old one is pushed up and off the screen with a special animation effect.

5. To illustrate another way of sending the message, this application has a simple HTTP client (Listing 37-5) that allows the user to enter any text, which is then routed via the servlet `SendMessage` (Listing 37-6) to the `MessageService` EJB. The rest of the data flow is as described in Steps 2 through 4.

## CODE WALKTHROUGH

By now you should be familiar with each of the Java technologies used in this application, except JavaFX, so I'll provide only very short explanations for the code listings.

The `PriceProvider` singleton bean shown in Listing 37-1 serves as an emulator of the data feed with stock quotes. Replace the random-number generator with a real-time Wall Street stock market feed, and this sample application will show the real data. I'd like to point out two annotations: @Startup and @Schedule. The first ensures that the Java EE application server automatically instantiates the PriceProvider bean whenever the server starts. The second is a calendar-based timer that will call the method getPriceQuote() every five seconds.

**LISTING 37-1: PriceProvider singleton bean**

```
@Singleton
@Startup
public class PriceProvider {

    @EJB
    private MessageService messageService;

    // In this example the method getQuotes() simply generates
    // prices, but in the real world it will get the quote
    // from some external data feed

    @Schedule(second = "*/5", minute="*", hour="*")
    public void getPriceQuote() {

        String price = Double.toString(generator.nextDouble() * 100.0);
        String symbol = symbols[generator.nextInt(symbols.length)];

        messageService.sendMessage(symbol + " " + price);
    }

    private static final Random generator = new Random();

    private static final String[] symbols =
                    {"AAPL", "MSFT", "YHOO", "AMZN", "MOT"};
}
```

The stateless session bean MessageService publishes the text message given as an argument to sendMessage() to the JMS topic that has been bound to the JNDI tree of GlassFish under the name jms/StockPrices. Both the topic connection factory and the topic objects are injected into the bean by the EJB container. The JMS topic will be mapped to the physical topic Prices of the MOM provider Open MQ.

**LISTING 37-2: Stateless bean MessageService**

```
@Stateless
public class MessageService {

    @Resource(mappedName = "jms/StockPrices")
    private Topic topic;

    @Resource(mappedName = "TopicConnectionFactory")
    private TopicConnectionFactory topicConnectionFactory;

    public void sendMessage(String text) {
```

*continues*

**LISTING 37-2** *(continued)*

```
        try {
            Connection connection = topicConnectionFactory.createConnection();
            Session session = connection.createSession(true, 0);
            MessageProducer producer = session.createProducer(topic);

            TextMessage textMessage = session.createTextMessage(text);
            producer.send(textMessage);

            connection.close();
        }
        catch (JMSException e) {
            throw new RuntimeException(e);
        }
    }
}
```

The web clients of this application are written in Java, JavaFX Script, and HTML. The Java class Messages is a part of the JavaFX applet that directly subscribes to the Open MQ topic Prices. Originally, I wanted the applet to use a JNDI call to GlassFish to get the topic jms/StockPrices from there. This would be a cleaner way of subscribing to the topic — no dependency on the particular MOM provider, and no client code changes needed should we decide to change the MOM provider or the application server.

Unfortunately GlassFish v3 doesn't offer a lightweight means of adding JNDI-related classes to the applet. It comes with the utility appclient, which simply packages 40 MB worth of Java classes into the one jar. Sending such a heavy extra weight over the network with the applet is not right, and that's why I decided to use a lighter solution: the applet's class Messages (Listing 37-3) doesn't perform JNDI lookup but directly connects to Open MQ. The Java class Messages uses an inner class called JMSListener and the interface MessageHandler.

**LISTING 37-3:** The Java client subscriber

```
public class Messages {

    public static void startListening(MessageHandler messageHandler)
                                                    throws Exception {
        JMSListener jmsListener = new JMSListener(messageHandler);

        ConnectionFactory connectionFactory = new ConnectionFactory();
        connectionFactory.setProperty(ConnectionConfiguration.imqAddressList,
                                            "mq://localhost:7676");

        connection = connectionFactory.createQueueConnection("admin","admin");

        Session session = connection.createSession(false,
                                            Session.AUTO_ACKNOWLEDGE);

        Topic topic = session.createTopic("Prices");
```

```
            MessageConsumer consumer = session.createConsumer(topic);

            consumer.setMessageListener(jmsListener);
            connection.start();
        }

    public static void stopListening() {
        try {
            connection.stop();
        }
        catch (JMSException e) {
            throw new RuntimeException(e);
        }
    }

    private static Connection connection;

    private static class JMSListener implements MessageListener {
        private MessageHandler messageHandler;

        private JMSListener(MessageHandler messageHandler) {
            this.messageHandler = messageHandler;
        }

        @Override
        public void onMessage(Message message) {

            TextMessage textMessage = (TextMessage) message;

            try {
                System.out.println("Got message: " + textMessage.getText());

                messageHandler.handle(textMessage.getText());
            }
            catch (JMSException e) {
                throw new RuntimeException(e);
            }
        }
    }
}

public interface MessageHandler {
    void handle(String message);
}
```

# Reading JavaFX Code

The JavaFX client shown in Listing 37-4 is responsible for the UI. It's deployed as an applet and is played in the client by the Java plug-in. Starting from Java 6 Update 10, this plug-in runs not as a part of the web browser, but as an independent JVM.

This applet is deployed on the server and is described in a special text file with the extension .jnlp (see Listing 37-7). The client's machine has to have the JavaFX run time installed to play this applet. Because you have the latest Java SE installed on your computer, you won't have any problem playing JavaFX applets. But users with older versions of Java are not guaranteed to have the same results. This is one of the reasons JavaFX has difficulties competing with Adobe Flex or Microsoft Silverlight in a non-corporate uncontrolled environment.

JavaFX Script can access the Java API and in this sample the JavaFX code communicates with the preceding Java message listener. JavaFX Script files are compiled into Java classes and then run on JVM. JavaFX developers need to have JavaFX SDK installed in addition to the run time.

The code in Listing 37-4 shows you the syntax of JavaFX Script. Variable declarations start with the keyword var, and specifying the data type is optional — the compiler will try to figure out what type to use based on assigned values.

The keyword bind represents binding — the value of the variable on the right is assigned to the variable on the left, and all the changes to the right-side values will be immediately reflected in the variable on the left.

Functions in JavaFX are similar to methods in Java, but they don't have to be defined inside a class and can just appear anywhere in the script. Functions can be defined dynamically, which makes them much like Java anonymous inner classes, but simpler. To call a function asynchronously, much as you would call Java's invokeLater(), just give this function FX.deferAction() as an argument, where FX is a class with system utilities. This is done at the beginning of Listing 37-4.

The instance of JavaFXMessageHandler is given to the class Messages (Listing 37-3), and every time the new message is published to the topic the addNewText() method is invoked.

---

**LISTING 37-4: The JavaFX client Main.fx**

```
class JavaFXMessageHandler extends MessageHandler {
    override public function handle(message:String):Void {
        FX.deferAction( function() { addNewText(message) } );
    }
}

Messages.startListening(new JavaFXMessageHandler());

var oldText = "";
var newText = "";

var oldTextOpacity = 0.0;
var oldTextYShift = -40.0;

var font = Font {
    name: "Verdana"
    size: 16
}

var oldTextLabel:Label = Label {
```

```
        font: font
        text: bind oldText
        textFill: Color.web("#808020")
        translateY: bind oldTextYShift
        opacity: bind oldTextOpacity
}

var newTextOpacity = 0.0;
var newTextYShift = 40.0;

var newTextLabel:Label = Label {
        textAlignment: TextAlignment.CENTER
        font: font
        textFill: Color.web("#808020")
        text: bind newText
        translateY: bind newTextYShift
        opacity: bind newTextOpacity;
}

var oldTextAnimation = Timeline {
        repeatCount: 1
        keyFrames: [
            at (0s) {
                oldTextOpacity => 1.0 tween Interpolator.LINEAR;
                oldTextYShift => 0.0 tween Interpolator.LINEAR;
            }

            at (1s) {
                oldTextOpacity => 0.0 tween Interpolator.LINEAR;
                oldTextYShift => -40.0 tween Interpolator.LINEAR;
            }
        ];
}

var newTextAnimation = Timeline {
        repeatCount: 1
        keyFrames: [
            at (0s) {
                newTextOpacity => 0.0 tween Interpolator.LINEAR;
                newTextYShift => 40.0 tween Interpolator.LINEAR;
            }

            at (.5s) {
                newTextOpacity => 1.0 tween Interpolator.LINEAR;
                newTextYShift => 0.0 tween Interpolator.LINEAR;
            }
        ];
}

function addNewText(text: String): Void {
        oldText = newText;
        newText = text;

        oldTextAnimation.playFromStart();
```

*continues*

**LISTING 37-4** *(continued)*

```
        newTextAnimation.playFromStart();
    }


    Stage {
        title: "Application title"

        scene: Scene {
            width: 600
            height: 100

            content: VBox {
                content: [
                    Stack {
                        nodeHPos: HPos.CENTER
                        content: [
                            Rectangle {
                                width: 600
                                height: 80
                                opacity: 0.3
                                fill: LinearGradient {
                                    startX: 0, startY: 0.0, endX: 0, endY: 80.0
                                    proportional: false
                                    stops: [
                                        Stop { offset: 0.0 color:
                                                    Color.web("#303030") }
                                        Stop { offset: 1.0 color:
                                                    Color.web("#FFFFFF") }
                                    ]
                                }
                            },
                            oldTextLabel,
                            newTextLabel ]
                    }]
                }
            }
        }

        onClose : function() { Messages.stopListening(); }
    }
```

The price quotes are displayed on a gray gradient background (see Figure 37-2) and each new price quote pushes the previous one from the screen. Both old and new message texts have animation effects (oldTextAnimation and newTextAnimation) that make the view more engaging.

The JavaFX UI components are not created to live inside a specific top-level container. You add a group of components to a *scene*, which is added to the *stage*. At run time the stage will be linked to a top-level container according to the platform on which the application has to work. A mobile device and a desktop computer will use different top-level containers to display your stage. Each of the components that you add to the scene is an instance of a Node class.

The content of a `Scene` is listed in its `content` property. The code in Listing 37-4 creates the `Stage` object and adds an instance of a `Scene`, which contains a `VBox` — a container with a vertical layout. Inside the `VBox` are three nodes: `Rectangle` with `LinearGradient` (a color effect changing from dark to light gray) and two `Label` nodes: `oldTextLabel` and `newTextLabel`.

Another interesting JavaFX component is `Timeline` — think of a reel of film in a projector. Spooling through frames rapidly produces the illusion of movement. If you need to repeat some actions in JavaFX you can create a `Timeline` with `keyFrames` that will occur at specific intervals.

The last line in the code of the `Stage` instance handles the `onClose` event. This event instructs the `Messages` class to stop listening to the price quotes.

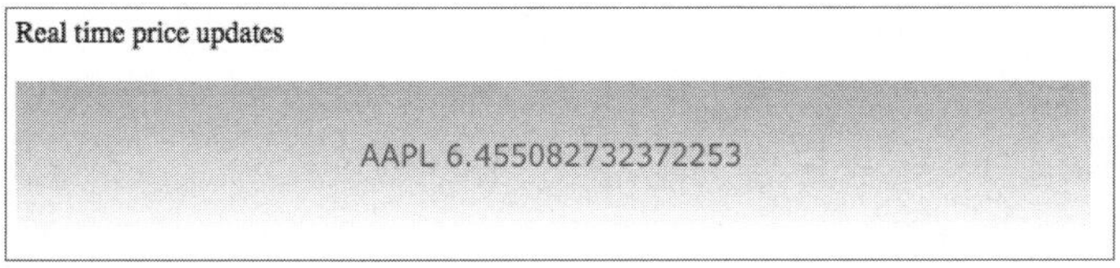

Real time price updates

AAPL 6.455082732372253

**FIGURE 37-2**

# The HTML Client

To provide another door to the messaging system you can use an HTML client that can send any text you want. This may be useful for managing the application. For example, an administrator may want to arrange it so that as soon as the client application receives the word STOP as a text message, it will stop listening to price quotes.

The simple HTML form in Listing 37-5 has just one input field, and when the user presses the Enter key the text is posted to the server by the action `send`.

**LISTING 37-5:** Index.html — the HTML client

```html
<html>
<head>
    <title>JMS Demo</title>
</head>
<body>
    Click this link to open <a href="prices.html">
                    JavaFX client consuming price quotes</a>
    <p>Enter any text in the input field below and watch how JavaFx
client will receive it</p>
    <form action="send" method="POST">
        <label title="Text to send">
            <input value="" name="text"/>
        </label>
    </form>
</body>
</html>
```

The Java EE application server will route all HTTP requests with the URL pattern `send` to the servlet `SendMessage` from Listing 37-6, which will get the text entered by the user and invoke `sendMessage()` on the session bean `MessageService`. This text will be published to the topic `jms/StockPrices` as will any other messages that originate from the singleton `PriceProvider`.

**LISTING 37-6:** SendMessage servlet

```java
@WebServlet("/send")
public class SendMessage extends HttpServlet {

    @EJB
    private MessageService messageService;

    protected void doPost(HttpServletRequest request,
    HttpServletResponse response) throws IOException, ServletException {
        String text = request.getParameter("text");
        messageService.sendMessage(text);

        response.sendRedirect("index.html");
    }
}
```

When this JavaFX applet is ready for deployment on the server, you need to add resources that are needed on the user's machine. Our `Main.fx` client from Listing 37-4 uses the JMS API to subscribe to the messages from the Open MQ MOM provider. Therefore the classes implementing the JMS API have to be downloaded to the user's computer along with `Main.fx`.

The JNLP file shown in Listing 37-7 has to be deployed on the server. It includes the `resources` section that lists what has to be downloaded to the client: the run time for JavaFX and the `javafx-ui.jar` file that includes our sample code and all related JMS supporting classes. The `<applet-desc>` tag includes the `main-class` parameter with a fully qualified name of the JavaFX applet itself with the name of the main class.

**LISTING 37-7:** JNLP deployment file

```xml
<?xml version="1.0" encoding="UTF-8"?>
<jnlp spec="1.0+">
    <information>
        <title>jms-send-receive</title>
        <vendor>practicaljava</vendor>
        <homepage href=""/>
        <description>jms send and receive</description>
        <offline-allowed/>
    </information>
    <resources>
        <j2se version="1.5+"/>
        <extension name="JavaFX Runtime"
href="http://dl.javafx.com/1.3.1/javafx-rt.jnlp"/>

        <jar href="javafx-ui.jar" main="true"/>
```

```
        </resources>
        <applet-desc name="javafx-ui"
        main-class="com.sun.javafx.runtime.adapter.Applet"
width="200" height="80">
            <param name="MainJavaFXScript" value="com.practicaljava.lesson37.ui.Main"/>
        </applet-desc>
        <update check="always"/>
    </jnlp>
```

The hyperlink in the main HTML page (Listing 37-5) downloads the HTML file `Prices.html` (Listing 37-8), which includes a special JavaScript function called `javafx` (its source code is available at `http://dl.javafx.com/1.3/dtfx.js`). This function is a part of the JavaFX deployment toolkit. It ensures that the client's computer has the right version of JRE and automatically generates the reference to the JNLP file shown in Listing 37-7.

**LISTING 37-8:** Prices.html

```
<html xmlns="http://www.w3.org/1999/xhtml" lang="en">
    <head>
        <title>Prices</title>
    </head>
    <body>
        <p>Real time price updates</p>

        <script src="http://dl.javafx.com/1.3/dtfx.js"
type="text/javascript" language="JavaScript"></script>
        <script type="text/javascript" language="JavaScript">
            javafx(
            {
                archive: "javafx/javafx-ui.jar",
                draggable: true,
                width: 600,
                height: 80,
                code: "com.practicaljava.lesson37.ui.Main",
                name: "Messages"
            }
            );
          A </script>
    </body>
</html>
```

# TRY IT

This is the final hands-on exercise in this tutorial. The goal is to build the application and make it work on your computer. This time you'll be building and deploying the application and starting the servers from the command window without any help from Eclipse IDE.

## Lesson Requirements

You should have Java and GlassFish v3 installed. You'll need to install Mercurial version control software to get the code for this example from the Google source control repository where all code samples used in this book are stored. You'll also need to install the build tool Maven.

> *You can download the code and resources for this Try It from the book's web page at* www.wrox.com. *You can find them in the Lesson37 folder in the download.*

## Hint

After this application is deployed from the command line, download the JavaFX plug-in for Eclipse IDE from `http://download.oracle.com/javafx/1.2/gettingstarted/eclipse-plugin` and try to create, deploy, and test this project inside Eclipse.

## Step-by-Step

1. Download and install the distributed source control management tool Mercurial from `http://mercurial.selenic.com`. In the Terminal window enter **hg –version** and you should see the version of Mercurial installed.

2. Check out the code samples for the book into a folder called `java24hourtrainer` from `http://code.google.com/p/practicaljava`. You can do this by entering the following command in the Terminal (command) window:

   **hg clone https://practicaljava.googlecode.com/hg/ java24hourtrainier**

3. Download and install JavaFX 1.3 SDK, available at `http://javafx.com/downloads/all` `.jsp?bundle=javafx_sdk`. In Windows, JavaFX SDK will be installed in the default location `c:\Program Files\JavaFX`, and in Mac OS in `/Library/Frameworks/JavaFX.framework`.

4. Check to see if you have the Maven build tool already installed on your computer by entering **mvn –v** at the command prompt. If you don't have it, download and install it from `http://maven.apache.org/download.html`. All you have to do is unzip the downloaded file into a directory and add Maven's `bin` directory to the system `PATH` variable. In Windows you do this via Control Panel, and on Mac OS by entering the following command in the Terminal window (enter the exact name of your maven directory):

   **export PATH=~/development/apache-maven-3.0/bin/:$PATH**

   You'll be using the Maven build scripts that were created specifically for this lesson. Maven is out of the scope of this tutorial, but if you are curious to see where all the build logic is located, open up the three files called `pom.xml` in subdirectories `lesson37`, *webdemo*, and `javafx-ui` under `java24hourtrainer`.

5. To build the project for this lesson, in the Terminal or command window go to `java24hourtrainer/java-ee/lesson37` and run `mvn install`.

6. As a part of Maven's install, it'll create a directory called .*m2*. Create a plain text file in this directory, named `settings.xml`, with the following content:

```
<settings>
  <pluginGroups>
    <pluginGroup>com.practicaljava.maven.plugin</pluginGroup>
  </pluginGroups>
</settings>
```

7. Change to the directory `java24hourtrainer/maven-plugins` and run `mvn install`.

   In several seconds Maven will have built two plug-ins — one for GlassFish and another for JavaFX.

8. Now go to the `/java-ee/lesson37/web-demo` directory and run the script to create a new domain in GlassFish; start it and deploy the web application there. In this example you are not going to run the instance of GlassFish that you've been using in previous lessons.

```
mvn gf:create-domain
mvn gf:start-domain
mvn gf:deploy
```

9. After the instance of GlassFish is running start Open MQ on port 7676 and its admin console, as described in the section "Administering Objects of Open MQ" in Lesson 30. You need to create a topic called `Prices` there.

10. Now start the admin console of GlassFish by entering the following URL in your web browser: `http://localhost:5000/`. Create there a `TopicConnectionFactory` and a topic `jms/StockPrices` mapped to `Prices`. This process was described in Lesson 31.

11. Finally, test this application from end to end. Make sure that the Open MQ and GlassFish servers are up and running, and point your web browser to `http://localhost:8080/javafx-web-demo/`. First you'll see a scary-looking message that an applet from `dl.javafx.com` is requesting access to your computer. Accept it and you'll see a simple web page with a hyperlink and an input field, as per Listing 37-5. Click the hyperlink and you should see price quotes being pushed to your JavaFX client every five seconds, as shown in Figure 37-2.

12. Test the second way of publishing messages through the HTTP request to the servlet. To do this, open another web browser page and direct it to the same URL: `http://localhost:8080/javafx-web-demo/`. Arrange both browsers on your computer monitor so you can see them at the same time. This time do not click the link, but type any text in the input field and hit the Enter key on the keyboard. The text you entered should be received and displayed by the JavaFX client in the second web browser.

 *Please select Lesson 37 on the DVD to view the video that accompanies this lesson.*

# Java Technical Interviews

Technical job interviewing is a game with well-defined rules. I've worn the hats of both interviewer and interviewee many times over the last 12 years of my Java career. In this lesson I'll share with you my views on hiring Java developers and on preparing for technical interviews.

Regardless of whether the IT job market is hot or not, there are some rules and techniques that can increase your interview success rate. The process of getting a job consists of three separate tiers:

1. Getting the interview
2. Interviewing successfully
3. Considering the offer

I can't stress enough how important it is to work on achieving each of these goals separately, one step at a time! Your résumé is the most important thing in the first step. Adjust it for each position you are applying for (no, I'm not asking you to lie). Make sure it's short and to the point (not more than two pages long).

## GETTING THE INTERVIEW

If you are applying for a Java developer's position, nobody needs to know the details of that Visual Basic project from 10 years ago. Always update your résumé based on the feedback you receive from recruiters or more experienced programmers.

There is a summary section on each résumé and many people just waste this space with some junk like "I'm looking for a challenging position that will let me improve my talents." What a waste! Use this summary line to show your relevant skills.

Say you've been specializing in Java messaging during the last two years, but this job posting requires web developers. Chances are that you've developed web applications before; highlight your web experience in the summary section of your résumé. The same day you may be responding to another ad, this one for people who know Java messaging. Modify your summary section accordingly and send a version of your résumé that emphasizes your experience with messaging.

Job requirements are more involved these days, and recruiting companies don't even want to submit your résumé to the client if you have "only" 8 out of 10 required skills. Read the requirements and highlight all the relevant skills you have. Do not be lazy; work with your résumé.

Networking is another great way to get an interview. This time I'm not talking about Java networking — I'm talking about meeting other IT people who may be hiring or know people who are hiring. Attend your local Java Users Group meeting, follow Java developers on Twitter, go to professional conferences and seminars.

## DOING WELL AT THE INTERVIEW

OK. The interview is scheduled, and now your main goal is to ace it. Remember, your interviewer has a difficult task: He needs to assess your technical skills within 30 to 60 minutes, so help him! Try to get as many technical details about the job as possible from your recruiter. If the position you are applying for requires knowledge of Java sockets, research working with non-blocking sockets. If they're building Java EE applications, find out which application server they use and read up on it.

Do your homework and prepare a short talk about some interesting and challenging technical problems you might have experienced in one of your college or real-world projects. If you didn't have any super-complex projects, just pick up a topic from one of the multiple online programmers' forums and research it. Another great source of Java tips and tricks is Josh Bloch's book *Effective Java*, Second Edition, Addison Wesley, ISBN: 0-321-35668-3.

For example, if you have prepared a talk on concurrent collections, you're not allowed to leave the interview without talking about this. But what if the interviewer won't ask you about Java concurrency? It doesn't really matter. Find a way to switch the conversation to the prepared topic and do your best. The interviewer will be happy because he doesn't need to think about what to ask next, and you're happy because you've had a chance to talk about a well-prepared subject.

Will this technique work all the time? No. But it'll work most of the time. Obviously you need to research the selected subject well, or you'll get fried. You must talk about technical challenges you've resolved. You need to remember that your interviewers have a difficult time trying to figure out your technical abilities in just 30 minutes. So, you need to help them out. Be in charge.

If you're a junior developer, spend some time answering the multiple-choice computer tests that are usually required for certification exams. You don't need to get certified, but all these books and online mock tests will help you pass similar tests offered by some job agencies. Find some sample interview questions online.

A technical interview is a game with known rules, but in many cases the interviewers are not prepared to run the interviews. Sometimes they just go by a prepared list of questions. Some interviewees take advantage of this and just spend some time studying introductory courses, and then memorize questions and answers for technical interviews. Believe it or not, in many cases this works.

What does a good enterprise Java developer have to know in addition to understanding the difference between abstract classes and interfaces? Usually employers are looking for people with knowledge of the following: Java Servlets, JSP, Spring framework, EJB, JMS, any commercial message-oriented middleware, JDBC, JNDI, HTML, XML, Hibernate, Ant or Maven build tools, SQL, one of the major application servers, and a couple of relational database management systems.

Understanding why a particular Java EE component is being used in your current project is equally important. If the interviewer asks you, "Why did you use EJB in this project?" please do not answer, "That decision was made before I joined the project." Have your own opinion and explain why you think it was a good or bad choice for this particular project.

Here's another tip: Don't critique the application architecture of your potential employer. You'll have plenty of chances to provide technical advice if you're hired, so just focus on getting an offer.

Be energetic during the interview and show your interest in the job. Even if you are a technical guru, don't behave as if you're doing the interviewer a favor just by showing up. Personality matters. People don't like prima donnas.

Be prepared to write code on a whiteboard and practice that skill. The interviewer may not ask you to do this, but it may be a good idea to start illustrating your thoughts on the board if there is one in the room. If there is no board, use your own notepad. Often interviewers are trying to judge how well you think and approach a problem more than how effectively you've memorized an algorithm, class name, or method arguments.

No need to rush. If you start writing a code fragment on a board, don't be afraid of making mistakes. Think aloud. It may be even beneficial for the interviewer to see how you can identify the wrong approach and then pick the right one. Practice explaining little code fragments to your friends or relatives; they don't need to know Java to participate in these role-playing games.

After the interview, as soon as you leave the building, take notes about what just happened. Don't postpone it until you get home; you may forget important details. Make a note to work on the questions you might have not answered correctly. These questions require your attention and research. Improve your technical skills after each interview.

## CONSIDERING THE OFFER

You've got an offer! Now think hard about whether you want to accept it. Have I mentioned that you should look for a new job not when your employer decides to let you go or your contract ends, but when you have a stable job, the sky is blue, and the grass is green? This gives you a tremendous advantage: You can consider the offer without being under pressure from unpaid bills.

Don't accept an offer just because the new job pays an extra $5,000 a year, which comes to less than $300 a month after taxes. But do accept the offer that will give you a chance to work with interesting technologies or business applications even if it won't pay you an extra dime.

Other nonmonetary factors of an offer are health benefits, flexible work hours, ease of commute, or simply a kinship that you feel with the people working for the potential employer. Believe it or not, some people won't accept offers from employers who require you to wear suit and tie. Just make a decision about what's more important for you — having an interesting job or being able to show off your latest tattoos.

No matter what your preferences are, take charge of your career and actively build it the way you want.

## INTERVIEWING ENTERPRISE DEVELOPERS

When the job market is healthy, major online job search engines show thousands of openings, and people are competing for these jobs. These days a seasoned developer has to know about 10 different tools or technologies to find a good job and feel relatively secure for a couple of years. Over the last several years I've interviewed lots of Java developers, and this is what I've noticed:

➤ People do not call themselves Java developers or programmer-analysts anymore — most of them prefer the title *Java architect*. Unfortunately, only some of them really understand how Java EE components operate and can suggest design solutions. Of course, knowledge of Java EE is not all that a Java architect should know.

➤ Job applicants are more senior, and I barely see any college graduates or junior programmers. Many of the junior positions are being outsourced and the number of graduates with computer science degrees has declined over the past several years.

➤ Having software certification does not make a résumé stand out. Actually, if a résumé starts with a list of certifications, most likely it's a beginner's. I'm not against certifications, as they help you learn a language or a tool, and show that you are willing to and can study. But a certificate doesn't make someone a skilled professional.

➤ With the introduction of middle-tier object-relational mapping frameworks such as Hibernate, many people don't even bother learning how database management systems work or how to write a SQL query that performs well — they just map Java classes to database tables.

➤ In a slow economy, be prepared to pass at least four interviews to get hired. Back in 1999 two good interviews would be enough; in 2001 it was very difficult to even get an interview, let alone a job!

➤ In 2010 a large portion of the development is done in India. Even though the total cost of development is not low despite the lower hourly rates of offshore developers, Western hiring managers unfortunately have an impression that local candidates must be flexible in their rates, too. Being a native English speaker is not enough for you to charge top dollar. Always be technically current, otherwise the more motivated guys from overseas will leave you in the dust.

Good knowledge of the business terminology of your potential employer is also important. I'm not sure about the Silicon Valley or Europe, but here in New York just being a techie may not be good enough to get you a senior job. Of course, interviewing with Google or Microsoft is an exception.

For example, if you're applying for a Java position in a financial brokerage company and don't know what a short sale is, this may be a deal breaker. If you are a senior developer you should be able to hit the ground running: Try to find out from your recruiter as many details as possible about the business. Do your homework, and you'll get the job! Recruiters are desperately looking for good programmers and you can be one of them.

# TO GET OR NOT TO GET CERTIFIED?

Any certification program is a business for the vendor that wants to sell training to award certificates. Oracle is no exception: you can find various certification programs to rate your Java skills. The following website offers various certification programs in Java SE and EE technologies: `http://education.oracle.com/pls/web_prod-plq-dad/db_pages.getpage?page_id=140#13`.

Although most certification programs require you to pass a multiple-choice computer test, some of them (such as those for Java EE architects) will give you a challenging task to design and program.

Overall I think it's a good idea to prepare yourself and go through the certification process, because it will definitely improve your understanding of the Java language or a specific enterprise technology or framework. In some areas it may also improve the performance of your résumé. It'll also help you slip through computer screening tests that are used by job placement agencies. Just check job postings from your potential employers to see if they insist on having certificates.

But I also want to caution you against overestimating the importance of getting Java certification. When I see a résumé that starts with a list of certificates, it tells me that this candidate is good… at passing multiple-choice tests. Having practical hands-on experience working on open-source or enterprise projects is a lot more valuable than any certificate you might have earned. If you have certificates — fine, but keep them somewhere at the end of your résumé rather than trying to present them as a major achievement.

# TECHNICAL QUESTIONS AND ANSWERS

Suggesting a list of technical questions for an interview is a risky business. Seasoned Java developers have different views on what's fair and what's not fair to ask. But junior developers who just completed a Java tutorial can definitely benefit from some guidance in preparing for Java job interviews.

The following are suggested technical interview questions and expected brief answers on various Java-related topics. The questions included in this section are those that I had to answer while working on various projects. In no way is this a complete list of possible questions, but it will definitely give you an idea of what to expect at an interview. Most of the answers to these questions can be found in this book, but some will require additional research.

**Q:** What's the difference between an interface and an abstract class?

**A:** An abstract class may contain code in method bodies, which is not allowed in an interface. With abstract classes you have to inherit your class from the abstract one because Java does not allow multiple inheritance. On the other hand, you can implement multiple interfaces in your class.

**Q:** How do you deploy a web application in the application server that you currently use?

**A:** In most Java EE application servers you create a web archive (war file) and copy it to the assigned directory per the application server documentation. (You should be able to explain the directory structure in a war file.)

**Q:** What's the usage of the keyword `static`?

**A:** It's used in declarations of methods and variables to make them available without creating an instance of the class. For example, the `main()` method is a `static` one. If a variable is `static`, its value is shared by all instances of the class.

**Q:** How can you force garbage collection?

**A:** You can't force garbage collection, but you can request it, because JVM does not guarantee that it'll be started immediately. Invoking `System.gc()` requests Java garbage collection.

**Q:** Explain the usage of event adapters.

**A:** Some `Swing` event listener interfaces declare multiple methods (for example, `WindowListener` has seven methods) and a class must implement all of them. Adapters already have all these methods predefined with empty bodies. So if a class needs to process just one of the `WindowListener` events, it has to override only the corresponding method of `WindowAdapter`.

**Q:** How do you decide if explicit casting is needed?

**A:** If you assign a superclass object to a variable of a subclass's data type, you need to use explicit casting. For example:

```
Object a;
Customer b;
b = (Customer) a;
```

Java generics eliminate the need for explicit casting. For subclass-to-superclass assignments the casting is performed automatically. You can also cast to interfaces that a class implements.

**Q:** Can you perform casting between objects of different types?

**A:** No, you can't. The objects can have a superclass-subclass relationship, or you can cast to interfaces implemented by a class.

**Q:** Can a Java class be inherited from two classes?

**A:** No, Java does not allow multiple inheritance, but a class can implement multiple interfaces, which, to some extent, can be used as a workaround.

**Q:** Both applets and Servlets are deployed on the server. What's the difference between the run-time environments of applets and Servlets?

**A:** Applets run in a JVM on the user's machine under control of a web browser, and they have security restrictions limiting access to a computer's devices. Servlets run on the server side under control of the Servlet container or Java EE Application Server.

**Q:** What's the difference between constructors and regular methods?

**A:** Constructors must have the same name as the class and cannot return a value. They are invoked only once, while regular methods can be invoked many times.

**Q:** What's the difference between the HTML methods `Get` and `Post`?

**A:** `Get` appends the parameters to the URL, and the resulting URL is bookmarkable. `Post` allows the sending of objects as well as text data, while `Get` works with text only.

**Q:** What's a cookie? Which Java components create them?

**A:** A cookie is an object that represents a name/value pair. Servlets, JSP, and JSF can create and send cookies to a web browser that saves them on the user's disk in a special directory. Cookies help a Servlet identify a user. For example, a bank can store your account number in a cookie file on your machine, so you do not need to enter it on a log-on screen.

**Q:** Can a non-abstract class have both abstract and concrete methods?

**A:** No, but only abstract classes can have abstract methods.

**Q:** Explain the use of Java packages.

**A:** Packages offer a way to organize multi-file projects. They also help in resolving naming conflicts when different packages have classes with the same names. Package access level also enables you to protect data from being used by unauthorized classes, permitting only the classes from the same package to see each other's member variables.

**Q:** Explain the usage of the keyword `transient`.

**A:** The `transient` keyword indicates that the value of this member variable does not have to be serialized with the object. When the class gets de-serialized, `transient` variables will be initialized with the default values of the variable data types (such as `0` for integers).

**Q:** What do you know about thread synchronization? Explain the difference between

```
public void synchronized myMethod() { ... }
```

and

```
public void myMethod() {
    ...
    synchronized (some_object) {... }
}
```

**A:** The keyword `synchronized` is used to prevent race conditions when more than one thread tries to update some values. Synchronized blocks are preferable to synchronized methods because they place locks for shorter periods. But before manually synchronizing blocks of code you should see if you can use one of the collection classes from the package `java.util.concurrent` as a better solution for dealing with race conditions.

**Q:** What's the difference between the methods `sleep()` and `wait()`?

**A:** The code `sleep(1000)` puts the thread aside for exactly one second. The code `wait(1000)` makes the thread wait for up to one second. A thread can stop waiting earlier if it receives the `notify()` or `notifyAll()` call. The method `wait()` is defined in the class `Object`, but `sleep()` is defined in the class `Thread`.

**Q:** What do you know about the method `invokeLater()`?

**A:** This method is defined in the class `SwingUtilities` and is used to ensure that `Swing` windows will be updated through the event-dispatching thread. You can also do this with the `SwingWorker` class.

**Q:** What's the difference between creating threads subclassing the class `Thread` and implementing the `Runnable` interface?

**A:** Thread creation with the class `Thread` requires that your class be inherited from it. Then you need to create an instance of your class and call its `start()` method. If a class implements the `Runnable` interface the procedure is different — you have to create the instance of your class, and the instance of the `Thread` object, passing the `Runnable` class to the latter. Using `Runnable` enables you to create threads from classes that have to be inherited from classes other than `Thread` classes.

**Q:** How can you create a thread that can return a value from its method `run()`?

**A:** You need to implement `Callable` interface.

**Q:** What would you use to compare two `String` variables — the `equals()` method, or the `==` operator?

**A:** I'd use `equals()` to compare the values of the `Strings`, and the `==` operator to check if two variables point at the same `String` object in memory.

**Q:** What do you know about the MVC design pattern?

**A:** MVC stands for the model-view-controller design pattern, which is used to separate presentation modules from business logic and data ones. The model part represents the data and the business logic of the application, the view is a visual representation (for example, a UI), and the controller accepts the data from the view and passes it to the model and vice versa. For example, a JSP page is a view, a Servlet is a controller, and a Java bean represents a model.

**Q:** How can you reduce the time spent by JVM on creating frequently used instances of some objects?

**A:** I'd create my own or configure existing object pools (e.g., DataSource or EJB objects can be configured to use object pools of a certain size).

**Q:** Will the following statement create the file `xyz.txt` on disk?

```
File a = new File("xyz.txt");
```

**A:** No, it just creates an object pointing to this file.

**Q:** How can a subclass invoke a method defined in a superclass?

**A:** Java has the keyword `super`. If a method has been overridden, but you'd like to invoke its version defined in the superclass, use the following syntax: `super.myMethod();`. To call a constructor of the superclass, just write `super();` in the first line of the subclass's constructor.

**Q:** What access level do you need to specify to ensure that only classes from the same directory can access the directory?

**A:** You do not need to specify any access level. In this case, Java will use the default package access level, which will guarantee visibility only to the classes located in the same directory (package).

**Q:** What's the use of JNDI?

**A:** JNDI is a Java API for naming and directory servers. It is used for finding Java objects by name in a distributed application. For example, you can use JNDI to get a reference to the DataSource or JMS objects.

**Q:** Do you have to invoke a method that reads a file inside the try/catch block?

**A:** You have to either put it in the try/catch block or declare that the calling method may throw an exception, for example:

```
void myMethod() throws IOException{...}
```

**Q:** If you need to catch more than one exception (such as FileNotFoundException and IOException), does the order of the catch statements matter?

**A:** Yes, it does. FileNotFoundException is inherited from IOException. The exception subclasses have to be caught first.

**Q:** Explain in detail the data workflow between a web page and a Servlet called FindBooks after the user presses Submit. (In this question interviewers can replace the web page and Servlet with any other client-server components. The main point is to find out if the job applicant understands the entire end-to-end data flow.)

**A:** The web browser connects to the server located at the specified URL, and if FindBooks has not been started yet, the Servlet container will start it, invoking the servlet's init() method followed by the service() method, which in turn calls doGet() or doPost(), depending on the method of HTTP request. The objects HTTPServletRequest and HTTPServletResponse are used for the interaction between the client and FindBooks. The Servlet's output can be sent back to the user by means of one of the methods of HTTPServletResponse, for example println().

**Q:** Explain the process of getting the data from a database table in a Java SE program using JDBC. Which classes and methods have to be used?

**A:** First you load the appropriate JDBC driver using Class.forName(). After that you get the Connection object using DriverManager.getConnection(). Then you create a Statement object and invoke one of its methods, like executeQuery() or executeUpdate(). Process the ResultSet, if any, and close the Connection, Statement, and ResultSet objects.

**Q:** What are the differences among the Java keywords final, finalize, and finally?

**A:** Depending on its position, the keyword final means either that the variable can be initialized only once, or that you cannot override a method, or that you cannot subclass a class.

The method finalize(), if defined in your class, is invoked by the garbage collector when it's ready to release a memory used by the instance of your class.

The keyword `finally` is used in a `try/catch` block to place code, such as code to close a stream, that must be executed whether the code in the `try` block succeeds or fails.

**Q:** Can you declare fields in an interface?

**A:** Yes you can, but they should be `final` and `static`.

**Q:** Can an inner class, declared inside a method, access local variables of this method?

**A:** It's possible only if the variables are `final`.

**Q:** Give an example of an anonymous inner class.

**A:** An event listener class can be created on the fly as an anonymous inner class, for example:

```
addActionListener (new ActionListener() {
        public void actionPerformed (ActionEvent e) {
                doSomething();}
            }
    );
```

**Q:** What could be used to keep track of sessions in web applications?

**A:** You can use cookies, URL rewriting, and the `HTTPSession` object.

**Q:** Will session management with cookies always work?

**A:** No, if a user disables cookies in the web browser, it won't work. In such cases application servers usually automatically switch to URL rewriting.

**Q:** How can you stop a long-running thread?

**A:** The class `Thread` has a deprecated method called `stop()`, but this method does not guarantee that the thread will be stopped. Depending on the process that is run by this thread, you could try to close connections or open streams, if any, or use the method `interrupt()`.

**Q:** When could a Java class be called a bean?

**A:** You call the class a bean if it has a nonargument constructor, implements the `Serializable` interface, and has public setter/getter methods for its private properties.

**Q:** What are the advantages of using JSP rather than Servlets?

**A:** JSP enables you to separate presentation from business logic and the resulting web page can be modified by people who do not know Java.

**Q:** Give an example that shows the difference between the use of the operators `&&` and `&`.

**A.** In the following code snippet the second expression in the `if` statement will not even be evaluated if variable a is `null`. If a single ampersand were used here we'd get a `NullPointerException`.

```
String a=null;
if (a==null && a.length()>10) {...}
```

**Q:** Name some predefined JSP variables.

**A:** `request, response, out, session...`

**Q:**   How do you deploy a JSP?

**A:**   You can place `.jsp` files in a document root directory of the Servlet container or application server, or create a war file.

**Q:**   Why is JSF preferable to JSP from the MVC design pattern perspective?

**A:**   JSF enforces separation of the presentation and the processing logic, while JSP doesn't.

**Q:**   What's the default port number that web servers use for HTTP-based communications?

**A:**   HTTP requests go through port 80, HTTPS ones through port 443.

**Q:**   What method of the Servlet class is an equivalent of a constructor in a regular Java class?

**A:**   The Servlet's method `init()` plays a similar role, but because all clients use the same instance of the Servlet, you should initialize only those variables that are allowed to have the same value for each user's request, such as the name of the database server.

**Q:**   Which is faster, array or `ArrayList`?

**A:**   Most likely array is faster. It can be used if you know in advance the number of elements in the array. `ArrayList` is an API on top of an array. You do not need to know its size in advance — new elements can be added as needed. Arrays work faster because JVM allocates memory only once for all elements. But to give you a better answer I'd have to write an appropriate benchmark in context to find out.

**Q:**   What do you know about Java reflection?

**A:**   Reflection is a way of finding information about a Java class during run time. For example, you can find out the constructors and the method signatures of a particular class. The class `Class` has such methods as `getConstructor()`, `getFields()`, `getMethods()`, and others.

**Q:**   What would you do if your Java program crashed during the run time with an "out of memory" error?

**A:**   I'd try to increase the size of the JVM's dynamic memory (heap) on program start-up using command-line parameters. For example, you can request the minimum heap size of 512 MB and the maximum heap size of 1024 MB as follows:

```
java –Xms64 –Xmx512 MyProgram
```

**Q:**   How can you ensure that only one instance of some class can be created in your application?

**A:**   You need to implement the singleton design pattern. Create a class with a private constructor and provide a public `Get` method that will return the only instance of this class, for example `MyClass.getInstance()`.

**Q:**   What's the major difference between a `Hashtable` and a `HashMap`?

**A:**   The `Hashtable` class is internally synchronized, while the `HashMap` is not.

**Q:**   Name some design patterns.

**A:**   Singleton, MVC, data transfer object, facade...

**Q:** The word stateless is used to describe a session EJB as well as HTTP protocol. What's the meaning of the word stateless in these two cases?

**A:** HTTP protocol is page-based, meaning that the web browser does not hold the connection between requests, but in the case of an EJB, *stateless* means that the session bean cannot be used to store the state of a particular client.

**Q:** Are Java objects passed by value or by reference?

**A:** Objects are passed by reference, but their reference variables are passed by value.

**Q:** How can a Java client access a message-driven bean?

**A:** Java clients don't access MDBs directly — they just place messages into a queue or publish them to topics, and the MDB retrieves them from there.

## EPILOGUE

The book is over. Even though it's rather small in size for the number of the covered subjects, I tried to touch on a wide spectrum of topics that most Java practitioners have to know. You may still need to do additional research on certain subjects, depending on your project needs, but at least now you know where to dig.

I really hope that you'll keep this book handy as a quick reference or for a refresher when it's time to hit the job market. No matter what your motivation is, have fun reading — I certainly had fun writing it. You can send thank-you notes and suggestions via e-mail to `yakovfain@gmail.com`. Thank you for reading my book!

# What's on the DVD?

This appendix provides you with information on the contents of the DVD that accompanies this book. For the most up-to-date information please refer to the ReadMe file located at the root of the DVD. Here is what you will find in this appendix:

➤ Using the DVD

➤ What's on the DVD

➤ Troubleshooting

## USING THE DVD ON A PC

To access the content from the DVD, follow these steps:

**1.** Insert the DVD into your computer's DVD-ROM drive. The license agreement will appear.

> *The interface won't launch if you have autorun disabled. In that case click Start ⇨ Run (For Windows Vista, Start ⇨ All Programs ⇨ Accessories ⇨ Run). In the dialog box that appears, type* `D:\Start.exe`. *(Replace D with the proper letter if your DVD drive uses a different letter. If you don't know the letter, see how your CD drive is listed under My Computer.) Click OK.*

**2.** Read through the license agreement, and click the Accept button if you want to use the DVD.

**3.** The DVD interface appears. Simply select the lesson video you want to view.

## USING THE DVD ON A MAC

To install the items from the DVD to your hard drive, follow these steps:

**1.** Insert the DVD into your computer's DVD-ROM drive.

**2.** The DVD icon will appear on your desktop; double-click to open.

**3.** Double-click the Start button.

**4.** Read the license agreement and click the Accept button to use the DVD.

**5.** The DVD interface will appear. Here you can install the programs and run the demos.

## WHAT'S ON THE DVD?

Most lessons in the book have a corresponding screencast that illustrates examples in the lesson and provides content beyond what is covered in print.

I recommend using the following steps when reading a lesson:

**1.** Read the lesson's text.

**2.** Watch the DVD and try to repeat all the instructor's actions on your computer.

**3.** Read the step-by-step instructions in the lesson's "Try It" section and complete the assignment on your own.

You can also download all the solutions to the "Try It" sections at the book's website. If you get stuck and don't know what to do next, visit the p2p forums (`p2p.wrox.com`), locate the forum for the book, and leave a post.

## TROUBLESHOOTING

If you have difficulty installing or using any of the materials on the companion DVD, try the following solutions:

➤ **Turn off any antivirus software that you may have running:** Installers sometimes mimic virus activity and can make your computer incorrectly believe that it is being attacked by a virus. (Be sure to turn the antivirus software back on later.)

➤ **Close all running programs:** The more programs you're running, the less memory is available to other programs. Installers also typically update files and programs; if you keep other programs running, installation may not work properly.

➤ **Reference the ReadMe:** Please refer to the ReadMe file located at the root of the CD-ROM for the latest product information as of publication time.

➤ **Reboot if necessary:** If all else fails, rebooting your machine can often clear any conflicts in the system.

# CUSTOMER CARE

If you have trouble with the CD-ROM please call the Wiley Product Technical Support phone number, (800) 762-2974. Outside the United States call 1 (317) 572-3994. You can also contact Wiley Product Technical Support at `http://support.wiley.com`. John Wiley & Sons will provide technical support only for installation and other general quality-control issues. For technical support on the applications themselves, consult the program's vendor or author.

To place additional orders or to request information about other Wiley products, please call (877) 762-2974.

# INDEX

# WILEY PUBLISHING, INC.
# END-USER LICENSE AGREEMENT

**READ THIS.** You should carefully read these terms and conditions before opening the software packet(s) included with this book "Book". This is a license agreement "Agreement" between you and Wiley Publishing, Inc. "WPI". By opening the accompanying software packet(s), you acknowledge that you have read and accept the following terms and conditions. If you do not agree and do not want to be bound by such terms and conditions, promptly return the Book and the unopened software packet(s) to the place you obtained them for a full refund.

1. **License Grant.** WPI grants to you (either an individual or entity) a nonexclusive license to use one copy of the enclosed software program(s) (collectively, the "Software") solely for your own personal or business purposes on a single computer (whether a standard computer or a workstation component of a multi-user network). The Software is in use on a computer when it is loaded into temporary memory (RAM) or installed into permanent memory (hard disk, CD-ROM, or other storage device). WPI reserves all rights not expressly granted herein.

2. **Ownership.** WPI is the owner of all right, title, and interest, including copyright, in and to the compilation of the Software recorded on the physical packet included with this Book "Software Media". Copyright to the individual programs recorded on the Software Media is owned by the author or other authorized copyright owner of each program. Ownership of the Software and all proprietary rights relating thereto remain with WPI and its licensers.

3. **Restrictions on Use and Transfer.**

(a) You may only (i) make one copy of the Software for backup or archival purposes, or (ii) transfer the Software to a single hard disk, provided that you keep the original for backup or archival purposes. You may not (i) rent or lease the Software, (ii) copy or reproduce the Software through a LAN or other network system or through any computer subscriber system or bulletin-board system, or (iii) modify, adapt, or create derivative works based on the Software.

(b) You may not reverse engineer, decompile, or disassemble the Software. You may transfer the Software and user documentation on a permanent basis, provided that the transferee agrees to accept the terms and conditions of this Agreement and you retain no copies. If the Software is an update or has been updated, any transfer must include the most recent update and all prior versions.

4. **Restrictions on Use of Individual Programs.** You must follow the individual requirements and restrictions detailed for each individual program in the "About the CD" appendix of this Book or on the Software Media. These limitations are also contained in the individual license agreements recorded on the Software Media. These limitations may include a requirement that after using the program for a specified period of time, the user must pay a registration fee or discontinue use. By opening the Software packet(s), you agree to abide by the licenses and restrictions for these individual programs that are detailed in the "About the CD" appendix and/or on the Software Media. None of the material on this Software Media or listed in this Book may ever be redistributed, in original or modified form, for commercial purposes.

5. **Limited Warranty.**

(a) WPI warrants that the Software and Software Media are free from defects in materials and workmanship under normal use for a period of sixty (60) days from the date of purchase of this Book. If WPI receives notification within the warranty period of defects in materials or workmanship, WPI will replace the defective Software Media.

(b) WPI AND THE AUTHOR(S) OF THE BOOK DISCLAIM ALL OTHER WARRANTIES, EXPRESS OR IMPLIED, INCLUDING WITHOUT LIMITATION IMPLIED WARRANTIES OF MERCHANTABILITY AND FITNESS FOR A PARTICULAR PURPOSE, WITH RESPECT TO THE SOFTWARE, THE PROGRAMS, THE SOURCE CODE CONTAINED THEREIN, AND/OR THE TECHNIQUES DESCRIBED IN THIS BOOK. WPI DOES NOT WARRANT THAT THE FUNCTIONS CONTAINED IN THE SOFTWARE WILL MEET YOUR REQUIREMENTS OR THAT THE OPERATION OF THE SOFTWARE WILL BE ERROR FREE.

(c) This limited warranty gives you specific legal rights, and you may have other rights that vary from jurisdiction to jurisdiction.

6. **Remedies.**

(a) WPI's entire liability and your exclusive remedy for defects in materials and workmanship shall be limited to replacement of the Software Media, which may be returned to WPI with a copy of your receipt at the following address: Software Media Fulfillment Department, Attn.: *Java Programming 24-Hour Trainer*, Wiley Publishing, Inc., 10475 Crosspoint Blvd., Indianapolis, IN 46256, or call 1-800-762-2974. Please allow four to six weeks for delivery. This Limited Warranty is void if failure of the Software Media has resulted from accident, abuse, or misapplication. Any replacement Software Media will be warranted for the remainder of the original warranty period or thirty (30) days, whichever is longer.

(b) In no event shall WPI or the author be liable for any damages whatsoever (including without limitation damages for loss of business profits, business interruption, loss of business information, or any other pecuniary loss) arising from the use of or inability to use the Book or the Software, even if WPI has been advised of the possibility of such damages.

(c) Because some jurisdictions do not allow the exclusion or limitation of liability for consequential or incidental damages, the above limitation or exclusion may not apply to you.

7. **U.S. Government Restricted Rights.** Use, duplication, or disclosure of the Software for or on behalf of the United States of America, its agencies and/or instrumentalities "U.S. Government" is subject to restrictions as stated in paragraph (c)(1)(ii) of the Rights in Technical Data and Computer Software clause of DFARS 252.227-7013, or subparagraphs (c) (1) and (2) of the Commercial Computer Software - Restricted Rights clause at FAR 52.227-19, and in similar clauses in the NASA FAR supplement, as applicable.

8. **General.** This Agreement constitutes the entire understanding of the parties and revokes and supersedes all prior agreements, oral or written, between them and may not be modified or amended except in a writing signed by both parties hereto that specifically refers to this Agreement. This Agreement shall take precedence over any other documents that may be in conflict herewith. If any one or more provisions contained in this Agreement are held by any court or tribunal to be invalid, illegal, or otherwise unenforceable, each and every other provision shall remain in full force and effect.